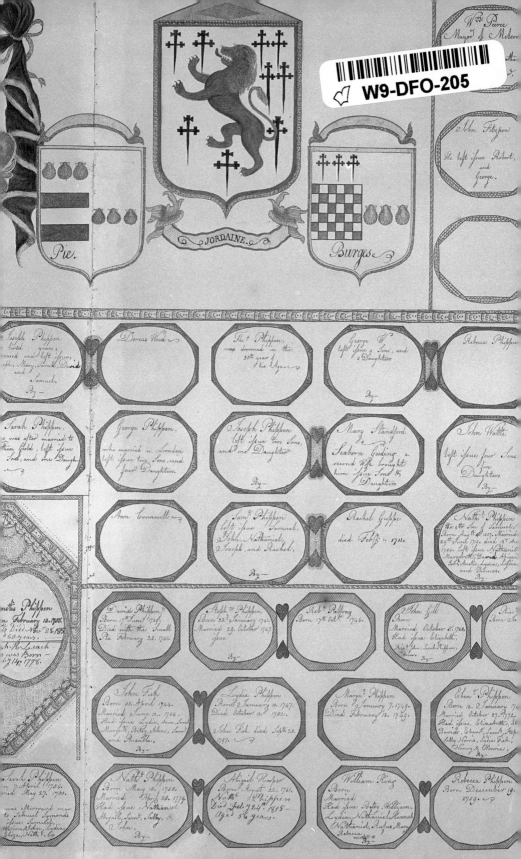

PHIPPEN GENEALOGY

ANCESTORS AND DESCENDANTS OF DAVID PHIPPEN
(C.1585–1650)

of MELCOMBE REGIS, DORSET, *and* HINGHAM
and BOSTON, MASSACHUSETTS

PHIPPEN GENEALOGY

ANCESTORS AND DESCENDANTS OF DAVID PHIPPEN
(C.1585–1650)

of MELCOMBE REGIS, DORSET, *and* HINGHAM
and BOSTON, MASSACHUSETTS

by

JOHN S. FIPPHEN
RICHARD C. FIPPHEN

Newbury Street Press
Boston 2017

ISBN-13: 978-0-88082-362-3
Library of Congress Control Number: 2017946412

Jacket and end paper artwork: John Symonds, American, 19th century,
*Genealogical Register with Coat-of-Arms of the Phippen and the Smith Families of
Salem, Massachusetts*, 1808; © 2017 Museum of Fine Arts, Boston.

NEWBURY STREET PRESS
imprint of New England Historic Genealogical Society
Boston, Massachusetts
AmericanAncestors.org

CONTENTS

PREFACE

Our journey to learn about the history of the Phippen family in England and America began in March 1975 in the stacks of the Northborough, Massachusetts Public Library. For over 40 years, my father and I have been gathering information on David Phippen, his ancestors and descendants. The journey has taken us from libraries and courthouses in Massachusetts; to Truro Cathedral in Cornwall; to vital records offices, historical societies, and cemeteries throughout New England; to the 1635 landing site in Hingham; to North Street in Boston's North End to see where the seventeenth-century Phippens lived and worked on what was then the Boston waterfront; to the streets of ancient Salem—called home by many Phippens since 1665; to House Island in Casco Bay where David's son Joseph fished in the mid-1600s; and to the Museum of Fine Arts in Boston to see the 1808 Phippen genealogical chart—to name just a few stops on this incredible voyage.

Along the way, we have had invaluable assistance from numerous individuals, both support staff at repositories and libraries as well as fellow Phippen descendants. I am grateful to all, but I want to express special gratitude to several. Nathaniel Taylor played a major role in researching and editing and made valuable contributions about the history of the family in England. Members of the staff of Newbury Street Press and the New England Historic Genealogical Society contributed in important ways. Ralph Crandall has been an inspiration and a good friend to both my father and me. Without his encouragement, this project would not have moved forward to publication. Numerous Phippen descendants have contributed to the project and I am very grateful for their assistance. I am especially indebted to Carol Phippen Silsby, for her extensive research in Maine vital records.

The Phippen surname has been spelled in numerous ways, both in England and America. Consistent surname spellings are (generally) the norm in the 20th and 21st centuries; not so in earlier times. David Phippen appears in the historical record at times as "David Phippeni" or "David Phippeny" (among others). Indeed, the facsimile of his signature, presumably taken from his will and reproduced in Winsor's *Memorial History of Boston* (vol. II, p. xii), clearly shows him signing his name as "David Phippeny."

Today, the surname has two principal spelling variants: *Phippen* and *Phippeney*. From the late 1600s, *Phippen* has been used by the descendants of Joseph[2] Phippen, while *Phippeney* (and its variants) has been used by the descendants of James[3] Phippeney. As a general rule, we have listed each numbered descendant with the spelling most commonly associated with that individual on the surviving historical record. Variations are often noted in the narrative to illuminate the spelling differences we encountered in the primary source material.

My *Fipphen* spelling is a relatively recent variant of *Phippen*. My great-great-grandfather's name appeared as Stephen *Fipphen* in his obituary in *The Concord Monitor* in 1907, but his gravestone and probate file show his name as Stephen *Phippen*. The story behind this change remains a mystery.

The publication of this volume marks the high point of our voyage, but not its end. I will be collecting corrections, additions, new material, etc. at phippengenealogy@gmail.com. In the short term, I am planning a Phippen genealogy blog to share new research, newly documented lines, and other topics of potential interest to Phippen descendants.

Finally, this preface would not be complete without a word about my collaborator, my friend, my Dad. From 1975 to 2010, we worked on this project together. He is the main reason why this volume has been published. Without his research, organization of the collected data, and writing of the original manuscript, this book would not have been possible. I am very sad that Dad did not live to see this stop on the journey. Yes, Dad, I am very pleased with the final product, as I know you are. We miss you.

Richard C. Fipphen
New York, New York
May 1, 2017

John S. Fipphen
(1927–2010)

List of Illustrations

Part I

The Phippen Family in England

CHAPTER 1

THE PHIPPEN GENEALOGICAL CHART OF 1808

A genealogical chart of the Phippen family—drawn in 1808 by John Symonds of Salem for Anstis Phippen and her husband Jonathan Smith—was the subject of an article published in 1868 by George D. Phippen of Salem, Massachusetts. The article appeared in *The Heraldic Journal*[1] and was titled "Fitzpen or Phippen, and Allied Families." The 1808 chart is a copy of an earlier version, drawn in 1768 by James Ford, a Salem schoolteacher, for David Phippen, Anstis Smith's father. The 1768 Ford copy suffered damage during the Revolutionary War and information was lost. The 1768 chart was itself a copy of the original genealogy prepared by Joseph Phippen, son of David1 Phippen, almost a century earlier.[2]

The *Heraldic Journal* article contained a partial genealogy of the Phippen family as well as a discussion of the history of the chart, which was presented in partial facsimile. Other than this short article, very little has been published on the Phippen family[3], with the exception of

---

[1]   George D. Phippen, "Fitzpen or Phippen, and Allied Families," *The Heraldic Journal* 4 [1868]: 1-20.

[2]   W.H. Whitmore, "Rev. Robert Jordan," *The New England Historical and Genealogical Register* 13 [1859]: 221-22.

[3]   There is a short genealogy of the family tucked into a footnote in Sidney Perley, *The History of Salem, Massachusetts,* 3 vols. (Salem, 1924–28), 2: 328–32; and another partial genealogy of the first few generations by Donald Lines Jacobus, "The Phippen Family and the Wife of Nathan1 Gold of Fairfield, Connecticut," *The American Genealogist* 17 [1940]: 1–19, with additional work by Jacobus in entries to his *History and genealogy of the families of old Fairfield,* 3 vols. (New Haven, Conn., 1930–32), 1: 476–78; 2: 2: 763; and 3: 262–63. Other twentieth-century studies of this family have only been compiled in manuscript, including a typescript series of

George Phippen's beautifully hand-lettered ledger book, dated 1848, in which he entered his notes and much more information. The book was formerly available in the library of the Essex Institute in Salem; unfortunately, it cannot now be located at that institution's successor, the Phillips Library of the Peabody Essex Museum.[4]

The 1808 Phippen chart is now in the Museum of Fine Arts, Boston, having been aquired by the museum in 1976. The chart is in a frame, 26.5" × 54.5", and—interestingly—contains much more information than was reproduced by George Phippen in the *Heraldic Journal* article. In addition to seventy-four elliptical or octagonal boxes containing names and genealogical information (plus two additional large decorated entries), there are eight elaborately painted coats of arms, and a great deal of painted and "pricked" ornamentation throughout the chart. See Plate IV for the complete Phippen chart. On Plates V and VI, we produce detail photographs of portions of the chart, showing the fine workmanship of the arms. Here, for the first time, we also provide a complete transcription of the genealogical information on the chart.

The chart requires some explanation. Each box contains information on a single individual. The boxes of married couples are next to each other and are linked by a design incorporating two hearts. No lines connect parents to children, and only rough placement clues indicate how individuals are connected to each other. The genealogical boxes are arranged into three "registers," or sections—an upper, middle, and lower section, each containing three rows of boxes—separated by heavy, ornamental lines. The upper register represents English ancestors or kin of the immigrant, David Phippen; the middle register represents his immediate descendants; and the lower register represents later members of the family. Within the lower register, another dividing line from upper left to lower right separates the material that would have been in the 1768 copy—made for David[5] Phippen (*Nathaniel*[4], *Samuel*[3], *Joseph*[2],

---

notes and correspondence by noted genealogist Winifred Lovering Holman, compiled around 1926, which are now among her papers in the collection of the New England Historic Genealogical Society (Mss A H63); and material collected by Anna Kingsbury around 1916, also held by NEHGS, in the Nickerson Collection (Mss SG Nic 30). Both collections have proved valuable.

4   We saw this manuscript once, in the 1980s. Following a request to locate it again, this manuscript has been extensively searched for (2006) by the staff at the Phillips Library of the Peabody Essex Museum, but without success.

5   The chart was briefly mentioned in a recent essay on the work of James Ford, compiler of the 1768 exemplar from which the existing 1808 copy was made: "James Ford, Salem Writing Master and Stonecarver," in Theodore Chase and Laurel K. Gabel, *Gravestone Chronicles II: More Eighteenth-century New England Carvers and an Exploration of Gravestone Heraldica* (Boston, 1997), 373–400, at 380 and 397–98.

David[1]) of Salem—and the 1808 copy made for his daughter Anstis[6] (Phippen) Smith and her husband Jonathan Smith. After the first two generations of American Phippens, those actually named in the chart are essentially limited to the direct line of ancestors of David[5] Phippen of Salem, along with the siblings of each of those Phippen ancestors. The new material added in the 1808 copy consists of information on the spouses and issue of the children of David[5] Phippen.

The coats of arms on the chart fall into two groups. The group of six coats of arms at upper left represents the Phippens and their English connections prior to emigration. This group, painted without crests or mantling, must have been copied from the 1768 chart, and may well have been taken from seventeenth-century drawings in possession of the New England family. These original six coats of arms, along with the English genealogical information in the top register, were almost certainly collected by the immigrant's brother, Rev. George Phippen of Truro, Cornwall, who may have given this information to his brother before emigration, or sent it to his brother and nephews after they emigrated. In contrast, the two much larger and more elaborate coats of arms in the bottom corners were likely added to the earlier version by the 1808 painter, John Symonds. The arms at right are simply another rendering of the Phippen or Fitzpen coat (with a crest which is not authentic); the arms at left represent Smith, for Jonathan Smith, for whom the 1808 copy was made. These Smith arms likely have nothing to do with Jonathan Smith of Salem; rather, they are drawn (perhaps at random) from one of the several coats of arms assigned to a Smith in the most popular book of English heraldry that was circulating in New England in the later 1700s— that is, the sixth edition of Guillim's *Display of Heraldry*, the source of most of the bogus coats of arms in New England from 1725 through the early nineteenth century.[6]

The genealogical information on the chart has obviously suffered from loss. Twelve of the seventy-four boxes for genealogical information are blank— nine of them in the top register. The top register is missing information that must have been one of the earlier versions of the chart. In particular, the names of the immigrant David Phippen and his wife

---

[6] On the rise of bogus arms after the appearance of Guillim's popular heraldry compendium, see "Headstones, Hatchments, and Heraldry, 1650–1850," in Chase and Gabel, *Gravestone Chronicles II*, 497–604, at 514–15, and note 30 at 596–97. These Smith arms are in John Guillim, *A Display of Heraldry*, 6th ed. (London, 1724), 403: arms confirmed to John Smith of Newcastle under Line, Staffordshire, in 1561: *barry of six, ermine and gules, a lion rampant crowned sable*. In the 1808 chart, the lion is proper (tawny-colored) and its crown is gold.

Sarah do not appear at all, although his parents, brother, and children do. It is possible that David's wife's surname, which remains unknown, might have been on the earlier, lost source of the 1808 copy.

The information on the 1808 chart agrees in some particulars with the pedigree of "Fitzpen alias Phippen," which was submitted by the immigrant's brother, Rev. George Phippen, for the 1620 Visitation of Cornwall.

Transcription of the 1808 Chart

Top Register, Left Side: Six coats of arms, in two groups of three, with a blank circular medallion in the center (surrounded by architectural ornament and mantling). The arms have names attributed to them on the chart. The attributed names are given here, with a simplified description of the arms (without "tinctures" or colors):

Arms

1. Peirce. *Two bends.*[7]
2. Fitzpen. *Two bars, in chief three escallops.*[8]
3. Holton. *On a bend, three eagles displayed.*[9]
4. Pie. *Impaled arms: "Fitzpen" as above, impaling on a fess, three escallops (for Pye of Saint Stephen's, Cornwall).*[10]
5. Jordaine. *A lion rampant among nine crosses crosslet fitchée.*[11]
6. Burges. *Impaled arms: A fess chequy, in chief three crosses crosslet fitchée (for Burgess of Truro); impaling Pye (as above, no. 4).*[12]

---

[7]   This appears to represent the family of Alice Peirce, wife of 'Henry Fitzpen,' the first person in the Visitation genealogy presented by George Phippen in 1620. The other Peirces in the chart appear to be her relatives, but have not been identified.

[8]   These are the same arms ascribed to himself by George Phippen in the 1620 Visitation of Cornwall, and used on his tomb and that of his brother Owen Phippen.

[9]   A Robert Holton is named on the chart as husband of Constance Peirce, who was probably related to Alice Peirce, claimed as wife of Henry Fitzpen in the 1620 Visitation pedigree. These arms therefore represent a collateral connection. These arms and the family to which they belong have not been found.

[10] These impaled arms represent the marriage of George Phippen to Jane Pye, and are also known to have been used on the marker for their tomb in the church of Saint Mary, Truro. These arms are the same as those used for the family of Pye of Saint Stephens in Brannel, Cornwall, in the 1620 Visitation of Cornwall: *see* J. L. Vivian, *The Visitations of Cornwall comprising the Heralds' Visitations of 1530, 1573 & 1620* (Exeter, Devon, 1887), 387.

[11] These arms are as rendered on George Phippen's tomb in Saint Mary's, Truro.

[12] No Burges appears named on the chart. However, George Fitzpen's wife Joan Pie appears to have previously beeen married to one Henry Burgess, while her sister Elizabeth Pie was married to a Thomas Burgess. Vivian, *The Visitations of Cornwall comprising the Heralds' Visitations of 1530, 1573 & 1620*, 63 (Burges), 387 (Pye),

Top Register, Right Side: Three rows of boxes, arranged 9, 8, and 8.

Top Register, Right Side, First Row

1. Wm. Peirce Mayor of Melcomb. Left issue Jonathan & Alexander.
2. Robt. Holton Gent. Died in Boloigne. Left issue Ann, Alexander, & George.
3. Constance Peirce Married Robt Holton. Left issue Samuel. Was afterward Married to Thomas Buckler; Lived 131[*sic*] Years.[13]
4. *Blank*
5. *Blank*
   [linked to]
6. Alice Peirce[14]
7. Robt Jordaine Gent. Left issue Robert.
   [linked to]
8. Cokers of ___ in Blandford, a second Wife brought him issue Henry.
9. John Pen, was Sherriff of London Anno. 1410.

Top Register, Right Side, Second Row

1. John Fitzpen He left issue Robert, John, and George.
   [linked to]
2. *Blank*
3. Robt Jordaine Mercht in Melcomb Left issue Cokers Jane & Edward
   [linked to]
4. *Blank*
5. *Blank*
6. *Blank*
7. Robt Fitzpen
   [linked to]
8. Cicely Jordaine

Top Register, Right Side, Third Row

1. *Blank*
2. Abel Phippen Married Jane Frances and had issue Elizabeth who died 2nd August 1636.
3. John Phippen Died Young.

---

and George D. Phippen, "Genealogical Gleanings in England," *Register* 49 [1895]: 240–46.

13 Boxes 2 and 3 in this row should be graphically linked, as containing spouses, but they are not. These people have not been identified.

14 Likely the "Alice Peirce, daughter of Thomas Peirce of Ireland" indicated in the 1620 Visitation pedigree as wife of Henry Fitzpen, but he does not appear on this chart.

4. Owen Phippen, who most valiently freed himself from the Turks.
5. *Blank*
6. *Blank*
7. Geo. Fitzpen called Phippen A.M.
8. Joan Pie daughter of Constance Pie

Middle Register: Three rows of boxes, arranged 10, 10, and 6.

Middle Register, First Row

1. Robt Phippen, who lost his life honourably in the King's service in the 28th year of his Age~
2. Joseph Phippen who lived ___ years; deceased and left issue, Joseph, Mary, Sarah, David and Samuel. By–
    [linked to]
3. Dorcas Wood~
4. Thos Phippen, was drowned in the 20th year of his Age.
5. George W left issue 9 Sons and 3 Daughters By–
    [linked to]
6. Rebecca Phippen
7. Benjm. Phippen, left issue 3 Sons, and 2 Daughters, By–
    [linked to]
8. Wellmith Youer~
9. Gamal Phippen left issue one Son and four Daughters, By–
    [linked to]
10. Sarah Purchase~

Middle Register, Second Row

1. Thomas Yow left issue one Son, and two Daughters, By–
    [linked to]
2. Sarah Phippen, who was after married to Nathan Goold, left issue two Sons, and one Daughter.
3. George Phippen, who married in London left issue two Sons and four Daughters.
4. Joseph Phippen left issue two Sons, and one Daughter By–
    [linked to]
5. Mary Standford ~ Seaborn Gooding a second Wife brought him issue Sons& Daughters
6. John Watti left issue four Sons & five Daughters By–
    [linked to]
7. Mary Phippen
8. Geo. Hodges left issue two Sons and four Daughters, By–
    [linked to]

9.   Sarah Phippen
10. David Phippen left issue ___ Sons By-

Middle Register, Third Row
1.   Ann Cromwell~
2.   Saml. Phippen left issue Samuel, John, Nathaniel, Joseph, and Rachel, By- [linked to]
3.   Rachel Guppe died Febr. 1. 1711.
4.   Nathl Phippen the 4th Son of Samuel. Born Augst 4th 1607. [corrected to Aug 4. 1677.] Married the 29th June 1710. died 13th August 1756. Left issue Nathaniel, Margaret, David, Abigail, Isrl, Anstis, Lydia, Lydia, and Thomas. By-
     [linked to]
5.   Margat Palfrey. Died Novm 30th 1753.

6.   *Blank*

Bottom Register: Three rows of cartouches, arranged 7, 6 and 10; two large double cartouches at left and right; two large coats of arms at left (Smith) and right (Phippen); compiler's colophons at bottom right.

Bottom Register, First Row
1.   David Phippen Jr. Born 17th June 1739. Died with the Small Pox February 25. 1761.
2.   Stephn Phippen Born 22d January 1741. Married 29. October 1767. issue ___ By-
     [linked to]

3.   *Reba Palfray. Born 17th Octr 1746.*
4.   John Gill Born ___ Married October 5. 1768. Had issue Elizabeth, Prisc., John, Sarah Phippen, Ann. By-
     [linked to]
5.   Prisc Phippen Born January 8. 1743.
6.   Saml Phippen Born December 28. 1745. Married ___ Had issue Samuel, Rebecca Maria By-
     [linked to]
7.   Polly Swain Born May 17. 1752. Samuel Phippen Died February 22. 1798.~

Bottom Register, Second Row
1.   John Fisk Born 30 April 1744. Married June 12. 1766. Had issue Lydia, Ann, Sarah, Margat, Betsy, John, Saml and Priscilla. By-
     [linked to]

2. Lydia Phippen Born January 10. 1747. Died October 13. 1782. John
    Fisk died Sept. 28. 1797.~
3. Margat Phippen Born January 7. 1749. Died February 13. 1749.
4. Ebenr Phippen Born 13. January 1750 Married October 27. 1772.
    Had issue Elizabeth, Ebenr, David, Ebenr, Saml, Stephn, Sally Norris,
    Lydia Fisk, Nancy, & Maria, By-
    [linked to]
5. Elizabeth Sims Born April 29. 1752.
6. Margt Phippen Born March 28. 1752.

Bottom Register, Third Row
1. Saml Hobbs Born Sept. 17th 1750. Was kill'd in the American War
    August 29. 1781. Left issue Sarah; Born April 15. 1782. By-
    [linked to]
2. Sarah Phippen. Born 7 April 1756. Married May 27. 1780. She was
    afterward married to Samuel Symonds had issue Saml Jr, Catherine,
    John, Lydia, Eliza, Nathl.
3. Nathl Phippen Born May 18. 1758. Married April 20. 1779. Had
    issue Nathaniel, Abigail, Saml, Sally, & John. By-
    [linked to]
4. Abigail Hooper Born August 22. 1761. Nathl Phippen Died Feby
    24th 1815- Aged 56 years.
5. William King Born ___ Married ___ Had issue Betsy, William, Lydia,
    Nathaniel, Hannah, Nathaniel, Rufus, Mary, Rebecca. By-
    [linked to]
6. Rebecca Phippen Born December 19. 1759.~
7. Elizath Phippen Born February 9th 1763. Died 31. March 1766.~
8. *Blank*
9. *Blank*
10. *Blank*

Large Cartouches
1. Jonathan Smith Born January 6. 1764. Married Sept. 6. 1789. To-
    Anstis Phippen Born February 13. 1755. [The following text, in
    different handwriting, was added at a later date.]
    Anstis Died Novr 28. 1815 Aged 60 years. Jona Smith was after
    Married May 19. 1816. To Sarah H. Leach- who was Born Feby 14.
    1778. Hannah Smith Mother of Jona, Died Novr 2. 1815. Aged 81
    years.
2. David Phippen 2. Son of Nathl. Born 10th Sept. 1710. Married
    4th May 1738. Left issue David, Stepn, Priscilla, Saml, Lydia, Margt,

Ebenr, Margt, Anstis, Sarah, Nathl, Rebecca, Elizath. By-
Priscilla Beckford Born August 8th 1719. Died April 16th 1781. Her
Husband died February 15th 1782.~

Colophons

1. Done for Jonathan Smith by John Symonds, 1808. Taken or Copied
   from one done for David Phippen, by James Ford in 1768.
2. This Genealogy was recorded by Joseph Phippen, who lived & died
   in New England, whose posterity where [*sic*] born there.

CHAPTER 2
THE EARLY PHIPPENS IN ENGLAND

In his 1868 genealogy, George D. Phippen wrote that "[t]he name Phippen is patronymic, and is a corruption of Fitz-pen or Fils-pen, (Fitz or Fils from the Latin Filius, meaning Son) being a Norman prefix to an old British name."[15] A few years earlier, in 1857, William Arthur's *An Etymological Dictionary of Family and Christian Names* gave the derivation of "Phippen" as "[a] corruption of *Fitz Penn,* from the Norman, *Fitz,* a son, and *Penn.* The son of *Penn.*"[16] This etymology was originally presented by the Rev. George Phippen, who submitted his family's pedigree under the name "Fitzpen" in the 1620 Visitation of Cornwall, and who chose the form "Fitzpen" for his own memorial tablet. Reaney's *Oxford Dictionary of English Surnames* cites the earliest documented instance of the name "Phippen" as "Nicholas Phippen" in the lay subsidy roll for Worcestershire in 1332,[17] which is a somewhat misleading reference because the name "Phippen" appears almost exclusively in Somerset and Dorset from the sixteenth century onward, with spellings *Fippen, Phepen, Phephyn, Phepyn, Phippen, Phippin,* and *Phippinge* all found there before 1600.[18]

---

[15] Phippen, "Fitzpen or Phippen, and Allied Families," *The Heraldic Journal* 4 [1868]: 10.

[16] William Arthur, *An Etymological Dictionary of Family and Christian Names: with an essay on their derivation and import* (New York, 1857), 217.

[17] P. H. Reaney and R.M. Wilson, *A Dictionary of English Surnames,* 3d ed., rev. (Oxford, 1997), 349, s. n. 'Phippen, Phippin.' The second reference is for a George Phippen, a student at Oxford in 1607, who is likely the brother of the immigrant David Phippen. Reaney's claim that "Phippen" derives from "'Phip-en,' a diminutive of 'Phipp,' a pet-form of 'Philip'" is not supported by any historical evidence. It is interesting to note that, in a separate publication, the same author notes that the name Okeford Fitzpaine appeared as "Occeford *Fyppyn*" in 1513. See P.H. Reaney, *The Origin of English Surnames* (London, 1967), 91.

[18] Federation of Family History Societies, *National Burial Index for England and Wales,* CD-ROM database, 2nd ed. (Coventry, Warwickshire, 2004); *see also,* T. L. Stoate, ed., *Dorset Tudor Subsidies Granted in 1523, 1543, 1593* (Bristol, Gloucestershire, 1982).

The 1808 Phippen chart, discussed in the previous chapter, implies
a derivation of the surname "Fitzpen" from the name "Pen"—hence the
box on the chart that states "John Pen, was Sherriff of London Anno.
1410," which was probably intended to indicate a male-line progenitor
or relative of the early Phippens. [19] The historical record supports the 1808
chart: a 'John Penne' was sheriff of London in 1410. [20] Also, a "Johannes
Penne" was returned to Parliament from Weymouth in 1421 and 1422
and a "Robertus Penne" was returned to Parliament from Melcombe
Regis in 1403, and from Weymouth in 1402, 1413, 1417, and 1419–21. [21]

While the evolution of the name "Phippen" has not been established
conclusively, the dual use of the names by "George Fitzpen alias
Phippen," brother of immigrant David Phippen, demonstrates George's
belief that "Phippen" was derived from an Anglo-Norman patronymic
"Fitzpen." Moreover, although George Phippen did not seek to claim
association, via the form of his surname or the arms he bore, with the
FitzPayns, we note that one prominent baronial family of Dorset and
Somerset, going back to the time of the Norman Conquest, bore the
surname FitzPayn. [22] While the evidence does not appear to establish a
connection between the Phippen/Fitzpen and FitzPayn families, [23] it
is worth noting that the surname Phippen does appear in an area of

---

[19]   Phippen chart, above, Top Register, First Row, no. 9.

[20]   *See The Survey of London by John Stow, Citizen of London,* ed. Ernest Rhys (London:
        J. M. Dent & Sons, 1912; work originally published 1598), 459. George D. Phippen
        observed that "[a]s all the other parts of the old record have been remarkably cor-
        roborated by the public archives, we infer that John Pen was not placed at the head
        of the list without authority." Phippen, "Fitzpen or Phippen, and Allied Families,"
        The Heraldic Journal 4 [1868]: 11.

[21]   *See* Public Record Office, *Return of Members of Parliament. Part I. Parliaments of
        England, 1213-1702* (London, 1878), 263, 265, 278, 289, 291, 294, 297, 299, and
        302.

[22]   On 'FitzPayn,' see *A Dictionary of English Surnames,* 335–36, s.n. 'Pain,' et al. 'FitzPayn'
        derives from the Norman given name 'Paien' (Latin 'Paganus').

[23]   The name Fitzpaine/FitzPayne appears, at times, to have been pronounced like
        "Phippen" or one of its variants, e.g., Fyppyn, Phippyn, Fippeny, and Fipany.
        Okeford Fitzpaine appeared as "Occeford *Fyppyn*" in 1513. *See* P.H. Reaney, *The
        Origin of English Surnames* (London, 1967), 91; George D. Phippen observed that
        the "chief seat of [the FitzPayn] family was called Fipany Okeford as late as 1600"
        ("Fitzpen or Phippen, and Allied Families," *The Heraldic Journal* 4 [1868]: 12). A
        compilation of 16th century court records from the diocese of Chester notes that
        "Wootton Fitzpaine" was known in the 16th century as "Wootton Phippyn." *See*
        Frederick J. Furnivall, *Child-Marriages, Divorces, and Ratifications, etc. in the Diocese of
        Chester, A.D. 1561-6* (London, 1897), xlv, n1. Bill Bryson has observed that "the
        strangest [village pronunciation] of all is Okeford Fitzpaine, Dorset, which many
        locals pronounce—for reasons no one can begin to guess at— 'fippeny ockford.'"
        Bill Bryson, *Mother Tongue: English & How It Got That Way* (New York, 1990), 206.

England where the earlier name "FitzPayn" had become rooted in local geography and history; thus, some account of the FitzPayns is provided here for context.

THE FITZPAYNS

A baronial FitzPayn family was prominent in Dorset and Somerset in the thirteenth and fourteenth centuries and appears to have been there since the time of the Norman Conquest.[24] A Robert FitzPayn was sheriff of Somerset and Dorset during the reign of Henry II. His grandson, Sir Robert FitzPayn (d. 1280 or 1281), fought in the Battle of Lewes in support of Simon de Montfort in the baronial party against King Henry III. His son and heir, also Sir Robert FitzPayn (d. 1315), is recognized by the *Complete Peerage* as the first Baron FitzPayn. According to the *Complete Peerage*, his manors included "Llanvair Discoed in Nether Gwent, Okeford Fitzpaine, Chelborough, Worth, and Wraxall, Dorset, Staple Fitzpaine, Cheddon Fitzpaine, Cary Fitzpaine, and Bridgehampton, Somerset, Poole Keynes and Stourton, Wiltshire [etc.]"[25] He was succeeded by his own son and heir, Robert, 2nd Baron FitzPayn (d. 1354), after which the barony of FitzPayn passed via daughters and cousins into the Chidiok and Grey families. Branches of this family also held lands in Frome Whitfield[26] and Kenticombe, Dorset.[27]

Robert, the second Baron Fitzpayn, is found in the 1327 lay subsidy for Dorset, holding lands in Wroxhale, Frome Whitfield, Okeford Fitzpaine, Chelborough, and Marshwood.[28] A William Fitzpayn is

---

[24] In *Domesday Book,* an Edmund fitzPayne "held ten hides and two valuable mills," according to C. G. Harfield, "William Belet: A Sergeant of the King's Retinue?" *Notes & Queries for Somerset and Dorset* 32 [1986]: 533–36, at 534. His "descendants' activities were not dissimilar to those of the Belet family," *i.e.,* they were royal sergeants who profited from their position.

[25] George Edward Cokayne, et al., *The Complete Peerage of England, Scotland, Ireland, Great Britain, and the United Kingdom, Extant, Extinct, or Dormant,* 2nd ed., 14 vols. (London, 1910–1998), 5: 448–64 (s. n. 'FitzPayn').

[26] An Arnald Fitzpayn, also called "Arnold of Frome," witnessed a number of charters printed in the *Cirencester Cartulary;* his apparent son, "Ralph son of Arnald Fispayn," made a grant to his brother Walter of eight acres of land in the "Field of Frome" around 1275. Michael McGarvie, "The Orchardleigh Charters," *Notes & Queries for Somerset and Dorset* 31 [1982]: 183–89 at 185.

[27] "The le Daneys family afterwards held of Robert FitzpPayn, one of de Percy's successors, in Kenticombe, Dorset." Rev. Sir Henry L.L. Denny, "Notes on the Family of Le Daneys," *Notes & Queries for Somerset and Dorset* 21 [1933]: 73, 76.

[28] *The Dorset Lay Subsidy Roll of 1327,* ed. Alexander R. Rumble (Dorchester: Dorset Record Society, 1980), 64 (Wroxhale), 1 (Frome Whitfield), 77 (Okeford Fitzpaine), 106 (Chelborough), 129 (Marshwood).

assessed in Dorchester and Fordyngtone in 1333.[29] The 2nd Baron
Fitzpayn was also assessed in the 1333 lay subsidy for Frome Whitfield,
Sutton Poyntz, and Okeford Fitzpayn.[30]

At least six former Fitzpayn manors in Dorset, Somerset, and
Devon still bear the name Fitzpayn: in Somerset, Cheddon Fitzpaine
(three miles north of Taunton), Staple Fitzpaine (five miles south of
Taunton), and Cary Fitzpaine (five miles north of Yeovil); in Devon,
Cheriton Fitzpaine (seven miles north of Exeter); and in Dorset,
Wootton Fitzpaine (two miles north of Lyme Regis) and Okeford
Fitzpaine (fifteen miles northeast of Dorchester).[31]

A popular work on Dorset recounts the local memory of one of
the baronial FitzPayns:

> Okeford Fitzpaine is one of Dorset's most attractive
> villages with timber-framed cottages, formed with locally
> made bricks, [and] has fought to retain its rural charm and
> solitude. Not only have the villagers tried to stop traffic
> rushing past ancient dwellings, but have successfully
> fought to have ugly overhead electric cables removed.
> Even the village post box is painted green rather than the
> traditional red. Twenty-five of the 18th century buildings
> are listed. In 1966 much of the village went under the
> hammer and was sold up for £166,000 but at the wish
> of the late Captain George Pitt-Rivers, who owned it,
> the properties were sold in lots to enable residents to
> purchase their own houses. One old man got his three-
> bedroomed thatched cottage for 1,500 pounds. Close by
> is a picnic site, high up on the famous Ridgeway—one
> of the country's ancient walks, which stretches from East
> Anglia to Devon.
>
> Villagers still chuckle when they retell the story of
> Robert son of Payn, one of the early Fitzpaines and a
> former landowner. He fought at the Battle of Lewes
> against King Henry III and was one of his captors.
> Analogous to a modern soldier 'borrowing' the sleeping-

---

[29] *The Dorset Lay Subsidy Roll of 1327*, ed. Alexander R. Rumble (Dorchester: Dorset
Record Society, 1980), 133 (Fordyngtone) and 137 (Dorchester).

[30] *The Dorset Lay Subsidy Roll of 1332*, ed. A. D. Mills (Dorchester: Dorset Record
Society, 1971), 2 (Frome Whitfield), 47 (Sutton Poyntz), and 65 (Okeford Fitzpaine).

[31] *See* A. D. Mills, *A Dictionary of British Place-Names* (Oxford, 2003).

out pass stamp in the Guard Room behind the military policeman's back, Robert of Payn and a man called Govis *'borrowed'* the King's seal and set it on a document excusing them from paying dues on their estates.

The sting in the telling of their amusing ruse was the rider stating that the grounds for the special indulgence were *'their good services to the King at Lewes.'*[32]

An article on the manor of Cheddon Fitzpaine gives a similar account of the family:

> Robert, 1st Lord Fitz-Payn . . . fought in the Welsh wars, 1282, and was summoned to Parliament as a baron, 1289. He was in the Scotch wars, 1303; was appointed governor of Corfe Castle, Dorset, 1305; installed K.B., 1306; appointed governor of Winchester Castle, 1307; and Steward of the Royal Household, 1308. In the same year he was dispatched on an embassy to the Papal Court at Rome. He died, 1316, and was succeeded by his son,
>
> Robert, 2nd Lord Fitz-Payn, then aged 28. In 1328, he gave the living of Cheddon [Fitzpaine] to John de Coteheye, the first rector of the parish whose name is recorded. Lord Fitzpayn served in the wars in Scotland and France, and before 1344 was a knight banneret. [sic] He married before 1323–4, Ela, who appears to have been a daughter of Sir Guy de Brian. In that year a settlement was made by lord Fitz-Payn and his wife under the terms of which, if they left no male heir, Cheddon and several other manors were to pass to Robert de Grey whose wife was a daughter of Sir Guy de Brian. Lord Fitz-Payn died 1354, leaving an only daughter, wife of Sir John Chideocke. Two years later, on the death of lady Fitz-Payn, Cheddon was inherited under the settlement by Robert de Grey, who thereupon assumed the name of Fitz-Payn.[33]

---

[32] "The Dorset Page," http://www.thedorsetpage.com/locations/Place/O020.htm (accessed 12 September 2010).

[33] A. W. Vivian-Neal, "The Church of Saint Mary, Cheddon Fitzpaine," *Notes & Queries for Somerset and Dorset* 23 [1941]: 199–205. This summary of the FitzPayn family is found at 200–1.

So, while the FitzPayns died out in the male line, the name was perpetuated among successors to the manor, though it was rare as a surname in Dorset and Somerset after the fourteenth century.

PHIPPENS IN SOMERSET AND DORSET

By the sixteenth century, the name "FitzPayn" had become quite rare while the name "Phippen" and its variants appear regularly. The published sixteenth-century Dorset lay subsidy rolls record several Phippens, including at least one association with an old FitzPayn manor: the lay subsidy of 1525 for the tithing of Wooton Fitzpaine shows a John Phepyn assessed £2 on goods (in addition to two men with the surname "Payn").[34] In 1545, John "Shypane" was assessed £1 in the same place.[35] In Dorchester in 1525, the same or another John Phephyn was assessed £1 on wages.[36] In Godmanston in 1598, John Fippen was assessed £1 on lands;[37] in Hawkechurche in 1543 and 1544, John Pheppyn was assessed £2.[38]

The National Burial Index ("NBI"), a compilation of burial records extracted from parish registers throughout England and Wales, shows concentrations of Phippens in several parishes of Dorset and Somerset between the years 1550 and 1670: in Dorset—Whitchurch and Melcombe Regis; in Somerset—Wrington, Wedmore, and various others.[39] Unfortunately, the NBI has as yet insufficient data for Devon

---

[34] *Dorset Tudor Subsidies,* 64.

[35] Ibid. There was also a Robert Payne.

[36] Ibid., 107.

[37] Ibid., 219.

[38] Ibid., 9. Two later Hawkchurch Phippens have wills recorded at the Archdeaconry Court of Dorset—the principal probate jurisdiction for the county. They are William Phippen, probated in 1667, and Alice Phippen, probated in 1672. See *A Calendar of Wills and Administrations Relating to the County of Dorset,* ed. Edward A. Fry, Index Library, vol. 22 (London, 1900).

[39] Federation of Family History Societies, *National Burial Index for England and Wales,* CD-ROM database, 2nd ed., (Coventry, 2004). The Phippen family of Wedmore, Somerset, has been identified as the origin of Judith (Phippen) (Hayward) Simonds, emigrant to Massachusetts in 1635, wife of James Hayward and then William Simonds, both of Woburn, Mass. The will of William Phipping of Wedmore, Somerset, proved 22 September 1647, mentions brother Joseph in Ireland and a daughter "Judah" in New England. "Notes," *Register* 66 [1912]: 87, citing *Matthew's Probate Acts,* vol. 5, 112. On 22 March 1634, Judith Phippen left London, at the age of 16, on the *Planter,* bound for New England (John C. Hotten, *The Original Lists of Persons of Quality [etc.] who went from Great Britain to the American Plantations* [New York, 1880, reprinted in 1962], 43). For the complete treatment of Judith Phippen, see Robert Charles Anderson, *The Great Migration: Immigrants to New England 1634-1635,* 7 vols. (Boston: New England Historic Genealogical Society, 1999-2011),

and Cornwall so it is not possible to identify parishes in those counties with similar early Phippen families.

One of the Dorset parishes above—Melcombe Regis—is identified as the birthplace of the Rev. George Phippen and his brother Owen Phippen on the two memorial tablets that were erected by George Phippen for himself and his brother Owen in the church of Saint Mary, Truro, Cornwall.[40] Two entries from the Melcombe Regis parish registers relating to the Phippens were noted by George D. Phippen in his 1868 *Heraldic Journal* article, namely the marriage record for Robert Phippen and Cecily Jordan, the parents of the immigrant David Phippen, and a baptism record for Cecily Phippen, daughter of Robert and Cicely (Jordan), dated 10 March 1593.[41] An English correspondent had apparently extracted this information on his behalf.[42]

Now, for the first time, the original Melcombe Regis parish registers have been reviewed, and all pertinent Phippen and Jordan records extracted.[43] There are two early register volumes: one for the church of Saint Mary, Melcombe Regis, and the other for the neighboring church of Saint Mary, Radipole, which was subordinate to Melcombe Regis after 1605 and appears to have overlapped in jurisdiction. Extractions from the two registers are presented here:

Register of Saint Mary's, Melcombe Regis *(marriages and burials start 1560; baptisms start 1595; register continues to 1640/41)*

1562, 3 April: John Jordine buried

1563[/64], 16 March Bartholomew **Jordon,** son of Thomas, buried

1563[/64], 16 March John **Jordon,** son of Thomas, buried

1564[/65], 8 January: Thomas Perrye and Alice **Jorden** married

1570, 11 April: William Chappell and Elizabeth **Jorden** married

1572[/73], 22 February: William **Jordon** buried

5: 456-57 (Judith Phippen), and Edward F. Johnson, *Genealogical Sketch of William Simonds* (Woburn, Mass., 1889), 3 *et seq.*

[40]   On the two memorials, see below.

[41]   Phippen, "Fitzpen or Phippen, and Allied Families," *The Heraldic Journal* 4 [1868]: 6, 13, 16.

[42]   Horatio G. Somerby may have extracted them. George D. Phippen refers to him as the source of some English material in the article, although the source of the parish register extractions is not made clear. Ibid. at 2.

[43]   Microfilm of the original Melcombe Regis parish registers is available from the Family History Library. *See* Family History Library film 2,427,538.

1573, 25 October: Ragnolde Vervill and Christian **Jorden** married

1575, 25 June: Henrie **Jorden** and Marie Myller married

1579, 13 November: Richard **Jordan,** son of Henry, buried

1580, 18 September: Robart Phippen and Cicely **Jordan** married

1589, 12 October: Robert **Jurder** buried

1591, 5 April: Anne **Jurden** buried

1593[/94], 16 February: Joanne **Jurdane** buried

1596, 2 June: Mary **Jurden,** daughter of Hugh, baptized

1596, 24 November: William **Phippen,** who "died coming from Portland," buried

1603, 3 July: Owen **Phippen** and Annis Cane married

1603, 27 October: John **Jorden,** son of Anthony, baptized

1604, 23 August: Catherine **Jurden,** daughter of Markes, baptized

Register of Saint Mary's, Radipole ("that part of the parish of Radipole which is called 'Melcombe Regis'") *(baptisms and burials start 1606; marriages start 1618; register continues to 1654)*

1607, 30 May: Edward **Phippen,** son of Robert, buried

1608, 10 November: Mary **Jordan,** daughter of Henry, baptized

1608, 16 April: Anne **Jurdan,** wife of Mark, buried

1608, 19 May: Cecily **Phippen,** wife of Robert, buried

1609[/10], 11 January: Annis **Phippen,** wife of Owen, buried

1609[/10], 8 February: Robert **Phippen** buried

1610, 25 December: Richard **Jordan,** son of Anthony, baptized

1614, 16 April: William **Jordan,** son of Anthony, baptized

1616[/17], 9 January: Rebacha **Jordan,** daughter of Anthony, baptized

1617, 18 December: Joseph **Jordan,** son of John, baptized

1619[/20], 20 March: Alice **Jordan,** daughter of Henry, baptized

1620, 20 May: _____, infant daughter of Henry **Jorden,** buried

1621, 25 April: Elizabeth **Jordan,** daughter of Henry, baptized

1623, 24 Dec: Rebecca **Jordan,** daughter of Henry, baptized

1628[/29], 3 March: Mary **Jordan**, daughter of Henry, buried

1629, 26 April: Friswell **Jordon**, widow, buried

1629, 3 May: Mary **Jordan**, daughter of Henry, baptized

1632, 27 June: Abel **Phippen** "of Weymouth" buried

1632, 16 July: Hugh **Jordon** buried

1632[/33], 6 January: Mary **Jordon** buried

1635, 19 June: Richard **Jordan**, son of Anthony and Frissell, buried

1638/39, 13 January: Rebecca **Jordan**, daughter of William and Lucy, baptized

1640, 24 February: Rebecca **Jordon**, daughter of William and Lucy, buried

1643, 9 April: Ruth **Jordan**, daughter of William and Lucy, baptized

1645, 25 September: _____ **Jorden**, infant son of William, buried

1648/49, 7 February: John **Jordan**, son of William, baptized

1650/51, 20 March: Mary **Jordan**, daughter of William, baptized

It will be noticed that the 1593 (or 1593/94) baptism record for David Phippen's sister Cecily, noted in 1868 by George D. Phippen, is not currently preserved in the original register. It is possible that it has been lost since 1868 with one or more leaves of the baptisms in the first Melcombe Regis register, since the currently preserved baptisms only begin in 1595. Nevertheless, the Phippen data presented here documents some of the immediate family of the immigrant David Phippen: the marriage and burials of his parents, one marriage of a brother (and the brother's wife's later burial), and the burial of another brother, previously unknown (Edward).

The parish records presented here do not conclusively show the immediate family of Cecily (Jordan) Phippen, although it is clear that there was a large Jordan family in and around Weymouth at this time. Bartholomew and John Jordan, sons of Thomas, who were buried together in 1564, were probably Cecily's brothers. In 1570, William Geordayne appears in a list of the freemen of the borough of Melcombe Regis, with Charles and Henry Geordaine appearing as inhabitants who were not borough freemen.[44] Thomas Jordan was not named in

---

[44] "Melcombe Regis town register [1564 to circa 1584]," a manuscript book of

the same list of inhabitants and may have died by the time his children were buried there in 1564. On the other hand, one list from the 1570s of the male inhabitants of the borough of Weymouth (not formally merged with Melcombe Regis until a few years later) names three contemporary adult Thomas Jordans, any one of whom may well have been Cecily's father.[45] Other Jordan records appear in this period: one Richard Jordan is named in a list of tariffs on the transportation of horses from the port in 1573, and Edmund Jordan in the same capacity in 1574.[46] A Richard Jordan was mayor of the borough of Melcombe Regis/Weymouth from 1596 to 1598.[47] It is likely that these Jordans were closely related to Cecily (Jordan) Phippen.

GEORGE PHIPPEN AND THE 1620 VISITATION OF CORNWALL

The traditional origins of the New England Phippen family have been recounted as they appear in a four-generation pedigree submitted by Rev. George Phippen (brother of immigrant David) to the 1620 Visitation of Cornwall. This pedigree was published twice in the nineteenth century in printed editions of the visitation, and twice more in New England in articles on the Phippen family.[48] The original manuscript of this Visitation is in the British Library.[49] A copy of the original manuscript, showing both the herald's drawing of the Phippen (or Fitzpen) arms and the original signature of Rev. George Phippen, is presented here for the first time (see Plate I).

The claims of the pedigree are reflected on the 1808 Phippen chart. Most importantly, the claim that the surname inherited by Rev. George Phippen was originally "Fitzpen" cannot be proved, since no

---

town records compiled by William Gregory of the mayoralty of the borough of Melcombe Regis (Cambridge, Mass.: Harvard University, Houghton Library, MS Eng 757), 19. This magnificent register contains several tax lists and lists of freemen and unfree men of the borough, as well as copies of documents relevant to the business of the port and borough, from 1564 through the 1570s, when William Gregory appears to have left the borough and taken the book with him.

45   "Fals suplicacion exhibited by the Inhabitants of Waimouth," undated, Melcombe Regis town register, Houghton MS Eng 757, 66–67.

46   Melcombe Regis town register, Houghton MS Eng 757, 146–47, 154.

47   George Alfred Ellis, *The History and Antiquities of the Borough and Town of Weymouth and Melcombe Regis* (Weymouth, 1829), 229 (list of mayors).

48   J. L. Vivian, *The Visitation of the County of Cornwall in the year 1620* (London, 1874), 71; J. L. Vivian, *The Visitations of Cornwall, Comprising the Heralds' Visitations of 1530, 1573 & 1620* (Exeter, 1887), 160. See also Phippen, "Fitzpen or Phippen, and Allied Families," *The Heraldic Journal* 4 [1868]: 3; and Phippen, "Genealogical Gleanings in England," *Register* 49 [1895]: 245.

49   British Library, MS Harley 1162, f. 84.

independent evidence of the surname "Fitzpen" anywhere in England, at any time, has ever been found. Likewise, the arms associated with the name are found uniquely in this Visitation pedigree, on the 1808 chart, and on the funeral monuments commissioned by Rev. George Phippen himself. It has also proved impossible to independently verify any of the specific ancestors claimed in the pedigree earlier than the parents of Rev. George Phippen and his siblings. The Phippen/Fitzpen ancestors, as given in the 1620 Visitation pedigree, are presented here:

First generation
Henry Fitzpen of St. Mary Ov'y in Devon = Alice, da. of _____
Peirse of Ireland.

Second generation
Jo: Fitzpen = _____ da. of _____

Third generation
Robt Fitzpen als Fippen of Wamouth in Com. Dorset = Cicilie da: of Tho: Jordan of Dorsetsh:

Fourth generation
Owen Fitzpen of Ireland 1 sonne.
David 2 sonne.
Geo: 3 sonne of Trouro in Cornwall, living 1620:
Cicilie a da:

[The pedigree is signed by "Geo: Fitzpen als Phippen."]

Of the pedigree's "Fitzpens," the first Henry Fitzpen is assigned a home that appears to be the parish now known as Ottery Saint Mary, Devonshire. Ottery's surviving parish register, which begins in 1601, shows nothing resembling the surnames of Fitzpen or Phippen, although there are many Pierces (spelled variously) present from the first years of the register onward. The 1808 Phippen chart displays a version of Peirce arms, and also shows apparent Peirce kin, not mentioned in this Visitation pedigree. Again, though, these Pierce arms cannot be assigned to any identifiable Pierce family, whether in Ireland or elsewhere. Further, while the Visitation pedigree shows the second generation, John Fitzpen, as having one son, Robert, the 1808 chart adds two other sons, John and George, who would be uncles of the immigrant David. None of these people, other than the immigrant's parents themselves, can be independently verified.

It is worth noting that the form "Fitzpen" is found almost exclusively connected to the Reverend George, and on a few New England records connected to his nephews there. Also, we have not located any English parish or other public records that use the "Fitzpen" variant of the surname. On the basis of the 1808 chart, the 1620 Visitation pedigree, the Melcombe Regis parish registers, and other information pertaining to Rev. George Phippen, the following summary of the known English family of David Phippen can be presented.

THE ENGLISH FAMILY OF DAVID PHIPPEN

1. ROBERT[A] **PHIPPEN,** perhaps originally of Weymouth, Dorset (as stated in the 1620 Visitation pedigree), was later of adjacent Melcombe Regis, where he married, on 18 September 1580,[50] **CECILY JORDAN,** said by Rev. George Phippen to be the daughter of Thomas Jordan of Melcombe Regis.[51] Their marriage record is the first time the name "Phippen" appears in the Melcombe Regis parish registers, which began only twenty years earlier. Cecily Jordan may well be sister to Bartholomew and John Jordan, sons of a Thomas Jordan, who were buried there in the 1560s. Other Jordans were buried or married in Melcombe Regis in this time, and various adult male Jordans, including a person or persons named Thomas Jordan, are found in surviving municipal records for the twin boroughs of Melcombe Regis and Weymouth. Cecily Phippen, "wife of Robert," was buried at Melcombe Regis on 19 May 1608.[52] Robert Phippen is likely the man of that name who was buried at Melcombe Regis almost two years later, on 8 February 1609/10.[53]

No records survive for Robert Phippen outside the parish register's notations of his marriage and burial, but he may well be the "Goodman Phippen" who appears in fiscal records of the expenditures of the mayor of the borough of Weymouth and Melcombe Regis[54] for the year ending Michaelmas 1604. These records show the payment of £2 9s 1d to "Goodman Phippen" for "byndinge the bridge pillers wth railes" and for "mendinge the Ramer and the Whele for the bridge."[55] If Robert

---

50   Register of Saint Mary's, Melcombe Regis (see Note 43 above).

51   Vivian, *The Visitation of the County of Cornwall in the year 1620,* 71.

52   Register of Saint Mary's, Radipole / Melcombe Regis (see Note 43 above).

53   Ibid.

54   The towns of Weymouth and Melcombe Regis were merged into a single borough during the reign of Elizabeth I (1571). *See* Samuel Lewis, *A Topographical Dictionary of England* (London, 1831), 4: 442-45.

55   Henry Joseph Moule, *Descriptive Catalogue of the Charters, Minute Books and Other Documents of the Borough of Weymouth and Melcombe Regis, A.D. 1252 to 1800, with extracts and some notes* (Weymouth, Dorset, 1883), 136.

Phippen was indeed a master carpenter as this record implies, he may well have passed the trade to his son David, who was also contracted to mend the borough's bridge a generation later, in 1631 and again in 1633 (see below).[56]

Children of Robert[A] and Cecily (Jordan) Phippen, apparently born at Melcombe Regis, Dorset:

2   i.   OWEN PHIPPEN, b. ca. 1582 (calculated by age at death, memorial tablet).

     ii.   DAVID[1] PHIPPEN, called "2 sonne" in the 1620 Visitation pedigree, hence he was b. between 1583 and 1590. (The emigrant to the Massachusetts Bay Colony, he is person number 1 in the next chapter.)

3   iii.   GEORGE PHIPPEN, b. in 1591 (memorial tablet).

     iv.   CECILY PHIPPEN, apparently bp. at Melcombe Regis 10 March 1593[/94?]. She appears to have been unmarried in 1620, but was married in 1650, when her brother George named her in his will, as "my sister Cecily Reignolds," leaving also a ring to her (unnamed) husband, showing that she was not then a widow.[57] Her spouse, place of residence, and family are unknown.

     v.   EDWARD PHIPPEN, "son of Robert," bur. at Melcombe Regis 30 May 1607.[58] His position in the birth order is unclear, since he did not survive to be named in the 1620 Visitation pedigree.

2. OWEN PHIPPEN (*Robert*[A]) was born about 1582, apparently at Melcombe Regis, Dorset; he died at Lamoran, Cornwall 17 March 1636/37, aged 54 years (according to the monument erected by his brother at Saint Mary's Church in Truro). He was buried at Saint Mary's 19 March 1636/37.[59] He married, at Melcombe Regis 3 July 1603,

---

[56]   It is possible that this 1604 record applies to David Phippen, but it is likely that he was only a youth in 1604 and unlikely to have been referred to as "Goodman."

[57]   One writer has claimed that Cecily Phippen married a Thomas Reynolds in 1594, and had a daughter Cecily Reynolds who arrived in Jamestown, Virginia in 1610. Given that Cecily Phippen, daughter of Robert Phippen, was born at about the same time (1593-94), she was obviously not the wife of Thomas Reynolds in 1594. *See* William G. Reynolds, *Reynolds History Annotated (1475-1977)* (Rockville, Md., 1978), 1, 105.

[58]   Register of Saint Mary's, Radipole / Melcombe Regis (see Note 43 above).

[59]   *The Register of Marriages, Baptisms & Burials of the Parish of St. Mary, Truro, Co. Cornwall, A.D. 1597 to 1837* (Exeter, 1940), 1: 275 ("Phippen, Owenus, Rectorii frater").

ANNIS CANE.[60] Annis Phippen, wife of Owen Phippen, was buried at Melcombe Regis 11 January 1609/10.[61] Owen Phippen may well have married again. As there are no other brothers shown in the Visitation pedigree signed by his brother George, he must be the father of the man named in his brother George's will as "my kinsman and brothers sonne Roger Phippen of Pennycomquicke" (near Exeter, Devon).

Owen Phippen was a mariner. In the Visitation of Cornwall of 1620, George Phippen referred to his brother Owen as "of Ireland," suggesting at least a temporary residence there. Yet in 1620, Owen Phippen would go even farther afield from his native Dorset. Years later, Owen Phippen's brother George caused the following memorial tablet (see Plate II) to be erected in the old church of Saint Mary, Truro, attesting to seven years of slavery and a daring escape from captivity under the corsairs of Algiers:

> To the pious and well deserved memory of Owen Fitz–Pen *alias* Phippen, who travelled over many parts of the world, and on the 24 of March 1620, was taken by the Turkes, and made a captive in Argier [*sic*]. He projected sundry plots for his libertie, and on the 17 of June 1627, with 10 other Christian captives, Dutch and French, (perswaded by his counsel and courage,) he began a cruel fight with 65 Turkes, in their owne ship, which lasted 3 howers, in which 5 of his company were slaine; yet God made him captaine, and so he brought the ship into Cartagene, being of 400 tons, and 22 ordnance. The King sent for him to Madrid, to see him; he was profered a capitaines place, and the King's favour, if he would turne Papist, which he refused. He sold all for £6000, returned into England, and died at Lamorran 17 March 1636.
>
> Melcombe in Dorset was his place of birth, Age 54, and here lies earth in earth.
>
> George Fitz-pen alias Phippen, ipsius frater et hujus ecclesiae rector, H. M. P. [*George Fitz-Pen alias Phippen, his brother and rector of this church, erected this monument.*][62]

---

60 Register of Saint Mary's, Melcombe Regis (see Note 43 above).
61 Register of Saint Mary's, Radipole / Melcombe Regis (see Note 43 above).
62 Daniel Lysons and Samuel Lysons, *Magna Brittannia* (London, 1814), 3: 2: 312-13. *See also* Joseph Polsue, *A Complete Parochial History of the County of Cornwall*, 4 vols. (Truro, 1867–72), 4: 255. The latter adds this heraldic information: "At the top of the monument are two shields, one charged with the arms of Fitz-pen, the

Child(ren) of Owen Phippen, perhaps by Annis Cane or by a later wife, include:

    i.   ROGER PHIPPEN, living at Pennycomquick, Devon, at the time of the will of his uncle George Phippen in 1650.

Owen Phippen's issue and kin appear to have continued in Cornwall and/or Devon at least into the eighteenth century, as may be implied by this comment in Joseph Polsue's *Parochial History of the County of Cornwall:*

> The Cornish branch of the Fitz-Pen family was short-lived, and its extinction gloomy. Near the close of the last century [i.e., the 18th] a man was found suffocated in a limekiln near Truro, into which he had crept for shelter and had fallen asleep; this was a poor, wandering, homeless maniac, called George Fitz-Pen, *alias* Phippen, *alias* Georgy Phipenny, the last representative of the brave Owen and the learned rector and master of the grammar School in 1625. In his lifetime he had been inoffensive and harmless, although he had to submit to much annoyance from school boys; he visited the neighbouring farm houses at certain seasons, and demanded with a show of authority, the payment of his rents; being well-known he was humoured in his notions, and his claims were readily compromised for a slice of cheese and a cup of cider. It is not known that he accepted parochial assistance, choosing rather to subsist for days together on the refuse of the markets.[63]

3. GEORGE PHIPPEN (*Robert*[A]) was born in 1591 (according to his own memorial tablet), and was 14 years of age upon his matriculation as a student at Exeter College, Oxford, on 6 February 1606/7.[64] As "George

---

other, *Or, a lion rampant between ten crosses crosslet sable,* being the arms of Adams." (These are, in fact, the Jordan arms found on the 1808 chart.) *See also* Fortescue Hitchins, *The History of Cornwall, from the earliest records and traditions, to the present time* (Helston, Cornwall, 1824), 2: 648.

[63] Polsue, *A Complete Parochial History of the County of Cornwall,* 4: 262.

[64] Joseph Foster, *Alumni Oxonienses: The Members of the University of Oxford, 1500–1714,* 4 vols. (Oxford, 1891), 3: 1160: "Phippen, George, of Dorset, pleb. EXETER COLL., matric. entry 6 Feb., 1606-7, aged 14; B.A. 27 Oct., 1610, M.A. 28 May,

Phippen" he took the degrees of bachelor of arts on 27 October 1610, and master of arts on 28 May 1614, and was ordained around the same time.

At some point after becoming a priest, he assumed the name "Fitzpen" in addition to Phippen: in 1620, as "George Fitzpen alias Phippen," he recorded a pedigree and arms in the Visitation of Cornwall (as discussed and reproduced above).

The Reverend George Phippen became lecturer of Saint Mary's, Truro, on 1 January 1619 and rector on 17 December 1624.[65] On 11 May 1625, he was also named the rector of the neighboring parish of Lamorran.[66] He was also master of the grammar school at Truro from 1621 to 1635. An inscribed communion table of oak and brass was among his gifts to Saint Mary's, still extant in 1840.[67] In 1645, in the course of the English Civil War, he was ejected as rector of Saint Mary's, stripped of some of his property, and "sequestered" for awhile to Saint Peter's, Berkhamstead, in Hertfordshire. He referred to this incident in his will as "the time of my imprisonment for myne adhering to Parliament." We do not know the length of his imprisonment. By the time of his second marriage in 1648, he had returned to Cornwall and was again vicar of Lamorran. He was still serving as rector at Lamorran when he wrote his will in 1650. He was buried at Lamorran on 28 September 1651.[68]

1614; rector of Truro St. Mary, Cornwall, 1629, sequestered to the rectory of Berkhampstead St. Peter, Herts, 1645, by the Westminster assembly of divines. See *Add. MS.* 15,669, p. 48; & Foster's *Index Eccl.*"

[65] *St. Mary, Truro Parish Register,* 1: ix ("1624. Geo. Phippen, *Rector*"); F.W.B. Bullock, *A History of the Parish Church of St. Mary, Truro* (Truro, 1948), 35.

[66] Bullock, *A History of the Parish Church of St. Mary, Truro,* 36.

[67] "Amongst the few notabilia within the church is the communion table, presented by the Rev. George Phippen, Rector. It is made of oak and encircled by a brass band, on which is very beautifully engraven in Greek capital letters, the 54th verse of the 6th Chapter of St. John's Gospel, 'whoso eateth my flesh and drinketh my blood hath eternal life, and I will raise him up at the last day'; thus perpetually affirming the sanction of the great head of the Christian Church, for the use of the sacrament in both kinds, (which the Roman Catholics have denied to the laity,) by affixing it to the very 'horns of the altar'. This table being made of *wood* escaped the violence of the commonwealth commissioners, who were authorised by an Act of Parliament to destroy all images and pictures in and about places of worship, and all altars of *stone*. Beneath the table is a brass plate, recording the burial of himself and wife, in a vault before prepared by themselves. . . ." "Notes relating to the Dominican Friary, in Kenwyn Street, and to St. Mary's Church, Truro, by Mr. Spry. Read July 3rd. 1840," *Twenty-Second Annual Report of the Royal Institution of Cornwall* (1840), 40–55. Placed online by Chris Bond, "A Cornish Sourcebook", at <http://cornovia.org.uk/htexts/spry01.html> (accessed 4 January 2006).

[68] Bullock, *A History of the Parish Church of St. Mary, Truro,* at 37.

George Phippen was married, first, apparently in 1621, to JOAN or JANE PYE, daughter of Anthony and Constance (Pound) Pye of Saint Stephens, Cornwall, and apparently widow of Henry Burgess.[69] The 1808 Phippen chart contains two coats of arms depicting her marriages to Burgess and to Phippen. She was buried at Truro 19 August 1636, the parish register referring to her as "Phippen, Jana uxor Georgii, *rectoris.*"[70] George Phippen married, second, at Helston, Cornwall 20 June 1648, MARY PENROSE, daughter of John and Jane (Trefusis) Penrose of Helston.[71] Both wives were gentlewomen, of families found in the Visitation of Cornwall. However, the Penrose arms are not found on the 1808 Phippen chart.

George Phippen's intended tomb in Saint Mary's[72] is marked by a brass plaque placed near the altar table he had given to the church (see Plate III). It bears two coats of impaled arms: first, the "Fitzpen" arms impaled with arms said to represent Jordan (for his mother), and second, the same "Fitzpen" arms impaled with those of Pye (representing himself with his first wife). The inscription is as follows:

EGO GEO. FITZPEN ALS PHIPPEN, 1591 DORSET
DE MELCOMB, 1614 IN ART. MAG. ET PRAEDICA.,
1624 HUIUS ECCL: RECTOR, ET IANA PIE 1621
UXOR MEA, HANC MENSAM 1628 ET SUB
EADEM SEPULCHRUM CONDIDIMUS.

JESU FILI DAVID TU SOLUS NOBIS VIA VERITAS
VITA.[73]

Translation: *I, George Fitzpen alias Phippen, [born] 1591 at Melcombe Regis, Dorset; Master of Arts (and licensed to preach) 1614; rector of this church 1624; and Jane Pye, my wife in 1621, have erected this [communion] table and the tomb below it in 1628.*

---

[69] Vivian, *The Visitations of Cornwall, Comprising the Heralds' Visitations of 1530, 1573 & 1620,* 387. Some connections of the family of Pye of Saint Stephen, Cornwall, are discussed by George D. Phippen in the "Genealogical Gleanings in England" passages on Burgess, Catcher, Pye, and Phippen, *Register* 49 [1895]: 240–46.

[70] *St. Mary, Truro Parish Register,* 1: 274.

[71] Helston Parish Register, from Cornwall Marriages, accessed via the Findmypast. co.uk website <www.findmypast.co.uk> (accessed 24 Sept. 2010) (marriage of George Phippen and Mary Penros); Vivian, *The Visitations of Cornwall, Comprising the Heralds' Visitations of 1530, 1573 & 1620,* 367 (Penrose).

[72] George Phippen was buried in Lamorran, not Saint Mary's.

[73] Polsue, *A Complete Parochial History of the County of Cornwall,* 4: 255. Translation: Nathaniel L. Taylor.

> *O Jesus, son of David: you alone are for us the way, the truth,*
> *and the life.*

When Saint Mary's parish became the seat of the newly created Anglican diocese of Cornwall in 1876, the old church was mostly demolished for the construction of the large neo-Gothic Truro cathedral; only a portion of the south aisle of the old parish church, incorporated into the cathedral, still stands today. Both Rev. Phippen's brass tomb marker and the remarkable tablet he erected to his brother Owen (quoted above) can be seen today in the cathedral's St. Mary's Aisle.[74]

George Phippen's will, written 20 July 1650, was proved at London before the Prerogative Court of Canterbury on 1 March 1651/52 by Mary Phippen, relict and executrix.[75] A partial abstract was published in 1895.[76] The complete text is given here:

> In thy name and with thy guidance, O my most gracious God, this twentieth day of July anno Domini 1650. I George Fitzpen alias Phippen of sound minde and otherwise enriched by thy bounty (praised by thy name) doe make this my last will and testament as followeth.
>
> First I commend my soule and body into thy gracious hands, both saved by the alone merritte of my sweete Jesus, being fully assured that for me *to live is Christ and to dye is gaine* (Phillipians 1, verse 21).
>
> Next, whereas John Catcher pretending against me an Oxford decree (voyd in itselfe), during the time of my imprisonment for myne adhering to Parliament, plundered me in corne and goods of all kinds, according to a shedule hereunto annexed, of the vallue of £210 7s. & 0d., for recovering whereof against him and other his agents I leave it to mine executrix hereafter named. Item to his sisters which had noe portions, viz. to Mr. William White, for his deceased wife Constance; to Margaret, Ellinor, Jane, Mary, and Honour, I give and bequeath freely all those my lands in Penansand [?] (by me dearly

---

74   Correspondence with Mr. Colin Reid, Truro Cathedral Communications Officer, April 2013.

75   Kew, The National Archives, PROB 11/221, Image Reference: 72; formerly PCC Bowyer 57.

76   Phippen, "Genealogical Gleanings in England," *Register* 49 [1895]: 244–46.

paid for) which were their father's, to have and to hold to them and their heires for ever. And all this I doe for them (God be my witness) not out of any checke of conscience that I ever wronged that family, for I did supply and support them for many years with mine own estate, so as they have spoken against me without a cause for my love they are my adversaries, but I give myself unto prayer the good God give them repentance and forgive them. Only this I doe in obedience to my God saying *be not overcome of evill but overcome evill with good* (Romans 12, verse last).

Item whereas I have charged my accompt in a Chancery amongst my disbursements with £50 lent unto Mrs. Margarett Catcher, widow, for which I have her bond, my will is that she upon the said bond be not charged by mine executrix.

Item I doe forgive unto Henry Pye of [St.] Stephens gent. all the mony which he oweth me by bond and accompt being about £100.

Item I doe forgive unto Mr. Henry Edmonds and Thomas Drake all the cost in law for a suite begun in the consistory of Exon. and finished with sentence for me in the Archds.

Item I doe forgive unto the executor or administrator of one Hercules Ash the money which he owed me, the severall bonds to be null.

Item to Mrs. Mary Woolcott I give fower yewes and a lamb to each yew. Item to every of my servants at my death I give a yew and lamb. Also to Robert Worth and to John Davis or Davey the Taylor to each a yew and lambe. Item towarde a stocke for the poore of Lamoran I give fower ewes and fower lambs. And unto the said poore in mony at my death or within a few dayes after twenty shillings.

Item to Joane Phippen, widow, I give all the remainder of my ewes and lambs (excepting such as may be killed at my funerall). Also I give unto her two piggs of at least halfe a yeare old and soe much other goods as may be worth forty shillings.

Item whereas there are two executions against Mr. Henry Edmonds aforenamed for thirty three pounds ten pounds whereof is assigned by me unto Ellinor Phippen now Ellinor George, in whose name the executions are, and now the rest I give also unto Francis George her husband.

Item unto my honoured friend Hugh Boscawen Esqr. I give my cabinett press, and unto his honourable lady my clocke. And I humbly pray his assistance unto my wife his near kinswoman and to my heirs. And for the good will of him that dwelt in the bush let the blessings come on head of him and all his.

Item I give and bequeath unto Anne Grosse the daughter of my brother in law Edward Grosse of Trurow all that cost old walls and plott of ground in Lemoyne (or Kenwyne?) streete sometime in the tenure of John Rankin and John Dainill and all my right and estate therein, to have and to hold the same unto the said Ann Grosse and her heires for ever.

Item to my kinsman and brothers sonne Roger Phippen of Pennycomquicke I give that silver bowle which was Mr. Upcottes, if it be not redeemed with fifty shillings before my death. Item I give and bequeath unto him the said Roger Phippen my land in Enoder called the greater Trewoone now in the tenure of Mary Thomas and all my right and estate therein to have and to hold the same unto the said Roger and his heires forever. Also I give unto him two milch kine and also soe much goods and necessaries as may bee thought worth five pounds.

Item for my brother David Phippen in New England I doe give and bequeath unto his eldest sonne the lesser Trewoone, unto his second sonne that Trewossa whereon the said Nicholas Clemowe liveth, and unto his third sonne the other Trevossa called Petherickes because it was sometimes in the tenure of one William Pethericke, to have and to hold the said tenements severally to them and to their severall heirs for ever. And if either of these there brothers dye without issue, my will is that that tenement shall descend unto the fourth sonne. And soe if another dye without issue to the next sonne. And to his daughter or daughters I give twenty pounds. Also to the eldest of these brothers I give my signet ring and to the second the silver seale which hangeth at my purse.

Item to my sister Cecily Reignolds I give my two biggest silver spoones. And I give my ring with deathes head unto her husband.

Item I give and bequeath unto Edmond Braine ten pounds, and to each of his brothers six pence, and to his sister six pence.

Item to my kinsman Thomas Phippen of Clemence I give and bequeath all my right in a field in Kenwyne which I hold of Mr. Pearce Edgcombe and which William Priske holdeth of me from yeare to yeare. Item I doe give unto him the remainder of the estate in Bridgend house in the said parish of Clemence after the decease of Ellinor George and of my wife if any remainder shalbe. And I also give unto him the furnace there at the expiration of the said estate. Item my prayer is that God would provide some able and faithfull minister to succeed me in Lamorran and my will is that all the bedsteads tables shelves dressers and benches be left unremoved in the parsonage house, excepting that furniture in the matted chamber and the table in the parlour and the greene bedstead, all which I give to my wife.

Item I have given and before my death have delivered unto Mary my wife a parcell of gold in these times worth near two hundred pounds to be disposed by her as her owne if I doe not take some convenient house and tenement for her. Also I give unto her dureing her life if she survive the affore named Ellinor George the house with the appurtenances called Bridgend house wherein the said Ellinor liveth, if the liveson the lease named soe long shall live she performing the condition in the said lease contayned. Item all the rest of my goods and chattels of what kinde soever within dourse and without quicke and dead, I give and bequeath unto Mary my wife. And I doe make and ordaine her to be my executrix of this my last will and testament, and doe hereby revoke and disanull all former wills by me made.

Item I doe desire Hugh Boscawen Esq. aforenamed, John Penros Esqr., and Edward Grosse gent., to be overseers of this my will and testament, that all things in the same way be duly performed according to myne intention to which purpose I give unto them and the survivor or survivors of them full power and authority to assist myne executrix in all that possibly they may doe; and to each of them for their payines I bequeath forty shillings to be putt into a ring as a small expression of my greate thankfullness.

In wittnes whereof I have written this my last will with my owne hand and have declared it to wittnesses herunto subscribed the day and yeare first above written.

Memorandum I have dealt soe bountifully by my wife in lieu of thirty pound per annum ioynture which in marriage I promised to leave unto her, and truly her vertuous and respectfull deportment towards me deserves well at my hands.

Also seeing my estate to be more than at first thoughte I give and bequeath unto the poore of Weymouth in Dorsett five pounds and to the poore of Melcombe there tenn pounds.[77] To the poore of Comborne three pounds and to the poore of Enoder forty shillings. Also I doe pray my brother John Penros to distribute of my money twenty pounds more unto the poore of twenty parishes where hee shall think fitt, recommending twenty shillings to each parish to be by the minister or otherwise disposed. And as a testimony of my love I give to every of his children twenty shillings apiece.

Geo: Phippen

Witnesses to this will are Hugh Boscawen, John Penros, Thomas Harvey.

This will was proved at London the first day of March in the yeare of our Lord God according to the English stile one thousand six hundred fifty one before Sir Nathaniell Brent Knight Doctor of Lawes, Master or Keeper of the Prerogative Court, by the oath of Mary Phippen the relict of the said deceased and executrix

---

[77] The records of the borough of Weymouth and Melcombe Regis record the legacy: on 20 January 1654 [new style] "was paid into Mr. Maior Wall by the Towne Clerke Twelve pounds of Mr. George Phippens Clerke his guift money to the poore of the Towne vizt Fower pounds for Weymouth poore and Eight pounds for Melcomb poore to bee lett out at Interest for the poores use." Maureen Weinstock, ed., *Weymouth & Melcombe Regis Minute Book 1625–1660* (Dorchester, Dorset, 1964), 95. Also noted by Henry Joseph Moule, *Descriptive Catalogue of the Charters, Minute Books and Other Documents of the Borough of Weymouth and Melcombe Regis, A.D. 1252 to 1800, with extracts and some notes* (Weymouth, Dorset, 1883), 118.

named in the said will, to whom was comitted administration of
all and singular the goods chattels and debts of the said deceased,
shee being first sworne well and truly to administer the same.

George Phippen appears to have had no children. However, his will
leaves legacies to many in-laws and Phippen kin, including a nephew
Roger Phippen (likely son of his brother Owen); unnamed sons and
daughters of his brother David in New England (suggesting he may
not have known their names or how many there were); his sister Cecily
Reynolds and her unnamed husband; and several in-laws among the
Boscawens, Pyes, and Penroses. He also names other Phippens—surely
kin—without specifying their kinship, who cannot be more concretely
placed in his family group:

- JOANE PHIPPEN, "widow"

- ELLINOR PHIPPEN, m. FRANCIS GEORGE; she may have been the Ellinor
  Phippin who was baptized in Cattistock, Dorset on 29 October
  1589, the daughter of John Phippin. The 1808 chart states that
  Robert Phippen had a brother John, which suggests that Ellinor
  Phippen and George Phippen may have been first cousins.[78]

- THOMAS PHIPPEN, "kinsman," "of Clemence" (perhaps St. Clement,
  near Truro)

In addition to these legatees of George Phippen, one other man
rounds out a list of apparent close kin, named "Phippen," who cannot
yet be placed confidently in the known family tree. He is named in the
1808 Phippen chart, although his parentage cannot be deduced from
the information there:

- ABEL PHIPPEN, named in the 1808 Phippen chart, and said there to
  have married JANE FRANCIS and to have had a daughter ELIZABETH
  PHIPPEN, who died 2 August 1636. An Abel Phippen, perhaps this
  man, was buried at Melcombe Regis 27 June 1632.[79] No records
  matching the marriage, or the death or burial of his daughter, survive
  in the Melcombe Regis parish registers. However, the common
  equivalence of the names "Jane" and "Joane," suggests that the
  "widow Joane Phippen" named in Rev. George Phippen's will could
  well be the widow of Abel Phippen.

---

[78] Dorset Family History Society, *Dorset Baptisms,* from the Parish Records Collection
1538-2005, accessed via the Findmypast.co.uk website <www.findmypast.co.uk>
(accessed 22 September 2010). The *Dorset Baptisms* database also has a baptism for a
Christopher Phippin, on 19 April 1592, at Cattistock, Dorset, son of John Phippin. Ibid.

[79] Register of Saint Mary's, Radipole / Melcombe Regis (see Note 43 above).

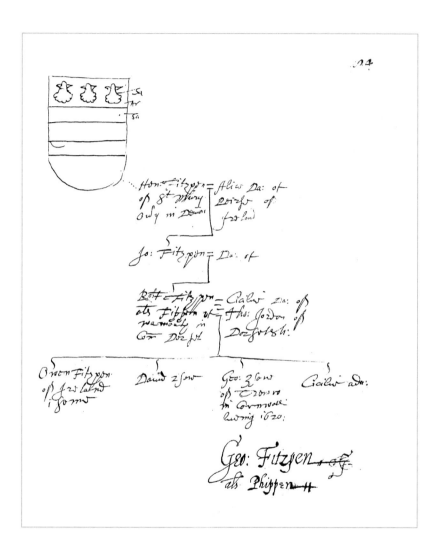

"Fitzpen" pedigree and arms, with autograph of Rev. George Phippen, from the original draft manuscript of the 1620 Visitation of Cornwall. © The British Library Board. Harley 1162 f84.

Stone tablet erected in memory of Owen Phippen
("Owen Fitz-Pen alias Phippen") by his brother, the
Rev. George Phippen, in the old parish church of St. Mary,
Truro. The tablet describes Owen's seven years of slavery and
his daring escape from captivity under the corsairs of Algiers.
The tablet is located in St. Mary's Aisle of the Truro Cathedral.
Photo credit: Paul Richards.

Brass plaque in St. Mary's Aisle, Truro Cathedral, placed
near the altar table he had given to the church, by the Rev.
George Phippen to mark his intended tomb. It bears two
coats of impaled arms: the "Fitzpen" arms impaled with
arms said to represent Jordan (for his mother), and the same
"Fitzpen" arms impaled with those of Pye (for his first wife).
Photo credit: Paul Richards.

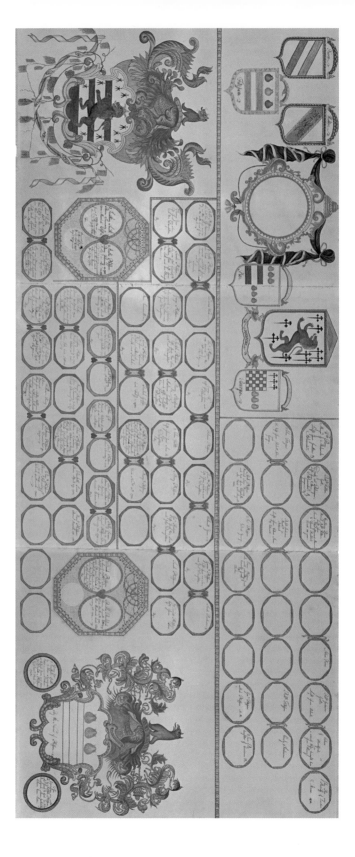

IV

Phippen Chart. Drawn and painted by John Symonds, Salem, Massachusetts, 1808; copied (with additions) from an earlier version by James Ford, Salem, 1768. Photograph © 2017 Museum of Fine Arts, Boston.

V

Phippen coat of arms with painter's colophons. Detail from the Phippen
Chart, drawn and painted by John Symonds, Salem, Massachusetts, 1808.
Photograph © 2017 Museum of Fine Arts, Boston.

Three Coats of Arms: 1. Phippen impaling Pye (representing the marriage
of Rev. George Phippen to Jane (Pye) Burgess, widow of Henry Burgess);
2. Jordaine (representing the mother of Rev. George and David Phippen,
Cecily (Jordan) Phippen); 3. Burgess impaling Pye (representing the first marriage
of Rev. George Phippen's first wife Jane Pye, to Henry Burgess of Truro).
Detail from the Phippen Chart, drawn and painted by John Symonds, Salem,
Massachusetts, 1808, copied from arms painted by James Ford, Salem, 1768.
Photograph © 2017 Museum of Fine Arts, Boston.

Elaborate octagonal cartouche depicting Anstis[6] Phippen and her husband, Jonathan Smith, of Salem—the patrons of the 1808 Phippen Chart. Note the elaborate "pricking" of the stippled field within the octagonal cartouche, creating a quilted effect on the paper. Simpler text areas include cartouches for Sarah[2] Phippen and her husband Thomas "Yow" at top, also with a colored and pricked heart design linking them. Detail from the Phippen Chart, drawn and painted by John Symonds, Salem, Massachusetts, 1808. Photograph © 2017 Museum of Fine Arts, Boston.

Oil portrait of Lydia[6] Phippen (1747–1782), wife of General John
Fiske, of Salem. She was the sister of Anstis[6] (Phippen) Smith
(1755–1815), for whom the Phippen Chart of 1808 was copied.
Pastel by Benjamin Blyth, c. 1770; photograph by Barbara Kennedy.
© 2017 Peabody Essex Museum, Salem, Massachusetts.

PART II

THE PHIPPEN FAMILY IN AMERICA

CHAPTER 3

DAVID¹ PHIPPEN

1. DAVID¹ PHIPPEN (*Robertᴬ*), second surviving son of Robert and Cecily (Jordan) Phippen, was born—probably at Melcombe Regis, Dorset—between 1583 and 1590. He died at Boston in the Massachusetts Bay Colony before 31 October 1650, when his will was proved.

Very little is known of David Phippen's life before his emigration to New England, as a middle-aged man, with some children who were already adults. Since his younger brother George attended Oxford in the 1600s and 1610s, David Phippen's immediate family was not without some means and social standing. Record of his marriage, to **SARAH** ___, which likely took place 1613–15, has not been located. But on 28 February 1617/18, David Phippen, surely the immigrant, appears in the minutes of the Melcombe Regis/Weymouth borough courts as a constable. On that date,

> E. Cuttance and Davy ffyppen, Constables, make presentment "that they did finde a legg and a shoulder of a calve sithence the time of Lent, killed by Walter Bythywood." The meat was seized and given to the poor.[80]

Some years later, still in Melcombe Regis, "David Fippen" appears in a different capacity—as a master carpenter overseeing bridge repairs and purchasing specialized timber on the borough's behalf. The minute book of the borough corporation (the mayor and aldermen) of Melcombe Regis records the following on 24 August 1631:

> It is agreed on by a grall Consent in a full assembly this present day that by reason the bridge in this Towne is

---

[80] Moule, *Descriptive Catalogue,* 58. The text is that of the abstract by Moule; that within the quotations is that of the orginal ledger. The borough court book that Moule selectively extracted is not available in print, so further mention of David Phippen as constable in earlier or later years cannot be sought.

decaying and stands in need of pmpt reparation threescore
Tonne of choice Timber shalbe with all Convenyent
speed bought either in the New forest or in the Isle of
Wight to be imployed in reparation thereof; and that
David Fippen shall be desyred to undertake the buying
thereof, and for that purpose to goe thither forthwith.
And that the Tresorer shall deliver him £10 in hand for
buying of the said Tymber, and shall pay him 2s 6d for
every day that he shall be imployed therin for his paynes
and expences, and all such other somes of money as he
shall lay out or agree for either for the tymber or for
Cariadge of the same both by sea and land or any other
wayes about this busynesse upon his accompt given in
for the same.[81]

On 16 December 1631, the borough corporation appointed two
burgesses to inspect the timber and to require "Fippen" to show them
his notes of disbursements and purchases.[82] The minutes do not mention
the results of any such audit, which was presumably satisfactory, because
two years later, David Phippen was contracted for similar work. On 26
April 1633, the corporation agreed that "that part of the Bridge next
to Waymouth syde shall wth all expedition be repayred and that Tho:
Lorelesse and David Fippen shall be Master Carpenters in the same."[83]
On 17 May 1633, the corporation decided that "David Fippen of this
Towne shall goe into the County of Southampton and buy where he
shall thinke fitt sixe Piles for the use of this Corporation to be imployed
about the repayring of the Bridge; And he is allowed two shillings p
the day for his Labour and expenses."[84] Even then the bridge was not
perfect—perhaps it was in constant disrepair—because on 17 October
1633, the borough court book noted that many persons "fell off the
Bridge" for "want of rails."[85]

By that date, David Phippen would no longer be available for further
borough contracts: the next spring, "Davide Phippen" emigrated as a
passenger on the ship *Recovery*, of London, which sailed from the port of
Weymouth and Melcombe Regis for New England on 31 March 1634.

---

[81]   *Weymouth & Melcombe Regis Minute Book*, 20.

[82]   Ibid., 21.

[83]   Ibid., 24; also noted in Moule, *Descriptive Catalogue*, 177.

[84]   *Weymouth & Melcombe Regis Minute Book*, 25.

[85]   Moule, *Descriptive Catalogue*, 177.

David Phippen was probably with his wife Sarah and, it is believed, six of their children.[86] A note in the surviving port book states that the passengers were

> All planters & have carried with them diverse sorts of household stuff, apparell & other provisions for the necessary use of themselves, their wives, children and servants, all which provisions are valued at their cost and their worth here, and are are allowed free of custom by their patent from His Majesty as by a letter received from the right worthy Sir John Worstenholme's certificate . . . appeareth. The value thereof is £920-06-08 as by these entries of every particular more plainly appeareth set down in this manner because the farmers [of Customs] are to have declarations from his Majesty.[87]

The earliest record of David Phippen in New England shows that he was one of the first settlers of Hingham, Massachusetts, where, on 18 September 1635 (when the first lots were drawn), five acres of land were granted to him.[88] The original Hingham lots were located on "the Cove on the north side of the road to Fort Hill."[89] According to George Lincoln's *History of Hingham, Massachusetts,* David Phippen's lot was situated on Town (North) Street, near the spot where St. Paul's Roman Catholic Church now stands.[90] "David Phippin" was made a freeman of the Massachusetts Bay Colony, along with seven other men from Hingham, on 3 March 1635/36.[91]

---

[86] Peter W. Coldham, "Genealogical Gleanings in England: Passengers and Ships to America, 1618–1668," *National Genealogical Society Quarterly* 71 [1983]: 163–92, at 171–72. The date of sailing is corrected, from 1633 to 1634, by John Plummer, "Identifying George P—?— of the *Recovery,* 1633 [1634]," *National Genealogical Society Quarterly* 77 [1989]: 249–55. Robert C. Anderson uses the corrected year in his accounts of *Recovery* passengers in *The Great Migration: Immigrants to New England, 1634–1635.*

[87] Coldham, "Genealogical Gleanings in England," *National Genealogical Society Quarterly* 71 [1983]: 171.

[88] Index to Proprietor's Grants of Land, *Hingham, Massachusetts Town Records, 1635-1830* [microform] (Boston, 1964), p. 16 (David Phippeny).

[89] Anna C. Kingsbury, "Fitzpen al's Phippen," Nickerson Collection, NEHGS, Mss SG Nic 30, Box C (Fitzpen/Phippen folder) (1916), p. 4.

[90] George Lincoln, *History of the Town of Hingham, Massachusetts,* 3 vols. (Hingham, Mass., 1893), 3: 112; Holman, "Phippen Papers" (Typescript, 1928, NEHGS MS A H63).

[91] Nathaniel B. Shurtleff, ed., *Records of the Governor and Company of the Massachusetts Bay in New England,* 5 vols. in 6 (Boston, 1853-54), 1: 371; Lucius R. Paige, "List of

The Hingham town records record "[t]he several parcels of land & meadow legally given unto David Phippeny by the town of Hingham":

> "for a houselot five acres of land" [September 1635]; "for planting land ten acres lying upon the Old Planter's Hill in the Plain Neck" [1635]; "for a Great Lot twenty acres of land, eighteen acres of it lying by Weymoth River. . . , the other two acres of it lying upon Squirrill Hill" [1635]; "for a small planting lot two acres of land lying in the Plain Neck by the Fresh River" [1635]; "four acres of salt marsh lying in the Home Meadow" [1635]; "two acres of salt marsh at Lyford's Liking Meadow over against Sagamore Hill southward as you go to the plain bushes" [no date]; "one acre and half of fresh meadow lying in Turkey Meadow" [5 March 1636[/37]]; "two acres of salt marsh at Conyehassett, it is the 24 lot in the first division . . . which said meadow was given in satisfaction for two acres of meadow at Nantascutt" [1647]; and "four acres of land more lying in the Home Neck, which he bought of Josiah Cobbitt" [no date].[92]

In 1639, Thomas Bushrode warned David Phippen, Joseph "Androws," and Henry Coggan to appear in the Quarterly Court held at Boston on 4 June 1639. Bushrode failed to appear to prosecute, so the court gave judgment of 10 shillings each to the defendants.[93] On 3 September 1639, Thomas Hammond of Hingham brought an action at the court at Boston against David Phippen "for trespasse wth his hogs in [Hammond's Indian] corne to the value of ƒ40s."[94] Hammond also brought suit at the same court against David Phippen and five others "for their fences being downe & unrepayred whereby all the trespasses have been don[e] upon the [plaintiff] to his dam[age]: 3*l*."[95]

Freemen," Register 3 [1849]: 89–96, 187–94, 239–46, 345–52, at 94; Anderson, *The Great Migration,* 5: 451 (David Phippen). "Thos. Ewer," David's future son-in-law Thomas Yeo, was also made a freeman on the same date.

[92]   Anderson, *The Great Migration,* 5: 451-52 (transcription of Index to Proprietor's Grants of Land, *Hingham, Massachusetts Town Records, 1635-1830* [microform] [Boston, 1964], 16 [David Phippeny]).

[93]   Shurtleff, *Records of the Governor and Company of the Massachusetts Bay in New England,* 1: 265; *Records of the Court of Assistants of the Colony of the Massachusetts Bay,* 3 vols. (Boston, 1901–28), 2: 82.

[94]   *Note-book Kept by Thomas Lechford, Esq., Lawyer, in Boston, Massachusetts Bay, from June 27, 1638, to July 29, 1641* (Cambridge, 1885), 175.

[95]   Ibid., 176.

On 13 September 1642, six men witnessed a deed made in New England by John Sibley of Salem regarding land in Bradpole, Dorset. The last three of the witnesses were "Ralph Sprage [of] Forington," "David Phippeni of Waymouth," and "Nicholas Upsall of Dorchester."[96] All three men were originally from Dorset. The Boston notary, William Aspinwall, presumably located three men from Dorset to make the deed more acceptable back in England. (Ralph Sprague of Charlestown was originally from Fordington St. George, and Nicholas Upsall of Dorchester in Massachusetts was originally from Dorchester in Dorset.) In this very unusual deed, David Phippen identified his parish of origin in England.[97]

The economic turmoil that hit the Massachusetts Bay colony starting in 1639–40, with the end of the Great Migration,[98] may have led David Phippen and his family to leave Hingham for Boston in 1641. On 27 September of that year, as shown in the Boston town records, "David Phippen [was] admitted to be a Townsman, and to have a howse lott, if it can be found."[99] The "Book of Possessions," Boston's annotated deed book from the 1640s and 1650s, shows "David Phippeni his possession within the limits of Boston," as follows: "One house and lott bounded by Valentine Hill northeast: the cove southeast: Mr. Wm Tings southwest: and John Oliver northwest."[100] George Lamb's *Series of Plans of Boston,* based on early town, county and colony records, including the Boston Book of Possessions, shows the location of the lot of "David Phippini" in 1645, on the Boston waterfront, north of Bendell's Cove and the Mill Creek.[101]

The Boston Book of Possessions also records an additional land acquisition in Boston by David Phippen in 1649. On 7 February 1649[/50?], John Milom of Boston sold

> unto David Phippeni of Boston a p'cell of land in Boston
> in length one hundred and two foote and in breadth at the

---

96   "A Volume Relating to the Early History of Boston Containing the Aspinwall Notarial Records from 1644 to 1651," in *Reports of the Record Commissioners of the City of Boston,* Vol. 32 (Boston, 1903), 162-163.

97   Anderson, *The Great Migration,* 5: 451.

98   Marion H. Gottfried, "The First Depression in Massachusetts," *The New England Quarterly* 9 [1936]: 655-678. For an excellent history of Boston during David Phippen's time there, see Darrett B. Rutman, *Winthrop's Boston: A Portrait of a Puritan Town, 1630-1649* (New York, 1972). See also Samuel G. Drake, *The History and Antiquities of Boston, from its settlement in 1630, to the year 1770* (Boston, 1856).

99   *Second Report of the Record Commissioners of the City of Boston; containing the Boston Records, 1634-1660, and the Book of Possessions,* 3rd ed. (Boston, 1902), 62-63.

100   Ibid., 11.

101   George Lamb, *Series of Plans of Boston showing existing ways and owners of property 1630–1635–1640–1645* (Boston, 1905), 14 (1645 Map).

high way nine foot nine ynches according as it laid out,
bounded with Bartholomew Barlow (*sic*) [in original] on
the southwest; the lott of David Phipeni on the northeast,
the highway southeast, and ------- on the northwest: and
this was by an absolute deed of sale dated 7 (12) 1649, and
sealed and delivered in presence of John Gore.[102]

The deed was apparently recorded on 15 March 1650.[103]

On 28 April 1645, David Phippen was granted "liberty of wharfing
before his propriety, neere the milne Creeke [Mill Creek]."[104] The Book
of Possessions notes that David Phippen's property adjoined "the cove"
on the southeast. The "cove" referred to was Bendall's Cove, where
Bendall's Dock was located, the principal dock for vessels, which was
later known as Town Dock. The dock extended inland as far as Dock
Square, part of Boston Harbor well into the eighteenth century, when
it was filled in and to become the site of Faneuil Hall. Named after
Edward Bendall, one of the most important persons active in the port of
Boston in the 1640s, Bendall's Cove was the principal wharfage section
of early Boston.[105] The "highway" referenced in the 1649 deed from
John Milom was presumably part of the street, bordering the waterfront,
later known as North Street, one of the three principal thoroughfares in
what is now Boston's North End.[106]

David Phippen must have been a man of considerable business
ability as the lots upon the cove were granted to the principal men of
the town, among whom were Valentine Hill and John Milom.[107] That

---

[102] *Second Report of the Record Commissioners of the City of Boston,* 11 (The Book of
       Possessions).

[103] Ibid.

[104] Ibid., 84.

[105] Robert C. Anderson, *The Great Migration Begins: Immigrants to New England 1620–
       1633,* 3 vols. (Boston: New England Historic Genealogical Society, 1995), 1: 155–
       56 (profile of Edward Bendall). On the development of the Boston waterfront in
       the 1640s, see Nancy S. Seasholes, *Gaining Ground: A History of Landmaking in Boston*
       (Cambridge, Mass., 2003), Chapter 3. Seasholes reprints a map created by Samuel
       C. Clough showing the Boston waterfront as it existed in 1648. Ibid., at 23.

[106] Annie H. Thwing, *The Crooked & Narrow Streets of the Town of Boston 1630–1822*
       (Boston, 1920), 33–34. Thwing states that David Phippen's property was on North
       Street, between Mill Creek and Cross Street. *See* Annie H. Thwing, *Inhabitants and
       Estates of the Town of Boston, 1630-1800* [electronic resource] (Boston, 2001), refer-
       ence 49626.

[107] Kingsbury, "Fitzpen al's Phippen," Nickerson Collection, NEHGS, Mss SG Nic
       30, Box C (Fitzpen/Phippen folder), 5; Nathaniel B. Shurtleff, *A Topographical and
       Historical Description of Boston* (Boston, 1871), 682.

David Phippen owned property on the Boston waterfront would be consistent with his apparent trade of carpenter, particularly with his expertise in maintaining waterfront works. It is quite likely that David Phippen was engaged in building and maintaining the nascent wharfs and bridges of Boston, and perhaps other ports in the colony.

In his description of the colonial Boston waterfront, historian Charles Andrews noted the wharf built by David Phippen:

> The waterfront of Boston . . . was gradually encircled with a line of wharves, numbering upward of thirty, amidst which stood out prominently the Dock, with its hoisting crane, at the foot of Dock Square and the market place, the predecessor of the old wharf (barricado) of 1672 and the Long Wharf of 1710. Some of these "wharves" were used as approaches to the many ferries that inter-linked the different parts of the irregular Boston peninsula with other parts of the mainland and with the islands. . . Others were sea-walls or jetties, at which small boats might tie up, such as were used to communicate with the larger vessels lying in the capacious harbor, where, it was estimated, 500 vessels could ride at anchor in good depth of water. Wharves of one kind or another were built before 1652 by Edward Bendall, Valentine Hill, John Milom, Walter Merry, Richard Bellingham, Edward Tinge, John Anderson, Christopher Lawson, George Halsall, Nicholas Upsall, David Phippen, Thomas Breedon, and others, either alone or with associates, sometimes (with the permission of the town) on their own properties facing the water, rights to which extended over the flats to the channel, and sometimes on land leased for the purpose and controlled under the terms of the indenture. Owners of private wharves were allowed to charge wharfage. Goods might also be landed anywhere along the shore or the banks of the rivers, and warehouses and other buildings were erected to receive them. Boston's waterfront became, as the years wore on, increasingly the center of a sea-going activity, with vessels coming and going, importing and exporting commodities and bringing into the community, not always to its advantage and sometimes to its discontent, a sea-faring element that often vexed the souls of the Puritan fathers. . .[108]

---

[108] Charles M. Andrews, *The Colonial Period of American History,* vol. 1 (New Haven, 1934), 514–15.

On 13 March 1647/48, "David Phipeny" was appointed a Boston constable,[109] an office he held thirty years earlier in Melcombe Regis.

The only known record of David Phippen's death is the (modern) entry appearing in the published Salem, Massachusetts vital records, which states that he died at Boston "about 1653."[110] The year is incorrect: David Phippen died, presumably at Boston, sometime between 7 February 1649[/50?], the date of the John Milom deed, and 31 October 1650, when his will was proved. The undated will of "David Phippeny" of Boston reads as follows:

> I the said David phippeni doe freely give unto my wife Sarah phippeny my wife the house that I now dwell in from end to end & my shop with with the shore being mine as also what tooles that are mine, and so there being an hundred foote taken out for to three houses uppon from the hygher end of it I meane westward, then what shalbe remaininge shall belong to the house given to my wife as her owne. The three houslotts is appointed one for Benjamin, another for Gamaliel, & the other to my sonne George, & another house being in the streete leading out to Roxbury uppon the left hand, in the outside of goodman Woodward, also I give unto Thomas Yeo my sonne in lawe that plotte of ground that is betweene goodman Batts & my selfe, from the streete backward fourty foote, also I give to my sonne George Vickars a Cowe to be made good by my wife to them. Also I leave my sonne Joseph Phippenie joint Execut[or] wth my wife pertaineing all my land in Hingham So I witnes this wth my hand
>
> [signed] David Phippeny.[111]

---

109 *Second Report of the Record Commissioners of the City of Boston,* 92. See also Robert F. Seybolt, *The Town Officials of Colonial Boston 1634-1775* (Cambridge, 1939), 15.

110 *Vital Records of Salem, Massachusetts to the end of the year 1849,* 6 vols. (Salem, 1916–25), 6: 137 ("native of England, h. Sarah, at Boston,---, abt. 1653").

111 Suffolk County Probate Records, New Series, vol. 1, 496–97. (The nineteenth-century transcription erroneously refers to George Vickars as George Rickard. The above transcription corrects the error.) This transcription of the will of David Phippen is from the "Nickerson Collection" manuscript prepared by Anna C. Kingsbury (SG NIC 31, R. Stanton Avery Special Collections, NEHGS, Boston). The will also appears in abstract form in "Abstracts from the Earliest Wills on File in the County of Suffolk, Mass.," *Register* 7 [1853]: 233. The signature of "David

The will was proved at Boston, 31 October 1650, and an inventory was accepted the same day, appraised by James Everill in the amount of £220.[112] The inventory of the estate of David Phippen is set forth below:

An Inventory of the goods & estate of David Phippeni
late of Boston Deceased Ano 1650

		£ s d
Imprimis in Ready money		05 – 00 – 00
Item	in weareing apparell	10 – 00 – 00
Item	his dwelling house with a p'cell of ground that is to lye for a highway	70 – 00 – 00
Item	a working shop	16 – 00 – 00
Item	a dwelling house wherein George Deere lives	22 – 00 – 00
Item	an hun^dd foote of ground given to Binge [Benjamin] & to Gamaliel & to George	10 – 00 – 00
Item	a p'cell of land conteining fourty fyve acres of upland & Marsh at Hingham	35 – 00 – 00
Item	a p'cell of land given unto his son in lawe Thomas Yew lyeing betweene his dwelling house & Bartholimew Barlow	08 – 00 – 00
Item	in working tooles in his shop	04 – 00 – 00
Item	two fether beds & boulsters & bedsteads & coverletts & blancketts lenterns & furniture	14 – 08 – 00
Item	in linen cloathes	07 – 00 – 00
Item	3 chestes & a case of bottles & a warming pan & two chaires one cushion & other smalethings att	01 – 10 – 00

Phippeny," presumably taken from his will, is reproduced in Justin Winsor, ed., *The Memorial History of Boston, including Suffolk County, Massachusetts. 1630–1880,* 4 vols. (Boston, 1880–81), 2: xii.

[112] Suffolk County Probate Records, New Series, 1: 497–98.

		£	s	d
Item	one bushell & halfe of malt two [b]ushell of Indian & a linnen bagg & 2 barrells	00	18	00
Item	foure bushells of wheate foure bushells of pease, two hogsheads	02	02	00
Item	a trundle bed	00	04	00
Item	a hogshead & a barrll & other implements	00	10	00
Item	one Cubbard	01	00	00
Item	one greate Chest & one table chaire	00	18	00
Item	2 boxes 2 Joint stooles & boxes for compasses	00	17	00
Item	2 bibles & other bookes 1$^£$ two fowling pieces a musket & sword 3$^£$ three brasse Kettles 3 brasse skilletts one frying pan 2$^£$ 3^s	06	03	00
Item	3yron potts 1 frying pan 1 spitt & otheryron	01	05	00
Item	in pewter 1$^£$ 10^s three pecks of wheate 3^s 9^d	01	13	09
Item	3 tubbs one Chaire 1 hand baskit 1 pale 1 pr of bellows & other smale things	00	15	00
Item	in timber	01	00	00
Item	oweing to him by Mr Hollard	00	16	00
Prised by us James Everill		**220**	**19**	**09**

This Inventory was accepted at a Court at Boston 31 (8) 1650

William Aspinwall

Recorder

Several deeds show the disposition of David Phippen's property after his death. On 24 October 1652, Sarah Phippeny of Boston, widow of David Phippeny, late of Hingham, deceased, with her son Joseph

Phippeny, also of Boston, sold the Hingham lot to Thomas Thaxter of Hingham.[113] On 9 April 1653, Sarah Phippin, widow, for £15, sold to John Hull of Boston, goldsmith, a house bounded upon the south by the sea, upon the north by the highway, and between the land of Richard Woodhowse and Jonathan Negoose.[114] On 3 December 1653, Sarah Phippin, widow, for £40, sold another waterfront house and parcel in Boston to Robert Saunderson of Boston, goldsmith. George Vicors and Rebeckah, his wife, who had an interest, together with "our mother Sarah Phippin," consented to the sale.[115] On 11 July 1654, "Sarah Fippenny" of Boston, widow, for £52, sold to Theodore Atkinson of Boston, "a dwelling howse orchard gardine & backside There unto Adioyneing containeing about halfe an Acker of Lande & towards the old winde mill in Boston." "gamaliel phipeny" and James Hill were witnesses.[116] After this last sale, widow Sarah Phippen apparently left Boston and married **GEORGE HULL** of Fairfield, Connecticut,[117] a prominent leader in the early years of both the Massachusetts Bay and Connecticut colonies.[118]

Sarah (___) Phippen's family connections are unknown. In a will dated 24 March 1651, Robert Shute of Boston named "Sara Phippeny" as a beneficiary in the amount of four pounds.[119] Also named were Rev. John Cotton, teacher of the First Church in Boston; Rev. John Wilson, Pastor of the First Church; Zachariah Sims, pastor of the church in Charlestown; Thomas Allen, teacher of the church in Charlestown; Richard Russell, friend; and brothers and sisters — Richard Shute, Thomas Shute, Marie Shute, and Sarah Hollyes. No relationship to Sarah Phippen is indicated.[120]

Sarah (___) Phippen's second husband George Hull died before 25 August 1659, when his inventory was taken (with movable goods of

---

113   Jacobus, "The Phippen Family," *The American Genealogist* 17 [1940]: 4 (source not cited).
114   Suffolk Deeds 3: 69–70.
115   Ibid., 3: 70–71.
116   Ibid., 2: 39–40.
117   Charles H. Weygant, *The Hull Family in America* (Pittsfield, Mass., 1913), 10.
118   Ibid., 11. *See also* Donald Lines Jacobus, *History and Genealogy of the Families of Old Fairfield,* 2 volumes in 3 (Fairfield, Conn., 1930), 1: 307–8. For a complete treatment of George Hull, *see* Anderson, *The Great Migration Begins,* 2: 1040–43.
119   "Abstracts from the Earliest Wills on File in the County of Suffolk, Mass.," *Register* 7 [1853]: 335.
120   Suffolk Probate Records, file no. 1651.

£58).[121] His will, the date of which has been obliterated, was probated
20 October 1659. It mentions his (then) wife Sarah, and children Josyas,
Cornelius, Mary, Martha, Elizabeth, and Naomey; he also left a legacy
to his cousin Jane (___) Pinckney. His son Cornelius Hull was named
as his executor.[122]

Sarah (___) (Phippen) Hull wrote her will following her husband's
death, and she died very shortly thereafter. Her estate was inventoried
on 25 August 1659, and her will, the date of which is obliterated in
the surviving copy, was probated on the same date as her husband's, 20
October 1659.[123] Here follows the will of Sarah (___) (Phippen) Hull:

The [date missing; top of page torn] 1659

I Sarah Hull of ffairefeild [...] wiffe unto Georg Hull late deceased
being [by the will of] God visseted with Sicknes but ha[ving] my
senses and perfect memory doe make this my last will.

I give and bequeath my house at Boston equally to be devided
betwixt all my children.

I give unto my sonn Gamaliell my cupboard which is in his owne
house. I give unto my sonn George Phippen my bedstead and
great chest which standeth in my house att Boston.

I give unto my daughter Rebeca my fetherbed and that which
appertayneth therunto: allsoe I give unto my daughter Rebecca
Vickers and my daughter Sarah Yow all my waring parrell both
linning and woolen equally betwixt them: as alsoe what other
goods was mine before the mariage of my late deceased husband,
to be alike devided betwixt my two forenamed daughters.

---

[121] Fairfield [Conn.] Probate District, Probate Book 1, pp. 56–58 (FHL Film 004,287).

[122] Spencer P. Mead, *Abstract of Probate Records at Fairfield, County of Fairfield, and State of Connecticut, 1648–1750* (typescript; reprint Salem, Mass., 1998), 7 (original record, Fairfield District probate book 1, 56).

[123] Fairfield District probate book 1, 61-62; Mead, *Abstract of Probate Records at Fairfield*, 7. Further inventories were taken 3 Jan. 1659[/60], and 14 Feb. 1660[/61], including a partial appraisal of "certain apparels of widow Ews now Mr. Goulds wyffe." See Box C, "Fitzpen/Phippen" folder, Nickerson Collection.

I give unto my daughter Sarah Yow ten pounds of my Estate at ffairefieild.

I alsoe give unto my Cossen Jane Pinkny thirty shillings. And the Remainder of my estate my will is shall be equally devided unto my foure sons (to witt) Beniamen Phippen Joseph: Gamaliell and Georg Phippin. I alsoe doe substitute and appoynt my cosen Phillip Pinkny to be my overseer of my whole Estate at ffairefeild which is or shall apear to be by my husbands will.

In witnes of all which I set to my hand

The mark of X Sarah Hull

In presence of
Cornelius Hull
Phillip Pinkny.[124]

The initial inventory of her estate was taken 25 August 1659 by Alexander Knowles and William Hill:[125]

The 25 August 1659:

The Estate of Sarah Hull late deceased in Fairfeild prized as followeth:

	£	s	d
Imprimis her apparell	11	4	0
Item 3 earthen milkpans		1	0
Item one pair of sissors and a Pin case			3
Item 2 earthen creampots		2	0
Item one blew rugg & 2 white blankets	3	0	0
Item 2 pillows	1	0	0
Item one brush		1	0
Item one chest		2	0

---

[124] Fairfield District probate book 1, 61. Also transcribed (less completely) by W. L. Holman (NEHGS: Holman MSS (Mss A H63), Phippen folder, "Notes Re George Hull," 5); *see also* Mead, *Abstract of Probate Records at Fairfield,* 7.
[125] Fairfield District probate book 1, 61–62.

	£	s	d
[page damaged; illegible]		4	0
[page damaged; illegible]		5	0
[page damaged; illegible] ... tubb		6	0
[page damaged; illegible]	1	0	0

[total: £17– 4s – 3d]

Alexander Knowles
William Hill

On 20 October 1659, the inventory was accepted on oath of Phillip
Pinkney, and Gamaliel Phippen was appointed administrator.[126]

An additional inventory of personal property, dated 3 Jan 1659/60,
was filed with the probate court of Hartford:

[Dorse:] An inventory of some of the estate of Mrs. Hulls of
ffairefeild, recorded 1659

An inventorie of certaine goods supposed to belonge to Mrs.
Hulls estate taken the 3d of Januarie 1659 by John Burr and
Alexander Knowels as followeth:

	£	s	d
Imprimis two chests	1	0	0
Item one table & a forme		12	0
Item one little jug			8
Item one fether bed, 2 pillows, one boulster, one blanket, one coverlidd	7	0	0
Item one linerie [?] cubbord		14	0
Item one chest		3	0
Item one smoking iron & henter [?????]		3	0
Item one great ketle and two litle ones	2	5	0
Item tow skelets		6	0
Item tow iron potts		18	0

---

[126]   Fairfield District probate book 1, 62.

	£	s	d
Item one kneding truf or leven tubb		4	0
Item one warminge pan		12	0
Item one spitt		3	0
Item 9 pewter platers	3	0	0
Item four earthen lighes & one brass plater		10	0
Item one flagon		6	0
Item three candlesticks		4	0
Item six pottengers & six sausers		6	0
Item three bassens, one candlepott, one fret, tow litle platers		8	0
Item one pestle & morter		5	0
Item one chafinge dish, 3 spounds		5	0
Item foure cusshins & one pincushinge	1	0	0
Item one boxe one flasket [?] one baskett		8	0
Item one bed, tow little boulsters, one blankett & one coverlid	2	0	0
Item one carpett one bearing blankett, one piece of a carpett	1	10	0
Item one cotton covering one cotton sheett and 2 sheets	2	10	0
Iteem one table cloath 2 napkins 6 pillowbears	1	4	0
Item 3 chaires 1 stoole 6 cushins		15	0
Item 3 books		6	0
Item one dester [?] & pear of toungs		3	0

[total: £29 – 0s – 0d]

A further list of additional clothing belonging to Sarah, then in the possession of her daughter, was appended to her probate file, as preserved at Hartford:

Certaine aparells of Sarah Ews widow of Fairefeild prized by John Burr & Alexander Knowels the 3d of January 1659 as followeth:

	£	s	d
Imprimis tow gowns three peticoats, three wastcoats, tow aprons, 1 hatt			
Item two linnie aperans, 5 hand cerchafes & other small linins		1	10 0
Item in Black silke		1	0 0

These inventories were sent to the high court at Hartford by overseers in Fairfield:[127]

Fairfeild the 14th of May 1660

Right worshipfull magestrats sitting in cort at Hartford: these are to informe you that there is certaine goods at fairfeild suposed to belonge to Mrs. Hulls estate late deceased which was not prized with the other goods presently after her decease. The said goods are prized by Alexander Knowels & John Bur and they are in Mr Goulds Custetie & he hath given bond for them or the value of them to be the Corts dispose as you for justic doe require. There is also certaine aparels of Widow Ews now Mr. Goulds wyffe which we prized and are also at the corts dispose. We heere send the inventorie of boath which you may understand them in your shicullers [?] and keep the bond to the Common welth in our hands till we have the determinacion of your cort and also the originall inventorie, so we humbly take our leave and wait

yours to comand .

Alexander Knowels
John Bur

---

127 Jacobus, "The Phippen Family," *The American Genealogist* 17 [1940]: 1.

These inventories reveal that Sarah (___) (Phippen) Hull was a well-dressed woman who lived in reasonable comfort relative to early colonial conditions, with a personal estate — largely clothes — valued at just over £60, plus desirable real estate in Boston.

Because of the naming of Pinckney "cousins" in the wills of George and Sarah Hull, it is often assumed that Sarah's maiden name was Pinckney. But the kinship could have linked *either* Sarah (___) (Phippen) Hull or George Hull to *either* Phillip Pinkney or Jane (___) Pinckney. It is probable that the connection is Sarah's since she chose this "cousin" as her overseer; however, no evidence concretely explains the Pinckney kinship nor provides a surname for Sarah. Unfortunately, the names of David Phippen and his wife Sarah are missing in the 1808 copy of the Phippen chart—otherwise Sarah's surname and origins might have been preserved.

After Sarah's death, her Boston property was sold to her son Benjamin² Phippen. On 3 June 1663, Joseph "Phippen als Fitzpen of ffamoth in Casco Bay," carpenter, "for and in the behalfe of himselfe and the rest of his Brothers and Sisters joint Executoʳˢ to the Estate of theire late deceased mother Mrs. Sarah Hull wife of Mr. George Hull late of ffairefeild in Connecticot," sold, for £102,

> a parcel of ground with the dwelling house on part thereof standing scituate lying and being neere unto the drawbridge in Boston aforesd. Containing in Length Seventy and Six foote or thereabout and in breadth twenty and four foot or thereabout, butting on the East on the Streete and on the land of James Robinson on the west, bounded by the land of Gamaliel Phippen als Fitzpen on the South and the land of Mary Paddy on the North and also one other parcel of ground Lying on the Easterly side of the sd. Streete wᵗʰ the Shop on part thereof standing containing thirty and one foote in breadth or thereabout and in length from the front unto low water marke . . .

to "Benjamin Phippen als ffitzpen of Boston," blockmaker. This deed was not recorded until 5 November 1677.[128]

---

[128] Suffolk Deeds 10: 212–13. The drawbridge near the Phippen property on the Boston waterfront was located on Ann (later North) Street, and crossed the Mill Creek. *See* Shurtleff, *A Topographical and Historical Description of Boston,* 113.

Children of David and Sarah (_____) Phippen, the first eight of whom were apparently born in England before 1634:[129]

    i. ROBERT[2] PHIPPEN, according to the Phippen chart, he "lost his life honourably in the King's service in the 28th year of his Age."

2   ii. JOSEPH PHIPPEN, b. about 1615.

    iii. THOMAS PHIPPEN, according to the Phippen chart, "was drowned in the 20th year of his Age."

    iv. Rebecca Phippen, b. about 1622. On 5 March 1639, Rebecca Phippen was awarded 20 shillings, to be paid by Richard Ibrooke for his "tempting 2 or more maydes [Rebecca Phippen and Mary Marsh] to uncleanness."[130] She m. about 1647, GEORGE VICKERS or VICKERY.[131] George Vickery was an early settler of both Salem and Marblehead,[132] and later lived in Boston and Hull. In 1651, George Vicars and Thomas Ewe, both of Boston, were presented in Court for sailing out of the harbor at Annisquam upon the Sabbath day morning.[133] On 17 July 1672, George Vickery and Rebecca his wife of Hull (alias Nantasket), granted to William Browne of Marblehead, for 8 pounds 10 shillings of current money of New England, 4 acres of land at Marblehead, with all meadows, timber, trees . . . commonages, fishing & appurtenances thereto belonging.[134] He "dyed suddenly" at Hull on 12 July 1679; on 29 July 1679, administration of the estate of George Vickery Sen[r], late of Hull, deceased, was granted to his widow Rebecca and his son Jonathan Vickery.[135] Inventory of his estate, valued at £220, was taken on 25 July 1679.[136] She survived him. The Phippen chart

---

[129] The birth order is based upon the order of the names on the 1808 Phippen chart.

[130] Shurtleff, *Records of the Governor and Company of the Massachusetts Bay in New England,* 1: 249.

[131] Mary L. Holman, "The Vickery Family of Marblehead, Massachusetts" (1926. G VIC 475, R. Stanton Avery Special Collections, NEHGS, Boston); Ethel F. Smith, *Early Families of Hull, Massachusetts* (Boston: New England Historic Genealogical Society, 2007), 183–85.

[132] George Vicary was of Marblehead in 1637/8. *See* Perley, *The History of Salem, Massachusetts,* 2: 2–3.

[133] Mary L. Holman, "The Vickery Family of Marblehead, Massachusetts"; Smith, *Early Families of Hull, Massachusetts,* 183–85.

[134] *Essex County Deeds, 1639-1678: Abstracts of Volumes 1-4, Copy Books, Essex County, Massachusetts* (Bowie, Md., 2003), 252 (abstracting Essex Deeds, 4: 31).

[135] Suffolk County Probate Records 12: 311 (Suffolk Probate docket no. 1106); Smith, *Early Families of Hull, Massachusetts,* 183–84.

[136] Suffolk County Probate Records 12: 312 (Suffolk Probate docket no. 1106).

states, "George W left issue 9 Sons and 3 Daughters By- Rebecca Phippen."

3   v.   BENJAMIN PHIPPEN, b. probably by 1625.
4   vi. GAMALIEL PHIPPEN, b. probably by 1627.
    vii. SARAH PHIPPEN, b. probably by 1630; m. (1) before Nov. 1650, THOMAS YEO of Boston. On 16 December 1653, Thomas Yeow of Boston, seaman, and Sarah his wife, in consideration of £140 paid by Phillip Wharton to satisfy Yeow's creditors and other consideration, sold to Wharton their dwelling house, and two small adjoining parcels of land, located on Conduit Street in Boston, along with the right to use the conduit for water.[137] After this transaction, Thomas and Sarah presumably removed to Fairfield, Connecticut, probably with her mother, widow Sarah Phippen. He died at Fairfield in 1658; the inventory of his estate was taken on 10 Sept. 1658.[138] Sarah m. (2) between Aug. 1659 and May 1660, NATHAN GOLD of Fairfield.[139] Major Nathan Gold was one of the leading citizens of seventeenth-century Connecticut.[140] In September 1692, "Sary" Gold testified in the Connecticut witchcraft trials.[141] She d. before 1 March 1693/4, when her husband made his will.[142] The 1808 Phippen chart states, "Thomas Yow left issue one Son, and two Daughters, By- Sarah Phippen, who was after married to Nathan Goold, left issue two Sons and one Daughter." Jacobus, however, traces one son and four daughters, all of whom left issue, by Nathan Gold.[143]

5   viii. GEORGE PHIPPEN, b. about 1633.
    ix. JOHN PHIPPEN, b. and d. at Boston in July 1637.[144]
    x.   JOHN PHIPPEN, b. and d. at Boston in July 1640.[145]

---

[137] *Suffolk Deeds*, 2: 305–6.

[138] Mead, *Abstract of Probate Records at Fairfield, County of Fairfield, and State of Connecticut, 1648–1750* (typescript; reprint Salem, Mass., 1998), 12 (Fairfield Probate Records, 1 (1648-56): 40).

[139] See Jacobus, "The Phippen Family," *The American Genealogist* 17 [1940]: 1–19, for an extensive treatment of the children and grandchildren of Sarah (Phippen) (Yeo) Gold and Nathan Gold.

[140] Ibid., 15; Jacobus, *History and Genealogy of the Families of Old Fairfield*, 1: 228–30.

[141] Jacobus, "The Phippen Family," *The American Genealoigst* 17 [1940]: 14; Jacobus, History and Genealogy of the Families of Old Fairfield, 1: 228–29.

[142] Jacobus, "The Phippen Family," *The American Genealogist* 17 [1940]: 14.

[143] Jacobus, "The Phippen Family," *The American Genealogist* 17 [1940]:15–18.

[144] *A Report of the Record Commissioners Containing Boston Births, Baptisms, Marriages, and Deaths, 1630-1699*, 5.

[145] Ibid., 9.

Chapter 4

The Second Generation

2. Joseph[2] Phippen (*David[1]*) was born perhaps by about 1615, probably at Melcombe Regis, Dorset, son of David and Sarah (___) Phippen. He likely came to New England with his father, mother, and family on the *Recovery*, sailing from Weymouth, Dorset, on 31 March 1634. He died at Salem, Massachusetts, between July and September 1687.[146]

The 1808 Phippen chart states that Joseph Phippen was the compiler of the original Phippen genealogical chart. It states: "This Genealogy was recorded by Joseph Phippen, who lived & died in New England, whose posterity where [sic] born there."

According to the 1808 chart, Joseph Phippen married **Dorcas Wood**, who is shown there to have been the mother of all his children.[147] Her parentage and connections are not known.[148] While Joseph's will names his wife Dorcas, she is several times called "Dorothy" in Boston records; it is probable that the same woman is intended.[149] Dorcas (Wood) Phippen survived her husband and was living in February 1692; her date of death is not known.

Joseph Phippen had attained his majority by 1637 when he was granted two acres of land in Hingham.[150] His land was located on

---

[146] *Vital Records of Salem, Massachusetts to the end of the year 1849,* 6: 137. The compilers of the *Vital Records of Salem, Massachusetts to the end of the year 1849* assumed that Joseph died in the same month that he made his will.

[147] *See also* Phippen, "Fitzpen or Phippen, and Allied Families," *The Heraldic Journal* 4 [1868]: 16; Winifred Lovering Holman, "Phippen papers" (Typescript, 1928, at NEHGS, MS A H63).

[148] Occasional assertions that she was daughter of Nicholas[1] Wood appear to be without foundation. Nicholas Wood's extant will does not name a daughter Dorcas Phippen.

[149] Jacobus discussed this point in "The Phippen Family," *The American Genealogist* 17 [1940]: 5–6. Jacobus correctly observed that some of Joseph's children gave the name Dorcas to children of their own, and that Joseph named only one wife on his genealogical chart.

[150] "Index to Proprietor's Grants of Land," *Hingham, Massachusetts Town Records, 1635–1830* [microform] (Boston, 1964), 70 (Joseph Phippeny).

Bachelor (now Main) Street, opposite what is now Water Street.[151] He removed to Boston about 1644[152] and was made a freeman there on 29 May 1644.[153] On 30 March 1647, Anchor Ainsworth of Boston, by a deed acknowledged before Governor John Winthrop, sold a house plot in Boston to Joseph Phippeni.[154]

By 1650, the year of his father's death, Joseph Phippen was in Casco Bay, Maine, apparently without his family, who remained in Boston. During that year, he acquired 100 acres of land at Purpooduck from George Cleeve, and also witnessed a 1650 deed from Cleeve to John Wallis.[155] The Purpooduck deed is not extant; the evidence of the transaction derives from a statement in a petition by Joseph's son David in 1687 that his father had purchased from George Cleeve 100 acres at Casco Bay thirty-seven years earlier, *i.e.* 1650, that the buildings and improvements on the property had been disturbed and destroyed in the late Indian war, and that on 5 August 1687, his father deeded the property to him. The David Phippen petition is referenced in a survey warrant issued by Governor Andros on 8 October 1687, directing the deputy surveyor to survey the 100 acres at Casco Bay for David Phippen. [156]

On 15 January 1652, Darothy Phippiney of Boston, "being in great want & distresse by reason of my husbands absence & losse at sea," mortgaged her house and land in Boston to Sampson Shoare of Boston.[157] The mortgage deed was witnessed by her brothers-in-law, "[g]ammalliel phipen" and "Benamen fippen." Over a year later, on 19 July 1653, "Joseph Phippeny of Boston, seaman, and Dorothie his wife" confirmed the sale of the dwelling house and half-acre of land to Sampson Shoare; he signed, she made her mark.[158]

---

[151] "Index to Proprietor's Grants of Land," *Hingham, Massachusetts Town Records, 1635–1830* [microform] (Boston, 1964), 70 (Joseph Phippeny); Lincoln, *History of the Town of Hingham*, 3: 112.

[152] Holman, "Phippen papers." 1644 is the likely date, based on the baptism records of his children.

[153] Shurtleff, *Records of the Governor and Company of the Massachusetts Bay in New England*, 2: 293; Lucius R. Paige, "List of Freemen," *Register* 3 [1849]: 190.

[154] *Second Report of the Record Commissioners of the City of Boston; containing the Boston Records, 1634-1660, and the Book of Possessions*, The Book of Possessions, p. 41; Samuel G. Drake, *The History and Antiquities of Boston* (Boston, 1856), 799.

[155] Sibyl Noyes, Charles Thornton Libby, and Walter Goodwin Davis, eds., *Genealogical Dictionary of Maine and New Hampshire* (Portland, Maine, 1928–39), 549; William Willis, *History of Portland, from 1632 to 1864*, 2d ed. (Portland, Maine, 1865), 97.

[156] "Land Warrants Issued Under Andros, 1687-1688," in *Publications of The Colonial Society of Massachusetts* 21 [1919]: 309–10.

[157] Suffolk Deeds, 1: 280–81.

[158] Suffolk Deeds, 1: 307–8.

Subsequent to this transaction, Joseph and his family removed to Falmouth, in Casco Bay, Maine, where Joseph and his sons engaged in farming and fishing at Purpooduck and House Island.[159] He was appointed a constable in 1661 for the Province of Maine, commissioner in 1663, and grand juror in 1664.[160] In the 1663 deed of sale of his mother's house and property in Boston to his brother Benjamin Phippen, Joseph referred to himself as Joseph "Phippen als Fitzpen of ffamoth in Casco Bay," carpenter.[161]

Joseph Phippen played a prominent part in the dramatic political and legal controversies that plagued the colonial Maine settlements during the middle of the seventeenth century. The settlements from Kittery to Casco Bay were the subject of hostile competition between competing land-proprietors, while the Massachusetts Bay Colony also sought to annex the territory.[162] From 1652 to 1658, Massachusetts secured the submissions of the towns from Kittery to Casco Bay,[163] but, by 1663, with the Puritans out of power in England, opposition to Massachusetts authority reached a critical stage. The opposition—led by the Rev. Robert Jordan and Henry Jocelyn—seceded from the authority of Massachusetts and sought the assistance of Charles II in establishing a new provincial government.[164] The Rev. Robert Jordan, one of the early settlers, was an Episcopal minister, one of the great land-proprietors of the Casco Bay region, and possibly a cousin of Joseph Phippen.[165] In addition, one of Robert Jordan's earliest conveyances of land was made to Joseph Phippen.[166]

---

[159] Phippen, "Fitzpen or Phippen, and Allied Families," *The Heraldic Journal* 4 [1868]: 7.

[160] Noyes, Libby, and Davis, *Genealogical Dictionary of Maine and New Hampshire,* 549.

[161] Suffolk Deeds, 10: 212-13.

[162] For background, *see* Charles E. Clark, *The Eastern Frontier: The Settlement of Northern New England, 1610–1763* (New York, 1970), 37-51; Henry S. Burrage, *The Beginnings of Colonial Maine 1602-1658* (Portland, Me., 1914); Willis, *History of Portland,* 62–167.

[163] Clark, *The Eastern Frontier,* 50.

[164] Willis, *History of Portland,* 121–22; William B. Jordan, Jr., *A History of Cape Elizabeth, Maine* (Portland, 1965), 24.

[165] Tristram Frost Jordan, *The Jordan Memorial: Family Records of the Rev. Robert Jordan, and His Descendants in America* (Boston, 1882). Rev. Jordan may have been a cousin of Joseph Phippen. The 1808 Phippen chart has two tablets of note; the first refers to one "Robt. Jordaine Gent." who "[l]eft issue Robert" and the second refers to "Robt. Jordaine," a merchant in Melcomb Regis, who had three children. George D. Phippen wrote that "[w]ithout doubt it was this connection with the Jordan family that induced Joseph Phippen to settle at Falmouth (Portland) with the Rev. Robert Jordan…." Phippen, "Fitzpen or Phippen, and Allied Families," *The Heraldic Journal* 4 [1868]: 7. *See also* W.H. Whitmore, "Rev. Robert Jordan," Register 13 [1859]: 221–22.

[166] Phippen, "Fitzpen or Phippen, and Allied Families," *The Heraldic Journal* 4 [1868]: 7. No evidence of the Robert Jordan/Joseph Phippen transaction has been discovered.

Accompanying the political battle was a major quarrel between Jordan and George Cleeve, another early settler, land proprietor, and former officeholder under the Province of Lygonia, over title to land in the region. Jordan was the chief proprietor on the south side of the Casco River, but he sought for many years to extend his domain as far north as the Presumpscot River, putting him into conflict with Cleeve and his tenants.[167] On 30 May 1660, Joseph Phippen was one of a group of distressed inhabitants of the town of Falmouth to petition the General Court at Boston for relief from the uncertainty caused by the claims of Cleeve and Jordan.[168] Joseph Phippen, a grantee of Cleeve on Purpooduck,[169] apparently lived on the disputed territory, and later removed to another part of Falmouth.[170] Joseph Phippen also owned House Island, which he no doubt used for fishing, until dispossessed by Sampson Penley in 1663.[171]

The political battle over the future of the region was perhaps the most intense in Falmouth. Willis observed that "[t]he spirit of party raged with more violence in Falmouth, probably, than it did in any other part of the county."[172] In 1663, "[t]he friends of Massachusetts succeeded in choosing two commissioners, Mr. Cleeves and Mr. Phippen, friendly to government, and in obtaining a vote to adhere to that jurisdiction." [173]

Others in Falmouth were strongly opposed to Phippen and Cleeve. In an (undated) petition to the General Court around this time, they voiced their displeasure:

> [T]he humble petition of divers inhabitants and freemen of Falmouth, humbly sheweth, That whereas there hath been a sad contention in these parts concerning government, Your petitioners most of them living upon their labour, and desirous rather to live in peace and learne to be obedient and submit to what government it shall please the Lord and our sovereign to appoint over us,

---

[167] Willis, *History of Portland,* 114–23.

[168] Massachusetts Archives Collection 3: 248; Willis, *History of Portland,* 124–25.

[169] Purpooduck was the aboriginal name for Spring Point, but was later extended to cover all of the northern shore of Cape Elizabeth. *See* Willis, *History of Portland,* 96.

[170] Willis, *History of Portland,* 125.

[171] Ibid., 135..

[172] Ibid., 154.

[173] Ibid. After a period of control by the King's commissioners, Massachusetts authority was fully re-established by 1668; by then, Joseph Phippen had relocated to Salem, Massachusetts. *See* Willis, *History of Portland,* 179–80.

than to contend or determine who are governors shall be, yet there hath latelie certaine men appeared in our names att ye Honorable General Court, and as we are informed, presented a petition which was without our consents or knowledge, for had ye government been settled and that we could have acted with freedom of spirit wee would never have dishonoured the Honourable General Court with men of such lives and conversations, as are first George Cleeves, who is upon record for breach of oath and accused of forgery. Mr. Phippen not many days before his departure was beating and drawing of ye blood of his Majestie's subjects and stands upon record for slandering ye deputie governor and was always a man of contention and strife since he came in our parts. John Phillips hath acknowledged himself guilty of keeping a woman which is none of his wife this fourteen years. These men cam in your names and exercise authoritie over us with many soare threatenings, wherefore our humble request is, That if itt please the Lord to continue us still under your government, you would be pleased to grant us the liberty that other of his Majestie's subject have, and you by Article granted, yt is freedom to vote for our officers and not such men imposed upon us, and we shall ever pray, &e.... [174]

Jordan's defiance of Massachusetts twice led to his arrest and imprisonment in Boston.[175] In 1663, Jordan and several others were indicted by a Massachusetts grand jury for renouncing the authority of the Bay Colony.[176] In June 1663, Joseph Phippen, Senior, of Falmouth and George Ingersoll of York were commissioned by the Massachusetts authorities to arrest Robert Jordan and to bring him to Boston for imprisonment. The full text of the warrant for Jordan's arrest is set forth here.

9:4:63
To Joseph Phippeny of Falmouth Senior & Georg Ingersoll In the Countie of York

---

[174] The original petition is contained in the Massachusetts Archives Collection, vol. 3, p. 287. It is transcribed in Willis, *History of Portland,* at 127–28.

[175] Jordan, *Jordan Memorial,* 72.

[176] Willis, *History of Portland,* 155; Jordan, A History of *Cape Elizabeth, Maine,* 24.

Whereas Robt. Jordan --- Falmouth Gent haveing entered into Articles of agreement wth us and oath of Freedom amongst us and accepted of Comission of Governm't from us and taken oath thereto notw[th]standing all w[ch]ye Said Robert hath falsified his trust & violated his oath to the great disturbance of his Majesties peace in these pts--- Wee therefore being intrusted & Comissionated by the General Court of the Massachusetts by power derived to them from his most excelent Ma[tie]. Cha:1 & confirmed by his Royal Matie that now is Cha:2. Doe hereby in his Majesties name Empower and Require you the S[d] Joseph to Arest apprehend Sieze and take into your Custodie the body of the s[d] Robert and him safely (wth all convenient Speed) to convey to Boston in the Massachusets Collony and to deliver the Said Robt. Jordan to Wilton Salter prison keeper there. And for the better effecting hereof you (or either of you) are further empowered to charge & require Such Ayde & asistance as you shall Se cause who are not to fayle therein at thier utmost perill:

Wm. Hathorne

9:4:63
To Joseph Phippeny

By Commission & power derived unto us from the Gen: Court of the Massachusets we doe in his mat[ies] name, empower & depute you Joseph Phippeny for the Serveing of all Warrants, Sumons & Attachmts wthin the Towne of Falmouth or depute whome you shall see meet as your Lawefull deputie for persecution thereof according to Lawe here established.

Wm. Hathorne
Elea: Lusher

Phippen completed his assignment,[177] later presenting Massachusetts authorities with a request that his expenses incurred in bringing Jordan to Boston be reimbursed. On 21 October 1663, Joseph Phippen was granted his bill of costs against Mr. Robert Jordan, "for bringing him to Boston, etc." in the amount of £12 19s.[178] The expenses from this endeavor were apparently not paid, for on 31 October 1667, Joseph Phippeny petitioned the General Court for satisfaction for his charges expended in the country's service relating to Mr. Robert Jordan. The court ordered that the treasurer pay Joseph Phippeny £20.[179]

In addition to his involvement in the area's political controversies, Joseph Phippen was a frequent litigant in the York county court. On 5 July 1658, Joseph Phippen was the plaintiff in an action of trespass brought against Richard Foxwell for taking away timber from Joseph's land, to the value of forty pounds.[180] On the same date, Joseph was presented at court for claiming that Mr. Bellingham, the deputy governor, advised him to "beat the said Foxwell & Manacle him, & carry him downe to his doore in a rope."[181] Further, Joseph was accused of "beating Mr. Ric: Foxwell & drawing blood from him," and of beating Foxwell again "when the [said] Foxwell came to forewarn him for Cutting of his Meddow."[182] The court then ordered that to prevent further trouble between Phippen and Foxwell, they should each post a bond in the amount of £100 along with a surety bond of £50, so that they would keep the peace.[183] On 12 July 1658, the court ordered that "all matters of difference betweene [Mr. Richard Foxwell and Joseph Phippenny] concerning titles of Land or otherwise" shall be referred to the next county court session, unless the General Court or the commissioners resolve the matter in the interim.[184] Finding itself incapable of resolving the dispute, for "want of evidence," on 4 July 1659, the court appointed Nicholas Shapleigh, Abraham Preble and Edward Rishworth to resolve the matter.[185]

---

[177] Jordan's petition for release from the prison at Boston, dated 4 September 1663, is transcribed in Jordan, *Jordan Memorial,* 72.

[178] Shurtleff, *Records of the Governor and Company of the Massachusetts Bay,* 4: 2: 94.

[179] Ibid., 359.

[180] Ibid., 62.

[181] Ibid., 63.

[182] Ibid., 63.

[183] Ibid., 63–64.

[184] Ibid., 68.

[185] Ibid., 77.

On 4 July 1659, Joseph Phippenny was presented at the York county court for "breeding a disturbance in the Towne Meeteing by flinging Mr. Jordans voats on the ground" and "for Casting aspertions upon Authority, to the greate disturbance of the peace of the Towne." Joseph Phippenny was "fined 10s for his offence."[186]

In 1663, Robert Jordan had brought suit at the York county court against Joseph Phippen and had attached Joseph Phippen's property, including his house, cattle, boats, corn and hay. Joseph Phippen petitioned the General Court for approval of a bond in the amount of £800 to secure Jordan's claim, if proven at the July 1664 court, on account of the perishable nature of his goods. On 21 October 1663, the General Court approved the petition and directed the constable to deliver up to Joseph Phippen for his use, his house, cattle, hay, land, boat and other goods.[187] At the July court, Jordan's case against Phippen was withdrawn.[188]

The court records for the 29 September 1663 session of the York court suggest that the political conflict raging in Falmouth was spilling over into the court. On 29 September 1663, Sampson Penley charged Joseph Phippeny, Senior with tearing down his fences and cutting down his timber; Phippen was found guilty. Sampson Penley also brought an action of battery against Joseph Phippeny, Senior, "for drawing blood" from him. The court again found for Penley. At the same court, the Town of Falmouth also brought charges against Joseph Phippeny for refusing to give an account to the Town of what he had gathered from the Town's lands. The court found for the Town of Falmouth. Joseph was ordered, in addition, to pay a judgment to George Munjoy for a debt of £17, to be paid in "Merchandable dry Codd fish att Currant price." Phippen did prevail on a claim for breach brought by Richard Foxwell.[189]

Court records for the 29 September 1663 court session also state, "Goodman Phippeny Complayned against by severall of his neighbours for his disorderly Carages & sleighting of Authority, denyed obedience thereto, refuseing to give in bond & makes not his appearance at the Court." The court ordered that Mr. Phippeny to be put in bond for £20 for his "good behaviour."[190] Mr. George Munjoy was given power "to

---

[186] Shurtleff, *Records of the Governor and Company of the Massachusetts Bay*, 4: 2: 81; Willis, *History of Portland*, 115–16.

[187] Shurtleff, *Records of the Governor and Company of the Massachusetts Bay*, 4: 2: 93–94.

[188] Ibid., 149.

[189] Ibid., 376.

[190] Ibid., 380.

do his Endeavor to take good security both of Mr. Cleeve & Phippenny to make their personall appearances to answere such things as shall at the next Court of Assotiats bee exhibited against them, the Complaints whereof with severall testimonys have beene presented att this present Court."[191]

In 1665, Joseph Phippen left Casco Bay for Salem, Massachusetts. On 1 November 1665, Joseph Phippeny was admitted as an inhabitant of the town of Salem, Massachusetts "to Inioy Comon privileges with other men."[192] On 8 July 1667, Mr. William Browne Jr., of Salem, merchant, conveyed, for £35, one and one-half acres of pasture land, as well as a salt marsh, both on Salem Neck, to Joseph Phippen,[193] who then erected a dwelling house on the lot, where he lived.[194]

Joseph Phipeny and his wife Dorcas were admitted to the First Church in Salem on 25 March 1668, having been dismissed from the Church of Boston on 6 August 1667.[195] The following is the record of the First Church:

> On the 25t[h] day of the 1 moneth at the time of the Sacrement of the Lords Supper was read letters of dismission from the Church of Boston, in the behalfe of Joseph Phipeny and Dorcas his wife, they having lived some considerable time here they were accepted by the vote of the Church unto membership in this Church, and then so they entred into covenant with this Church.[196]

A few years later, Joseph found himself at the center of controversy at the First Church, which led to his excommunication. From the records of the First Church in Salem:

> The case of Brother Phipeny was considered, he having long absented himself from the Lords Supper upon occasion of a difference between him and Brother H.

---

[191] Ibid., 380.

[192] *Town Records of Salem, Massachusetts, 1634–1691,* 3 vols. (Salem, Mass., 1868–1934), 2: 58.

[193] Essex Deeds 3:197-99; Sidney Perley, "Salem in 1700. No. 21," *Essex Antiquarian* 9 [1905]: 163; Essex Society of Genealogists, Inc., *Essex County Deeds 1639-1678: Abstracts of volumes 1–4, Copy Books, Essex County, Massachusetts* (Westminster, Md., 2003), 184.

[194] Perley, "Salem in 1700. No. 21," *Essex Antiquarian* 9 [1905]: 163.

[195] Richard D. Pierce, ed., *The Records of the First Church in Salem, Massachusetts 1629–1736* (Salem, 1974), 118.

[196] Ibid.

Skery about which much time was spent and many of the Brethren did speak The issue was he not making any acknowledgement of his Error to Satisfaction He was by a clear vote of the Church layd under a censure of Admonition from Ephesians 5:14: Warn the unruly and from I Corinthians 11:31.[197]

On 25 February 1674, Joseph Phippen was excommunicated by the First Church of Salem:

Joseph Phipeny being layd under an Admonition for his unruliness in rising up against . . . and the law and withdrawing communion from the Church and being called to appear before the Church meeting severall times, He not at all coming and giving very perverse answers to the Brethren that were sent from the Church to him, and utterly refusing so much as to come to the Church meeting, it was unanimously judged by the Church that He did not hear the Church and so was by a generall vote Excommunicated at this time.[198]

Joseph Phippen, Sr., was among those signing a petition in June 1680 urging the town to erect another meetinghouse.[199]

On 27 August 1669, Joseph Phippeney was chosen as a constable in the town of Salem for the following year.[200] On 4 April 1671, he was chosen as an overseer of highways.[201] He also served as a juryman in 1667 and 1668, and as a grand juryman in 1672.[202] In June 1679, Joseph Phipen and Reuben Guppy were witnesses against William Nick, who was presented to the Salem court for being "disguised in drink."[203] Also in 1679, Joseph Phippen took the inventory of the estate of Mr. Robert Starr, who had been murdered by the "barbearious heathens."[204] In 1683, Joseph Phippen, sr., of Salem, filed a complaint against John Hopman for nonperformance of an indenture, whereby Hopman was

---

[197] Richard D. Pierce, ed., *The Records of the First Church in Salem, Massachusetts 1629–1736* (Salem, 1974), 133.

[198] Ibid., 140.

[199] George Francis Dow, ed., *Records and Files of the Quarterly Courts of Essex County, Massachusetts,* 9 vols. (Salem, Mass., 1911–21), 7: 402–3.

[200] *Town Records of Salem, Massachusetts, 1634–1691,* 2: 103.

[201] Perley, *The History of Salem, Massachusetts,* 2: 6.

[202] Ibid., 9–10.

[203] Dow, *Records and Files of the Quarterly Courts of Essex County, Massachusetts,* 7: 238.

[204] Ibid., 239.

to serve him as a servant for four years, but had withdrawn from his service without giving satisfaction. At its November 1683 session, the Salem court rendered a verdict for Joseph Phippen, and the defendant was ordered to serve his full time according to the indenture.[205]

Not many years after the devastation and depopulation of the Casco Bay settlements during King Philip's War, a group of Salem men petitioned the General Court of the Massachusetts Bay Colony for permission to establish a plantation at the bottom of Casco Bay on the river Swegustagoe. Joseph Phippen was apparently the lead petitioner. The group also included Francis Neale, Sr., George Ingersoll, John Pickering, Jonathan Marston, Robert Nickles, Jonathan Ingersoll, Jonathan Wales, Nathaniel Wales, Francis Neale, Jr., John Johnson, John Royall, and Jonathan Putnam. The petition was granted on 11 June 1680, with the petitioners to receive five miles square and two adjacent islands, with the proviso that the proprietors settle twenty or thirty families, with an able minister, within two years.[206] Upon learning that the proprietors "were not approved by those of Casco Bay, who favoured Gorges' claim," the General Court granted the township on the north of Casco Bay.[207] One Salem historian wrote of this enterprise:

> It is significant that, within three years of the time when some of the bloodiest murders of the whole war had occurred around Casco Bay and the country had been depopulated and deserted, a group of men had arranged to push their way back. It is typical of the indomitable spirit of the early settlers . . .[208]

This settlement was begun in August 1680, and in the following month, the plantation was given the name North Yarmouth.[209] Rowe's history of North Yarmouth states that an earlier settlement of the Wescustogo area, subsequently broken up on account of King Philip's War, had been formed as the result of an ancient grant of land given by either Gorges or his son to a body of proprietors represented by Joseph Phippen.[210] Rowe notes that no record of this grant has been found.

---

[205] Ibid., 9: 112.

[206] Shurtleff, *Records of the Governor and Company of the Massachusetts Bay*, 5: 273. *See also* James Duncan Phillips, *Salem in the Seventeenth Century* (Cambridge, Mass., 1933), 248–49; Perley, *The History of Salem, Massachusetts*, 3: 96–97.

[207] Joseph B. Felt, *The Annals of Salem, from its first settlement* (Salem, Mass., 1827), 265–66.

[208] Ibid.

[209] William Hutchinson Rowe, *Ancient North Yarmouth and Yarmouth, Maine 1636–1936, A History* (Yarmouth, Me., 1937), 31-33.

[210] Ibid. at 31.

Joseph Phippen died, presumably at Salem, between 21 July 1687, when he made his will, and 15 September 1687, when his will was proved. His will named his wife Dorcas and five children:[211]

> In the name of God Amen. This twenty first of July in the
> yeare of our Lord One Thousand Six Hundred Eighty
> Seaven I Joseph Phippen Senr of the towne of Salem in
> the County of Essex in New England Blockmaker being
> strickened in years and accompanied with illness w^ch
> accompanies Old age Butt of good and perfect memory
> Blessed be Almighty God for the same and calling to
> remembrance the incertainte state of this Transitory Life
> and that all flesh must yield unto death which it shall please
> God to call Doe make Constitute and Ordaine this my
> Last will and Testament In manner and forme following,
> revoking and annulling by these presents all and every
> testament and testaments will and wills heretofore by me
> made and declared either by word or writing and this to be
> taken onely for my last will and testament and none other
> and first being penitent and sorry from the bottome of my
> heart for my sinns past most humbly desiring forgiveness
> for the same. I Give and Comitt my soule unto Almighty
> God my saviour in whome and by the merritts of Jesus
> Christ my saviour I trust and believe assuredly to be saved,
> and my body to the earth from whence itt was taken to
> be buryed in such desent and Xhian [Christian] manner
> as to my Executrix here after named shall be thought
> meet and convenient. And now for the settling of my
> temporal estate, such goods, chattells & debts as itt hath
> pleased God to give me Doe Order Give and Dispose
> in same in manner and forme following. First I will that
> those debts and and dues as I owe in right or Conscience
> to any manner of person or persons whatsoever shall be
> well and truly paid or ordained to be paid in convenient
> time after my decease by my excutrix hereafter named.
> Item I give and bequeath unto my dearely beloved wife
> Dorcas Phippen all my housing lands chattel and debts
> (vizt) all my whole estate during her natural life- both
> reall & personall, to be disposed of by her as she shall think

---

[211] William Hutchinson Rowe, *Ancient North Yarmouth and Yarmouth, Maine 1636–1936, A History* (Yarmouth, Me., 1937), 31-33.

meete for her comfortable being in this world during her naturall life If she continues remaining a widdow, (but if should marry again then only one third according to law.

Item after my wife Dorcas Phippen her decease I give unto my eldest sonn, Joseph if his mother doe not marry againe after my decease a double portion of what shall be left after her decease But if she marry againe then my desire is my eldest son Joseph to receive his share into his hand and to for me [sic] according to this my last will and testament.

Item I give unto my two sonns David & Samuell equally between them what shall be remaining after my eldest sonn Joseph hath received his double portion as above mentioned.

Item I give unto my two daughters after myne and my wifes decease before my sonns have as above written as follows out of my estate To my daughter Mary fower pounds and to my daughter Sarah eight pounds And as for what money I have I have [sic] and give itt to my wife Dorcas to be att her disposall my funeral charges Doctor and other expenses being first paid out during her naturall life. But if she shall marry againe then my desire is and my will she shall have one third and my three sonnes the remainder My eldest sonn to have a double portion thereof whether before his mothers death if she marry againe; and also after her decease if she marry not againe of what shall then be remaining.

Item I constitute my Dearly beloved wife Dorcas Phippen to be my full and whole Executrix of this my Last will and testament And doe desire my three sonnes Joseph David and Samuel to be assistant & helpful to their mother during her naturall life in all things may continue her naturall life; for the receiving and paying of debts; and in what else may be for her comfort and in witness of the truth hereof I Joseph Phippen have hereunto sett my hand & seal this 21th of July 1687.

Signed Joseph Phippen with his seal and signed and sealed in the presence of us Phillipp Cromwell John Pickering Senr Francis Neale Senr

By his excellency.

The above named Phillipp Cromwell John Pickering Senr &
Francis Neale Senr. Witnesses to this will appeared before me
and made oath that they saw the above written Joseph Phippen
signed Sealed & declare this writing to be his last will and
testament & att the time of his doing thereof he was of sound &
perfect mind and memory to the best of their perceiving.

Sworn th 15ᵗʰ of September 1687 before me E. ANDROS. [212]

The probate of Joseph Phippen's will, along with the inventory of
his estate, is on file in the Suffolk County Court in Boston, and
is as follows:[213]

The probate of the will of Joseph Phippen and the administration
granted thereon to his wife Dorcas Phippen Executrix

Sir Edmund Andros, Knt, Capt General and Governour in chief
of his Majesties Territory and Dominion of New England to
all to whome this shall come or may concern Greeting: Know
ye that on the fifteenth day of September in the yeare of our
Lord one thousand six hundred eighty and seven before me att
Boston in the county of Suffolk in the dominion aforesaid the
will of Joseph Phippen Senior Late of Salem in the county of
Essex within the dominion aforesaid to these presents annexed
was proved, approved and allowed who having while he lived and
at the time of his death goods rights or credits in diverse parts of
said Dominion. The administration of all and singular the goods
rights and Credits the said deceased and his will in any manner
concerning was comitted unto Dorcas Phippen wife of the said
deceased Executrix in the same will named will [*sic*] and truly to
administer the same and to make a true and perfect inventory of
all and singular the goods rights and credits of the said deceased
and the same to exhibit unto the secretarys office of the said
Dominion by the seventeenth day of March next And also to
render a true account thereof upon oath.

---

[212] Suffolk Probate Records 10: 108–9, docket no. 1595.
[213] Suffolk Probate Records 10: 110–11 (inventory). During the administration of Sir
     Edmund Andros (1686 to 1689), all estates in the Dominion of New England were
     probated in Suffolk County.

In witness where of I have hereto sett the seal of the office for probate of wills and Granting administration dated the sixteenth day of September Amo Dni 1687.

An apprizall of the goods and estate of the estate of M[r] Joseph Phippen Sen[r] as itt was apprized by M[r] Phillipp Cromwell and M[r] John Pickering this Twenty First of July 1687 in M[r] Joseph Phippen his life time :

	£	s	d
His now Dwelling House and Land there unto belonging with the wharfe, wearhouse, shop & other buildings there upon	100	-	-
An acre of Marsh in the Northfield	10	-	-
The bedding in the New Rooms (vizt) One feather bed, one boulster two pillows one pair of sheets, three blankets one ruggee curtains [?], and bedstead	10	-	-
His wearing apparrell	12	-	-
A pair of Andirons in the room,	-	10	-
a bed boulster, blanketts, skirts, and rugg& bedstead, & pillows in the outward Room and bedstead	8	-	-
Pewter	2	-	-
Warming pan, chafing dish, skimer, & milker,	1	-	-
Three small Brass Kettles,	2	10	-
5 iron potts	1	5	-
Earthen & tin ware	-	5	-
4, Remnants osearge and one remnant of ticking, 5 pieces of ghinting,	5 3	10	-
two chests,	1	5	-
a piece of coarse Diaz one piece of Holland & a piece of Dowley,	2	-	-

	£	s	d
Two Trammells, a pr of doggs tongs, fire shovel, & bellows,	-	12	-
two musquetts	1	4	-
	£161	**11**	**-**
One cow,	1	15	-
two books,	1	-	-
Halfe a boat,	5	-	-
the tools in the shopp,	13	15	-
a pigg, 1 - -			
remnants of searge, one remnant of sheffield. one remnant of flannel. & six pound of thread,	6	-	-
an old flock bed & appurts,	-	15	-
a thousand of boards	1	10	-
[total]	**£23**	**-**	**-**

This inventory on the others side and above written was apprized in Mr Joseph Phippen his life time by us and Mr Phippen did show them to us the 21th of July 1687 as witness our hands

Phillip Cromwell,
John Pickering Senr.,
Francis Neal Senr.

The house and lot on Salem Neck were devised to his three sons. David and Samuel released their interest to Joseph, the oldest son, on 15 January 1694/95.[214] On 8 December 1696, Joseph Phippen sold the house, lot and wharf, for £94, to Obed Carter, of Salem, fisherman.[215]

On 7 February 1692/93, Dorcas Phippen of Salem, widow, and administratrix of the will of her late husband Joseph Phippen, along with her sons Joseph, David, and Samuel Phippen, sold one and one-half acres of salt marsh in what was called the North Field, to Samuel Stone of Salem, yeoman.[216]

---

[214] Perley, "Salem in 1700," *Essex Antiquarian* 9 [1905]: 163; Essex Deeds, 11: 173.
[215] Perley, "Salem in 1700," *Essex Antiquarian* 9 [1905]: 163; Essex Deeds, 11: 178.
[216] Essex Deeds, 9: 69.

Joseph Phippen had a number of different occupations over the course of his life, including seaman, carpenter, and blockmaker.

The 1808 Phippen chart states, "Joseph Phippen who lived___ years; deceased and left issue, Joseph, Mary, Sarah, David and Samuel. By- Dorcas Wood."

Children of Joseph and Dorcas (Wood) Phippen, born at Hingham or Boston:

  i. CHILD³, bur. at Hingham 27 April 1642.²¹⁷

6 ii. JOSEPH PHIPPEN, bp. at Hingham in Aug. 1642.²¹⁸

  iii. MARY PHIPPEN, bp. at Hingham 5 March 1643/44;²¹⁹ m. (1) JOHN WALLIS of Falmouth, Maine. The 1808 Phippen chart has "Watti" in error and states, "John Watti left issue four Sons & five Daughters By – Mary Phippen." John Wallis, a fisherman, was closely associated with the Phippens. Their nine Wallis children and their many descendants are treated in detail by John Bradley Arthaud.²²⁰ They took refuge from the Indian War in Gloucester, Mass., where John Wallis died, 13 Sept. 1690.²²¹ His widow Mary and son Josiah Wallis gave administration bond on 29 March 1691, with her brother David Phippen as surety.²²² Mary m. (2), before 24 July 1692, as his second wife, SAMUEL MORGAN of Beverly, Mass.; on that date, the First Church of Beverly recorded that she was "received to or communion by letters of dismission from Gloster church." ²²³"Mary Morgan alias Phipen" was named in an agreement of her three brothers, dated 15 Jan. 1694/95, which refers to her receipt of her father's bequest. The agreement also stated that the care of their

---

²¹⁷ C. Edward Egan, Jr., ed., "The Hobart Journal," *Register* 121 [1967]: 3–25 *et seq.*, at 14. (The name of the buried child is not named.)

²¹⁸ Ibid., 15.

²¹⁹ Ibid.

²²⁰ John Bradley Arthaud, "The John Wallis Family of Cape Ann," *Register* 152 [1998]: 286–310, 391–414; 153 [1999]: 29–51, 183–206, 293–318.

²²¹ *Vital Records of Gloucester, Massachusetts to the end of the year 1849,* 3 vols. (Salem, Mass., 1923), 3: 315.

²²² Essex County Probate Records, file no. 28850; Jacobus, "The Phippen Family," *The American Genealogist* 17 [1940]: 7.

²²³ Edgar Allen Poe Yates, "Some Collated Notes Regarding the Early Essex County Morgans" (bound typescript at NEHGS, 1907), 23–24. "Beverly First Church Records," *Essex Institute Historical Collections* 35 [1899]: 177–211 et seq., at 206. Walter Goodwin Davis misdated this to 1694, in *Ancestry of Sarah Stone* (Portland, Maine, 1930), 30.

mother, Dorcas, was provided by her brother David Phippen.[224]
Samuel Morgan of Beverly died before 16 Dec. 1698, when his
will, naming his wife Mary, was proved.[225] Mary m. (3), at Beverly
18 Aug. 1700 [intentions], JOHN BLACK of Beverly,[226] and "[there]
Lived Until har deth," according to her next-door neighbor, in a
deposition given 70 years later.[227] She had nine children by Wallis,
and no children by Morgan or Black.[228] Two of the Wallis children
were named Dorcas and Joseph, after Mary's parents.

    iv. SARAH PHIPPEN, bp. at the First Church of Boston 9 Feb. 1644/45;[229]
m. at Salem 24 Sept. [1668], GEORGE HODGES.[230] The 1808 Phippen
chart states, "Geo Hodges left issue two Sons and four Daughters,
By- Sarah Phippen."

7   v. DAVID PHIPPEN, bp. at the First Church of Boston 4 April 1647.[231]

8   vi. SAMUEL PHIPPEN, bp. at the First Church of Boston 6 May 1649.[232]

    vii. ELIZABETH PHIPPEN, b. at Boston, 10 June 1652;[233] d. 14 July 1653.[234]

3. BENJAMIN[2] **PHIPPEN** (*David*[1]) was born probably by 1625, son of
David and Sarah (____) Phippen; he lived in Boston, Massachusetts. He
married, first, **WILMOT EWER** or **YEO**. He married, second, **ELEANOR**
____.[235] He died before 21 October 1678, when administration of his

---

224 Essex Deeds 10: 114, 15 January 1694/95.

225 Essex County Probate Records, file no. 18748.

226 *Vital Records of Beverly, Massachusetts to the end of the year 1849,* 2 vols. (Topsfield, 1906), 2:37, 214.

227 George Freeman Sanborn, Jr., "Mary (Phippen) (Wallis) Black," *Register* 153 [1999]: 291–92.

228 Arthaud, "The John Wallis Family of Cape Ann," *Register* 152 [1998]: 286 et seq.; see Nathaniel L. Taylor and John Fipphen, "Another Husband for Mary (Phippen) (Wallis) (Morgan) Black: Samuel[2] Morgan (Robert[1]) of Beverly, Mass.," *Register* 160 [2006]: 99–100.

229 *Boston Births, Marriages, and Deaths, 1630–1699,* 19 (Sarah was "aged about 5 days"). In the baptism records for Sarah, David, and Samuel, the First Church of Boston records refer to Joseph Phippeny as a member of the Church of Hingham.

230 *Vital Records of Salem, Massachusetts to the end of the year 1849,* 3: 506, 4: 188 (the record states the year as between 1665 and 1669); Jacobus, "The Phippen Family," *The American Genealogist* 17 [1940]: 7.

231 *Boston Births, Marriages, and Deaths, 1630–1699,* 26 ("aged about 7 wks").

232 Ibid., 30 ("aged about 7 days"). The First Church records erroneously give his name as Joseph.

233 Ibid., 37.

234 Ibid., 42.

235 Jacobus, "The Phippen Family," *The American Genealogist* 17 [1940]: 7–8.

estate was granted to his widow "Elinor" Phippen.[236] Widow Eleanor Phippen married, second, before 22 November 1684, **NATHANIEL JEWELL** of Boston,[237] by whom she had a son George, born at Boston 28 April 1685.[238]

On 16 August 1659, Benjamin ffitzpen als Phippen of Boston, block maker, with consent of his wife Willomett, for £54, sold land with a dwelling house in Boston, to James Robinson of Boston, seaman.[239] The deed is given here in its entirety:

> This Indenture made the sixteenth day of August in the yeare of our Lord one thousand six hundred fifty and nine between Beniamin ffitzpen, als Phippen of Boston in the county of Suffolk in New England Block maker of the one part and James Robbinson of the same Boston seaman of the other part wittnesseth that the said Beniamin ffitzpen als Phippen with the free voluntary will & consent of Willomett his wife for and in consideration of the summe of fifty & fowre pounds sterling by ye value therof in monney & other currant pay of & in New England, in hand well & truly paid, before the sealing & deliuery Hereof the receipt whereof is hereby acknowledged, Hath giuen, granted bargained, sold, Aliened Enfeoffed Assigned set ouer and confirmed unto the said James Robbinson his heires executors administrators and assignes a peice or pcell of ground containing in length on the easterly side thereof fourty & seuen foote or there abouts and in length on the Westerly side thereof fourty & seuen foote or thereabout containing also in breadth on the Northerly side therof Thirty and Eight foot or thereabouts, and on the South Side therof fourty foot or thereabout, together with the dwelling house, one P^t of the said ground standing the said house & ground scituate liing, and being Neare the Mill Creek in Boston aforesaid and bounded by the lands of Mary Paddy widdow on the northerly-side thereof & ye lands of the said Beniamin on the Easterly side therof the lands of Samuell Bennit on the Southerly side thereof and the lands of George ffitzpen, als Phippen on the

---

[236] Suffolk Probate Records 12: 32 (Suffolk Probate docket no. 989).

[237] Nathaniel Jewell is named as the husband of "Elnor Phippin" in a deed dated 22 November 1684, by which the heirs of Gamaliel Phippen sold to Job Prince the remaining interest in property adjoining that of Eleanor Phippen and formerly belonging to Gamaliel's widow Sarah. See Suffolk Deeds 13: 232–33.

[238] Boston Births, Marriages, and Deaths, 1630–1699, 166 (birth of George Jewell).

[239] Suffolk Deeds, 4: 22–24.

Westerly side thereof with all and singular the priuiledges and
appurtenances to the same belonging, And also all the estate
Right title interest use property possession claime & demand
whatsoeuer of him the said Beniamin ffittzpen als Phippen in or
to the same or any part or pcell thereof. To haue and to hold
the said peice or pcell of ground with the dwelling house now
theron standing with the priuiledges therunto belonging and the
appurtenances therto appertaining unto the said James Robbinson
his heires Executors administrators & assignes from the day of
the date hereof for euer to the onely proper use and behoofe of
the said James Robbinson his heires executors administrators and
assignes for euer, And the said Beniamin ffitzpen als Phippen for
himselfe his heires executors administrators and euery of them
doth Couenant promise to and with the said James Robbinson
his heires executors administrators and assignes that hee the
said Beniamin ffitzpen als Phippen at the time of the sealing &
delivery of these presents was the true and rightfull owner of the
above bargained premisses and that the same is free & cleare &
freely & clearely acquitted exonerated and discharged of & from
all and all manner of former and other, bargaines, sales, gifts,
grants, leases, Assignements, Mortgages, wills, Extents, Judgments,
executions, forfeitures, seisures, Joyntures, power & thirds of
Willomet his now wife to be claimed, or challenged, of or in or
to the premisses or any p^t therof, And of and from all and singular
& other charges, titles, troubles, and incumbrances, whatsoeuer,
had made done or suffered to be done by the said Beniamin
ffitzpen als Phippen, or any other pson or psons whatsoeuer, by
his or theire means, default, consent or procurement, And against
him the said Beniamin ffitzpen als Phippen his heires executors
& administrators and euery other person & persons Whatsoever
lawfully claiming from by or under him them or any of them
shall and will warrant and for ever defend by these presents. And
lastly the said Beniamin ffitzpen als Phippen for himselfe his heires
executors and administrators doth Covenant & promise to and
with the said James Robbinson his heires executors administrators
and assignes That they shall and may forever after the day of the
date herof quietly and peaceably haue Hold use ocupy posesse
& Enioy the said bargained premisses and every part and pcell
thereof with the appurtenances and priviledges thereto belonging
to his and theire own prper use and behooffe without the let suite
trouble, molestation, denyall contradiction interuption euiction

ejection or disturbance of the said Beniamin ffitzpen als Phippen his heirs executors administrators or any other person or persons Haueing claiming or pretending to haue any estate right title interest claime or demaund of in or to the same or any pt. or pceel thereof from by or under him them or any of them In wittnesse whereof the said Beniamin ffitzpen als Phippen hath here unto put his hand and seale the two and twentieth day of August in the yeare of our Lord one thousand six hundred ffity and nine. Beniamin Phippen and seale.

Signed sealed and deliuered and possession giuen to the within named James Robbinson by the within named Beniamin ffitzpen als Phippen of the within named peice of ground and dwelling house in the presence of us.

Edmund Jackson.
Thomas Barlow.
William Pearse.

This deed was acknowledged by the aboue named Beniamin ffitzpen als Phippen to bee his act and deed and by Willomett his wife to be with her free voluntary will and consent the. Before mee.

This conveyance aboue written was acknowledged to the act & deed of Benjamin ffiuepeny the 1ˢᵗ day of January. 1661. before mee Jo: Endicott Govr.

His wife doth acknowledge ye like as witnesse my hand. Entred & Recorded the. 22ᵗʰ of July 1662. Edw. Rawson Secreʸ.[240]

Benjamin Phippen apparently operated an ordinary (tavern), presumably on his property along the Boston waterfront. On 12 November 1659, in an action brought against Benjamin Phippeny and John Andrews by Richard Brackett and Samuel Bass, on behalf of the town of Braintree, "for giving John Frizell so much licquors as made him druncke, & occasioned his miserable freizing, the Court, on a hearing of the case & evidences, doe find for yᵉ defendants [with] costs of Court."[241]

---

[240] Suffolk Deeds, 4: 22–24.

[241] Shurtleff, Records of the Governor and Company of the Massachusetts Bay, 4: 1: 401–2.

On 28 April 1673, Benjamine Phippeny was granted liberty to keep a cook shop and "to sell strong beere with his victualls."[242] Permission was granted again in April 1674, on 26 April 1675, and on 24 April 1676.[243] "Widdow Phippany" was licensed to sell "Beere & Cyder" on 26 April 1680,[244] and was approved to "keepe [a] house for publique entertainemt" on 25 April 1681.[245] The inventory of Benjamin Phippen's estate included "one barrel of Cider and three [barrels] of beare," valued at £2, 6s.[246]

On 28 January 1666/67, "Benjamine Phipinye," "Gamaliell Phippinye" and nine others were granted "liberty to wharfe or make dockes . . . before theire owne landes between the mill Creeke & John Phillips dock."[247] Samuel Clough's reconstructed map of Boston in 1676 identifies the location of "B. Phippeni's Wh[ar]f" on the Boston waterfront, not far from the Great Drawbridge and the Mill Creek.[248] He was in the Boston tax lists of 1674 and 1676.[249]

On 26 October 1674, the town of Boston issued a warrant to "ye Constable to leauy 20s. on Benja. Phippany for annoyinge his Neighb^rs & ye lane neere his hous by his hogstie."[250]

Administration of the estate of Benjamin Phippen, late of Boston, deceased, was granted to Elinor Phippen, his relict, on 21 October 1678.[251] The inventory of his estate, taken on 26 October 1678, valued his estate at £348, 13s. His "House, land, Wharfs and shops" were valued at £300.[252]

---

242 A Report of the Record Commissioners of the City of Boston, containing the Boston Records from 1660 to 1701 (Boston, 1881), 76.

243 Ibid., 87, 95, 100.

244 Ibid., 139.

245 Ibid., 145. For the history of ordinaries in seventeenth-century Boston, *see* Gavin R. Nathan, *Historic Taverns of Boston* (New York, 2006), 3–4. Nathan notes that there were 27 licensed establishments in 1677. Annie Haven Thwing observed that this area of Boston (now North Street) was "famous for its wharfs and taverns." *See* Thwing, *The Crooked & Narrow Streets of the Town of Boston 1630–1822*, 34.

246 Suffolk Probate Records 12: 225 (Suffolk Probate docket no. 989).

247 *A Report of the Record Commissioners of the City of Boston, containing the Boston Records from 1660 to 1701*, 33.

248 Seasholes, *Gaining Ground: A History of Landmaking in Boston*, 25. The Clough map is also accessible at the Massachusetts Historical Society's on-line map collection: www.masshist.org/online/massmaps/doc-viewer.php?old=1&item_id=1788

249 First *Report of the Record Commissioners of the City of Boston*, 2d. ed., 35, 38, and 63.

250 *A Report of the Record Commissioners of the City of Boston, containing the Boston Records from 1660 to 1701*, 89.

251 Suffolk Probate Records 12: 32 (Suffolk Probate docket no. 989).

252 Ibid., 225.

On 10 July 1697, Nathaniel Sherman and Mary his wife, Benjamin Sherman and Rebecca his wife, and James Phippen, all of Stratford, Connecticut, and Nathaniel Baldwin and Sarah his wife, of Milford, Connecticut, conveyed for £40, 10s. to Michael Shaller of Boston. The deed states that Benjamin Phippen, late of Boston, block maker, father of the said James, Mary, Rebecca, and Sarah, died intestate; that he possessed a dwelling house, land, and two shops, near the Drawbridge in Boston; that the Court had settled the estate of Benjamin Phippen on 6 February 1678; and that the estate was to be divided equally except a double share to the eldest son, that the two shops were divided equally among Sarah Baldwin, Mary Sheman, James Phippen, and Rebecca Sherman, and the house and land were appointed to the eldest son Benjamin Phippen (two-fifths), and to Thomas, John and Joseph Phippen (one-fifth each); and that the said eldest son Benjamin Phippen, by his will dated 14 Jan 1683/84, devised two-fifths of his property to his oldest sister Sarah Baldwin and the remainder to his brothers and sisters, James Phippen, Mary Sherman, and Rebecca Sherman, equally. [253]

A second deed, dated 10 July 1697, from the same grantors, recites similar facts, and adds that whereas, John and Joseph Phippen "went to Sea and have been long absent, unheard of, and as it is supposed and presumed they are Dead and Intestate," the said grantors, as the only heirs, conveyed to Michael Shaller the two-fifths that belonged to John and Joseph. [254]

The 1808 Phippen chart states, "Benjm. Phippen left issue, 3 Sons and 2 Daughters, By- Wellmith Youer." Wilmot's maiden name is possibly Ewer or Yeo. The name of Sarah[2] Phippen's husband, Thomas Yeo, was spelled Yow on the chart; it is possible that Wilmot's name was Yow on the original chart and miscopied as Youer. [255]

Children of Benjamin and Wilmot (Ewer) Phippen, born at Boston: [256]

    i.   DAVID[3] PHIPPEN, b. 6 Nov. 1651; d. young.

[253] Suffolk Deeds 14: 410–13; Jacobus, "The Phippen Family," *The American Genealogist* 17 [1940]: 8.

[254] Suffolk Deeds 14: 413–415; Jacobus, "The Phippen Family," *The American Genealogist* 17 [1940]: 8.

[255] Jacobus, "The Phippen Family," *The American Genealogist* 17 [1940]: 7–8.

[256] Unless noted otherwise, information about children is from Boston Vital Records 1630–1699, 33 (birth of David), 40 (birth of Benjamin), 44 (baptism of Benjamin), 46 (birth of Benjamin), 47 (death of Benjamin), 49 (baptism of "Benjamin of

ii.   BENJAMIN PHIPPEN, b. 6, bp. at the First Church 10 April 1653; d. 28
      May 1654.

iii. BENJAMIN PHIPPEN, b. 19, bp.at the First Church 28 Jan. 1654/55; d.
      20 Sept. 1655.

iv.   BENJAMIN PHIPPEN, b. 15 July 1656, d. unm. in 1694. His will, dated
      14 Jan. 1683/84, gave his [step] "mother Elenor Phippen twenty
      shillings to buy her a gold Ring," bequeathed two-fifths of his
      estate to his eldest sister Sarah Baldwin, and gave the remainder to
      his brother James Phippen and sisters Mary Sherman and Rebecca
      Sherman, to be divided equally. Administration of the estate of
      Benjamin Phippen, late of Boston, mariner, deceased, was granted
      on 9 June 1694, to his executor Ralph Carter.[257]

v.   SARAH PHIPPEN, b. 13 April 1658; m. NATHANIEL BALDWIN, bp.
      at Milford, Conn., 22 March 1648, son of John Baldwin, Sr..[258]
      Jacobus lists seven children, born at Milford, Conn.[259]

vi.   MARY PHIPPEN, b. about 1660; m. at Stratford, Conn. 30 June
      1680 or 30 June 1681, NATHANIEL SHERMAN,[260] b. at Stratford 21
      March 1656, son of Samuel and Sarah (Mitchell) Sherman.[261] She
      d. before 26 Nov. 1707, when he m. (2), at Stratford, Abigail (Burr)
      (Lockwood) Hanford of Fairfield.[262] He d. at Stratford 17 April
      1712.[263]

9   vii. JAMES PHIPPENEY, b. 30 Jan. 1663/4. James and his descendants
      consistently spelled their name as "Phippeney" or "Phippeny," and
      are so named in this volume.

viii. REBECCA PHIPPEN, b. 10 Aug. 1666; m. at Stratford, Conn. 6 June
      1683, BENJAMIN SHERMAN,[264] b. 29 March 1662, brother of her sister

---

Mrs. Phipeny of the New Ch[urch]"), 52 (death of Benjamin), 55 (birth of
Benjamin), 64 (birth of Sarah), 89 (birth of James), and 101 (birth of Rebecca).

[257] Suffolk Probate Records 13: 432–33 (Suffolk Probate docket no. 2150).

[258] Jacobus, "The Phippen Family," *The American Genealogist* 17 [1940]: 9.

[259] Ibid.

[260] Lorraine Cook White, ed. "Stratford 1639-1840," *The Barbour Collection of Connecticut
      Town Vital Records,* vol. 41 (Baltimore: Genealogical Publishing Co., 2000), 205,
      transcribing from two sources with different dates.

[261] Ibid., 220; Samuel Orcutt, *A History of the Old Town of Stratford and the City of
      Bridgeport, Connecticut,* 2 vols. [hereafter *History of Stratford*] (New Haven, 1886), 2:
      1283–84.

[262] "Stratford 1639-1840," *The Barbour Collection of Connecticut Town Vital Records,* vol.
      41, 220; Jacobus, "The Phippen Family," *The American Genealogist* 17 [1940]: 9;
      Orcutt, *History of Stratford,* 2: 1284. Jacobus states that they had no issue, but Orcutt
      lists a child Comfort Sherman, b. abt. 1682.

[263] "Stratford 1639-1840," *The Barbour Collection of Connecticut Town Vital Records,* vol.
      41, 220.

[264] Ibid., 205, 217.

Mary's husband.[265] They had 13 children.[266] She d. 5 Aug. 1739, age 75; he d. 29 Aug. 1741 in his 80th year.[267] Jacobus lists thirteen children, born at Stratford.[268]

Children of Benjamin and Eleanor (____) Phippen, born at Boston:[269]

ix.   THOMAS PHIPPEN, b. 1 Dec. 1671; d. unm. in 1714, when administration of his estate was granted to William Cotton of Portsmouth and his wife Anna. He was a mariner and lived in Boston. His will, made on 21 Oct. 1695 as he prepared to go to sea, gave half his estate to "Mrs." Ann Carter, daughter of Ralph Carter, probably his intended bride, with legacies to her relatives and others, and two shillings apiece to his brother James Phippen and his sisters Sarah Phippen, Mary Phippen, and Rebecca Phippen.[270]

x.   JOHN PHIPPEN, b. 1 June 1673; presumed dead by 1697.

xi.   JOSEPH PHIPPEN, b. 30 Nov. 1676; presumed dead by 1697.

4. GAMALIEL[2] **PHIPPEN** (*David*[1]) was probably born by 1627, son of David and Sarah (____) Phippen. He lived at Boston, Massachusetts, where he died between 11 November 1671 and 30 January 1671/72. He married, by 1649, **SARAH PURCHASE**, who was baptized at Dorchester, Dorset 6 August 1626, the daughter of Aquila and Anne (Squire) Purchase.[271] She died at Boston 17 January 1682/83.[272]

Like his father David, Gamaliel Phippen lived and worked along the Boston waterfront. On 28 January 1666/67, "Gamaliell Phippinye," "Benjamine Phipinye," and nine others were granted "liberty to wharfe or make dockes . . . before theire owne landes between the mill Creeke & John Phillips dock."[273] Samuel Clough's reconstructed map of Boston in 1676 indicates that "G. Phippeni" and "B. Phippeni" owned nearby

[265]   Ibid., 217; Orcutt, *History of Stratford,* 2: 1284.

[266]   Jacobus, "The Phippen Family," *The American Genealogist* 17 [1940]: 9–10.

[267]   Orcutt, *History of Stratford,* 2: 1284.

[268]   Jacobus, "The Phippen Family," *The American Genealogist* 17 [1940]: 9–10.

[269]   *Boston Vital Records 1630–1699,* 120 (birth of Thomas), 129 (birth of John), and 139 (birth of Joseph).

[270]   Suffolk Probate Records 18: 321-22 (Suffolk Probate docket no. 3596); Jacobus, "The Phippen Family," *The American Genealogist* 17 [1940]: 10.

[271]   Anderson, *The Great Migration Begins: Immigrants to New England 1620-1633,* 3: 1527–28.

[272]   "Old Gravestones," *Register* 25 [1871]: 88–89; Suffolk Probate Records 9: 146 (date of grant of administration).

[273]   *A Report of the Record Commissioners of the City of Boston, containing the Boston Records from 1660 to 1701* (Boston, 1881), 33.

wharfs along the Boston waterfront, not far from the Great Drawbridge and the Mill Creek.[274]

The Suffolk County probate files contain a transcription of the will of Gamaliel Phippen, which was made on 11 November 1671 and proved on 1 February 1671/72:[275]

> The Last Will and Testament of Gamaliell Phippen of Boston Senior Being in perfect memory I doe leave unto my Beloved wife Sarah Phippen my whole Estate of housing lands vessells and moveables Soe long as she Continues a Widdow to mayntaine and bring up my Children that is to say: Hannah, Rebecca, and Gamaliell Elizabeth Ann and Mehitabell Alsoe I doe give unto my Sonne Gamaliell all my working tooles which belonges to my trade in case hee followes it: otherwise if hee like any other trade better hee shall have the worth of them Alsoe I give to my wife in case shee changes her Condition ffifty pounds out of my Estate to dispose of as shee shall see good then the Remaynee of the Estate is equally to bee Divided And also my Daughter Sarah Horton my Daughter that is married In case the Estate arriseth to more then I have already given her to her portion shee shall bee equally with my abovesaid Children: Also I doe request my Loving friends Richard Knight Bricklayer and Edward Rainsford to bee the Overseers of this my will

> 11:9: mo: 1671   Gamaliell Phippen

> Witnes Hugh Drury
>   Benjamin Thompson

On 30 January 1671[/72], administration of the estate of Gamaliell Phippen, late of Boston, deceased, was granted to Sarah Phippen.[276] On 31 January 1671[/72], the inventory of the estate of Gamaliell Phippeny of Boston Blockmaker was presented to the court by Sarah Phippen. The estate, valued at £495, 12s, and 6d, included the dwelling house and land on the "west Side of the highway," valued at £200, and a warehouse, lean-to, wharfing, and land on the "East Side of the Highway," valued at £150.[277]

---

[274] Seasholes, *Gaining Ground: A History of Landmaking in Boston,* 25.

[275] Suffolk Probate Records 7: 187 (will). A brief transcription of Gamaliel Phippen's will appears in W.L. Holman's unpublished research. Winifred Lovering Holman Papers (Mss 920), R. Stanton Avery Special Collections, NEHGS, Boston, Phippen folder, "Phippin Notes," p. 8. Daughter Sarah's married name (Houghton) was transcribed incorrectly in the probate records.

[276] Suffolk Probate Records 7: 187.

[277] Ibid., 188–89 (inventory).

On 4 July 1672, Robert Haughton of Boston sold to Sarah Phipany of Boston, widow and sole executrix of her late husband, Gamaliel Phipany, a warehouse and land located near the Draw Bridge in Boston, which Gamaliel Phipany, late of Boston, deceased, had sold to Haughton on 13 March 1670.[278] The Boston tax list of 1676 includes "widdow Phippenny."[279]

On 3 April 1676, Robert Haughton, mariner, and Sarah Phippeny, widow of Gamaliel Phippeny, both of Boston, mortgaged to Simon Lynde of Boston, merchant, "all that great warehouse Leanto and wharfe with the ground & fflatts on which they stand . . being neere the draw bridge in Boston . . and at present in the occupation of James Loyd Merchant, bounded North Easterly with a little warehouse wharfe ground and fflatts in our own occupation; North westerly with the highway, South westerly with widdow Milam & Benjamin Gibbs and South Easterly with the River or harbour before Boston."[280]

On 11 March 1680/81, Sarah Phippen of Boston, widow; Sarah Haughton of Milford, Connecticut, widow; William Gibson of Boston, Massachusetts, cordwainer, and his wife Hannah; and Elisabeth Phippen, Ann Phippen, and Mehetabel Phippen, all of Boston, spinsters, conveyed to Job Prince of Boston, mariner, part of the house and land, located near the Drawbridge in Boston, now occupied by the said Sarah Phippen, and bounded, in part, by the house and land of Eloner Phippen.[281]

On 31 July 1683, adminstration of the estate of Sarah Phippen was granted to Joseph Bridgham and William Gibson, both of Boston.[282] The inventory of her estate, valued at £265, was presented to the court on 20 December 1683. The principal item in the estate was her husband's warehouse, smith's shop and the land they stood on, valued at £200.[283]

On 12 June 1684, William Gibson of Boston, cordwainer, and Joseph Bridgham of Boston, tanner, administrators appointed by the court in Boston to make sale of the estate of the late Gamaliel Phippen deceased to pay debts, for £60, sold a shop with wharf, located near the Draw Bridge in Boston, to John Orris of Boston, blocksmith. The heirs consented to the sale and signed as Elizabeth Spencer, Ann Phippen,

---

[278]   Suffolk Deeds 6: 316.
[279]   *First Report of the Record Commissioners of the City of Boston.* 2d. ed. (Boston, 1881), 63.
[280]   Suffolk Deeds 9: 435–36.
[281]   Ibid., 13: 221–22.
[282]   Suffolk Probate Records 9: 146 (administration).
[283]   Ibid. at 240 (inventory).

Mehittable Phippen, "Job Prince, Husband to Rebecka Phippen formerly Soe called," and by Joseph Phippen "husband to Elizabeth one of the Daughters of Gamaliel Phippen." The acknowledgements were taken on 8 May 1685, of "The Severall daughters of Gamaliel Phippeny viz Elizabeth Rebeckah Ann and Mehittable together with Job Prince husband to sd Rebecca, and Joseph Phippen husband to Eliza."[284]

On 22 November 1684, Benjamin Smith of Milford, Connecticut, tailor, and Sarah his wife; William Gibson of Boston, cordwainer, and Hannah his wife; Elizabeth Spencer of Boston, widow; and Ann Phippen and Mehitable Phippen of Boston, spinsters, referring to the deed of 11 March 1680/81, in which Sarah Phippen late of Boston, widow, deceased, Sarah Haughton (now wife of said Benjamin Smith), and the others sold to Job Prince, sold the remainder of the house and land to Job Prince.[285]

About 1870, several old gravestones were discovered during building construction on Carlton Place, near Eliot Street, in Boston. Most of the stones had the "old-fashioned death's head" over the inscription. One of the gravestones had the following inscription: "Here lyeth buried ye body of Sarah Phippen, ye wife of Gamaliel Phippen, aged 55 years. Died January ye 17,----."[286]

The 1808 Phippen chart states, "Gamal. Phippen left issue one Son and four Daughters, By-- Sarah Purchase." It is known that he had six daughters that grew to marry, and that no sons survived.

Children of Gamaliel and Sarah (Purchase) Phippen, born at Boston:[287]

> i.   SARAH[3] PHIPPEN, bp. 30 Dec. 1649, aged about 6 days; m. (1) at Cambridge, Mass. 8 Sept. 1668, ROBERT HOUGHTON,[288] b. about 1642, son of Richard Houghton of Boston;[289] he d. at Milford,

[284]   Suffolk Deeds 13: 343.
[285]   Ibid., at 13: 232–33.
[286]   "Old Gravestones," *Register* 25 [1871]: 88–89.
[287]   Unless noted otherwise, information on children is from Boston Vital Records 1630-1699, 30 (baptism of Sarah), 33 (birth of Gamaliel), 37 (death of Gamaliel), 39 (baptism of Gamaliel), 41 (birth of Hannah), 44 (baptism of Hannah ["Anna"], 55 (birth of Rebecca), 63 (baptism of Rebecca), 69 (birth of Elizabeth), 72 (baptism of Elizabeth), 89 (birth of Gamaliel), 101 (birth of Ann) and 108 (birth of Mehitable). Baptisms were recorded at the First Church, Boston.
[288]   *Vital Records of Cambridge, Massachusetts to the end of the year 1850,* 2 vols. (Boston, 1914), 2: 207, 308.
[289]   James Savage, *A Genealogical Dictionary of the First Settlers of New England,* 4 vols. (Boston, 1860-62; reprinted Baltimore, 1977), 2: 378.

Conn. about 1678 (estate inventoried).[290] She m. (2) at Milford 9
Feb. 1682, BENJAMIN SMITH,[291] b. about 1633, son of William and
Magdalen (_____) Smith. He had married (1), at Milford 21 Oct.
1660, Mary Baldwin.[292] Sarah (Phippen) Houghton was admitted
to the Milford Church 20 Oct. 1677.[293] Jacobus lists three children
by her first husband and four by her second husband.[294]

  ii. GAMALIEL PHIPPEN, b. 12, bp. 14 March 1651/52; d. 8 Sept. 1652.

 iii. HANNAH PHIPPEN, b. 25, bp. (as Anna) 31 July 1653; m. at Boston in
1672, WILLIAM GIBSON. He d. at Milford 18 Sept. 1703. Jacobus lists
fifteen children.[295]

 iv. REBECCA PHIPPEN, b. 12 Feb., bp. 1 March 1656/57; died at Milford
17 Oct. 1712, aged about 54 years.[296] Jacobus claims that she married
SAMUEL BALDWIN, b. about 1645, son of John Baldwin, Sr.; however,
that marriage is highly improbable, since Rebecca would have
been only 14 years of age when Samuel died at Milford on 16 Jan.
1671/72.[297] She m. (1) at Boston about 1678, JOB PRINCE of Boston,
bp. 22 Aug. 1647, son of "Elder" John and Alice (Honour) Prince.
He died at sea in 1693.[298] She m. (2) ENS. GEORGE CLARK, widower
of Deborah Gold, daughter of Nathan and Sarah[2] (Phippen) Gold.
Mrs. Rebeckah Clark, discharged from the First Church in Boston,
was admitted to the Milford church 30 Nov. 1701. Jacobus lists
seven children for Rebecca and Job Prince, all born at Boston.[299]

  v. ELIZABETH PHIPPEN, b. 10,[300] bp. 15 Aug. 1659; living in 1733; m. (1)
ABRAHAM SPENCER, who d. in 1683;[301] m. (2) between 12 June 1684

---

[290] Jacobus, "The Phippen Family," *The American Genealogist* 17 [1940]: 11.

[291] White, Lorraine Cook, ed. "Milford 1640-1850," *The Barbour Collection of Connecticut Town Vital Records,* vol. 28 (Baltimore: Genealogical Publishing Co., 2000), 166; Jacobus, History and Genealogy of the Families of Old Fairfield, 1: 477.

[292] "William Smith of Jamaica," *The American Genealogist* 25 [1948]: 70–90, at 70–71.

[293] Jacobus, "The Phippen Family," *The American Genealogist* 17 [1940]: 11.

[294] Ibid., at 11–12.

[295] Ibid., 12. Sir Winston Churchill was one of their descendants. See "The American Ancestry of Mr. Winston Churchill," *The New York Genealogical and Biographical Record* 73 [1942]: 163.

[296] Morris W. Abbott, *Milford Tombstone Inscriptions* (Milford, Conn., 1967), 34.

[297] Jacobus, "The Phippen Family," *The American Genealogist* 17 [1940]: 12.

[298] Smith, *Early Families of Hull, Massachusetts,* 159.

[299] Jacobus, "The Phippen Family," *The American Genealogist* 17 [1940]: 12–13.

[300] Also found in "Early Records of Boston," *Register* 13 [1859]: 220.

[301] Thomas B. Wyman, *The Genealogies and Estates of Charlestown in the County of Middlesex and Commonwealth of Massachusetts, 1629-1818,* 2 vols. (Boston, 1879), 2: 886.

and 8 May 1685, JOSEPH[4] PHIPPEN, grandson of her uncle Joseph[2] Phippen, *i.e.* her first cousin once removed.[302]

vi.   GAMALIEL PHIPPEN, b. 16 Feb. 1663; d. between 11 Nov. 1671 (when he was named in his father's will) and 11 March 1680/81.

vii. ANN PHIPPEN, b. 28 April 1666; m. at Boston 16 May 1686, WILLIAM WHEELER;[303] Jacobus lists four children.[304]

viii. MEHITABLE PHIPPEN, b. 27 April 1668. (Published Boston vital records erroneously show her parents as *Daniel* and Sarah Phippen.) Mehitable died at Milford 15 Dec. 1721, in her 54th year.[305] She m. (1) THOMAS FORD, d. probably at Boston after 8 June 1692; she m. (2) CAPT. SAMUEL CLARK, b. at Milford 4 Aug. 1666, son of Thomas and Hannah (Gibbard) Clark, and nephew of Ens. George Clark, husband of Deborah[3] Gold. He d. at Milford 29 May 1725. Mehitabel Clark was received into the Milford Church from the Church in Boston in 1697. Jacobus lists one son by Ford (who died young) and ten children by Clark.[306]

5. GEORGE[2] PHIPPEN (*David[1]*) was born about 1633 and died at Hull, Massachusetts 24 December 1704, son of David and Sarah (___) Phippen.[307] He married (perhaps in London) before 3 February 1659/60, **ELIZABETH** ____.[308] She died at Hull 20 August 1714.[309]

George Phippen, a mariner, lived at Boston, then at Falmouth, Maine. He was likely preparing to leave Boston when, on 3 February 1659/60, as "George ffitzpen als Phippen of Boston," seaman, with consent of his wife Elizabeth, he sold land in Boston for £9,10s to James Robinson of Boston, seaman:

---

[302] Jacobus, "The Phippen Family," *The American Genealogist* 17 [1940]: 13.

[303] *Boston Births, Marriages, and Deaths, 1630-1699,* 172.

[304] Jacobus, "The Phippen Family," *The American Genealogist* 17 [1940]: 13.

[305] "Milford 1640-1850," *The Barbour Collection of Connecticut Town Vital Records,* vol. 28, 63 (date of death stated as 16 Dec. 1721); Abbott, Milford Tombstone Inscriptions, 33.

[306] Ibid.; Jacobus, "The Phippen Family," *The American Genealogist* 17 [1940]: 13–14.

[307] Vital Records of *Hull, Massachusetts to the end of the year 1849* (Boston, 1911), 65.

[308] Phippen genealogical chart of 1808 (see Chapter 1).

[309] *Vital Records of Hull, Massachusetts to the end of the year 1849,* 65. The name is spelled "Fippeny" in the Hull record. No first name is given, but "wid. of" is followed by a blank, followed by "Aug. 20, 1714."

This indenture made the Second day of ffebruary in the yeare of our Lord one Thousand Six hundred ffifty and nine Between George ffitzpen als Phippen of Boston in the County of Suffolk in New England seaman of the one part and James Robbinson of the same Boston seaman of the other part.

Witnesseth that the said George ffitzpen als Phippen with the free voluntary will and consent of Elizabeth his wife for and in consideration of the summe of Nine pounds ten shillings sterling by the value thereof in monney and other pay currant of and in New England in hand paid by the said James Robbinson unto the said George ffitzpen als Phippen before the sealing and delivery hereof Hath given granted bargained sold aliened enfeofed assigned set over and confirmed, and by these presents doth give grant bargaine sell alien enfeofe set over & confirme unto the said James Robbinson his heires executors administrators or assignes a peice or parcell of ground lying and being in Boston aforesaid containing in length fourty foot or thereabout and in breadth fourty foot or thereabout butting on the lands of Mary Paddy widdow on the North End the lands of Samuel Bennett on the South East bounded by the lands of Gamaliell ffitzpen, —on the Northwest, and the lands of the said James Robbinson on the South East with all and singular the privileges & appurtenances to the same belonging and also all the estate right title interest use pperty posession claime and demand, whatsoeuer of him the said George ffitzpen als Phippen in or to the same or any part or pcell thereof. To have and to hold the said peice or pcell of ground as aforesd with the appurtenances and priviledges to the same belonging unto the sd James Robbinson his beires executors administrators and assignes from the day of the date hereof for ever. To the onely pper use and behoof of the said James Robbinson his heirs executors administrators and assigns for ever.

And the said Georg ffitzpen als Phippen for himselfe his heires executors and administrators and for every of them doth Covenant and promise to and With the said James Robbinson his heires executors administrators and assignes That hee the said George ffitzpen als Phippen at the time of the sealing and delivery heerof was the true and rightfull

owner of the aboue bargained premisses, and that the same
is free and cleere & freely & clearely acquitted exonerated
and discharged of and from all and all manner of former
and other bargaines, sales. gifts, grants, Leases, assignements,
mortgages, wills, entailes, Judgm^{ts}, forfeitures seizures,
Joyntures, Power and thirds of Elizabeth his now wife to be
claimed or challenged of in or to the premisses or any part
or pcell thereof and of and from all and singular other titles
troubles charges Incumbrances and demands, whatsoeuer
had done made or suffered to be done by the said George
ffitzpen als Phippen, or any other pson or psons whatsoeuer
by his or their Act, meanes consent or procurement, And
against him the said George ffitzpen als Phippen his heires
executors and administrators and all and every other pson
or psons lawfully claiming from by and under him, them, or
any of them shall and will, warrant and for ever defend by
these presents.And lastly the said George ffitzpen als Phippen
for himselfe his heires executors and administrators doth
covenant and pmise to and with the said James Robbinson
his heires executors administrators and assignes That they
shall and may for euer after the day of the date hereof quietly
and peaceably haue hold use occupy possess and injoy the
said bargained premisses & every part and pcell thereof with
the appurtenances and priviledges thereto belonging to his
and their own pper [*sic*] use and behooffe without the let
suite trouble molestation denyall, contradiction, interuption,
eviction, ejection, or disturbance, of the sd George ffitzpen
als Phippen his heires executors administrators or any pson
or psons hauing claiming or pretending to haue any estate
right title interest claime or demand of in or to the same or
to the same or any part or parcell thereof from by or under
him them or any of them.

In wittnesse wherof the said George ffitzpen als
Phippen hath herunto put his hand and seale the Third day
of ffebruary in the yeare of our Lord abouewritten 1659.
George Phippen & a seale.

This deed was acknowledged by the aboue Named George
ffitzpen ats Phippen to be his act and deed and by Elizabeth
his wife to bee with her free voluntary consent. the 3rd day of
february, 1659. Before me. Humphrey Atharton. Signed sealed

> *and delivered and possession given of ye within named peice of ground by the within named Georg ffitzpen als Phippen to the within named James Robbinson in the presence of us. The mark of T. G. Thomas Gold. The mark of Pilgrim. S. Simkings. William Pearse.*[310]

By April 1660, George Phippen was working in Falmouth, Maine as a fisherman. On 5 April 1660, "Geo. Phippeney" and three other men, who had been "Joynt partners" in a "fishing vioage," having received "for the Carijng on & Mangeing wrof... seuerall necessarys & puissions of Capt Bryan Pendleton to the valew of Twenty pounds 3s 11d. . .", pledged "to pay or Cause to be payd the aboue named some of 20 3 11 vnto Capt Bryan Pendleton or his assignes, In good M^{r}chandable fish to bee Deliuerd at Cape Porpus, at prise Currant, at or before the 26th day of May next Insewing."[311]

In 1662, "Geo Phipenny" of Falmouth signed a petition to the General Court in Boston requesting that the Massachusetts government protect the inhabitants of Maine from Ferdinando Gorge's commissioners.[312] In November 1666, George Phippenny was a defendant in an action brought to the Casco court by John Williams.[313] He was of Merriconeag Neck before 1672.[314] Andrew and George Phippeny were at Mare Point, Maine, within the limits of what was later called the Pejepscot purchase, by the early 1670s.[315] Driven off by the outbreak of hostilities along the Maine frontier, he fled to Hull, Massachusetts, where he took the oath of allegiance on 21 April 1679.[316]

In February 1692/93, George Phippen signed a petition from the town of Hull supporting the repeal of the law prohibiting the taking of mackerel during the months of May and June.[317]

---

[310] Suffolk Deeds 4: 24–26. The deed was recorded 22 July 1662.

[311] York Deeds, 18 vols. (Portland, 1887-1910), Book 1, folio 91.

[312] *Province and Court Records of Maine* (Portland, 1991), 1: 198–99; Massachusetts Archives Collection 3: 269.

[313] *Province and Court Records of Maine*, 1: 318.

[314] York Deeds, Book 12, part 1, folio 1 (reference to "Meadow wch George Phepeny has formerly mowd").

[315] George A. Wheeler et al., *History of Brunswick, Topsham, and Harpswell, Maine, including the ancient territory known as Pejepscot* (Boston, 1878), 18 (citing York County Records, 2: 90).

[316] Noyes, Libby, and Davis, *Genealogical Dictionary of Maine and New Hampshire, 549; see also A Volume of Records Relating to the Early History of Boston, Containing Miscellaneous Papers* (Boston, 1900), 175–76.

[317] Massachusetts Archives Collection 61: 365.

On 23 March 1694, George Phippen petitioned the General Court for a license to keep a public house, "having received great losses by the French enemy last October, his wife being very lame and he very poor." The Hull selectmen supported Phippen's petition.[318]

The Phippen chart states, "George Phippen, who married in London left two Sons and four Daughters." The will of widow Elizabeth (____) Phippen, dated 20 May 1714, named her son James (executor); daughters Elizabeth Coms, Mary, and Ruth; and granddaughter Elizabeth Coms.[319]

Children of George and Elizabeth (____) Phippen, born at Falmouth or Hull:

10   i.   JAMES[3] PHIPPEN, b. about 1660.
        ii. SARAH PHIPPEN, d. at Hull 14 Jan. 1694.[320]
        iii. ELIZABETH PHIPPEN, m. THOMAS COOMES; she d. 10 June 1724.[321]
        iv. MARY PHIPPEN, unm. in 1714.
        v.   RUTH PHIPPEN, unm. in 1714.
        vi. (perhaps) ANDREW PHIPPEN, living with George Phippen at Mare Point; he d. before 1714.[322]

---

[318] Smith, Early *Families of Hull,* 149.
[319] Suffolk Probate Records, 18: 367, 369–70, file no. 3621; Jacobus, "The Phippen Family," *The American Genealogist* 17 [1940]: 18.
[320] *Vital Records of Hull, Massachusetts to the end of the year 1849,* 65.
[321] Ibid., 64 ("Elisabeth, w. of Thomas, and d. of G[e]org[e] and Elisabeth Pipen, June 10, 1724").
[322] No additional children are mentioned in their mother's will of 1714, but the 1808 Phippen chart stated that George Phippen had two sons. *Genealogical Dictionary of Maine and New Hampshire* mentions a *John* Phippen attested at Mare Point (list 191, cited on 549), but suggests "John" was a mistake for "George."

CHAPTER 5

THE THIRD GENERATION

6. JOSEPH[3] **PHIPPEN** (*Joseph*[2], *David*[1]) was baptized at Hingham, Massachusetts in August 1642, the son of Joseph and Dorcas (Wood) Phippen.[323] He died, presumably at Salem, Massachusetts, before 1724; on 27 June 1724, Damaris Phippen, widow of Joseph Phippen of Salem and "formerly widow of Thomas Searl late of Salem," quit to Henry West certain Searle property and mentioned Searle children.[324]

Joseph Phippen married, first, probably at Falmouth, Maine, by about 1664, **MARY STANFORD**, daughter of Thomas Stanford of Purpooduck.[325] He married, second, probably at Falmouth, 22 December 1670, **SEABORN GOODEN**.[326] He married, third, at Salem, 14 April 1686, **DAMARIS (BARTLETT?) SEARLE**,[327] widow of Thomas Searle and probably daughter of Nicholas Bartlett.[328]

Joseph stayed in Falmouth after his father left for Salem in 1665.[329] He lived at Purpooduck, in Falmouth, for many years until driven by

---

[323] Egan, "The Hobart Journal," *Register* 121 [1967]: 15.

[324] Essex Deeds 42: 241.

[325] Noyes, Libby, and Davis, *Genealogical Dictionary of Maine and New Hampshire*, 549, 655. *See also* York Deeds, Book 17, folio 150, in which Mary[4] (Phippen) (Searl) English refers to herself as the granddaughter of Thomas Sanford, formerly of Falmouth, Maine.

[326] *Vital Records of Salem, Massachusetts to the end of the year 1849*, 3: 429, 4: 190. Although the date of Joseph's second marriage is reflected in the published Salem vital records, Joseph was still of Falmouth in 1670; this marriage most likely took place in Falmouth, not Salem.

[327] *Vital Records of Salem, Massachusetts to the end of the year 1849*, 4: 190, 293. The marriage record lists Joseph as "Joseph, sr." Although his father Joseph was still living at the time of this marriage, he undoubtedly went by "Joseph, sr.," to distinguish himself from his eldest son Joseph, who was probably about 21 years old at the time.

[328] Noyes, Libby, and Davis, *Genealogical Dictionary of Maine and New Hampshire*, 78; Jacobus, "The Phippen Family," *The American Genealogist* 17 [1940]: 6; Perley, *The History of Salem, Massachusetts*, 2: 391.

[329] Noyes, Libby, and Davis, *Genealogical Dictionary of Maine and New Hampshire*, 549.

the Indian War to Salem.[330] Willis states that in 1675, Joseph Phippen and family were one of forty families in the town of Falmouth; they were living on the south side of the Fore River.[331]

On 28 December 1674, William Browne, Sr., of Salem, merchant, conveyed a dwelling house with 52 rods of land and an orchard in Salem to Joseph Phippen, Jr., of Salem, fisherman.[332] Joseph "Phipeny" was received into membership of the First Church on 21 April 1679.[333] He was made a freeman on 19 May 1680.[334] He was chosen an overseer of highways on 8 March 1685/86,[335] and served as a juryman in 1683 and a grand juryman from 1683 to 1685.[336]

On 15 January 1694/95, Joseph Phippen of Salem, fisherman, for one half of his late father's house and land conveyed to him by his brothers David and Samuel, sold his "late homestead" to his two brothers; Damaris Phippen released any claim. David Phippen, shipwright, and Samuel Phippen, blockmaker, conveyed all rights to their father's estate to "Our eldest brother" Joseph Phippen of Salem, fisherman, for one-half rights in the estate.[337] On 8 December 1696, Joseph Phippen of Salem, fisherman, sold the house, land, and wharf in Salem that were formerly the property of his father, Joseph Phippen, deceased, to Obed Carter of Salem, fisherman, for £94.[338] On 14 December 1700, Joseph Phepeny, Sen[r.] of Salem, mariner, sold to John Higginson, Jun[r], of Salem, merchant, 100 acres of land at Purpooduck, in the township of Falmouth, "the Land . . . the s[d] Phepeny built on lived on & improved for many Years before the First Indian War. . ."[339]

The 1808 Phippen chart states, "Joseph Phippen left issue two Sons, and one Daughter By- Mary Standford ~ Seaborn Gooding a second Wife brought him issue Sons & Daughters."

[330] Phippen, "Fitzpen or Phippen and Allied Families," *The Heraldic Journal* 4 [1868]: 17. G. D. Phippen states that Joseph left Falmouth in 1676.

[331] Willis, *History of Portland*, 199–200.

[332] Essex Society of Genealogists, Inc., *Essex County Deeds 1639-1678: Abstracts of volumes 1-4, Copy Books, Essex County, Massachusetts* (Westminster, Md., 2003), 305; Essex Deeds, 4: 357. The deed was recorded on 19 January 1675[/76].

[333] Pierce, ed., *The Records of the First Church in Salem, Massachusetts 1629–1736*, 147.

[334] Shurtleff, *Records of the Governor and Company of the Massachusetts Bay in New England*, 5: 540; Lucius R. Paige, "List of Freemen," Register 3 [1849]: 245–46.

[335] Perley, *The History of Salem, Massachusetts*, 2: 7.

[336] Ibid., 9–10.

[337] Essex Deeds 10: 113, 11: 173.

[338] Perley, "Salem in 1700," *Essex Antiquarian* 9 [1905]: 163; Essex Deeds, 11: 178.

[339] York Deeds, Book 13, folio 213.

Children of Joseph and Mary (Stanford) Phippen, probably born
at Falmouth:

11   i.   JOSEPH[4] PHIPPEN, b. about 1665.

     ii.   MARY PHIPPEN, b. about 1667; she m. (1), about 1687, JOHN
SEARL;[340] she m. (2) at Salem 20 Dec. 1693[/94], JOSEPH
ENGLISH,[341] son of Clement and Mary (Waters) English.[342] She was
living on 13 May 1735, when she signed a deed transferring land in
Purpooduck next to the harbor and adjoining land of "our Father
Joseph Phippen"[343]

     iii.   SON. The 1808 Phippen chart indicates that Joseph and Mary had
two sons; probably d. young.

Children of Joseph and Seaborn (Gooden) Phippen, born at
Salem (except as noted):[344]

12   iv.   DANIEL PHIPPEN, b., probably at Falmouth, 20 Dec. 1671; bp. 16
Nov. 1679.

13   v.   SAMUEL PHIPPEN, b. 20 Sept. 1674.

     vi.   SARAH PHIPPEN, b. 8 Oct., bp. 16 Nov. 1679; m. at Salem 8 June
1699, BENJAMIN ENGLISH,[345] who was b. there 19 Oct. 1676, son of
Clement and Mary (Waters) English.[346]

     vii.   DORCAS PHIPPEN, b. 22 Dec. 1678, bp. 16 Nov. 1679; d. at Wallingford,
Conn. in 1760; she m. (1) at Milford, Conn. (where she had cousins
living) 24 Sept. 1706, JONATHAN LINSLEY of Branford,[347] who d. 3

---

[340] Jacobus, "The Phippen Family," *The American Genealogist* 17 [1940]: 6. Mary apparently had two children by her first husband, both born at Salem: i) *Mary Searl*, b. 18 July 1688; d. June 1690; ii) *John Searl*, b. 15 Sept. 1690. They are listed in the published Salem vital records as the children of Joseph and Mary (Searl) English. *See Vital Records of Salem, Massachusetts to the end of the year 1849*, 1: 282; 5: 231, and Perley, *History of Salem*, 3: 35.

[341] *Vital Records of Salem, Massachusetts to the end of the year 1849*, 3: 337, 4: 293.

[342] Perley, *The History of Salem, Massachusetts*, 3: 35.

[343] York County Deeds, Book 17, Fol. 150.

[344] *Vital Records of Salem, Massachusetts to the end of the year 1849*, 2: 164 (John "Phipeny," Anne "Phipeny"), 165 (Rachel "Phippeny"), 166 (Daniel, Dorcas, Israel), 169 (Samuel, Sarah). Although Daniel's birth is contained in the published Salem vital records, it is most likely that he was born in Falmouth, Maine, given that his family did not move to Salem until 1674. The children were baptized at the First Church of Salem. *See* Pierce, *Records of the First Church in Salem,* 33 (Daniel, Dorcas, Sarah, John), 35 (Rachel), 36 (Anne).

[345] *Vital Records of Salem, Massachusetts to the end of the year 1849,* 3: 336, 4: 191.

[346] Ibid., 1: 282; Perley, *The History of Salem, Massachusetts,* 3: 35.

[347] White, Lorraine Cook, ed. "Branford 1644-1850," *The Barbour Collection of Connecticut Town Vital Records,* vol. 3 (Baltimore: Genealogical Publishing Co., 1995), 182.

May 1725; she m. (2) at Branford 21 June 1726, JACOB JOHNSON, who d. at Wallingford 26 July 1749. Jacobus lists five children by her first husband, and one by the second.[348]

    viii. JOHN PHIPPEN, bp. 16 Nov. 1679.

14   ix. ISRAEL PHIPPEN, b. 17 July 1681.

    x. RACHEL PHIPPEN, bp. 12 Aug. 1683.

    xi. ANNE, bp. in Feb. 1683/84.

Children of Joseph and Damaris (Bartlett?) (Searle) Phippen, born at Salem:[349]

    xii. ELIZABETH PHIPPEN, b. 15 Feb. 168_.

    xiii. SUSANNA PHIPPEN, b. 2 July 168[7], bp. at First Church 10 July 1687;[350] she m. at Salem 2 Dec. 1718, as his second wife, HENRY WEST.[351] West, a shoemaker and sadler, had married first, at Salem, 2 Feb. 1704/5, Judith Poor.[352] Judith (Poor) West was born at Newbury, Mass. 22 May 1681, dau. of John and Mary (Titcomb) Poor.[353] Judith d. at Salem 27 Jan. 1715,[354] four days after her last child was born.[355] On 10 May 1719, Susannah (Phippen) West sought "to renew her covenant with God" at the First Church of Salem; she was received into communion on 7 June 1719.[356] Susanna (Phippen) West died before 22 Dec. 1726, when Henry West married, as his third wife, at Salem, RUTH (MARSTON) PHIPPEN, widow of Susanna's brother Benjamin.[357]

15   xiv. BENJAMIN PHIPPEN, b. 29 Sept. 1688.

---

[348] Jacobus, "The Phippen Family," *The American Genealogist* 17 [1940]: 6–7.

[349] *Vital Records of Salem, Massachusetts to the end of the year 1849,* 2: 165 (birth of Benjamin), 166 (birth of Elizabeth), 169 (birth and baptism of Susanna).

[350] Pierce, *Records of the First Church in Salem,* 38.

[351] *Vital Records of Salem, Massachusetts to the end of the year 1849,* 4: 191, 454.

[352] Ibid., 4: 205, 454.

[353] *Vital Records of Newbury, Massachusetts to the end of the year 1849,* 1: 428; Alfred Poore, *A Memoir and Genealogy of John Poore: Ten Generations: 1615–1880* (Salem, 1881), 10.

[354] *Vital Records of Salem, Massachusetts to the end of the year 1849,* 6: 323.

[355] Poore, *A Memoir and Genealogy of John Poore,* 10.

[356] "Fragment of a Diary Kept by Rev. Samuel Fiske of Salem, 1719–1721," *Essex Institute Historical Collections* 11 [1872]: 284.

[357] *Vital Records of Salem, Massachusetts to the end of the year 1849,* 4: 191, 454.

7. DAVID³ PHIPPEN (*Joseph²*, *David¹*) was baptized, at the age of 7 weeks, at Boston, Massachusetts 4 April 1647, son of Joseph and Dorcas (Wood) Phippen.[358] David Phippen died at New Casco, Maine 10 August 1703, in an Indian attack.[359]

He married at Salem, Massachusetts 26 June 1672, **ANNE (CROMWELL) AGER,** widow of Benjamin Ager, and daughter of Thomas and Ann Cromwell.[360] The Phippen chart states, "David Phippen left issue ___ Sons. By – Ann Cromwell." She was his widow in 1719; her date of death is unknown.[361]

David Phippen was of Casco Bay in July 1667 when his father, then of Salem, Massachusetts, deeded land to him and his brother, Joseph Phippen.[362] He removed to Salem soon thereafter; in 1668, he and his father were both signatories to a petition to the General Court by many Salem inhabitants against the imposition of duties on imports.[363]

His house in Salem was located at the intersection of the "Highway to [the] River" (now Central Street) and Main Street (now Essex Street). Benjamin Browne of Salem, merchant, conveyed the lot, with house and stable, to David Phippen of Salem, shipwright, before 1693. At David Phippen's death in 1703, the house and land were valued at £95.[364] David Phippen's widow, Anne Phippen, and the surviving children (Thomas Phippen, mariner; William Furneux, ropemaker, and wife Abigail; Benjamin Ropes, cordwainer, and wife Anne; and John Webb, seaman, and wife Elizabeth), all of Salem, conveyed the house and lot to Capt. John Brown of Salem, merchant, on 27 May 1714 for £80.[365] David Phippen also owned four adjoining lots along the South River, which he acquired very early, one being conveyed to him by Edmund Batter on 3 May 1679.[366]

On 31 August 1672, for £105, David Phippen of Salem, shipwright, conveyed to Joseph Wild of the Island of Jamaica, mariner, "the good

---

[358] *Boston Births, Marriages, and Deaths, 1630–1699,* 26.

[359] Noyes, Libby, and Davis, *Genealogical Dictionary of Maine and New Hampshire,* 7, 549; Willis, History of Portland, 312–14.

[360] *Vital Records of Salem, Massachusetts to the end of the year 1849,* 4: 189; Perley, The History of Salem, Massachusetts, 2: 143, 327.

[361] Perley, *The History of Salem, Massachusetts,* 2: 327–28.

[362] Noyes, Libby, and Davis, *Genealogical Dictionary of Maine and New Hampshire,* 549.

[363] "Petitions Against Imposts, 1668," *Register* 9 [1855]: 81–91 at 85.

[364] Sidney Perley, "Salem in 1700. No. 28," *Essex Antiquarian* 11 [1907]: 109–11.

[365] Ibid., at 109–10.

[366] Sidney Perley, "Salem in 1700. No. 27," *Essex Antiquarian* 11 [1907]: 66–75, at 69, 74.

Sloope called the gift of Salem of the burthen of thirty three Tuns or thereabout's now Riding at an Anchor in the harbor of Boston. . . . "[367]

On 17 May 1679, for £125 sterling, David Phippen of Salem, shipwright, conveyed to Robert Hodge, mariner; Nehemiah Willoughby, merchant; Eleazer Gedney, shipwright; and Francis Skerry, yeoman, all of Salem, the ketch *Francis and Mary* of Salem, which was riding at anchor in the South River, by the wharf of David Phippen, who had "lately built & launched" it. The deed describes the ketch as "its hull, finished & fitted for the sea, with all carpenter work, boat & masts & yards."[368]

David Phippen was a Salem constable in 1678,[369] chosen clerk of the market on 23 July 1680,[370] and served as a juryman in 1681.[371]

David Phippen apparently moved to Boston before the turn of the century, then returned to Casco Bay. On 5 October 1698, his tax was abated in Charlestown.[372] On 24 February 1700/1, the town treasurer of Salem took a bond of Mr. David Phippen of Boston and Jonathan Pickering of Salem for the £30 left by Mr. Cromwell toward a Latin school.[373] David Phippen was of Casco Bay, late of Boston, in May 1702 when Hannah Cromwell brought suit for dower against David Phippen and his wife and the Salem Pickerings.[374]

On 8 October 1687, upon the petition of David Phippen of Salem, shipwright, Sir Edmond Andros directed that a survey be taken of the land at Casco Bay granted to David's father in 1650 by George Cleeve. The Andros warrant is as follows:

> Sr Edmund Andros Kn^t Capt Generall & Govern^r in Chiefe
> of his Majestyes Territory and Dominion of New England
> to Mr Richard Clements Deputy Surveyor Whereas David
> Phippen of Salem in the County of Essex shipwright hath
> by his Peticon sett forth that his father Joseph Phippen
> sen^r about thirty seven yeares since purchased of George
> Cleve a parcel of Land in Caskobay Conteyneing One

---

[367] Suffolk County Deeds 7: 337-38.

[368] Essex Society of Genealogists, Inc., *Essex County Deeds, 1675: Abstracts of Volume 5, Copy Books, Essex County, Massachusetts* (Westminster, Md., 2008), 25 (*citing* Essex Deeds, 5: 154); *see also* Perley, *The History of Salem, Massachusetts,* 2: 363.

[369] Perley, *The History of Salem, Massachusetts,* 2: 402.

[370] Ibid., 189.

[371] Ibid., 9.

[372] Wyman, *Genealogies and Estates of Charlestown,* 2: 748.

[373] Perley, *The History of Salem, Massachusetts,* 3: 358.

[374] Noyes, Libby, and Davis, *Genealogical Dictionary of Maine and New Hampshire,* 549.

hundred Acres the which by himselfe & Children was quietly possessed and buildings and other improvements made thereon untill disturbed and Destroyed by the late Indian warr And that the fifth day of August last past his said father did by Deed Give and Grant the same to the peticoner And praying a confirmacon for the same under his Majestye These are therefore to Authorize and Require yow to survey & lay out for the said David Phippen the said One hundred Acres of Land and to make a Plat or Draft thereof and the same to Returne to the Surveyors Office at Boston that a confirmacon may be there upon granted to the Peticoner as Desired and for so Doeing this shall be yor warrant Given under my hand and seale at Boston the 8th day of October 1687.[375]

The map of David Phippen's property, consisting of 102¼ acres at Long Creek, Falmouth, is in the Massachusetts Archives.[376]

Before his return to Maine, David Phippen acquired more land in the Casco Bay area. In 1689 and 1690, Francis Neal, George Felt, and Jenkin Williams sold David Phippen a large tract of land on the Presumpscot River, which they had acquired from Nanaadionit and Wavaad Button, Indian sagamores, in 1672.[377] On 19 December 1693, Thomas Mason sold him seven acres of land in the Town of Casco and sixty acres on the northern side of the Presumpscot River.[378] David Phippen removed to Casco Bay, no doubt to improve upon his estate. He lived near the fort at Falmouth, on the east side of the Presumpscot River and nearly opposite Staple's Point.[379]

---

[375] Julius Herbert Tuttle, "Land Warrants Issued under Andros, 1687–1688," *Publications of the Colonial Society of Massachusetts* 21 [1919]: 292–363 at 309–10.

[376] Massachusetts Archives, Maps and Plans, 3rd Series, vol. 37, p. 19.

[377] Willis, *History of Portland,* 113; Harriet Ruth Waters Cooke, *The Driver Family: A Genealogical Memoir of the Descendants of Robert and Phebe Driver, of Lynn, Mass. with an Appendix, Containing Twenty-three Allied Families, 1592–1887* (New York, 1889), 440–41.

[378] The Mason deed is referenced in the sale of partial interests in several Casco Bay properties of David Phippen by John Green of Salem, and his wife Anna, daughter of David Phippen, to James Brickell of Falmouth, trader, dated 25 April 1730. See York Deeds, Book 13, folio 206–7.

[379] Noyes, Libby, and Davis, *Genealogical Dictionary of Maine and New Hampshire, 549; Maine Historical and Genealogical Recorder* 5 [1888]: 35–36; Willis, History of Portland, 310.

On 10 August 1703, all the settlements from Casco to Wells were attacked by the French and Indians, resulting in 73 deaths and 94 settlers taken.[380] Under a flag of truce, David Phippen and a Mr. Kent were killed. Willis's *History of Portland* describes the event as follows:[381]

> The whole country, from Purpooduck Point to Spurwink, was covered with woods, except the few spots which the inhabitants had cleared. This afforded facilities to the Indians for concealment and protection. From these coverts they made their sudden and cruel visits, then returned to mingle again with the other wild tenants of the forests, beyond the reaches of pursuit. The enemy next directed their attention to the fort at New Casco. This was the most considerable fort on the eastern coast, and was the central point of defense for all the settlements upon Casco bay; under its protection, several persons had collected to revive the fortunes of the town. Major March commanded the garrison at this time, consisting of but thirty-six men. The enemy practiced a stratagem in hopes of taking the fort without loss of life, and for this purpose their able chiefs, Moxus, Wanungonet, and Assacombuit sent a flag of truce to the commanding officer, soliciting a conference, under pretence that they had something important to communicate. At first, Major March declined the invitation, suspecting some treachery, but afterward, as they seemed to be few in number and unarmed, he concluded to meet them, taking the precaution to post two or three sentinels, where they might be ready in case of danger. On his arrival at the place of meeting, they saluted him civilly, but immediately drew their tomahawks from under their robes, and violently assaulted him, while others in ambush shot down one of the sentinels. March, being a man of uncommon strength as well as courage, wrested the tomahawk from one of the assailants and successfully defended himself until Sergeant Hook arrived from the fort with a file of ten men and rescued him from his perilous situation. Mr. Phippen and

---

[380] Noyes, Libby, and Davis, *Genealogical Dictionary of Maine and New Hampshire,* 7.
[381] Willis, History of Portland, 312–14. Mr. Kent was possibly John Kent from Newbury, Mass. *Ibid.* at 314.

Mr. Kent, who accompianed Major March, being less able from advanced age to resist this savage attack were overpowered and slain.

Penhallow wrote of the slaughter of Phippen and Kent: "Mr. Phippen and Mr. Kent, who accompanied [Major March], were attacked by others, and soon fell by their fury; for being advanced in years, they were so infirm, that I might say of them as Juvenal did of Priam, they had scarce blood enough left to tinge the knife of the sacrifice."[382]

After David Phippen's death, the family returned to Salem. On 27 September 1703, Anne Phippen of Salem gave administration bond with Thomas Phippen and Benjamin Ropes. David Phippen's estate was valued at £125 19s.[383]

Children of David and Anne (Cromwell) Phippen, born at Salem:[384]

    i. DAVID[4] PHIPPEN, b. 14 April 1673; probably d. young.

16   ii. THOMAS PHIPPEN, bp. in Aug. 1675.

    iii. ANN PHIPPEN bp. 19 May 1678; m. (1) at Salem 10 March 1694/95, BENJAMIN ROPES,[385] who was b. at Salem 22 Feb. 1669/70, son of John and Lydia (Wells) Ropes.[386] Benjamin Ropes d. 20 Nov. 1717.[387] Ann m. (2), at Salem 26 July 1718, JOHN GREEN,[388] a mariner, who was b. there 12 Sept. 1695, son of John and Hannah (Dodge) Green.[389]

    iv. CROMWELL PHIPPEN, bp. 5 Oct. 1679; probably d. young.

    v. JOSEPH PHIPPEN, bp. Aug. 1681; probably d. young.

    vi. JANE PHIPPEN, bp. 7 Oct. 1683; probably d. young.

    vii. ABIGAIL PHIPPEN, bp. 2 Aug. 1685; m. at Salem 2 Oct. 1707, WILLIAM FURNEUX/FURNACE.[390]

    viii. ELIZABETH PHIPPEN, bp. in May 1689; m. at Salem 18 Oct. 1705, JOHN WEBB,[391] who was b. there 17 April 1676, son of Daniel and

---

[382] Samuel Penhallow, *The History of the Wars of New-England with the Eastern Indians* (Cincinnati, 1859; originally published in Boston, 1726), 20.

[383] Essex Probate Records, file no. 21744.

[384] *Vital Records of Salem, Massachusetts to the end of the year 1849,* 2: 164 (Thomas, Ann, Cromwell, Joseph, Jane, Abigail, Elizabeth, Sarah, all with surname spelled "Phipeny"), 166 (David). Baptisms were all held at the First Church of Salem.

[385] Ibid., 4: 188, 268.

[386] Ibid., 2: 246.

[387] Ibid., 6: 192.

[388] Ibid., 3: 446, 4: 268.

[389] Ibid., 1: 388.

[390] Ibid., 3: 394, 4: 188.

[391] Ibid., 4: 189, 443.

Mary (Beckett) Webb.[392] Elizabeth (Phippen) Webb d. at Salem in Nov. 1773, aged 90 years.[393]

ix. SARAH PHIPPEN, bp. in May 1691; probably d. young.[394]

x. JOHN PHIPPEN, birth date unknown, but from the birth dates of his siblings, it would appear to be approximately 1687. This estimate would make him 16 years of age at the time of the Indian massacre. The casualty list states that "Mr. David Phippeny and son John" were among the inhabitants of Casco who were killed by the Indians, 10 August 1703.[395]

8. SAMUEL[3] PHIPPEN (*Joseph[2], David[1]*), blockmaker, son of Joseph and Dorcas (Wood) Phippen, was baptized at Boston, Massachusetts 6 May 1649 at the age of about 7 days.[396] He died at Salem, Massachusetts 1 February 1717/18, aged 68.[397] He is buried in the Charter Street Burial Ground in Salem.[398]

Samuel married at Salem 1 February 1676/77, **RACHEL GUPPY,**[399] who was probably born at Salem about 1659, daughter of Reuben and Eleanor (Ellen) Guppy.[400] She died 1 February 1710/11, aged 52.[401]

They lived in Salem, where he was a constable in 1685.[402] He was also a juryman in 1683 and was named clerk of the market on 9 April 1683.[403] Samuel Phippen died intestate, and administration of his estate was granted on 26 February 1717/18 to his sons Samuel, John, and Nathaniel.[404]

---

[392] *Vital Records of Salem, Massachusetts to the end of the year 1849*, 2: 402.

[393] Ibid., 6: 316 (Essex Gazette, Issue of 30 November 1773).

[394] George D. Phippen named her as a daughter of Samuel[3] and Rachel (Guppy) Phippen. "Fitzpen or Phippen, and Allied Families," *The Heraldic Journal* 4 [1868]: 18.

[395] Noyes, Libby, and Davis, *Genealogical Dictionary of Maine and New Hampshire*, 7, 549.

[396] *Boston Births, Marriages, and Deaths, 1630–1699*, p. 30. (He is erroneously listed in the record as Joseph.)

[397] *Vital Records of Salem, Massachusetts to the end of the year 1849*, 6: 139.

[398] Perley Derby, "Inscriptions from Charter Street Burial-Ground, Salem, Mass.," *Essex Institute Historical Collections* 13 [1877]: 67 et seq., at 108.

[399] *Vital Records of Salem, Massachusetts to the end of the year 1849*, 3: 453, 4: 191.

[400] Her year of birth is calculated from her age at death, which appears on her gravestone in the Charter Street Burial Ground, Salem, Mass. *See also* Perley, *The History of Salem, Massachusetts*, 2: 118.

[401] *Vital Records of Salem, Massachusetts to the end of the year 1849*, 6: 139; Perley, "Charter Street Inscriptions," *Essex Institute Historical Collections* 13 [1877]: 108.

[402] *Records and Files of the Quarterly Courts of Essex County*, 9: 566.

[403] Perley, *The History of Salem, Massachusetts*, 2: 9, 189.

[404] Essex Probate Records, file no. 21765.

On 30 March 1681, William Brown, Sr. of Salem, Esq., sold ten poles of land with a dwelling house and fence in Salem to Samuel Phippen, blockmaker.[405]

Sidney Perley discussed the Samuel Phippen house as it stood in 1700 in his detailed house-by-house description of Salem in 1700, as follows:[406]

> *Samuel Phippen House.* This lot belonged to Samuel Archer of Salem April 27, 1665, when he conveyed that part of it lying east of the dashes to James Browne of Salem, merchant.[407] Mr. Browne was murdered in Maryland Nov. 12, 1675. By an agreement between his widow and children this lot, then called the great garden, was released to his daughter Elizabeth Browne Sept. 15, 1694.[408] Miss Browne conveyed the land to Samuel Phippen (or, Phippeny), sr., of Salem, blockmaker, Oct. 6, 1699.[409]
>
> That part of the lot lying westerly of the dashes remained the property of Samuel Archer until his death in December, 1667, when it was valued at five pounds. The estate was insolvent, and William Browne, sr., of Salem, esquire and merchant, the principal creditor, took the place. Samuel Archer's widow, then Susannah, wife of Richard Hutchinson, released her dower interest in the lot to Mr. Browne July 5, 1669.[410] He erected a house upon the lot, and, for eighty pounds, conveyed the house and this part of the lot to Mr. Phippen, who owned the remainder of this lot, March 30, 1681.[411]
>
> Sept. 27, 1687, Samuel Archer (or, Archard) of Salem, house-carpenter, eldest son of the deceased Samuel Archer, released the land to Mr. Browne.[412] Samuel Phippen died Feb. 1, 1717–8, at the age of sixty-eight, intestate. The house and an old shop and the land were then appraised at eighty pounds. The real estate was divided among his children May 21, 1733, when it was valued at one hundred and

---

[405] Essex Deeds 7: 27.
[406] Sidney Perley, "Salem in 1700. No. 26," *Essex Antiquarian* 11 [1907]: 12, 15.
[407] Essex Deeds, 2: 111.
[408] Ibid., 10: 69.
[409] Ibid., 13: 229.
[410] Ibid., 7: 27.
[411] Ibid., 146.
[412] Ibid., 3: 75.

twelve pounds and ten shillings. The house and the land
around it were assigned to his son Nathaniel Phippen of
Salem, cooper. Nathaniel Phippen died in 1756, possessed
of the house and land around it, which was described in
the inventory of his estate as "One Old houfe & Land in y^e
Lane former Saml Phippens dec^d," and valued at sixty-five
pounds, six shillings and eight pence. In his will he devised
his real estate to his children, David, Israel, Thomas, Margaret
and Anstes. In the division of the real estate, Nov. 15, 1759,
this old house and the land around it were assigned to son
Thomas Phippen, who then lived in the house.[413] The
executor of the will of David Phippen of Salem, gentleman,
deceased, brought suit against Thomas Phippen; and, May
13, 1785, this lot with the old house thereon, was set off to
the estate in satisfaction of the judgment.[414] July 9, 1785,
the executor of David Phippen's will, for sixty-four pounds,
ten shillings and six pence, conveyed the lot and buildings
thereon to John Fisk of Salem, merchant;[415] and the house
was gone before 1792, when Mr. Fisk sold the lot.

On 8 September 1677, "Sam^ll Phippeny his wife [was] appointed
to sett In ye Southrmost of ye Woemens pewes In ye west gallery of
ye meetinghouse:"[416] In June 1680, Samuell Phipin was among those
signing a petition urging the town to erect another meetinghouse.[417]

The 1808 Phippen chart states, "Saml. Phippen left issue Samuel, John,
Nathaniel, Joseph, and Rachel, By- Rachel Guppe. Died Febr. 1. 1711."

Children of Samuel and Rachel (Guppy) Phippen, born at Salem: [418]

17   i.   SAMUEL[4] PHIPPEN, b. 12 Dec. 1677, bp. 11 June 1682.
         ii. JOHN PHIPPEN, b. 4 Oct. 1679, bp. 11 June 1682; d. 6 Aug. 1684.[419]
         iii. STEVEN PHIPPEN, b. 9 May, bp. 11 June 1682; d. 30 Aug. 1682.[420]

---

[413]   Essex Deeds, 111: 1.
[414]   Ibid., 144: 187.
[415]   Ibid., 47.
[416]   *Salem Town Records,* 2: 242.
[417]   Dow, *Records and Files of the Quarterly Courts of Essex County, Massachusetts,* 7: 402–3.
[418]   Baptisms were at the First Church of Salem. *Vital Records of Salem, Massachusetts to
         the end of the year 1849,* 2: 165 (John [record does not name him but says "ch. of
         Samuel, bp. Dec – 1685"]), 166 (John), 167 (John, Joseph), 168 (Rachel, Nathaniel,
         Rachel), 169 (Samuel, Steven); *Salem First Church Records,* 34 (Samuel, John, Steven),
         38 (Nathaniel).
[419]   *Vital Records of Salem, Massachusetts to the end of the year 1849,* 6: 137.
[420]   Ibid., 139.

iv. RACHEL PHIPPEN, b. 5 Aug. 1683; d. 24 July 1685.[421]

18 v. JOHN PHIPPEN, b. 25 Dec. 1685; bp. in Dec. 1685.

19 vi. NATHANIEL PHIPPEN, b. 4, bp. 7 Aug. 1687.

vii. RACHEL PHIPPEN, b. 13 Sept. 1693; in 1749, she was listed as a spinster in Salem.[422]

20 viii. JOSEPH PHIPPEN, b. 9 Feb. 1696/97.

9. JAMES³ PHIPPENEY (*Benjamin², David¹*) was born at Boston, Massachusetts 30 January 1663/4, son of Benjamin and Wilmot (Ewer) Phippen.[423] He died at Stratford, Connecticut 12 August 1717.[424] He married JOANNA ____. He was in Stratford as early as 15 December 1685, when his land ownership there was first recorded.[425] James Phippeney and his wife were admitted members of the Stratford Congregational Church on 7 April 1696.[426] They resided at Old Mill Green.[427] Widow Joanna (____) Phippeney made oath to the inventory of James Phippeney's estate on 3 June 1718.[428] She married, second, on 8 March 1722, LEMUEL SHERWOOD.[429] She died at Stratfield, Connecticut 9 May 1727.[430]

James "Fippen" was one of Jacob Leisler's fifty militiamen in the rebellion of 1689,[431] which resulted in a temporary (1689–91) change in control of the colonial government of New York after the overthrow of James II and the Dominion of New England under Governor Andros.[432]

Children of James and Joanna (____) Phippeney, born at Stratford:[433]

i. JOANNA⁴ PHIPPENEY, b. 17 Jan. 1695/96; m. at Stratford 26 Dec. 1723, JOHN FAIRCHILD.[434]

---

[421] Ibid., 138.

[422] Perley, *The History of Salem, Massachusetts*, 2: 328.

[423] *Boston Births, Marriages, and Deaths, 1630-1699*, 89.

[424] "Stratford 1639-1840," *The Barbour Collection of Connecticut Town Vital Records*, vol. 41, 205.

[425] Orcutt, *History of Stratford*, 2: 1268.

[426] Ibid.

[427] Ibid.

[428] Jacobus, *History and Genealogy of the Families of Old Fairfield*, 1: 477.

[429] Ibid.

[430] Ibid.

[431] Kenneth Scott, "Jacob Leisler's Fifty Militiamen," *Record* 94 [1963]: 65-72 at 68, 72.

[432] For background, *see* Michael Kammen, *Colonial New York: A History* (New York, 1975), 118–27.

[433] "Stratford 1639-1840," *The Barbour Collection of Connecticut Town Vital Records*, vol. 41, 205 (births of Joanna, Mary, Benjamin, Sarah, James).

[434] Ibid.

ii.   MARY PHIPPENEY, b. 27 Sept. 1697; m. at Stratfield 28 May 1719,
      JONADAB BASSETT.[435]

21   iii.   BENJAMIN PHIPPENEY, b. 14 Jan. 1701/2.

iv.   SARAH PHIPPENEY, b. 30 March, bp. at Stratfield 20 May 1705;[436] d. at
      New Milford, Conn. 27 Jan. 1743/44;[437] m. at Trumbull (recorded
      in New Milford), 6 Jan. 1740/41,[438] as his second wife, SAMUEL
      PRINDLE, who was b. 23 Sept. 1702, son of Samuel and Dorothy
      (Plumb) Prindle of New Milford.[439]

22   v.   JAMES PHIPPENEY, b. 10 Aug. 1710. After his mother's death earlier in
      the year, on 22 August 1727, James made choice of Jonadab Bassett
      to be his guardian.[440] On 13 Feb. 1729/30, Jonadab Bassett was
      relieved from guardianship, and John Fairchild was appointed.[441]

vi.   SON.

vii.   SON. Their father's probate mentions, without naming them, four
      sons and three daughters.[442] These last two may have died soon
      thereafter; they cannot be traced.

10. JAMES[3] **PHIPPEN** (*George*[2], *David*[1]) was born about 1660, son of
George and Elizabeth (___) Phippen. He lived at Hull, Massachusetts,
where he was a boatman. James Phippen married before 1693, **JOANNA**
____.[443] James died at Hull 29 December 1735.[444] Joanna died there 25
September 1735.[445]

On 9 May 1700, Joseph Bosworth of Hull sold land in Hull,
including a house and barn, to James Phippen.[446] On 16 November
1716, along with Elizabeth Coomes, Jr., of Hull (his niece), James sold

---

[435]   Jacobus, *History and Genealogy of the Families of Old Fairfield,* 1: 478.

[436]   Ibid.

[437]   Ibid.

[438]   White, Lorraine Cook, ed. "New Milford 1712-1860," *The Barbour Collection of
        Connecticut Town Vital Records,* vol. 30 (Baltimore: Genealogical Publishing Co.,
        2000), 167; Jacobus, *History and Genealogy of the Families of Old Fairfield,* 1: 478.

[439]   "New Milford 1712-1860," *The Barbour Collection of Connecticut Town Vital Records,*
        vol. 30, 127.

[440]   Mead, *Abstract of Probate Records at Fairfield,* 78 (Fairfield PR 7: 22).

[441]   Ibid.

[442]   Jacobus, *History and Genealogy of the Families of Old Fairfield,* 1: 477.

[443]   Noyes, Libby, and Davis, *Genealogical Dictionary of Maine and New Hampshire,* 549.
        She may have been Joanna Chamberlain, daughter of Henry and Sarah (Jones)
        Chamberlain of Hull. *See* Smith, *Early Families of Hull,* 68–69.

[444]   *Vital Records of Hull, Massachusetts to the end of the year 1849,* 72.

[445]   Ibid.

[446]   Suffolk Deeds, 19: 357.

a house and land in Hull—probably inherited from his mother—to Thomas Binney, inn holder.[447] On 10 December 1701, James Phippen also sold land to William Chamberlain, Jr. of Hull.[448] In all these deeds, James Phippen is called a mariner.

In 1717, James Phippen deposed that he formerly lived at Mare Point (Maine) and knew Nicholas White. In 1735, he sold 1,000 acres of land there to Aaron Cleveland.[449]

James Phippen made his will on 15 November 1735; it was proved on 5 January 1735/36:

> In the name of God Amen I James Phippeney being but weak & decaying in body. . . [make bequests] to my two daughters and the children of my Daughter decd that is to say to my daughter Sarah Bell . . . to Elisabeth Lobdel. . . the children of my daughter Joanna Adams decd . . . [and name] my well beloved Sons in law John Bell & Joseph Lobdell to be joynt Executrs. . . .[450]

In an inventory of his estate, dated 6 January 1735/6, his estate was valued at £328, including his house and land at £130.[451]

Children of James and Joanna (___) Phippen, born at Hull:

    i. SARAH[4] PHIPPEN, b. 22 Jan. 169[3/9]4;[452] she m. at Boston, Mass. 8 Aug. 1715, JOHN BELL.[453]

    ii. ELIZABETH PHIPPEN, b. 18 March 1695/96;[454] m. at Hull 5 April 1719, JOSEPH LOBDELL.[455]

    iii. JOANNA PHIPPEN, b. 30 Nov. 1698;[456] m. at Hull 18 Dec. 1718, WILLIAM ADAMS.[457]

---

[447] Ibid., 33: 109.

[448] Ibid., 44: 182.

[449] Noyes, Libby, and Davis, *Genealogical Dictionary of Maine and New Hampshire,* 549.

[450] Suffolk Probate Records 32: 315–17.

[451] Suffolk Probate Records 32: 498.

[452] *Vital Records of Hull, Massachusetts to the end of the year 1849,* 17; Willard S. Allen, "Records of Hull, Mass.," *Register* 27 [1873]: 360–63 at 361 (birth of "Sarah Fipenny").

[453] *Boston Marriages 1700–1751,* 2 (spelled as "Phipeny" on marriage but "Phippeny" on marriage intention).

[454] *Vital Records of Hull, Massachusetts to the end of the year 1849,* 17; Allen, "Records of Hull, Mass.," 362 (birth of "Elizabeth Fipieng").

[455] *Vital Records of Hull, Massachusetts to the end of the year 1849,* 46, 51.

[456] *Vital Records of Hull, Massachusetts to the end of the year 1849,* 17; Allen, "Records of Hull, Mass.," 363 (birth of "Joannah Fipeny").

[457] *Vital Records of Hull, Massachusetts to the end of the year 1849,* 46.

CHAPTER 6

THE FOURTH GENERATION

11. JOSEPH[4] **PHIPPEN** (*Joseph*[3-2], *David*[1]) was probably born in Falmouth, Maine, about 1665, son of Joseph and Mary (Stanford) Phippen.[458] He died at Fairfield, Connecticut in February 1732/33. The will of Joseph Phippen of Fairfield, dated 3 and proved 6 February 1732/33, named his wife Elizabeth and his sister, Mary English.[459]

Joseph Phippen married between 12 June 1684 and 8 May 1685, his first cousin once removed **ELIZABETH**[3] **(PHIPPEN) SPENCER,** daughter of his great-uncle Gamaliel[2] Phippen (*David*[1]) and Sarah (Purchase) Phippen. Elizabeth was born at Boston, Massachusetts 10 August 1659. Her first husband was Abraham Spencer, who died in 1683.[460] Joseph Phippen was in Fairfield as early as 1698.[461]

Child of Joseph and Elizabeth (Phippen) (Spencer) Phippen, born at Salem, Massachusetts:

>   i. JOSEPH[5] PHIPPEN, b. 3 March 1686;[462] d. at Fairfield 10 July 1712, aged 26 years.[463] Administration of his estate was granted to his father on 7 Aug. 1712.[464]

---

[458] Jacobus, *History and Genealogy of the Families of Old Fairfield,* 1: 478, mistakenly assigned him as son of Benjamin[2] Phippen, but the reference in his will to sister Mary English shows him to be son of Joseph[3] Phippen, apparently born in Maine. Jacobus corrected this error in "The Phippen Family," *The American Genealogist* 17 [1940]: 6.

[459] Jacobus, "The Phippen Family," *The American Genealogist* 17 [1940]: 6; Holman, Phippen Notes.

[460] Sources are provided in the section on Elizabeth[3] Phippen above.

[461] Holman, Phippen Notes.

[462] *Vital Records of Salem, Massachusetts to the end of the year 1849,* 2:164.

[463] Francis F. Spies, *Fairfield, Fairfield Co., Conn. inscriptions from the graveyards arranged with notes and index* (Hastings-on-Hudson, N.Y., 1934), 38. His gravestone is located in the Old Burying Ground of Fairfield. It is the oldest known extant Phippen gravestone in the United States.

[464] Mead, *Abstract of Probate Records at Fairfield,* 204 (Fairfield Probate Records 5 (1702–50): 384.

12. DANIEL[4] **PHIPPEN** (*Joseph*[3–2], *David*[1]) was probably born at Falmouth, Maine 20 December 1671, son of Joseph and Seaborn (Gooden) Phippen.[465] He died at Boston, Massachusetts 24 December 1702.[466] He married **ELIZABETH** ____, whose identity has not been ascertained. They lived in Boston. In 1696, "Danill Phipenny" signed a petition of Boston inhabitants requesting that the law relating to building with brick be repealed.[467] Elizabeth Phippen married second, at Boston, 2 August 1704, **BENJAMIN SIMPSON**.[468]

Children of Daniel and Elizabeth (____) Phippen, born at Boston:[469]

     i.   DANIEL[5] PHIPPEN, b. unk.; d. 13 August 1696.

23   ii. DANIEL PHIPPEN, b. and bp. 18 Oct. 1696.

    iii. MARY PHIPPEN, b. 2 and bp .3 July 1698.

    iv. JOSEPH PHIPPEN, b. 28 May 1701.

    v. ELIZABETH PHIPPEN, bp. 22 June 1701.

13. SAMUEL[4] **PHIPPEN** (*Joseph*[3–2], *David*[1]) was born at Salem, Massachusetts 20 September 1674, son of Joseph and Seaborn (Gooden) Phippen.[470] He died there 17 September 1704.[471] He married at Salem 12 June 1701, **ELIZABETH ENGLISH**,[472] daughter of Clement and Mary (Waters) English, who was born at Salem 9 February 1670/71;[473] she died there between 30 October 1727, when she made her will, and 7 February 1727/28, when her will was proved.[474]

[465] *Vital Records of Salem, Massachusetts to the end of the year 1849,* 2: 166.

[466] Robert J. Dunkle and Ann S. Lainhart, *Deaths in Boston, 1700-1799* (Boston, 1999), 2: 719.

[467] "Petition of Boston Inhabitants in 1696, that the Law Relating to Building with Brick be Repealed," *Register* 16 [1862]: 84–87 at 86.

[468] *Boston Marriages 1700–1751,* 15.

[469] *Boston Births, Marriages, and Deaths, 1630–1699,* 228 (Daniel), 241 (Mary); Boston Births 1700–1800, 9 (Joseph);"Records of the Old South Church in Boston," *Boston Church Records,* CR_ROM (Boston, 2002) (death of Daniel, baptisms of Daniel, Mary and Elizabeth). Elizabeth's baptism record lists her as the daughter of Daniel and *Mary,* which appears to be an error. In addition, the Boston town records have no record of Elizabeth's birth, and the Old South Church records have no baptism record for Joseph. Perhaps Elizabeth (the mother) gave birth to twins in 1701, with only the younger Elizabeth surviving.

[470] *Vital Records of Salem, Massachusetts to the end of the year 1849,* 2: 169.

[471] Ibid., 6: 139.

[472] Ibid., 4: 191, 3: 337.

[473] Ibid., 1: 282; Perley, *The History of Salem, Massachusetts,* 3: 35.

[474] Essex Probate Records, file no. 21746; Holman, Phippen Notes.

Samuel Phippen left no will, nor was there any administration granted on his estate. There are no records of any deeds for him in Essex County, Massachusetts. Elizabeth (English) Phippen's will states:

> I Elizabeth Phippen of Salem . . . widow being weak . . . ordain this my last will . . . Imp^rs I give to my well beloved Daughter Sarah Williams the wife of Zerubbabel Williams . . . to my well beloved Daughter Abiell Phippen whom I . . . ordain . . . Executrix signed by mark. Wit: Sarah Connaway, Lydia Henfield, John Nutting.[475]

Children of Samuel and Elizabeth (English) Phippen, born at Salem:

    i. SARAH[5] PHIPPEN, b. in July 1702;[476] bp. 4 Oct. 1702;[477] m. at Salem 6 Aug. 1725, ZERUBBABEL WILLIAMS,[478] who was b. at Salem 28 Nov. 1702, son of Isaac and Mary (Endicott) Williams.[479]

    ii. ABIEL PHIPPEN, b. 13 Nov. 1704 (after her father died),[480] bp. 15 July 1705; m. at Boston 17 April 1729 (intentions 12 April), as his second wife, DAVID CHAPIN of Boston,[481] who was b. 2 July 1690, son of Caleb and Sarah (____) Chapin of Boston.[482] David Chapin had married, first, at Boston 2 June 1720, Margaret Pope.[483]

14. ISRAEL[4] PHIPPEN (*Joseph*[3–2], *David*[1]) was born at Salem, Massachusetts 17 July 1681, son of Joseph and Seaborn (Gooden) Phippen.[484] Suffolk land records show that he died before 16 July 1712. On that date, David Craigie of Boston, mariner, and Deborah his wife, with Sarah Phippen, widow of Boston, sold all rights to a certain house in Boston to Daniel

---

[475] Essex Probate Records, file no. 21746. The partial transcription appears in Holman, Phippen Notes.

[476] *Vital Records of Salem, Massachusetts to the end of the year 1849,* 2:169.

[477] Richard D. Pierce, *The Records of the First Church in Salem, Massachusetts, 1629–1736* (Salem, 1974), 47.

[478] *Vital Records of Salem, Massachusetts to the end of the year 1849,* 4:191, 477.

[479] Ibid., 2: 435.

[480] Ibid., 165.

[481] *Boston Marriages 1700–1751,* 166; *Vital Records of Salem, Massachusetts to the end of the year 1849,* 3: 201, 4: 188.

[482] *Boston Births, Marriages, and Deaths, 1630–1699,* 189.

[483] *Boston Marriages 1700-1751,* 98; Gilbert Warren Chapin, The Chapin Book of Genealogical Data (Hartford, 1924), 90.

[484] *Vital Records of Salem, Massachusetts to the end of the year 1849,* 2:166.

Loring of Boston.[485] Also, on 14 April 1715, Abigail Walter of Boston, widow, sold to Sarah Phippen, also a widow, land on Marlboro Street, Boston, near the widow Mann.[486]

Israel Phippen was married at Boston 30 October 1707, by Rev. Benjamin Wadsworth, to **SARAH MAN**, daughter of Nathaniel and Deborah (___) Man of Boston.[487] She d. at Boston 1 November 1718.[488] On 13 January 1718[/19], John Man, mariner, was appointed administrator to the estate of his sister Sarah Phippen, a widow, with Samuel Greenleaf Butcher and Thomas Thatcher, both of Boston, as his sureties.[489]

Child of Israel and Sarah (Man) Phippen, born at Boston:

    i.   DEBORAH[5] PHIPPEN, b. 30 Aug. 1708;[490] m. at Boston 18 July 1728, SAMUEL HEWES.[491] She died before 5 Dec. 1734, when Samuel m. (2) Elizabeth Tew.[492]

15. BENJAMIN[4] **PHIPPEN** (*Joseph*[3-2], *David*[1]) was born at Salem, Massachusetts 29 September 1688, son of Joseph and Damaris (Searl) Phippen.[493] He died intestate by 1726. Benjamin Phippen married at Salem 1 November 1715, **RUTH MARSTON**,[494] who was born about 1690, daughter of Deacon John and Mary (Turner) Marston.[495]

Benjamin was a fisherman and cordwainer.[496] On 22 January 1717, Deacon John Marston and wife Mary of Salem deeded to Benjamin Phippen, fisherman and son-in-law, a quarter-acre, and six poles of land in Salem fronting on the east on a lane and butting on the west on land of William West, on the south, land of Samuel Phippen and on the north, by land of Mr. Brays.[497] On 8 December 1719, Benjamin Phippen of Salem, fisherman, mortgaged land there to William Bowditch;

---

485 Suffolk Deeds 27: 167.

486 Ibid., 28:79.

487 *Boston Marriages 1700–1751*, 14.

488 Dunkle and Lainhart, *Deaths in Boston, 1700-1799*, 2: 719.

489 Suffolk Probate Records, file no. 4127.

490 *Boston Births 1700–1800*, 57.

491 *Boston Marriages 1700–1751*, 144.

492 Eben Putnam, *Lieutenant Joshua Hewes: a New England pioneer, and some of his descendants* (New York, 1913), 113.

493 *Vital Records of Salem, Massachusetts to the end of the year 1849*, 2: 165.

494 Ibid, 4: 188, 66.

495 Nathan Washington Marston, *The Marston Genealogy* (South Lubec, Me., 1888), 470.

496 Perley, *The History of Salem, Massachusetts*, 2: 328.

497 Essex Deeds 33: 74; *Marston, Marston Genealogy*, 472.

the mortgage was released in 1722.[498] On 26 March 1722, Benjamin Phippen of Salem, fisherman, sold land there to Samuel Browne. Ruth his wife released her rights and signed by mark.[499] Benjamin Phippen lived at the east end of the parish, and his land bounded that of Rachel Phippen.[500]

Widow Ruth Phippen married, second, at Salem 22 December 1726, **HENRY WEST**,[501] widower of Susanna Phippen, Benjamin's sister. On 2 January 1738 Benjamin Phippen of Salem, cordwainer, as administrator of the estate of his father Benjamin Phippen, deceased, sold land in Salem to Thomas Bistrell and Henry West, both of Salem. Documents for the sale indicate that Ruth, wife of Henry West, sadler, and widow of said deceased, quit her rights to the land.[502]

Children of Benjamin and Ruth (Marston) Phippen, born at Salem:[503]

24   i.   BENJAMIN[5] PHIPPEN, bp. 28 April 1717.
       ii.   ELIZABETH PHIPPEN, bp. 7 Sept. 1718; m. at Salem (int. dated 30 Aug. 1738) 18 Sept. 1738, DANIEL PARROT.[504]
      iii.   RUTH PHIPPEN, b. about 1719; d. unm. 10 Dec. 1785, aged 66 years. [505]

16. THOMAS[4] **PHIPPEN** (*David*[3], *Joseph*[2], *David*[1]) was baptized at Salem, Massachusetts in August 1675, son of David and Anne (Cromwell) Phippen.[506] He married at Salem in October 1706, **MARY (LINDALL) GEDNEY**,[507] widow of Nathaniel Gedney. Mary Lindall was born at Salem 7 April 1674, daughter of Timothy and Mary (Veren) Lindall.[508] She died at Salem 19 March 1722/23, aged 49 years,[509] and was buried in the Charter Street Burial Ground in Salem.[510]

[498]   Essex Deeds 36: 190.
[499]   Ibid., 40: 24.
[500]   Essex PR, no. 21743.
[501]   *Vital Records of Salem, Massachusetts to the end of the year 1849,* 4: 191, 454.
[502]   Essex Deeds 77:253.
[503]   *Vital Records of Salem, Massachusetts to the end of the year 1849,* 2: 165 (Benjamin), 166 (Elizabeth); *Salem First Church Records,* 56 (baptism of Benjamin), 57 (baptism of Elizabeth).
[504]   *Vital Records of Salem, Massachusetts to the end of the year 1849,* 4: 158, 189.
[505]   Ibid., 6: 139; Perley, *The History of Salem, Massachusetts,* 2: 328.
[506]   *Vital Records of Salem, Massachusetts to the end of the year 1849,* 2: 164.
[507]   Ibid., 4: 191, 3: 410.
[508]   Ibid., 1: 524; Perley, *The History of Salem, Massachusetts,* 2: 298.
[509]   *Vital Records of Salem, Massachusetts to the end of the year 1849,* 6: 138.
[510]   "Charter Street Burial-Ground Inscriptions," *Essex Institute Historical Collections* 13 [1877]: 108.

In 1722, the assessors' book notes "Thomas Phippen, a long time gone; tax abated, nine shillings." In 1725, Thomas Phippen had been absent from the country more than two years; during this time, his wife having died, his children lived with their grandmother, Mrs. Mary Lindall. At that time, Thomas's son Nathan, being fourteen years of age, was apprenticed to Joshua Dodge of Boston, Massachusetts.[511]

Thomas Phippen's wherabouts became known by 1731; he was working as a shipwright in Cecil County, Maryland. On 13 September 1731, Thomas Phippen, "living on Elke river in the County of Sissill in the Plantation of Merliand Shipwright" sold his interests in his father's properties in Casco Bay, Maine to John Higginson of Salem, Gent.[512]

Children of Thomas and Mary (Lindall) (Gedney) Phippen, born at Salem:[513]

    i.   MARY[5] PHIPPEN, bp. 21 Nov. 1708; m. at Salem after 10 Oct. 1730, EDWARD ROSE.[514]

    ii. THOMAS PHIPPEN, bp. 28 Jan. 1710/11; probably d. young.

    iii. NATHAN PHIPPEN, bp. 19 Oct. 1712; living in Boston in 1737;[515] apprenticed to Joshua Dodge of Boston in 1725.[516]

17. SAMUEL[4] PHIPPEN (*Samuel[3], Joseph[2], David[1]*) was born at Salem, Massachusetts 12 December 1677, son of Samuel and Rachel (Guppy) Phippen,[517] and died at Salem in 1732. On 20 January 1732, Samuel Phippen, guardian of Rebecca, Jonathan, and Atwater Phippen, gave guardianship bond, with John Phippen and Nathaniel Phippen as surety.[518]

---

[511] John Adams Vinton, *The Giles Memorial* (Boston, 1864), 320–21.

[512] York Deeds, Book 14, folio 252–53.

[513] *Vital Records of Salem, Massachusetts to the end of the year 1849* 2: 167 (birth of Mary), 168 (baptism of Nathan), 169 (baptism of Thomas); *Salem First Church Records,* 53 (baptism of Nathan). Vinton's *The Giles Memorial* (320–21) lists another child for Thomas and Mary: a daughter Sarah, born about 1707, who married ____ Williams. This is most likely the Sarah Phippen, daughter of Samuel and Elizabeth (English) Phippen (q.v.), who married Zerubbabel Williams.

[514] *Vital Records of Salem, Massachusetts to the end of the year 1849,* 4: 190, 271. Intentions were filed on 10 Oct. 1730; there is no record of the date of marriage.

[515] Perley, *The History of Salem, Massachusetts,* 2: 328.

[516] Vinton, *The Giles Memorial,* 321.

[517] *Vital Records of Salem, Massachusetts to the end of the year 1849,* 2: 169.

[518] Essex Probate Records, file no. 21762.

He married first, at Salem in 1708, **MARY BEADLE**,[519] who was born at Salem 21 May 1678, daughter of Samuel and Hannah (Lemon) Beadle.[520] No death record for Mary has been found, but she must have died shortly after the birth of her daughter Mary in 1715.

Samuel Phippen married, second, at Salem 20 March 1717/18, **REBECCA (ATWATER) BEADLE**,[521] widow of Lemon Beadle. Lemon Beadle, who died at Salem on 17 November 1717, aged 36 years,[522] was the brother of Samuel's first wife, Mary.[523] She died after the birth of their sixth child, Mehitable, in 1727. Mehitable's baptism record refers to her as the "dau. of Samuel and Rebecca, deceased."[524]

Samuel Phippen acquired the house formerly owned by John Cromwell. A discussion of this property is found in Sidney Perley's thorough review of early eighteenth-century Salem:[525]

> Mr. Cromwell . . . died, possessed of the house and entire lot, Sept. 30, 1700. In his will he devised the estate to his cousins, Ann, wife of David Phippen, and Jane, wife of Jonathan Pickering. Jonathan Picketing was a ship-carpenter, and lived in Salem. For forty pounds, he and his wife Jane conveyed one-half of the house and lot to Samuel Phippen, jr., of Salem, mariner, April 18, 1712.[526] The next day, Mr. Phippen, for a similar consideration, bought the other half interest of widow Anne Phippen of Salem.[527] Mr. Cromwell's widow, Hannah Cromwell, of Salem, for twenty pounds, had released her life interest in the estate to Mr. Phippen, called a fisherman, April 10, 1712.[528] Mr. Phippen was already living in the house. For eighty pounds, Mr. Phippen mortgaged the estate to Capt. William Pickering of Salem, mariner, March 29,

---

[519] *Vital Records of Salem, Massachusetts to the end of the year 1849,* 3: 94, 4: 191 (day and month missing in record).

[520] Ibid., 1: 81; Perley, *The History of Salem, Massachusetts,* 2: 386.

[521] *Vital Records of Salem, Massachusetts to the end of the year 1849,* 3: 94, 4: 191.

[522] Ibid., 5: 78.

[523] Perley, *The History of Salem, Massachusetts,* 2: 386.

[524] *Vital Records of Salem, Massachusetts to the end of the year 1849,* 2: 168.

[525] Sidney Perley, "Salem in 1700. No. 25," *Essex Antiquarian* 10 [1906]: 159–60.

[526] Essex Deeds 24: 196.

[527] Ibid., 23: 261.

[528] Ibid., 23: 261.

1714.[529] Mr. Pickering foreclosed the mortgage by taking
possession of the premises; and, with Samuel Phippen of
Salem, then called a blockmaker, conveyed, for eighty-five
pounds, the house, shop and land around them to Joseph
Phippen of Salem, cooper, April 1, 1719.[530] Mr. Phippen
lived here, being at this time a mariner. He died in 1734,
possessed of the estate. The house was then valued at sixty
pounds, and the shop at twenty-five pounds. His widow,
Susanna Phippen, continued to live here. Mr. Phippen's
heirs, Joseph Phippen, mariner, and Sarah Phippen,
spinster, heirs of Joseph Phippen, deceased son of the
deceased, and Sarah Dean, spinster, heiress of Sarah Dean
(wife of Thomas Dean, who joins in the deed), deceased,
daughter of the deceased Joseph Phippen, sr., all of Salem,
for seventy-five pounds, quitclaim their interest in the
land (no house being mentioned) to Abraham Watson of
Salem, gentleman, Dec. 12, 1782.[531]

Children of Samuel and Mary (Beadle) Phippen, born at Salem:[532]

25   i.   SAMUEL⁵ PHIPPEN, bp. 7 Jan. 1710/11.
        ii. JOSEPH PHIPPEN, bp. 14 June 1713; living in 1732 when his father
             died;[533] Joseph probably d. in 1773. On 7 Dec. 1773, Atwater
             Phippen was appointed administrator for the estate of Joseph
             Phippen, mariner. Inventory of his estate was as follows: bed,
             bedstead, and bedding, £6 10s 4d; men's apparel and pewter, £4 8s
             2d; china, "Delph," and glassware, £2 10s 2d; household furniture,
             table linen, £12 0s 6d; two hogsheads of rum, £32 5s 4d; silver and
             gold, £2 18s 3d; women's apparel, £6 13s 8d; cash received from
             Andrew Preston £7 4s 0d. The total was £74 10s 5d.[534]
        iii. MARY PHIPPEN, bp. 14 Aug. 1715; m. at Topsfield, Mass. 7 May
             1735, JOHN AVERILL,[535] who was b. at Topsfield 24 April 1711, son

[529]   Essex Deeds, 49: 158.
[530]   Ibid., 36: 96.
[531]   Ibid., 40: 82.
[532]   *Vital Records of Salem, Massachusetts to the end of the year 1849,* 2: 167 (Joseph, Mary),
        168 (Samuel).
[533]   Perley, *The History of Salem, Massachusetts,* 2: 328.
[534]   Essex PR, no. 21753.
[535]   *Vital Records of Topsfield, Massachusetts to the end of the year 1849,* 2 vols. (Topsfield,
        1903), 1: 118, 177.

of John and Anne (Greensleet) Averill.[536] Mary (Phippen) Averill
d. at Westminster, Vt. 18 Sept. 1809.[537] John Averill d. there 2 Sept.
1797.[538] Their sixth child, Anna[6] *Averill*, b. autumn of 1751, was said
to be the first child born in Westminster.[539]

Children of Samuel and Rebecca (Atwater) (Beadle) Phippen, born
at Salem:[540]

iv.   RUTH PHIPPEN, bp. 21 Dec. 1718; m. at Salem 5 June 1740, MASCOLL
WILLIAMS,[541] who was b. at Salem 4 Aug. 1717, son of Isaac and
Sarah (Mascoll) Williams.[542] He d. at Salem and was buried on 13
Feb. 1799, aged 81 years.[543] Mascoll Williams was a bookbinder,
stationer, and book dealer in Salem.[544] Ruth (Phippen) Williams,
widow of Mascoll Williams, died in the Salem poor house in Dec.
1811.[545]

v.   REBECCA PHIPPEN, bp. 4 Dec. 1720; m. at Salem 3 Dec. 1741,
ROBERT ALLEN.[546]

vi.   JONATHAN PHIPPEN, bp. 1 July 1722; living in 1732 when his father
died.

vii. ATWATER PHIPPEN, bp. 28 June 1724; apparently d. young.

viii. ATWATER PHIPPEN, bp. 5 June 1726; d. at Salem 15 Dec. 1806, aged
81 years.[547] He m. (1) at Salem 20 March 1750, OLIVE BUTLER,[548]
who was bp. at South Berwick, Maine 31 March 1728, dau. of
Thomas and Mehitable (____) Butler.[549] She d. at Salem 9 Sept.

536   Ibid., 1: 10;   Clara A. Avery, *The Averell-Averill-Avery Family: A Record of the Descendants of William and Abigail Averell of Ipswich, Mass.,* 2 vols. (Cleveland, 1914), 1: 121–23.

537   Avery, *The Averell-Averill-Avery Family,* 1: 186.

538   Ibid.

539   Ibid., 190.

540   *Vital Records of Salem, Massachusetts to the end of the year 1849,* 2: 165 (baptisms of both Atwaters), 167 (baptism of Jonathan), 168 (baptisms of Ruth, Rebecca and Mehitable).

541   Ibid., 4: 191, 476.

542   Ibid., 2: 433; Perley, *The History of Salem, Massachusetts,* 3: 16.

543   *Vital Records of Salem, Massachusetts to the end of the year 1849,* 6: 336.

544   Perley, *The History of Salem, Massachusetts,* 3: 16.

545   *Vital Records of Salem, Massachusetts to the end of the year 1849* 6: 337 ("Williams, wid. Mascoll, Esq., at the poorhouse. Issue of Dec. 3, 1811." The death notice appeared in the *Salem Gazette.*

546   Ibid. 3: 47, 4: 190.

547   Ibid., 6: 137.

548   Ibid., 3: 174, 4: 188.

549   George H. Butler, *Thomas Butler and His Descendants: A Genealogy of the Descendants*

1790 of "bilious diarrhea," at age 61 years.[550] He m. (2) at Salem 7 Nov. 1791, his cousin MARTHA[6] PHIPPEN[551] (*Israel[5], Nathaniel[4], Samuel[3], Joseph[2,] David[1]*). Martha (Phippen) Phippen survived him and died at Salem 25 Feb. 1847, aged 92 years.[552]

Atwater Phippen was a frequent Salem municipal officeholder: he was surveyor of highways from 1779 to 1783, and surveyor of boards from 1775 to 1783; he was measurer of wood in 1782, and in charge of supplies for soldiers' families in 1779.[553] He was listed as manufacturing glue in 1773. He also kept a meticulous record of the rainfall in Salem, month by month.[554] The Rev. William Bentley, in commenting upon an apparent hurricane, wrote in his diary for 10 October 1804 that "Mr. Atwater Phippen who for many years has noticed the fall of rain, distinguished the rain of yesterday as the greatest he ever knew, four inches fell in the day & three inches in the night."[555] Atwater Phippen is probably the Mr. Phippen that Bentley mentions as having dined with him on 4 July 1803, with the comment that he was nearly 80.[556] His will, made 30 Nov. 1799, was probated 19 Jan. 1807. He named his wife Martha as his sole heir.[557] They left no issue. He was listed in the 1790 census, in Salem, with one male over 16 and two free white females.[558]

    ix.   MEHITABLE, bp. 9 July 1727.

18. JOHN[4] PHIPPEN (*Samuel[3], Joseph[2], David[1]*) was born at Salem, Massachusetts 25 December 1685, son of Samuel and Rachel (Guppy) Phippen.[559] He died in 1755.[560]

---

      of Thomas and Elizabeth Butler of Butler's Hill, South Berwick, Me., 1674–1886 (New York, 1886), 9, 17.

550 *Vital Records of Salem, Massachusetts to the end of the year 1849*, 6: 138 (Salem Gazette, 13 Sept. 1790). Rev. John Prince, pastor of the First Church, recorded her death on 9 Sept. 1790, age 61 years. "List of Deaths Recorded by the Rev. John Prince, Pastor, First Church in Salem," *Essex Institute Historical Collections* 9 [1869]: 95.

551 *Vital Records of Salem, Massachusetts to the end of the year 1849*, 4: 188,190.

552 *Vital Records of Salem, Massachusetts to the end of the year 1849*, 6: 138.

553 Essex County, Massachusetts officers and committees 1775-1783 (Mss A 7772). R. Stanton Avery Special Collections, NEHGS, Boston.

554 Joseph B. Felt, *Annals of Salem*, 2d ed., 2 vols. (Salem, 1849), 2: 99, 169.

555 William Bentley, *The Diary of William Bentley, D.D., Pastor of the East Church, Salem, Massachusetts*, 4 vols. (Gloucester, Mass., 1962), 3: 116.

556 Ibid., 3: 30.

557 Essex Probate Records, file no. 21742.

558 1790 U.S. Census, Salem, Essex County, Massachusetts, roll 4, p. 586.

559 *Vital Records of Salem, Massachusetts to the end of the year 1849*, 2: 167.

560 Perley, *The History of Salem, Massachusetts*, 2: 328.

John Phippen married at Salem 23 November 1709,[561] ELIZABETH
HARTSHORN, who was born at Reading, Massachusetts 20 December
1686, daughter of Benjamin and Elizabeth (Browne) Hartshorn.[562] She
was John's widow in 1759;[563] she died at Salem 14 July 1760.[564]

Various sources list John Phippen as a housewright, joiner, and
shipwright. A house that he built stands today on Hawthorne Boulevard
in Salem, around the corner from the Essex Institute. He purchased
land in Salem on 23 July 1711 from John Richards.[565] On 2 April 1714,
he sold rights to a house in Salem to Nathaniel Phippen, cooper.[566]

He made his will on 10 January 1754, which was proved on 9 July
1755. The will mentioned his four children—John Phippen, Elizabeth
Cook, Rachel Cook, and Hannah Roberts—giving each 10 shillings.
His wife Elizabeth received the remainder of his estate.[567]

On 19 May 1756, Elizabeth Phippen, widow of John, late of Salem,
housewright, deceased, sold property to Jonathan Gardner.[568] In 1759,
she again sold land of her late husband.[569]

Children of John and Elizabeth (Hartshorn) Phippen, born at
Salem:[570]

> i. ELIZABETH[5] PHIPPEN, bp. 15 April 1711; m. at Salem 24 Dec. 1730,
> BENJAMIN COOK,[571] who was b. there about 1705, son of John
> and Hannah (Dean) Cook. Benjamin Cook was a fisherman and
> mariner. Elizabeth was living in 1766, and her husband was living
> in 1799.[572]

---

[561] *Vital Records of Salem, Massachusetts to the end of the year 1849*, 3: 472, 4: 189.

[562] *Vital Records of Reading, Massachusetts to the end of the year 1849* (Boston, 1912),
120. For discussion of her parentage, see John S. Fipphen, "Elizabeth, Wife of John
Phippen," *The Essex Genealogist* 2 [1982]: 27.

[563] Perley, *The History of Salem, Massachusetts*, 2: 328.

[564] *Vital Records of Salem, Massachusetts to the end of the year 1849*, 6: 140 ("Mrs. Phippen,
July 14, 1760.")

[565] Perley, "Salem in 1700. No. 26, *Essex Antiquarian* 11 [1907]: 16–17; Essex Deeds 22:
278.

[566] Essex Deeds 28: 22.

[567] Essex Probate Records, file no. 21750.

[568] Essex Deeds 102: 264.

[569] Ibid., 108: 25.

[570] *Vital Records of Salem, Massachusetts to the end of the year 1849*, 2:165 (baptism of
Benjamin) 166 (baptisms of Elizabeth, Hannah, Ebenezer, and James), 167 (baptism
of John), 168 (baptism of Rachel), 169 (baptism of Susanna).

[571] *Vital Records of Salem, Massachusetts to the end of the year 1849*, 3: 239, 4: 189.

[572] Perley, *The History of Salem, Massachusetts*, 2: 43–44.

    ii. RACHEL PHIPPEN, bp. 11 Oct. 1713; d. before 1782;[573] m. at Salem 18 Sept. 1732, JAMES COOK,[574] who was b. at Salem 22 March 1709/10, son of Joseph and Margaret (Cox) Cook.[575] Both were living in 1768.[576]

    iii. HANNAH PHIPPEN, bp. 30 Dec. 1716; m. at Salem 7 July 1737, JOSEPH ROBERTS.[577]

26   iv. JOHN PHIPPEN, bp. 15 March 1719.

    v. BENJAMIN PHIPPEN, bp. 29 Oct. 1721; died before 10 Jan. 1754, when his father made his will.

    vi. EBENEZER PHIPPEN, bp. 2 Aug. 1724; died before 10 Jan. 1754, when his father made his will.

    vii. JAMES PHIPPEN, bp. 23 April 1727; died before 10 Jan. 1754, when his father made his will.

    viii. SUSANNA PHIPPEN, bp. 14 Dec. 1729; died before 10 Jan. 1754, when her father made his will.

19. NATHANIEL⁴ PHIPPEN (*Samuel³, Joseph², David¹*) was born at Salem, Massachusetts 4 August 1687, son of Samuel and Rachel (Guppy) Phippen,[578] and died at Salem 14 August 1756, aged 69 years.[579] Nathaniel married at Salem 29 June 1710, **MARGARET PALFREY**,[580] who was born at Salem, Massachusetts 15 November 1687, daughter of Walter and Margaret (Manning) Palfrey.[581] She died 30 November 1753.[582]

Nathaniel Phippen was a cooper. Among numerous references in town records, he provided fire buckets to the town in 1730, for which, on 2 February 1729/30, the town treasurer was ordered to pay him 48

---

[573] Perley, *The History of Salem, Massachusetts*, 2: 44.

[574] *Vital Records of Salem, Massachusetts to the end of the year 1849*, 3: 240, 4: 190.

[575] Ibid., 1: 203.

[576] Perley, *The History of Salem, Massachusetts*, 2: 43–44.

[577] *Vital Records of Salem, Massachusetts to the end of the year 1849*, 4: 189, 261..

[578] Ibid., 168.

[579] Perley, *The History of Salem, Massachusetts*, 2: 328; the 1808 Phippen chart records the date of death as 13 August 1756. *See also Vital Records of Salem, Massachusetts to the end of the year 1849*, 6: 138 (date of burial, 16 August 1756). Another entry in the *Vital Records of Salem, Massachusetts to the end of the year 1849* erroneously states that he died about February 1755.

[580] *Vital Records of Salem, Massachusetts to the end of the year 1849*, 4: 154, 190.

[581] Ibid., 2: 136; Perley, *The History of Salem, Massachusetts*, 3: 150.

[582] 1808 Phippen chart.

shillings.[583] Nathaniel and his wife Margaret were admitted to the First Church of Salem on 3 July 1715.[584]

Nathaniel Phippen placed the following advertisement in the *Boston Evening-Post* on 1 and 8 November 1742:[585]

TO BE SOLD,

A Likely healthy Negro Man, of about 25 Years old, of a midling Stature, and speaks good English. He is a good Cook, a Musician, and a Cooper by Trade. Enquire of Nathaniel Phippen in Salem, living near the Common.

The following bill of sale was presented in an article in *The Liberator* in 1858:[586]

KNOW ALL MEN, That I, Nathaniel Phippen, of Salem, in ye County of Essex, Cooper, in consideration of forty pounds to me already paid by Nathaniel Archer, of said Salem, Gentleman, Have Sold and Delivered and hereby Do Sell, Convey and Confirm unto ye s'd Nath'l Archer, my negro man, named Titus, aged about thirty-eight years, being a servant for Life, with his Apparel. To hold ye s'd Negro as a servant for Life with all his Apparel, to him ye s'd Nath'l Archer and to his Heirs and Assigns and as his and their proper Estate, and for his and their only use, benefit and behoofe, free of all incumbrances. And I hereby covenant with ye s'd Nath'l Archer that ye s'd Negro is every way sound and well: That I am ye lawful owner of ye same Negro, and have good right and lawful authority to sell him with this Apparel in manner and form aforesaid: And further, that I, my Heirs, Ex'rs and Adm'rs, shall and will warrant this sale to and for ye s'd Nath'l Archer and his Heirs and Assigns against all persons.

In Witness Whereof, I hereto put my hand and seal, this thirteenth day of April, A.D. 1756.

NATH'L PHIPPEN

583 *Essex Institute Historical Collections* 2 [1860]: 104, extract published under header "A Caveat to the Steam Fire Engines of Our Day." "Order to the treasurer to pay Nathaniel Phippen 48 s for 24 water buckets for the town's use in case of fire" (citing town records for 2 Feb. 1729/30).

584 *Records of the First Church in Salem, Mass.*, 241.

585 *Boston Evening-Post*, 1 Nov. and 8 Nov. 1742.

586 *The Liberator*, 27 Aug. 1858.

Signed, Sealed and Del'd in presence
of us-this paper being stampt with ye
three penny stamp.

DAVID PHIPPEN,
SAM'L ARCHER.

Nathaniel Phippen made his will on 17 February 1755. He named
his children— Abigail, David, Israel, Thomas, Margaret, and Anstis—as
well as the children of his son Nathaniel (Joshua, Hardy, Joseph, and
Seath). David Phippen and Israel Phippen were appointed executors.
The will was proved 18 October 1756. The detailed inventory of his
estate, both real estate and personal property, is here given in full:[587]

An Inventory of Reall & Personall Estate of M[r] Nath[l]
Phippen late of Salem Dec[d]

	£	s	d
At the warfe			
The Coopers Shop & Garden with thirty feet of warfe front		80	
The Joyner Shope & warfe to run to the south six foot short of the maine ware-houee from hence on a straight line to the west of the warfe	66	13	4
The Great warehouse & all the remaining part of the warfe	226	13	4
The Gundelo etc		6	
500 feet of board & plank		17	4
4 1/2 hundred of Hhd hoops	1	7	
4 hundred barrel Do		12	
10 fifth Hogshead	2	13	4
1 1/2 hogshead Salt	1	6	
one old house & land in the lane formerly Samuel Phippen's Deceased	65	6	8
The House Coopers shops Barn Garden etc in the main street	256	13	4
The common right in ths great pasture	10		

---

[587] Essex Probate Records, file no. 21760.

	£	s	d
a cow & 26 hundred of hay	4	13	4
four coard of wood	2	13	4
3 thod *of* red Oke hogshead staves	5	12	
Coopers tule in the shop	3	6	8
Sundry old trushoops heading & staves etc in the Coopers shop	2		
Bettle & wedges & ax		5	4
Two Shoat	1	4	
1 feather bed wt 69 1/2 pound @ ¼	4	12	8
1 Do wt 72 @13	3	16	
one Do wt 86 @ 12	4	6	
one wooling rugg		8	
one Do.	8		
1 Quilt	6	8	
1 Green Rugg		8	
1 pr old Blankets		6	8
1 Quilt	10	8	
1 Sute Callico Curtins		10	8
1 Do 10	8		
3 pilabors		4	
1 Linning sheet		9	4
Carried Over	749 1	1	
Brought over	749 1	1	
2 pr Toocloth Sheets		14	8
2 pr Do	13	4	
1 pr Cotton linning Do		12	
1 Bedsted & Laping		17	4
1 Do	16		
1 Desk 26/8 1 Tea Table 14/8	2	1	4
1 Walnut Table (Dearfeet)		18	8
1 Do old fashion		17	4
1 Large Looking glass		16	

	£	s	d
Clostool & pan		8	
6 black Chars		8	
2 Walking Cains		1	4
Gun Sword & Contouchbon		9	4
pr hand iorns		8	
8 Joyners Chars & 1 Great Do	1	6	8
2 Wine Glasses			6
1 Small Pole table		6	
1 Old chest drawers		6	8
10 Eathem plates & 2 dishes		7	8
pr hand ioms		6	8
5 pictures & stand		1	4
4 Old chairs		2	8
1 Bedsted & Laping		16	
2 Leather buckets		7	4
31 lb pewter @ 1/4 pd	2	1	4
13 lb Do @ 91/2 pd		10	3
1 Brass Cittle wt 22 @ 1/4 pd	1	9	4
1 Small Do wt 12 @ 1/4 pd		16	
1 pr Brass Candle Sticks		6	
1 old pr Do		3	4
1 Brass Skillet & frame		3	4
1 pr Iorn Doggs		6	
2 Trammels		2	8
1 old Chafindish		1	4
2 pr old tongs & shovell		4	
1 frying pan		2	
5 Iorn baking pans		8	
3 Iorn Skillits		3	4
2 Small pots & pot hooks		6	
1 pot large		3	4
1 warming pan		4	8

	£	s	d
2 Bon Ioms & heaters		6	
1 pine table		2	8
2 Do 2		8	
[carried over]	771	6	2

	£	s	d
Brought over	771	6	2
1 Black Jarr		2	
12 old chars		8	
1 old great chare			11
1 old jack		4	
large bible		4	
2 small Do		2	11
1 Large Exposition on 2 Epistles of Peter		6	
Sundry Small books		5	4
pr Small Stilyards		2	8
3 Earthen Muggs			9
1 Cadlepot			6
2 Milk pans			8
Small Spit 14d & Bucket 8d		1	10
1 Kersey Great Coat		18	8
1 Sute of Broad Cloth Cloaths	1	9	4
1 Kersey Coat		9	4
1 Black Cloath Coat & Jacket	1	7	14
1 homspun Jacket		1	4
1 Bever Hat 12/ 1 Old Do 1/4		13	4
1 Linning Jacket & 4 Shurts		16	
Totle Sum	779	11	1

Salem, Novb^r 1. 1757

David Phippen
Israel Phippen
Jos. Grafton
Jona Gardner
Jos. Hodges

The 1808 Phippen chart states, "Nathl Phippen the 4th Son of Samuel. Born Augst 4th 1607. [corrected to Aug 4. 1677.] Married the 29th June 1710. died 13th August 1756. Left issue Nathaniel, Margaret, David, Abigail, Isrl, Anstis, Lydia, Lydia, and Thomas. By- Margat Palfrey. Died Novm 30th 1753."

Children of Nathaniel and Margaret (Palfrey) Phippen, born at Salem:[588]

27   i.   NATHANIEL[5] PHIPPEN, b. 5 July 1711.

        ii.   MARGARET PHIPPEN, b. 15 June 1713; died unm. in 1764. Administration of her estate was granted to David Phippen of Salem on 28 Dec. 1764.[589]

28   iii. DAVID PHIPPEN, b. 18 Sept. 1715.

        iv.   ABIGAIL PHIPPEN, b. 16 Sept. 1717; m. (1) at Salem 11 Oct. 1739, NATHANIEL PIKE,[590] who was bp. at Salem 5 Feb. 1715/16, son of Nathaniel and Margaret (King) Pike.[591] Abigail m. (2) in on or before 1756, JOHN WARD of Marblehead, Mass.,[592] who was b. 21 June 1729, son of Deacon Joshua and Sarah (Trevett) Ward.[593]

29   v.   ISRAEL PHIPPEN, bp. 17 July 1720.

        vi.   ANSTIS PHIPPEN, bp. 7 June 1724; died unm. 18 April 1775.[594] Her will, dated 18 April 1775, gave one-half right in the house where she lived to her nephew, Thomas Phippen, Jr. She made William Phippen, Thomas Phippen's brother, her executor as well as giving him the other half of her house. To Rebecca Phippen, wife of Thomas Phippen, Jr., she gave her program gown. To her sisters, Abigail Ward and Martha Phippen, she left a gold necklace, wearing apparel, and furniture, to be divided equally between them. The will was probated 12 July 1782. No reason is apparent for the seven-year delay in probating her will.[595]

---

[588] *Vital Records of Salem, Massachusetts to the end of the year 1849,* 2: 165 (birth of Abigail, baptism of Antsis), 166 (birth of David and baptism of Israel), 167 (birth of Margaret, baptism of Lydia), 168 (birth of Nathaniel), 169 (baptism of Thomas).

[589] Essex Probate Records, file no. 21758.

[590] *Vital Records of Salem, Massachusetts to the end of the year 1849,* 4: 188, 198.

[591] Ibid., 2: 178; Perley, *The History of Salem, Massachusetts,* 3: 396.

[592] Perley, *The History of Salem, Massachusetts,* 2: 328.

[593] *Vital Records of Salem, Massachusetts to the end of the year 1849,* 2: 390; Perley, The History of Salem, Massachusetts, 2: 101–2.

[594] Perley, *The History of Salem, Massachusetts,* 2: 328; *Vital Records of Salem, Massachusetts to the end of the year 1849,* 6: 137 (buried 20 April 1775).

[595] Essex Probate Records, file no. 21741.

vii. LYDIA PHIPPEN, bp. 17 Sept. 1727; d. young, as she was not mentioned in her father's will.

viii. LYDIA PHIPPEN, b. say 1729. The Phippen chart lists two Lydias; she also apparently died young, as she was not mentioned in her father's will.

30 ix. THOMAS PHIPPEN , bp. 17 Jan. 1730/31.

20. JOSEPH[4] PHIPPEN (*Samuel[3], Joseph[2], David[1]*) was born at Salem, Massachusetts 9 February 1696/7, son of Samuel and Rachel (Guppy) Phippen.[596] He died in the spring of 1734.[597] Administration of his estate was granted on 8 June 1734.[598] Joseph married at Salem 18 January 1719/20, SUSANNA HARTSHORN,[599] who was born at Reading, Massachusetts 21 September 1692, daughter of Benjamin and Elizabeth (Brown) Hartshorn.[600] Joseph Phippen was a cooper in Salem.

Children of Joseph and Susanna (Hartshorn) Phippen, born at Salem:[601]

31 i. WILLIAM5 PHIPPEN, b. 23 Sept. 1721.

ii. SUSANNA PHIPPEN, b. 7 July 1723.

iii. SARAH PHIPPEN, b. 25 June 1726; m. at Salem 31 July 1751, Capt. THOMAS DEAN JR.[602] Sarah d. at Salem 18 March 1752.[603] Thomas Dean m. (2) at Salem 9 April 1754, MARY CASH.[604]

iv. JOSEPH PHIPPEN, b. 18 Dec. 1730.

[596] *Vital Records of Salem, Massachusetts to the end of the year 1849,* 2: 167.

[597] Perley, *The History of Salem, Massachusetts,* 2: 329.

[598] Essex Probate Records, file no. 21752.

[599] *Vital Records of Salem, Massachusetts to the end of the year 1849,* 3: 472, 4: 190. First Church records give the date as 15 Jan. 1719/20.

[600] *Vital Records of Reading, Massachusetts to the end of the year 1849,* 121.

[601] *Vital Records of Salem, Massachusetts to the end of the year 1849,* 2: 167 (birth of Joseph), 169 (births of William, Susanna, and Sarah).

[602] *Vital Records of Salem, Massachusetts to the end of the year 1849,* 3: 287, 4: 191.

[603] Ibid., 5: 200.

[604] Ibid., 3: 195, 287.

21. BENJAMIN[4] PHIPPENEY (*James*[3], *Benjamin*[2], *David*[1]) was born at Stratford, Connecticut 14 January 1701/2, son of James and Joanna (____) Phippeney.[605] He married at Stratford 30 January 1726/27 REBECCA BOSTWICK of New Milford, Connecticut,[606] who was baptized at Stratford 21 August 1709, daughter of Joseph and Ann (Buss or Burr) Bostwick.[607]

Benjamin was part of a group that established a new church in 1747 at North Stratford.[608] Benjamin Phippeney lived in Unity Parish, Stratford, until 1760, when he removed to New Milford, where he purchased 200 acres.[609]

Children of Benjamin and Rebecca (Bostwick) Phippeney, born at Stratford:[610]

	i.	ANN[5] PHIPPENEY, b. 15 Nov. 1727; she m. at Unity Parish in July 1750, NEHEMIAH BENNIT.[611]
32	ii.	JOSEPH PHIPPENEY, b. 11 June 1730.
33	iii.	ARCHIBALD PHIPPENEY, b. 21 Oct. 173[3].
	iv.	EUNICE PHIPPENEY, b. 3 May 1742; m. at North Stratford 5 Oct. 1760, ZADOCK BLACKMAN, son of Timothy and Beulah (____) Blackman. Eunice petitioned for divorce in August 1769 on the ground of desertion.[612]
34	v.	BENJAMIN PHIPPENEY, b. 9 June 1744.
	vi.	BETTY (or RUTH) PHIPPENEY, b. 26 Feb. 1746.
	vii.	REBECCA PHIPPENEY, b. 18 May 1749; m. at New Milford 18 Oct. 1764, DAVID BOTSFORD.[613]

---

605   "Stratford 1639-1840," *The Barbour Collection of Connecticut Town Vital Records*, vol. 41, 205.

606   Ibid.

607   Henry A. Bostwick, *Genealogy of the Bostwick family in America: the descendants of Arthur Bostwick of Stratford, Conn.* (Hudson, N.Y., 1901), 122; Jacobus, History and Genealogy of the Families of Old Fairfield, 1: 93.

608   Orcutt, *History of Stratford*, 2: 1015.

609   George N. Mackenzie, *Colonial Families of the United States of America*, 7 vols. (Baltimore, 1912), 3: 402.

610   "Stratford 1639-1840," *The Barbour Collection of Connecticut Town Vital Records*, vol. 41, 205.

611   Frederic W. Bailey, ed., *Early Connecticut Marriages as Found in Ancient Church Records Prior to 1800*, 7 vols. (New Haven, Conn., 1896–1906), 7: 95. *See also* Jacobus, *History and Genealogy of the Families of Old Fairfield*, 1: 74.

612   Donald L. Jacobus, "Connecticut Divorce Records," *The American Genealogist* 32 [1956]: 155–57 at 157.

613   "New Milford 1712-1860," *The Barbour Collection of Connecticut Town Vital Records*, vol. 30, 167.

22. JAMES⁴ PHIPPENEY (*James³, Benjamin², David¹*) was born at Stratford, Connecticut 10 August 1710, son of James and Joanna (_____) Phippeney.⁶¹⁴ On 22 August 1727, he chose Jonadab Basset, his sister Mary's husband, to be his guardian. On 13 February 1729/30, Jonadab Basset was discharged as his guardian, and John Fairchild of Stratford was appointed in his place.⁶¹⁵

James Phippeney married at Unity Parish (Stratford), Connecticut 14 July 1734, **HANNAH SMITH** of Hartford, Connecticut,⁶¹⁶ daughter of Philip and Mary (Robinson) Smith.⁶¹⁷

Children of James and Hannah (Smith) Phippeney, born at Stratford:⁶¹⁸

      i.   HANNAH⁵ PHIPPENEY, b. 3 Aug. 1735.

      ii. MARY PHIPPENEY, b. 28 Nov. 1737.

35   iii. JAMES PHIPPENEY, b. in May 1743.

36   iv. NEHEMIAH PHIPPENEY, b. in March 1746.

      v. DAVID PHIPPENEY, b. in June 1750; d. in Oct. 1771.

---

⁶¹⁴ "Stratford 1639-1840," *The Barbour Collection of Connecticut Town Vital Records,* vol. 41, 205.

⁶¹⁵ Mead, *Fairfield Probate Abstracts,* 78 (Fairfield Probate Records 7 (1721-50): 22, 72).

⁶¹⁶ "Stratford 1639-1840," *The Barbour Collection of Connecticut Town Vital Records,* vol. 41, 205; Bailey, *Early Connecticut Marriages,* 7: 93 (date of marriage is stated as 18 July 1734).

⁶¹⁷ Lucius Barnes Barbour, *Early Families of Hartford, Connecticut* (Baltimore, 1977), 547–48.

⁶¹⁸ "Stratford 1639-1840," *The Barbour Collection of Connecticut Town Vital Records,* vol. 41, 205 (births of Hannah and Mary); Orcutt, *History of Stratford,* 2: 1268 (births of James, Nehemiah and David).

CHAPTER 7

THE FIFTH GENERATION

23. DANIEL[5] **PHIPPEN** (*Daniel*[4], *Joseph*[3–2], *David*[1]) was born at Boston, Massachusetts 18 October 1696, son of Daniel and Elizabeth Phippen.[619] He can be presumed to have died by 1736, when his wife remarried. Daniel Phippen was married by Rev. Mr. Benjamin Wadsworth at Boston 5 February 1718/19 to **RACHEL MARSHFIELD**,[620] who was born at Springfield, Massachusetts 4 August 1692, daughter of Josiah and Rachel (Gilbert) Marshfield.[621] Rachel married, second, at Boston 21 October 1736, **JOHN WADLEIGH**,[622] who was probably the John Wadleigh born at Salisbury, Massachusetts 14 August 1691, son of John and Abigail (___) Wadleigh.[623]

Children of Daniel and Rachel (Marshfield) Phippen:

 i RACHEL[6] PHIPPEN, b. ca. 1719, d. 29 Aug. 1721. Her gravestone is in the Ancient Burying Ground in Hartford, Conn.[624]

 ii. MARY PHIPPEN, b. 6 March 1721;[625] m. at Salisbury 8 April 1742, SAMUEL WAIT of Amesbury, Mass.[626]

24. BENJAMIN[5] **PHIPPEN** (*Benjamin*[4], *Joseph*[3–2], *David*[1]) was baptized at Salem, Massachusetts 28 April 1717, son of Benjamin and Ruth

---

[619] *Boston Births, Marriages, and Deaths, 1630–99,* 228.

[620] *Boston Marriages 1700–51,* 77.

[621] *Vital Records of Springfield, Massachusetts to the end of the year 1849,* 1: 43, *Early Families of Hartford, Connecticut,* 387.

[622] *Boston Marriages 1700-51,* 199; *Vital Records of Salisbury, Massachusetts to the end of the year 1849* (Topsfield, Mass., 1915), 456, 505 (spelled "Phippeny" and "Fippen").

[623] *Vital Records of Salisbury, Massachusetts to the end of the year 1849,* 245.

[624] "Center Burying Ground," *Hartford Courant,* 26 June 1897, 12 (accessed from ProQuest Historical Newspapers); Findagrave.com (memorial# 16963121).

[625] *Vital Records of Amesbury, Massachusetts to the end of the year 1849,* 248.

[626] *Vital Records of Salisbury, Massachusetts to the end of the year 1849,* 351, 506 (spelled "Fippen").

(Marston) Phippen.[627] Since there is no vital record in Salem or record of probate in Essex County for Benjamin, his place and date of death are unknown. He was a cordwainer in Salem.[628] Perhaps he was the Benjamin Phippeny who was living in the north suburbs of Halifax, Nova Scotia in 1752, with a woman and two female children under the age of 16.[629]

Benjamin Phippen married at Salem 5 July 1739 (intentions published 10 February 1738/39), **HANNAH BECKET**,[630] daughter of William and Mary (Mascoll) Becket of Salem.[631]

Child, born at Salem:

    i. MARY[6] PHIPPEN, bp. 6 July 1743;[632] apparently m. by 1767, WILLIAM HOLMAN, who was b. at Salem 9 Sept. 1740, son of Gabriel and Elizabeth (Reeves) Holman.[633] He is probably the William Holman who died 4 Jan. 1827, aged 86, at the almshouse at Salem, a Revolutionary War veteran.[634] Children (surname *Holman*): 1. *Mary,* bp. 11 March 1768; 2. *Esther,* bp. 3 Dec. 1769; 3. *Sarah,* bp. 11 Aug. 1771; 4. *Elizabeth,* bp. 24 Jan. 1773; 5. *William,* bp. 16 Oct. 1774; 6. *Jacob,* bp. 18 March 1776; 7. *Esther,* bp. 14 Dec. 1777; 8. *Nancy,* bp. 20 Jan. 1782; 9. *Hannah,* bp. in Oct. 1786.[635]

25. SAMUEL[5] PHIPPEN (*Samuel*[4-3], *Joseph*[2], *David*[1]) was baptized at Salem, Massachusetts 7 January 1710/11, son of Samuel and Mary (Beadle) Phippen.[636] He died at Westminster, Vermont 2 March 1804, in his 94th year,[637] and was buried in Westminster Old Cemetery.[638]

---

[627] *Vital Records of Salem, Massachusetts to the end of the year 1849,* 2: 165.

[628] Perley, *The History of Salem, Massachusetts,* 2: 329.

[629] *Collections of the Nova Scotia Historical Society* 8 [1895]: 246–61 at 247.

[630] *Vital Records of Salem, Massachusetts to the end of the year 1849,* 3: 96, 4: 189.

[631] Perley, *The History of Salem, Massachusetts,* 2: 224.

[632] *Vital Records of Salem, Massachusetts to the end of the year 1849,* 2: 167; "Salem Baptisms," *Essex Institute Historical Collections* 22 [1885]: 177 et seq., at 23 [1886]: 245.

[633] *Vital Records of Salem, Massachusetts to the end of the year 1849,* 1: 444.

[634] Ibid., 5: 338.

[635] Ibid., 1: 443–44.

[636] Ibid., 2: 168.

[637] Vermont Vital Records. (The very early records for Vermont are on individual cards with no reference information.) Gravestone information copied from cemetery marker, Westminster (Vt.) Old Cemetery.

[638] Cemetery marker, Westminster (Vt.) Old East Parish Cemetery.

Samuel Phippen removed to Topsfield, Massachusetts, and married there 7 September 1738, **EMMA AVERILL,**[639] daughter of John and Anne (Greensleet) Averill, who was baptized at Topsfield in May 1715.[640] She died at Westminster in April 1799.[641] Emma was the sister of John Averill, husband of Samuel's sister Mary.

Samuel Phippen is listed as being in the militia in Topsfield in 1745. In September 1747, Samuel and his wife "Amy" and four children were warned out of Boxford, Massachusetts, and told to return to Topsfield. On 1 March 1763, this article appeared on the Topsfield town meeting warrant: "To see if the town will purchase the house and privilages that belongs to Samuel Phippen for the use of a school house for the inhabitants of the north side of the river in said town at a price agreed upon and also agree upon some proper method to provide a school house for inhabitants on the south side of the river." No action was taken.[642]

Samuel Phippen removed from Topsfield to Lunenburg, Massachusetts, then to Northfield, Massachusetts, and finally to Westminster in Windham County, Vermont, where he settled in a place that became known as "Phippen Hill." The family was there as early as 1772, as appears from a deed from Samuel Phippen to Ephraim Ranney.[643] He was a member of the Baptist Society of Westminster at the time of its organization in 1784. He was enumerated (along with the separate households of his sons Samuel Junior, Joseph, and Atwater) in the 1790 census of Westminster.

Children of Samuel and Emma (Averill) Phippen, born at Topsfield:[644]

    i. MERCY[6] PHIPPEN, b. 31 Jan. 1738/39; bp. at Christ Church, Topsfield 12 Oct. 1746; m. (1) ABIJAH LOVEJOY; m. (2) her double first cousin ASA AVERILL, who was b. about 1739, son of John and Mary (Phippen) Averill. She was dead by 1799. The story behind her second marriage is as follows:

---

[639] *Vital Records of Topsfield, Massachusetts to the end of the year 1849,* 177.

[640] Ibid., 11.

[641] Cemetery Marker, Westminster (Vt.) Old East Parish Cemetery.

[642] George Francis Dow, *History of Topsfield* (Topsfield, 1940), 137, 299, 351.

[643] A. M. Hemenway, ed., *Vermont Historical Gazetteer* 5 vols. (Burlington, Vt., 1868-91) 5 [1891]: 588-89, 619.

[644] Information about births and Ruth's baptism is from *Vital Records of Topsfield, Massachusetts to the end of the year 1849,* 87; information about other baptisms is in Avery, *The Averell-Averill-Avery Family,* 1: 194.

The bride concealed herself in some place where there was absolute privacy, stripped herself of everything given her by her late husband, and her marriage ceremony was performed with their hands meeting outside the place of concealment. She then clothed herself in attire provided by her new husband, and thus evaded the responsibility for the debts of his predecessor.[645]

    ii.   MARY PHIPPEN b. 3 July 1740; bp. at Christ Church 12 Oct. 1746; m. JOHN PETTY.

37   iii.   SAMUEL PHIPPEN, b. 20 Jan. 1742/43; bp. at Christ Church 12 Oct. 1746.

38   iv.   JOSEPH PHIPPEN, b. 21 April 1745; bp. at Christ Church 12 Oct. 1746.

    v.   HANNAH PHIPPEN, b. 4, bp. 13 Dec. 1747.

    vi.   MEHITABLE PHIPPEN, b. 19, bp. 22 April 1750.

    vii.   SARAH PHIPPEN, b. 10, bp. 16 Sept. 1753.

    viii.   RUTH PHIPPEN, bp. 9 Nov. 1755; d. at Topsfield 15 June 1757.[646]

39   ix.   JONATHAN ATWATER PHIPPEN, b. 15, bp. 21 May 1758.

26. JOHN[5] PHIPPEN (*John[4]*, *Samuel[3]*, *Joseph[2]*, *David[1]*) was baptized at Salem, Massachusetts 15 March 1719, son of John and Elizabeth (Hartshorn) Phippen.[647] He married at Salem 10 December 1742, **HANNAH HOOPER**,[648] who was baptized 18 September 1720, daughter of Charles and Hannah (Neal) Hooper.[649] He died late in 1760; administration of his estate was granted on 2 January 1761 to Hannah Phippen, widow; Jonathan Very, cordwainer; and David Phippen, joiner, all of Salem.[650]

Children of John and Hannah (Hooper) Phippen, born at Salem:[651]

    i.   ABIGAIL[6] PHIPPEN, b. about 1744; m. at Salem 9 Aug 1762, Capt. BENJAMIN WEST,[652] who was bp. 14 Jan. 1738/39, son of John and

---

645 Avery, *The Averell-Averill-Avery Family*, 1: 296

646 Ibid.; *Vital Records of Topsfield, Massachusetts to the end of the year 1849*, 245.

647 *Vital Records of Salem, Massachusetts to the end of the year 1849*, 2: 167.

648 Ibid., 3: 517, 4: 189.

649 Ibid., 1: 449.

650 Essex County Probate Records, file no. 21751.

651 Perley, *The History of Salem, Massachusetts*, 2: 329 (births of Abigail, Hannah, Elizabeth; information about Samuel); *Vital Records of Salem, Massachusetts to the end of the year 1849*, 2: 169 (birth of Susannah).

652 *Vital Records of Salem, Massachusetts to the end of the year 1849*, 4: 189, 453.

Mary (Dean) West.[653] Benjamin West d. 22 March 1809, aged 70 years.[654] Abigail West d. 1 Dec. 1797.[655] (The marriage record gives her name as Hannah, while the marriage intention gives it as Abigail.)

    ii. HANNAH PHIPPEN, b. about 1746; d. 14 Jan. 1816, aged 70 years, of "numb palsy";[656] m. at Salem 22 March 1767, WILLIAM MATTHEWS,[657] who d. at sea on board the schooner Alice in July 1793.[658]

    iii. SAMUEL PHIPPEN, b. about 1748; living in 1761; no further information.

    iv. ELIZABETH PHIPPEN, b. about 1750.

    v. SUSANNAH PHIPPEN, b. 19 Dec. 1751; m. at Salem 25 July 1773, THOMAS HOVEY.[659]

27. NATHANIEL[5] **PHIPPEN** (*Nathaniel*[4], *Samuel*[3], *Joseph*[2], *David*[1]) was born at Salem, Massachusetts 5 July 1711, son of Nathaniel and Margaret (Palfrey) Phippen.[660] He was living in Boston in 1745 and 1747. He returned to Salem, where he was a cooper, the trade of his father.[661] He died after 1749, when he was in Boston, and before 18 February 1755, when his own father died.[662] His father's will made the following bequest:

> I having advanc'd to my son Nathanael in his lifetime, one hundred pounds two shillings, being the Balance of his account with me; I hereby Give to Joshua, Hardy, Joseph & Seath, the Children and legal Representatives of the sd Nathanael, so much of my Estate as (the sd sum being accounted as part) will amount to One full seventh part of my whole Estate, and no more, to be equally Divided among them & their Heirs.[663]

---

[653] Ibid., 2: 410.
[654] Ibid., 6: 322.
[655] Ibid., 6: 322 (gives her age as 50, yielding approximate birth year of 1747).
[656] Ibid., 6: 61.
[657] Ibid., 4: 76, 189.
[658] Ibid., 6: 62.
[659] Ibid., 3: 521, 4: 191.
[660] Ibid., 2: 168.
[661] Perley, *The History of Salem, Massachusetts*, 2: 329.
[662] *Vital Records of Salem, Massachusetts to the end of the year 1849*, 6: 138.
[663] Essex Probate Records, no. 21760 (Nathaniel's will), no. 21747 (later guardianship of three youngest children).

Nathaniel Phippen married at Salem 16 October 1734, SEETH HARDY,[664] who was born at Salem 7 February 1712/13, daughter of Joseph and Sarah (Pickering) Hardy.[665] Seeth died 26 September 1755.[666]

Children of Nathaniel and Seeth (Hardy) Phippen, born at Salem: [667]

    i.   SEETH[6] PHIPPEN, b. 12 Jan. 1736; m. at Salem 17 Feb. 1754, as his second wife, THOMAS NEEDHAM,[668] who was bp. at Salem 27 Oct. 1728, son of George and Rachel (Gould) Needham.[669] Thomas had m. (1) at Salem 13 July 1751, MARY TWIST; he m. (3) at Salem 4 Aug. 1779, LYDIA LEFAVOUR.[670]

40   ii.   HARDY PHIPPEN, b. 25 Feb. 1740. On 13 July 1759 he was of Marblehead, Mass., "upward of 14 years of age," and had his uncle Israel[5] Phippen appointed as guardian.

41   iii.   JOSHUA PHIPPEN, b. 27 Jan. 1742.[671] On 13 July 1759 he was of Danvers, Mass., "upward of 14 years of age," and chose Benjamin Ropes as his guardian.[672]

    iv.   JOSEPH PHIPPEN, b. 15 March 1747.[673] On 13 July 1759 he was listed as under 14 years of age when Benjamin Ropes was appointed his guardian. He was a shipmaster of Salem and of Danvers in 1759. He was lost at sea 12 May 1783 while making passage from Virginia.[674]

---

[664] *Vital Records of Salem, Massachusetts to the end of the year 1849,* 3: 467, 4: 190. Another record gives the marriage date as 16 Oct. 1736, which seems unlikely with the birth of daughter Seeth on 12 Jan. 1736.

[665] Harrison Ellery and Charles P. Bowditch, *The Pickering Genealogy: being an account of the first three generations of the Pickering family of Salem, Mass.,* 3 vols. (Cambridge, Mass., 1897), 1: 104; *Vital Records of Salem, Massachusetts to the end of the year 1849,* 1: 404.

[666] H. Claude and Edwin Noah Hardy, *Hardy and Hardie: Past and Present* (Concord, N.H., 1977), 1002.

[667] Notes of John Fipphen on the George D. Phippen manuscript.

[668] *Vital Records of Salem, Massachusetts to the end of the year 1849,* 4: 116, 191.

[669] Ibid., 2: 99.

[670] Ibid., 4: 116.

[671] The guardianship appointments for Hardy, Joshua and Joseph are in Essex Probate Records, no. 21747.

[672] *Vital Records of Salem, Massachusetts to the end of the year 1849,* 2: 167.

[673] His grave, at the Charter Street Burial Ground in Salem, states that he was 24 years of age at death, yielding an approximate birth year of 1759. Perley, "Charter Street Burial Ground Inscriptions," *Essex Institute Historical Collections* 13 [1877]: 108. The gravestone states that he died 11 May 1783.

[674] Ellery and Bowditch, *The Pickering Genealogy,* 1: 212; William Leavitt, "History of the Essex Lodge of Freemasons," *Essex Institute Historical Collections* 3 [1861]: 126. The Lodge record states his year of birth as 1750.

28. DAVID⁵ PHIPPEN (*Nathaniel⁴, Samuel³, Joseph², David¹*) was born at Salem, Massachusetts 18 September 1715, son of Nathaniel and Margaret (Palfrey) Phippen.[675] He was baptized 25 September 1715 at the First Church in Salem.[676] He died, a widower, at Salem 15 February 1782, aged 65 years.[677]

David Phippen married at Salem (intentions published 4 March 1737[/38])[678] 24 May 1738, **PRISCILLA BICKFORD,**[679] daughter of John and Rebecca (Pinson) Bickford of Reading, Massachusetts.[680] She died 16 April 1781.[681]

A joiner by trade, David Phippen was prominent in Salem affairs. He served as a selectman in 1767, as town clerk in 1780, as assessor from 1779 to 1781, and as surveyor of boards from 1775 to 1781.[682] He was also deacon of the East Parish Church in Salem and is often referred to as "Deacon David Phippen." David Phippen was also a member of the Salem fire club before 1766.[683]

David Phippen appears to have been wealthy and made several substantial property transactions. On 27 January 1740, Sarah Montgomery conveyed a house and land on Lowder's Lane (later Elm Street) to David Phippen for £65. Deacon Phippen apparently removed the house shortly afterward. This lot was adjacent to the house and land formerly owned by Samuel³ Phippen.[684] In 1762, David Phippen, with the consent of his wife Priscilla, sold to Richard Derby of Salem two

---

[675] *Vital Records of Salem, Massachusetts to the end of the year 1849,* 2: 166.

[676] Pierce, *Salem First Church Records,* 55; Walter Beadle, *Samuel Beadle Family* (Wilmington, Del., 1970), 117 (a facsimile of the hand¬written baptismal record from the First Church in Salem, Mass.).

[677] *Vital Records of Salem, Massachusetts to the end of the year 1849,* 6: 137. See also, *The Salem Gazette,* 21 Feb. 1782. His death notice stated: "Died, on Friday last, Deacon DAVID PHIPPEN of this town, in the 66th year of his age."

[678] *Publishments of the Intentions of Marriage of the Town of Salem,* __ vols. (Salem, 1891), 1: 22.

[679] *Vital Records of Salem, Massachusetts to the end of the year 1849,* 3: 109, 4: 189; *Vital Records of Reading, Massachusetts to the end of the year 1849,* 286, 418.

[680] The 1808 Phippen chart states her date of birth as 8 Aug. 1719; the published Salem Vital Records contain a baptism record for "Priscilla, d. John, bp. Sept. 7, 1718" (*Vital Records of Salem, Massachusetts to the end of the year 1849,* 1: 92). Perley provides a third date, 8 August 1717. See "Beckford-Bickford Genealogy," *Essex Antiquarian* 8 [1904]: 60–64 at 60.

[681] 1808 Phippen chart.

[682] Essex County, Massachusetts officers and committees 1775–1783.

[683] James Duncan Phillips, *Salem in the Eighteenth Century* (Salem, 1937), 190-91.

[684] Perley, "Salem in 1700. No. 26," *Essex Antiquarian* 11 [1907]: 12–21 at 15–16; Essex Deeds 81: 104.

parcels of land in Salem located at the head of Union or Long Wharf, giving Derby control over prime Salem wharf property. The property description refers to "Phippen's Wharf."[685] On 14 March 1763, Joseph Trask of Salem, mariner, for £53 6s 8d, conveyed a house and lot in Salem to David Phippen of Salem, gentleman.[686] On 25 December 1769, David Phippen, for £83 6s 8d, conveyed the house and lot to widow Priscilla Hodges of Salem.[687] The house was gone before 1807.[688]

David Phippen was one of the signatories to a July 1768 document protesting a vote of the Salem town meeting to support a vote in the Massachusetts House of Representatives declining to rescind a January 1768 resolution urging the other colonies to join in a petition to the King.[689]

On June 21, 1774, David Phippen and other members of the "patriot party" in Salem signed an address to Thomas Gage, the royal governor of Massachusetts, rejecting the idea that Salem should benefit by the closing of the port of Boston as the result of the enactment of the Boston Port Act, one of the "Intolerable Acts."[690]

On 18 May 1776, David Phippen, John Fisk (his son-in-law), and Richard Derby Jr., Esq., all of Salem, gave a bond for £2,000 for the Massachusetts Sloop *Tyrannicide*, which was a privateer commissioned by order of the Massachusetts General Court to cruise along the coasts of America for defense of the seacoast and to capture British ships and cargoes during the Revolutionary War.[691] Captain John Fisk was the ship's commander. The *Tyrannicide* was the first of two vessels commissioned by the Massachusetts Bay Colony as state vessels of war. Owned by Richard Cabot, the vessel was described as modest but with a formidable name. In June 1776, the Yankee craft, which apparently mounted fourteen guns and had a crew of about one hundred men, captured a cutter bound from Halifax to New York with important documents and materials on board. During the same cruise, on 13 June

---

[685] James Duncan Phillips, *The Life and Times of Richard Derby, merchant of Salem, 1712–1783,* (Cambridge, 1929), 68–70; Phillips, "Derby Wills and Land Titles," Essex Institute Historical Collections 66 [1930]: 68–70.

[686] Perley, "Salem in 1700. No. 15," *Essex Antiquarian* 8 [1904]: 66–78, at 72; Essex Deeds 111:167.

[687] Perley, "Salem in 1700. No. 15," *Essex Antiquarian* 8 [1904]: 72; Essex Deeds 127:41.

[688] Perley, "Salem in 1700. No. 15," *Essex Antiquarian* 8 [1904]: 72.

[689] Phillips, *Salem in the Eighteenth Century,* 293–95.

[690] Ibid., 321–27. *See also The Essex Gazette,* 14–21 June 1774. The petition was also signed by Atwater Phippen, Samuel Phippen, and David Phippen's son-in-law John Fiske.

[691] William Bell Clark, ed., *Naval Documents of the American Revolution,* 11 vols. to date (Washington, D.C., 1964–), 5: 140–41.

1776, the *Tyrannicide*, following an hour-long battle, captured the British packet schooner *Despatch* after her master, Captain Gutteridge, had been killed. The *Despatch* was carrying eight carriage and twelve swivel guns and thirty-one men. In July 1776, the ship captured the British armed ship *Glasgow*, and the following month took the brig *St. John* and the schooner *Three Brothers*. In 1777, the *Tyrannicide*, with the brig *Massachusetts*, captured the bark *Lawnshade*. On 29 March 1779, when off Bermuda, she fought and captured the British brig *Revenge*, which carried fourteen guns and eighty-five men. The gallant *Tyrannicide* was caught in the Penobscot Bay fiasco of 14 August 1779, the largest naval operation undertaken by the Americans during the war. The ship was burned to prevent capture by the British.[692]

David Phippen's will, written 17 November 1781 and probated 4 March 1782, is as follows:

> In the Name of God Amen this 17th day of November AD 1781. I David Phippen of Salem in the County of Essex and State of Massachusetts bay in New England Gentleman being weak in Body but through God's goodness of perfect mind and Memory; considering the mortality of my Body and that it is appointed unto all Men once to die. Do now make and ordain this my last Will and Testament. In the first place I commit my Soul unto the hands of God who gave it, and my Body to the Earth to be buried in a decent Christian manner. And as to that Worldly Estate which it hath pleased God to Bless me, I give demise and dispose of in the manner following.
>
> After my Funeral Charges and all my just Debts are paid the Remainder of my Estate both Real and Personal I give to my Children to be Equally divided between them Viz: Samuel Ebenezer Nathaniel Priscilla Lydia Margaret Anstis Sarah & Rebecca. Finally I hereby Constitute and Appoint my Son Ebenezer Phippen Executor of this my last Will & Testament, be it remembered that each Child is to account for what they have received of me.
>
> Signed Sealed Published and pronounc'd & delivered by the said David Phippen as his last Will and Testament in presence of Ab^m Watson, Henry Skerry, John Archer Junr.[693]

---

[692] Edgar Stanton Maclay, *A History of American Privateers,* (New York, 1899), 139-41.

[693] Essex Probate Records, file no. 21745.

Deacon Phippen's estate was valued at £2,277 12s. The estate included his "Mansion House and barn with 35 poles of land" (£1,000) and "[t]he Shop with the Wharf and Land being about 19 poles, having an incumbrance of a cartway out to Capt. Derby's Wharf" (£360). The estate also included "One large Frame, containing the Genealogy of y^e: Phippen Family."[694]

The genealogy of the Phippen family in David Phippen's estate was commissioned by him in 1768 and was done by Salem schoolmaster and heraldic painter James Ford. The now lost 1768 genealogy was the basis for the 1808 chart commissioned by the husband of his daughter Anstis (Phippen) Smith. The 1808 chart states the following information for David Phippen: "David Phippen 2. Son of Nathl. Born 10th Sept. 1710. Married 4th May 1738. Left issue David, Stepn, Priscilla, Saml, Lydia, Margt, Ebenr, Margt, Anstis, Sarah, Nathl, Rebecca, Elizath. By-Priscilla Beckford Born August 8th 1719. Died April 16th 1781. Her Husband died February 15th 1782. ~"

Children of David and Priscilla (Bickford) Phippen, born presumably at Salem:[695]

    i.   DAVID[6] PHIPPEN, b. 17 June 1739; d. 25 Feb. 1761, aged 21 years, of smallpox. David Phipen, Jun'r was a member of Capt. Goodhue's Company in the French and Indian War, and was paid £10 for his service in the expedition to Canada in 1757.[696]

    ii. STEPHEN PHIPPEN, b. 22 Jan. 1741; m. at Salem 29 Oct. 1767, REBECCA PALFREY.[697] The 1808 Phippen chart states that they had children, but none have been identified. He was a cabinetmaker, living in Salem.[698] He died before 2 Aug. 1774, when administration of the estate of Stephen Phippen of Salem, cabinetmaker, was granted to David Phippen, gentleman (his father). After the death of his father David, administration of the estate passed to his brother Ebenezer on 6 Dec. 1782.[699] The 1808 Phippen chart states: "Stephn Phippen Born 22d January 1741. Married 29. October 1767. issue ___ By-Reba Palfray. Born 17th Octr 1746."

694 Essex Probate Records, file no. 21745.

695 The information on the children is from the 1808 Phippen chart and the notes of John Fipphen on the George D. Phippen manuscript. The birth records, with one exception, do not appear in the published Salem vital records.

696 Phillips, *Salem in the Eighteenth Century,* 209–10.

697 *Vital Records of Salem, Massachusetts to the end of the year 1849,* 4: 153, 191.

698 Ethel Hall Bjerkoe, *The Cabinetmakers of America* (Garden City, N.Y., 1957), 170.

699 Essex Probate Records, file no. 21769.

iii. PRISCILLA PHIPPEN, b. 8 Jan. 1743; she m. at Salem 5 Oct. 1768, JOHN
GILL[700]. Priscilla Gill d. at Salem 24 April 1826, aged 84 years.[701] The
1808 Phippen chart states: "John Gill Born ___ Married October
5. 1768. Had issue Elizabeth, Prisc., John, Sarah Phippen, Ann. by –
Prisc Phippen born January 8. 1743."

42   iv. SAMUEL PHIPPEN, b. 28 Dec. 1745.

v. LYDIA[6] PHIPPEN, b. 10 Jan. 1747;[702] m. at Salem 12 June 1766, Capt.
(later Gen.) JOHN FISKE.[703] John Fiske was a distinguished citizen
of Salem. He was a sea captain, commander of the *Tyrannicide* and
the *Massachusetts* during the Revolution, a major-general in the
militia, and after the war, a successful Salem merchant.[704] As a young
married woman, Lydia (Phippen) Fiske sat for a pastel portrait by
artist Benjamin Blyth (see Plate VIII). This portrait was acquired
by the Essex Institute of Salem in 1913. Lydia (Phippen) Fiske d.
at Salem 13 Oct. 1782.[705] John Fiske m. (2) at Manchester, Mass. 11
Feb. 1783, Martha (Lee) Hibbert of Manchester, widow of Capt.
Jeremiah Hibbert.[706] She d. at Salem 30 Nov. 1785, age 32 years. [707]
John Fiske m. (3) at Marblehead 18 June 1786, Sarah (Wendall)
Gerry of Marblehead, widow of John Gerry.[708] John Fiske d. at
Salem 28 Sept. 1797.[709] His third wife survived him and died in
Feb. 1804, aged 59 years.[710]

Their large family is recorded in John Fiske's Bible, which was
published by Eben Putnam in *Genealogical Magazine* in 1916,
along with a plate of Lydia (Phippen) Fiske's portrait.[711] The 1808

---

[700] *Vital Records of Salem, Massachusetts to the end of the year 1849,* 3: 417, 4: 190.

[701] Ibid., 5: 280.

[702] *The Vital Records of Salem, Massachusetts to the end of the year 1849,* 2: 167, show the
date as 7 Jan. 1747.

[703] Ibid., 3: 361; 4: 190.

[704] For more detailed biographical information on General Fiske, *see* James Duncan
Phillips, *Salem and the Indies; The Story of the Great Commercial Era of the City* (Boston,
1947), 86–88, and Frederick C. Pierce, *Fiske and Fisk Family* (Chicago, 1896), 82,
102–4.

[705] *Vital Records of Salem, Massachusetts to the end of the year 1849,* 5: 248.

[706] Ibid., 3: 361.

[707] Ibid., 5: 248.

[708] Ibid., 3: 361.

[709] Ibid., 5: 248.

[710] Ibid., 5: 248.

[711] See Eben Putnam, "Maternal Line of Ancestry of Lydia (Phippen) Fisk," *Genealogical
Magazine* 3 [1916]: 185 and plate opposite; and "Records from Family Bibles: Bible
of General John Fisk, 1744–1808," *Genealogical Magazine* 3: 186–87. The portrait is
owned by the Peabody Essex Museum of Salem, Mass., but its current whereabouts
have not been ascertained.

Phippen chart states: "John Fisk Born 30 April 1744. Married June 12. 1766. Had issue Lydia, Ann, Sarah, Margat, Betsy, John, Saml and Priscilla. By – Lydia Phippen Born January 10. 1747. Died October 13. 1782. John Fisk died Sept. 28. 1797.~"

  vi. MARGARET PHIPPEN, b. 7 Jan. 1749; d. 13 Feb. 1749.

43 vii. EBENEZER PHIPPEN, b. 13 Jan. 1750.

  viii. MARGARET PHIPPEN, b. 28 March 1752; d. unm. 23 April 1842, aged 90 years.[712]

  ix. ANSTIS PHIPPEN, b. 13 Feb. 1755; m. at Salem 6 Sept. 1789, JONATHAN SMITH,[713] who was bp. at Salem 8 Jan. 1764, son of George and Hannah (Bickford) Smith.[714] Anstis (Phippen) Smith died at Salem 28 Nov. 1815, aged 60, after what appears to have been a difficult illness.[715] The Rev. William Bentley wrote in his diary for 1 Dec. 1815:

> This is the most remarkable case of Dropsy I have known. She has been tapped 26 times & had discharged 83 gallons. The returns were every fortnight for the last part of the time. She was not a woman of large system nor very full habit. She married at full age & never had any children. Her reputation good.[716]

The elaborate 1808 Phippen chart was made for Jonathan and Anstis (Phippen) Smith (see Plate IV). Anstis (Phippen) Smith died childless, and when Jonathan Smith married again, at Salem, 19 May 1816, to SARAH H. LEACH, daughter of John and Sarah Leach,[717] he added the information on his second wife to the chart (see Plate VII). Jonathan Smith died 11 Sept. 1840, aged 76.[718]

  x. SARAH PHIPPEN, b. 7 April 1756; m. (1) at Salem 28 May 1780, Capt. SAMUEL HOBBES,[719] who was bp. at Salem 15 Oct. 1758, son of John and Elizabeth (___) Hobbes. Sarah m. (2) at Middleton, Mass. (int. dated 13 Nov. 1784, SAMUEL SYMONDS of Middleton,[720]

---

[712] *Vital Records of Salem, Massachusetts to the end of the year 1849,* 6: 138.

[713] Ibid., 4: 188, 324.

[714] Ibid., 2: 302.

[715] Ibid., 6: 232. Notice of her death appeared in the 30 Nov. 1815 issue of the *Salem Gazette.*

[716] *The Diary of William Bentley,* 4: 363.

[717] *Vital Records of Salem, Massachusetts to the end of the year 1849,* 3: 596, 4: 324.

[718] Ibid., 6: 235

[719] Ibid., 3: 503, 4: 191. The 1808 Phippen chart states the date as 27 May 1780.

[720] *Vital Records of Salem, Massachusetts to the end of the year 1849,* 3: 504; *Vital Records of Middleton, Massachusetts to the end of the year 1849* (Topsfield, Mass., 1904), 87, 111.

who was b. there 28 Feb. 1756, son of Samuel and Lydia (Perkins) Symonds.[721] The 1808 Phippen chart states: "Saml Hobbs Born Sept. 17th 1750. Was kill'd in the American War August 29. 1781. Left issue Sarah; Born April 15. 1782. By – Sarah Phippen. Born 7 April 1756. Married May 27. 1780. She was afterward married to Samuel Symonds had issue Saml Jr, Catherine, John, Lydia, Eliza, Nathl."

44   xi.   NATHANIEL PHIPPEN, b. 18 May 1758.

      xii. REBECCA PHIPPEN, b. 19 Dec. 1759; m. at Salem 10 March 1785, WILLIAM KING,[722] son of William and Anstis (Crowninshield) King.[723] William King was a craftsman in Salem, and later, by 1805, an itinerant profilist.[724] He was also apparently unable to establish himself in his native Salem. The following colorful description of King appeared in *Antiques* in 1927:

> William....perhaps by spontaneous divergence from the family type, seems to have manifested many characteristics of the migratory tumble-weed. He was, in short, a vagabond. He is first mentioned in Bentley's diary, November 20, 1787, when it is noted that, after having been absent in the West Indies, 'William King about four years ago returned and married a daughter of Deacon Phippen, by whom he had one child and prospect of another.' Apparently this prospect proved uncongenial to William. He unceremoniously deserted his family and, leaving a letter declaring his 'intention to abscond,' made off as swiftly as a horse and sulky, purloined from a neighbor, would carry him.[725]

King was apprehended in East Haven, Conn., and returned to his family in Salem.[726] On 6 July 1796, William Bentley noted in his diary:

> News from Philadelphia, that Wm King, belonging to a good family in this Town, after having dragged his family from Town to Town, left a note that he was going to drown

---

[721] *Vital Records of Middleton, Massachusetts to the end of the year 1849,* 53.

[722] *Vital Records of Salem, Massachusetts to the end of the year 1849,* 3: 573, 4: 190.

[723] Harriet Ruth Waters Cooke, *The Driver Family: A Genealogical Memoir of the Descendants of Robert and Phebe Driver* (New York, 1889), 237.

[724] D. Brenton Simons, "New England Silhouettes: Profile Portraits ca. 1790-1850," NEXUS 9 [1992]: 100-6 at 105-6.

[725] [Unsigned], "The Serpent Bests William King," *Antiques* 12 [1927]: 202.

[726] *The Diary of William Bentley,* 1: 81.

himself & disappeared. It is supposed that he means to ramble unincumbered. The family are to return to Salem.[727]

William apparently deserted his family again; he was in Portsmouth briefly in 1805, and in 1806, he was advertising in Hanover, N.H. He may have headed to a southern state at some point in his travels. His fate is unknown. William and Rebecca had six children, including NATHANIEL PHIPPEN[7] KING (1796–1819), also a Salem craftsman. Rebecca (Phippen) King moved to Boston, and died there on 5 Jan. 1839.[728] The 1808 Phippen chart states: "William King Born ___ Married ___ Had issue Betsy, William, Lydia, Nathaniel, Hannah, Nathaniel, Rufus, Mary, Rebecca. By – Rebecca Phippen Born December 19. 1759.~"

    xiii. ELIZABETH PHIPPEN, b. 9 Feb. 1763; d. 31 March 1766.[729]

29. ISRAEL[5] **PHIPPEN** (*Nathaniel*[4], *Samuel*[3], *Joseph*[2], *David*[1]) was baptized at Salem, Massachusetts 17 July 1720, son of Nathaniel and Margaret (Palfrey) Phippen.[730] He was dead by 8 December 1767, when his brother David Phippen was granted administration of the estate of Israel Phippen of Marblehead, Massachusetts.[731]

Israel Phippen married at Salem 11 April 1745, **ELIZABETH TREVITT**.[732] He was a merchant in Marblehead.[733]

Children of Israel and Elizabeth (Trevitt) Phippen, born at Marblehead:[734]

    i. ELIZABETH[6] PHIPPEN, b. and d. same day.

    ii. ISRAEL PHIPPEN, bp. 21 Sept. 1746; apparently d. young.

    iii. ISRAEL PHIPPEN, bp. 22 Oct. 1751.

    iv. MARTHA PHIPPEN, bp. 7 July 1754; m. at Salem 7 Nov. 1791, ATWATER[5] PHIPPEN, son of Samuel[4] Phippen [No. 17].[735]

---

[727] *The Diary of William Bentley*, 2: 191.

[728] *Vital Records of Salem, Massachusetts to the end of the year 1849*, 1: 91–94; Ethel Hall Bjerkoe, *The Cabinetmakers of America* (Garden City, N.Y., 1957), 138; Simons, "New England Silhouettes," *NEXUS* 9 [1992]: 106.

[729] 1808 Phippen chart.

[730] *Vital Records of Salem, Massachusetts to the end of the year 1849*, 2: 166.

[731] Essex Probate Records, no. 21479.

[732] *Vital Records of Salem, Massachusetts to the end of the year 1849*, 4: 189, 399.

[733] Perley, *The History of Salem, Massachusetts*, 2: 328.

[734] Unless noted otherwise, information about children is from *Vital Records of Marblehead, Massachusetts to the end of the year 1849*, 3 vols. (Salem, Mass., 1903–8), 1: 396.

[735] *Vital Records of Salem, Massachusetts to the end of the year 1849*, 4: 188, 190.

30. THOMAS[5] **PHIPPEN** (*Nathaniel*[4], *Samuel*[3], *Joseph*[2], *David*[1]) was baptized at Salem, Massachusetts 17 January 1730/31, son of Nathaniel and Margaret (Palfrey) Phippen.[736] He died about 1793.[737] He married, first, at Salem 2 November 1749, **MARGARET DRIVER**,[738] who was baptized there 7 February 1724/25, daughter of Thomas and Mary (Ingalls) Driver.[739] Margaret died between the birth of her last child (baptized in April 1763) and April 1766, when Thomas married, second, at Salem 12 April 1766, **SARAH (INGALLS) SMITH**, widow of John Smith.[740] John Smith had married Sarah Ingalls at Salem 7 August 1755.[741] Sarah was blind for many years. On 26 December 1798, the Rev. William Bentley noted in his diary, "Blind Mrs Phippen is to be buried today."[742] Thomas Phippen was a cooper in Salem.

On March 25, 1765, Thomas Phippen sold to David Phippen his mansion house bounded on the west by Louder's Lane.[743]

On 17 December 1793, Sarah Phippen, widow, sold land in Marblehead, Massachusetts, called "Ingalls Farm," to Samuel Sewall of Marblehead.[744]

Children of Thomas and Margaret (Driver) Phippen, born at Salem:[745]

45   i.   THOMAS[6] PHIPPEN, bp. 1 March 1752.

46   ii.   WILLIAM PHIPPEN, b. 27 Feb. 1752/53, bp. 1 March 1752[/53].

       iii. JAMES PHIPPEN, bp. 21 April 1754; d. at Salem 10 April 1756, aged 2 years.[746]

       iv. JAMES PHIPPEN, bp. 13 April 1760; drowned in 1770.[747]

       v.   CHILD PHIPPEN, bp. 17 April 1763.

---

[736] Ibid., 2: 169; Perley, *The History of Salem, Massachusetts,* 2: 328.

[737] Perley, *The History of Salem, Massachusetts,* 2: 328.

[738] *Vital Records of Salem, Massachusetts to the end of the year 1849,* 3: 315, 4: 191.

[739] Ibid., 1: 265.

[740] Ibid., 4: 191.

[741] Ibid., 3: 526, 4: 323.

[742] *The Diary of William Bentley,* 2: 290.

[743] Cooke, *The Driver Family,* 90.

[744] Ibid.

[745] Unless noted otherwise, information about children is from *Vital Records of Salem, Massachusetts to the end of the year 1849,* 2: 166, 169.

[746] Ibid., 6:137.

[747] Cooke, *The Driver Family,* 90.

Child of Thomas and Sarah (Ingalls) Phippen, born at Salem:

>   vi.   OLIVE PHIPPEN, bp. 19 April 1767;[748] d. at Salem 14 June 1802, aged
>   35 years, of scarlet fever.[749] Olive m. at Salem 2 March 1790, ISAAC
>   PERKINS, JR.,[750] who was bp. at Topsfield, Mass. 11 Jan. 1756, son of
>   Isaac and Elizabeth (Perkins) Perkins.[751] Isaac Perkins, Jr., m. (2) at
>   Salem 25 Feb. 1806, ANNA LEE,[752] who d. as his widow at Salem 29
>   Dec. 1831, aged 75.[753]

31. WILLIAM[5] **PHIPPEN** (*Joseph*[4], *Samuel*[3], *Joseph*[2], *David*[1]) was born at
Salem, Massachusetts 23 September 1721, son of Joseph and Susannah
(Hartshorn) Phippen.[754] He died in 1748.[755]

William Phippen married at Salem 4 April 1744, **ELIZABETH
BUSH,**[756] who was probably born at Salem about 1718, daughter of
Eastick Bush.[757] Elizabeth married, second, at Salem 27 June 1749,
SAMUEL BAGNEL.[758] She married, third, at Danvers, Massachusetts 26
July 1776, **JOHN MASURY,**[759] who was born at Salem 27 September
1715, son of John and Kezia (Woodbury) Masury. John Masury died
in Salem 28 September 1797, aged 82 years and "blind with age."[760]
Elizabeth (Bush) (Phippen) (Bagnel) Masury died at Salem 24 February
1812.[761] On that date William Bentley noted:

---

[748]   *Vital Records of Salem, Massachusetts to the end of the year 1849,* 2: 168; "Salem
        Baptisms," *Essex Institute Historical Collections* 22 [1885]: 245.

[749]   *Vital Records of Salem, Massachusetts to the end of the year 1849,* 6: 130; George
        Augustus Perkins, *The Family of John Perkins of Ipswich, Massachusetts,* 3 vols. (Salem,
        Mass., 1882–89), 2: 40.

[750]   *Vital Records of Salem, Massachusetts to the end of the year 1849,* 4:179, 190. (Perkins,
        The Family of John Perkins of Ipswich, Massachusetts, 2:40, says marriage date was 27
        March.)

[751]   *Vital Records of Topsfield, Massachusetts to the end of the year 1849,* 1: 80.

[752]   *Vital Records of Salem, Massachusetts to the end of the year 1849* 3: 599, 4: 178. (Perkins,
        The Family of John Perkins of Ipswich, Massachusetts, 2:40, says the marriage year was
        1805.)

[753]   *Vital Records of Salem, Massachusetts to the end of the year 1849,* 6: 128.

[754]   Ibid., 2: 169.

[755]   *The Diary of William Bentley,* 4: 85.

[756]   *Vital Records of Salem, Massachusetts to the end of the year 1849,* 3: 172, 4: 191.

[757]   Perley, *The History of Salem, Massachusetts,* 3: 33; *The Diary of William Bentley,* 4: 85,
        records that Elizabeth was born before 1718 and that she was 94 at her death.

[758]   *Vital Records of Salem, Massachusetts to the end of the year 1849* 3: 70, 4: 191.

[759]   Ibid., 3: 70, 4: 73.

[760]   Ibid., 2: 60; *The Diary of William Bentley,* 4: 85.

[761]   *Vital Records of Salem, Massachusetts to the end of the year 1849,* 6: 60. The record says,
        "Elizabeth (Bush), wid. John, formerly w. _____ Phippen and S. Bagnall Feb. 24
        1812, a 94 y." This age at death yields a birth year of 1718.

This day died Elizabeth Masury. She was a Bush & in 1744 married William Phippen, in 1749, Samuel Bagnel, & in 1776, John Masury. By the two first she had Children. Her husband Masury died in 1797, aet 82. This woman was born before the building of our Meeting House in 1718 & her age is given as 94. Her husband was blind many years & depended on her activity for his support. For several years she has been the charge of her daughter & and has had relief from friends & has been on our Parish list either herself or Husband since the Bills have been recorded in 1791 & what before is uncertain, surely above twenty years. Elizabeth lived with her first husband, W. Phippen, from 1744 to 1748, with her second, Thomas Bagnel, from 1749 to 1755, and with her third, John Masury, from 1776 to 1797, 21 years.[762]

Child of William[5] and Elizabeth (Bush) Phippen, born at Salem:

    i. ELIZABETH[6] PHIPPEN, b. before 1749; m. at Danvers 20 Dec. 1770, JOHN SWINERTON, JR.[763]

32. JOSEPH[5] PHIPPENEY (*Benjamin[4], James[3], Benjamin[2], David[1]*) was born at Stratford, Connecticut 11 June 1730, son of Benjamin and Rebecca (Bostwick) Phippeny.[764] Joseph Phippeny married 29 March 1759, **MEHITABLE ("MABEL") FAIRCHILD.**

By the time of the Revolution, this Joseph Phippeney had migrated to the Lake George region of New York. He appears to have been the Joseph "Phippany" who is said to have been the first settler, in 1784, of the area now incorporated as Dresden, Washington County, New York, at the foot of South Bay on Lake George.[765] He was enumerated in the 1800 census as living in Westfield in Washington County.[766]

Joseph Phippeney was of Putnam, Washington County, when he wrote his will 7 May 1810; it was recorded 24 May 1811 and probated

[762] *The Diary of William Bentley,* 4: 85.
[763] *Vital Records of Danvers, Massachusetts, to the End of the Year 1849,* 2 vols. (Salem, Mass., 1909–10), 2: 217, 284.
[764] Bostwick, *Genealogy of the Bostwick family in America,* 122–23.
[765] James Sullivan, ed., *History of New York State, 1523–1927,* 6 vols. (New York, 1927), vol. 3, chap. 3, based on the account in J. H. French, *Gazetteer of the State of New York* (Syracuse, N.Y., 1860).
[766] 1800 U.S. Census, Westfield, Washington Co., N.Y.

four days later.[767] The will names wife Mabel and two daughters
(Rebecca and Nobi) and their husbands; the two named daughters
were to inherit his farm in equal portions. Joseph had other children
alive at the time — including Eunice (Phippeny) Gilbert, although he
did not name the others in his will, as they were not living with or near
him. The will was witnessed by a Benjamin Phippeny, who, although no
relationship is stated, is likely either Joseph's brother Benjamin or the
latter's son (also named Benjamin), although he might also be David
Benjamin (see below).

Children of Joseph and Mehitabel (Fairchild) Phippeney (list
likely incomplete):

  i. EUNICE[6] PHIPPENEY, bp. at Unity Parish, Stratford, Conn. 23 March
      1760;[768] m. in March 1780, TRUMAN GILBERT; d. in Portage County,
      Ohio 17 Oct. 1840.[769] Not named in her father's will.

 ii. CHARITY PHIPPENEY, bp. at Unity Parish 15 Sept. 1765.[770]

iii. REBECCA PHIPPENEY; named in her father's will, with husband JOHN
      MCCLINTOK.

 iv. NOBI PHIPPENEY; named in her father's will, with husband JOHN
      MARTIN.

33. ARCHIBALD[5] **PHIPPENEY** (*Benjamin*[4], *James*[3], *Benjamin*[2], *David*[1]) was
born at Stratford, Connecticut 21 October 173[ ], son of Benjamin and
Rebecca (Bostwick) Phippeney; he died after 1810.[771] He was living in
New Milford, Connecticut, at the time of the 1790, 1800, and 1810
censuses[772]. Archibald married 9 May 1753, **CHARITY STRATTON** of
Stratford, second daughter of Thomas and Mary (Johnson) Stratton.
They lived in Stratford, Trumbull, and New Milford.[773]

---

767 Washington County, N.Y., Will Book 2, 354–55. Posted 17 March 2001 to
     Washington County, N.Y. message board on Ancestry.com by Robert Clemons.
768 Orcutt, *History of Stratford*, 2: 1267–68.
769 Homer W. Brainard, Harold S. Gilbert, and Clarence A. Torrey, *The Gilbert Family:
     Descendants of Thomas Gilbert* (New Haven, Conn., 1953), 225.
770 Orcutt, *History of Stratford*, 2: 1267–68.
771 "Stratford 1639-1840," *The Barbour Collection of Connecticut Town Vital Records*, vol.
     41, 205.
772 1790 U.S. Census, New Milford, Litchfield Co., Conn., p. 72.
773 Bostwick, *Genealogy of the Bostwick family in America*, 123; Orcutt, *History of Stratford*,
     2: 1267–68.

In 1768 Archibald Phippany appears to have run afoul of the law:

Whereas it is represented to this Assembly that Archibald Phipany, of Stratford in the county of Fairfield, was before the superior court held at Fairfield on the last Tuesday save one in February, 1768, duly convicted of counterfeiting the bills of credit of the Province of New York, by force of which conviction the estate of the said Phipany by writs of attachment served on the estate that belonged to the said Phipany demanding, as it is represented, greater damages than are justly due to the creditors; that four of said actions are now depending before Fairfield county court, and sundry judgments &c. have been rendered against him by justices of the peace, which judgments &c. have been satisfied out of said estate &c.: Whereupon this Assembly do appoint Gold Sellick Silliman, Esqr., of said Fairfield, who is hereby impowered and directed to examine into the matters aforesaid, and to make a reasonable and proper defence on the part of said Phipany in the actions depending against him as aforesaid, and to take all proper measures to make a reasonable and proper saving of the said estate for the benefit of this Colony, and make report of his doings therein to this Assembly at their next sessions.[774]

Children of Archibald and Charity (Stratton) Phippeney:[775]

  i. **NEHEMIAH**[6] **PHIPPENEY,** bp. 21 April 1754; d. in Oswego Co., N.Y. 16 Jan. 1839; m. 29 July 1784, **HANNAH TAYLOR** of Woodbury, Conn.[776] Nehemiah was a soldier in the Revolutionary War and subsequently a pensioner. He enlisted 22 April 1777 for eight months from New Milford as a private in Eleazer Warner's Company, Col. Herman Swift's Regiment in Connecticut, and saw service in the Battle of Brandywine. He was discharged 9 Jan. 1778.[777] Although he may have had children, none survived.

---

[774] *The Public Records of the Colony of Connecticut, from April 1636 to October 1776,* 15 vols. (Hartford, Conn., 1850–90), 13: 101.

[775] Bostwick, *Genealogy of the Bostwick family in America,* 123; Orcutt, History of Stratford, 2: 1267–68.

[776] Bailey, *Early Connecticut Marriages,* 3: 118.

[777] U.S. Revolutionary War Pension Application no. S14179.

He is probably the Nehemiah Phippeny listed in New Milford in the 1790 census, and in Aurelius, Cayuga Co., N.Y. in the 1810 census.[778]

    ii.   HULDAH PHIPPENEY, b. 2 June 1757.

    iii. CHARITY PHIPPENEY, b. 7 Sept. 1759.

47   iv. DAVID PHIPPENEY, b. in 1762.

    v.   CHARITY PHIPPENEY, b. in Aug. 1765; m. 6 Dec. 1785, JAMES BELL.

    vi. BENJAMIN PHIPPENEY, b. 9 Jan. 1767.

48   vii. ASAHEL PHIPPENEY, b. about 1772.[779]

   viii. DAUGHTER PHIPPENEY, bp. at New Milford 26 Aug. 1775.

    ix. ANN PHIPPENEY.

    x.   HANNAH PHIPPENEY.

49   xi. WILLIAM PHIPPENEY, b. say 1780.

34. BENJAMIN[5] PHIPPENEY (*Benjamin[4], James[3], Benjamin[2], David[1]*) was born at Stratford, Connecticut 9 June 1744, son of Benjamin and Rebecca (Bostwick) Phippen. He is very likely the "Benjamin Phippene Jr." who married at New Milford, Connecticut 23 September 1767, **HANNAH WELLER.**[780]

This Benjamin appears to be the Benjamin Phippeny (sometimes "Fippeny") enumerated in the 1790, 1800, and 1810 censuses for Rutland County, Vermont (1790 in Fair Haven, 1800 and 1810 in West Haven). He is shown as head of household with a wife and children, among whom may be the "D. B." or "David Benjamin" Phippeney listed below. In 1810, either Benjamin[5] or his son [David] Benjamin[6] witnessed the will of Joseph[5] Phippeney at Putnam in Washington County, New York.

Apparent child of Benjamin and perhaps Hannah (Weller) Phippeney:

50   i. DAVID BENJAMIN[6] PHIPPENEY.

---

[778] 1790 U.S. Census, New Milford, Litchfield Co., Conn., p. 14.

[779] Elizabeth P. Ellsberry, *Addison County, Vermont: Cemetery Records of New Haven* (Chillicothe, Mo., ca. 1965), vol. 3, online at *www.Ancestry.com.*

[780] Bailey, *Early Connecticut Marriages,* 3: 114.

35. James⁵ Phippeney (*James⁴⁻³*, *Benjamin²*, *David¹*) was born at Stratford, Connecticut in May 1743, son of James and Hannah (Smith) Phippeney. U.S. censuses from 1790 to 1820 indicate that he was living in New Milford, Connecticut, during that period. James married at New Milford 16 September 1772, **Rosannah Brownson**.[781]

Children of James and Rosannah (Brownson) Phippeney, born at New Milford: [782]

51   i.   Joel⁶ Phippeney, b. 7 Aug. 1773.

      ii.   Abigail Phippeney, b. 29 Jan. 1775; m. Thomas Davis of New Milford.

      iii. Esther Phippeney, b. 27 March 1777.

52   iv.   Peter Phippeney, b. 31 Jan. 1779.

      v.   Clotilda Phippeney, b. 6 Aug. 1782; d. at Washington, Conn. 10 Nov. 1847, aged 65 years.

36. Nehemiah⁵ Phippeney (*James⁴⁻³*, *Benjamin²*, *David¹*) was born at Stratford, Connecticut in March 1746, son of James and Hannah (Smith) Phippeney. He died at Fairfield, Connecticut 2 February 1809, aged 63 years.[783] He married, first, 14 February 1771, **Lydia Davis**, who was born 19 June 1735, daughter of Jabez Davis. He married, second, at Fairfield 14 June 1795, **Johanna Parmiter**. Johannah or "Hannah" (Parmiter) Phippeney died at Fairfield 14 May 1808, aged 65 years.[784] Nehemiah "Phipeny" is listed in the 1790 census as a resident of Fairfield.[785]

Children of Nehemiah and Lydia (Davis) Phippeney, born at Fairfield:

      i.   Hannah⁶ Phippeney, b. 13 Oct., bp. 29 Dec. 1771. Child, born out of wedlock: Julia-Ann⁷ Phippeney, b. at Fairfield 29 July 1807, m. John S. Cogswell.[786]

---

[781] "New Milford 1712-1860," *The Barbour Collection of Connecticut Town Vital Records*, vol. 30, 167; Orcutt, History of Stratford, 2: 1267–68.

[782] Ibid.

[783] Jacobus, *History and Genealogy of Families of Old Fairfield, Connecticut*, 763.

[784] Ibid.

[785] 1790 U.S. Census, Fairfield, Fairfield Co., Conn., Roll: M637_1, p. 29.

[786] White, Lorraine Cook, ed. "Fairfield 1639-1850," *The Barbour Collection of Connecticut Town Vital Records*, vol. 12 (Baltimore: Genealogical Publishing Co., 1998), 108.

    ii. EUNICE PHIPPENEY, bp. 3 July 1774.
   iii. DAVID PHIPPENEY, bp. 10 May 1778.
   iv. MARY PHIPPENEY, bp. 31 Aug. 1779.

CHAPTER 8

THE SIXTH GENERATION

37. SAMUEL[6] **PHIPPEN** (*Samuel*[5-3], *Joseph*[2], *David*[1]) was born at Topsfield, Massachusetts 20 January 1742/43 and baptized there 12 October 1746 with several of his siblings. He was the son of Samuel and Emma (Averill) Phippen. He died at Watertown, Jefferson County, New York 23 July 1820.[787] He lived for many years at Westminster, Vermont, where he married, 5 September 1784, **RUTH LANE.** She died at Watertown, New York 10 September 1839.

Samuel Phippen served in the French and Indian War, being listed in a group of men who enlisted at Topsfield on 18 February 1760 for "the total reduction of Canada."[788] According to his pension application file, he was a lieutenant in the Revolutionary War, in a company commanded by Capt. Azariah Wright. On the march to Quebec in September 1775, Captain Wright became ill with smallpox and Lieut. Phippen assumed command of the company. He also fought in the Battle of Stillwater. In 1781, he was with Captain Beck's company and then appointed lieutenant in Capt. Abner Seeley's company of Rangers. In a sworn deposition, John Goold stated that Samuel Phippen was the brother-in-law of Captain John Petty, and that Samuel served under Petty in 1777. He was also said to have been a lieutenant in Wait's Battalion of the Vermont militia during the Revolutionary War.[789]

On 20 December 1791, Samuel Phippen deeded to Samuel Phippen Jr. house lot no. 30 and lot no. 16 in the second range, on Main Street in the village of Westminster, Vermont.[790] His household was enumerated in Westminster, Windham County, in the 1790 and 1800 censuses. In 1808 he removed to Watertown in Jefferson County, New York.

---

[787] U.S. National Archives, Revolutionary War Pension Application file W19985.
[788] Dow, *History of Topsfield*, 173.
[789] All these data are taken from Revolutionary War Pension Application file W19985.
[790] Town clerk of Westminster, Vt., correspondence dated 17 December 1976.

Children of Samuel and Ruth (Lane) Phippen, born at Westminster:[791]

    i. SARAH[7] PHIPPEN, b. 2 Aug. 1783; m. JOHN SINCLAIR.

    ii. ZUBA PHIPPEN, b. Nov. 1785; m. WILLIAM MORSE.

53   iii. ASEPH PHIPPEN, b. 21 Aug. 1787.

    iv. SUSAN PHIPPEN, b. 30 May 1789; m. IRA URVIS.

    v. ENOS PHIPPEN, b. 31 March 1793; m. SUSAN STORY.

54   vi. HORATIO PHIPPEN, b. 18 Sept. 1796. (Horatio deposed that he was the sixth of his parents' children.)

    vii. AMELIA PHIPPEN, b. 22 Dec. 1799; d. in Aug. 1801, aged 2 years 7 months 13 days; bur. in Old East Parish Cemetery, Westminster.[792]

    viii AMELIA PHIPPEN, d. 24 July 1802.

    ix. CHESTER PHIPPEN, b. 11 July 1806; d. unm. at Hounsfield, N.Y. 25 July 1881, aged 79 years.

38. JOSEPH[6] **PHIPPEN** (*Samuel*[5-3,] *Joseph*[2], *David*[1]) was born at Topsfield, Massachusetts 21 April 1745, and baptized there 12 October 1746 with several of his siblings. He was the son of Samuel and Emma (Averill) Phippen. He died at Westminster, Vermont 17 May 1826.[793]

He lived in Lunenburg and then Northfield, both towns in Massachusetts, before he removed to Westminster, Vermont, by 1775. He served as a soldier in the Westminster militia in the Revolutionary War under Captain Azariah Wright.[794]

Joseph Phippen married, first, in 1777, **SILENCE PAUL,** known as Liley, who was born at Dighton, Massachusetts about 1758, daughter of James and Sarah (White) Paul.[795] He bought a farm among the hills in West Parish near the town of Rockingham, Vermont, about the time of his marriage. For many years he attended church with his wife and family at Saxton's River Village in that town.[796] He was a member of the Baptist Society at the time of its organization in 1784. Silence (Paul) Phippen died at Westminster 27 June 1822.[797]

---

[791] Notes of John Fipphen on George D. Phippen manuscript.

[792] Cemetery marker, Old East Parish Cemetery, Westminster, Vt.

[793] Vermont Vital Records.

[794] *DAR Patriot Index* 3; Hemenway, *Vermont Historical Gazetteer,* 5: 588.

[795] *Vital Records of Topsfield, Massachusetts to the end of the year 1849,* 2: 78.

[796] Edward J. Paul, "Notes on the American families of Paul or Paull," 6 vols. (Manuscript, 1897). Boston: New England Historic Genealogical Society, Mss 282 [hereafter Paul-Paull MS], 2: 78.

[797] Vermont Vital Records.

Joseph Phippen married, second, his sister-in-law **MARY PAUL**. He is buried in the West Parish beside his first wife, Silence, having had no children by his second marriage.[798]

Children of Joseph and Silence (Paul) Phippen, born at Westminster:[799]

55   i.   JOSEPH[7] PHIPPEN, b. 29 April 1780.

56   ii. BENJAMIN PHIPPEN, b. 6 Oct. 1781.

57   iii. JONATHAN PHIPPEN, b. 11 July 1783.

        iv. SILENCE ("LILEY") PHIPPEN, b. 25 March 1785; m. (1) _____ CROWELL; m. (2) SILAS PRATT; she d. at Newstead, N.Y. 21 Dec. 1870. Children by her first husband (surname *Crowell*): 1. *Hiram*; 2. *Bolinda*; 3. *Maria*; 4. *Miranda*. Children by her second husband (surname *Pratt*): 5. *Leonard*; 6. *Orvilla*; 7. *Julia*.

        v.   LUCY PHIPPEN, b. 5 Dec. 1786; m. JOHN WOOD, who was b. at Rockingham, Vt. In Aug. 1786, son of Barnabas and Sarah (Holt) Wood. They lived at Ira, Vt., where he was a farmer. She d. at Ira 27 Sept. 1828. Children (surname *Wood*): 1. *Joseph*; 2. *Anna*; 3. *Bezaleel*.

        vi. ZILPHA PHIPPEN, b. 8 March 1789; d. 5 April 1859; m. (1) DANIEL STRATTON; m. (2) JOB PARKHURST, who was b. 29 Nov. 1793, son of Lemuel and Anna (Wheeler) Parkhurst. Children by her first husband (surname *Stratton*): 1. *Isaac*, living at Westminister in 1885; 2. *Daniel*, living at Athens, Vt., in 1885; 3. *Miriam*. Children by her second husband (surname *Parkhurst*): 4. *Joseph Phippen,* d. at 11 years of age; 5. *Alvan*, b. at Westminster 14 Dec. 1828; 6. *Joseph Phippen.*

        vii. POLLY PHIPPEN, b. 29 Jan. 1791;[800] m. (1) LUCIUS CROWELL; m. (2) _____.

58   viii. ISAAC PHIPPEN, b. at Rockingham 15 Feb. 1793.

        ix. NANCY PHIPPEN, b. 25 March 1795; d. at Angelica, N.Y.; m. EDWARD DODD.

        x.   ANN PHIPPEN, b. 7 April 1797; d. unm. at Westminster in 1852.

59   xi. CALVIN PHIPPEN, b. 4 May 1799.

        xii. BETSEY PHIPPEN, b. 3 June 1801;[801] d. at Antwerp, N.Y. 8 Feb. 1894;[802] m. DALMANUTHA BENT, who was b. at Mount Holly, Vt. 5 Aug. 1801, son of David and Lucy (Fletcher) Bent; Dalmanutha d.

---

[798] Paul-Paull MS, 2: 78.

[799] Unless noted otherwise, data on children are from Paul-Paull MS, 2: 78, 79, 81.

[800] Vermont Vital Records.

[801] Allen H. Bent, *The Bent Family in America* (Boston, 1900), 150.

[802] Ibid.

at Antwerp, where they resided, 6 January 1883. Children (surname *Bent*): 1. *Curtis Rinaldo*, b. 23 Aug. 1820; 2. *Martha Jane*, b. 24 May 1822; 3. *Mary Eliza*, b. 29 June 1826; 4. *Erva Adeline*, b. 29 Dec. 1828; 5. *Matilda Eveline*, b. 5 May 1830; 6. *Esther Caroline*, b. 26 Sept. 1834; 7. *Hartwell Fletcher*, b. 9 May 1837; 8. *Lavilla Maria*, b. 25 June 1844.[803]

xiii.   HIRAM PHIPPEN, d. in infancy.[804]

39. JONATHAN ATWATER[6] **PHIPPEN** (*Samuel*[5–3], *Joseph*[2], *David*[1]) was born at Topsfield, Massachusetts 15 May 1758, son of Samuel and Emma (Averill) Phippen.[805] He died at Westminster, Vermont 26 July 1827, aged 69 years.[806] Jonathan settled at Westminster in Windham County, Vermont, in 1781.

He married, first, in 1785, **MARY "MOLLY" AVERILL,** daughter of Asa and Anna (Chaffee) Averill.[807] They settled on "Phippen Hill" not far from the farm of James Richardson.[808] Mary (Averill) Phippen died at Westminster 14 July 1807, aged 39 years.[809] Jonathan married, second, at Westminster 6 April 1808, **HANNAH WASHBURN,** who was born at Leicester, Massachusetts 5 June 1762, daughter of Seth and Mary (Harwood) Washburn.[810] She died at Westminster 24 July 1850, aged 88.[811]

Jonathan Phippen was a Revolutionary War soldier and a member of the Westminster militia company under Captain Azariah Wright in 1775.[812]

Children of Jonathan Atwater and Mary (Averill) Phippen, born at Westminster:

i.   ANNA[7] PHIPPEN, b. 15 April 1787;[813] d. at Westminster 10 May 1821;[814] m. 30 Jan. 1810, JOHN WOOD.[815]

---

803   Information supplied by correspondence with Marilyn Putnam of Antwerp, N.Y., 1977.
804   Paul-Paull MS, 2: 79.
805   *Vital Records of Topsfield, Massachusetts to the end of the year 1849,* 1: 87, 88.
806   Cemetery marker, East Parish Cemetery, Westminster, Vt.
807   Paul-Paull MS, 2: 88.
808   Hemenway, in *Vermont Historical Gazetteer,* 5: 588.
809   Cemetery marker, East Parish Cemetery, Westminster, Vt.
810   *Vital Records of Leicester, Massachusetts, to the End of the Year 1849* (Worcester, Mass., 1903), 99.
811   Vermont Vital Records.
812   Hemenway, in *Vermont Historical Gazetteer* 5: 588.
813   Paul-Paull MS, 2: 88.
814   Ibid.
815   Vermont Vital Records.

60   ii.   CLARK PHIPPEN, b. 24 Jan. 1789.[816]

      iii.   PRISCILLA PHIPPEN, b. 10 March 1791;[817] m. JOSEPH STAUNTON. In 1822 she was listed as a member of the Congregational Church in Crown Point, N.Y.[818] She is buried in White Church Cemetery, Crown Point.

      iv.   HANNAH PHIPPEN, b. 3 Oct. 1793;[819] m. 27 Nov. 1817 IRA KITTREDGE. Children (surname *Kittredge*): 1. *George;* 2. *Lucia A.;* 3. *Milo.*[820]

      v.   MARY PHIPPEN, b. 17 April 1796;[821] d. at Lyndon, Vt. 24 March 1850; m. at Westminster 16 March 1820, JOSEPH IDE of Sheffield, Vt., who was b. at Westminster 22 Feb. 1797, son of Ichabod and Phebe (_____) Ide.[822] They left no issue.[823]

61   vi.   DAVID ATWATER PHIPPEN, born 2 Jan. 1798.[824]

62   vii.   SAMUEL PHIPPEN, born 7 Oct. 1799.[825]

40. HARDY[6] **PHIPPEN** (*Nathaniel*[5-4], *Samuel*[3], *Joseph*[2], *David*[1]) was born at Salem, Massachusetts 25 February 1740, son of Nathaniel and Seeth (Hardy) Phippen. He married at Marblehead, Massachusetts 4 February 1766, **MARY (STEVENS) ASHTON**.[826] Mary Stevens had previously married, at Marblehead, 15 December 1763, William Ashton.[827]

Hardy Phippen was a fisherman and resided at Marblehead. He was lost at sea shortly before 4 September 1775, when administration was granted to his widow, Mary Phippen, who gave bond with Thomas Stevens and Joshua Phippen.[828] She married third, at Manchester, Massachusetts 28 September 1775, William Stone.[829]

---

[816]   Paul-Paull MS, 2: 88; *Vermont Vital Record* says 4 Jan. 1788.

[817]   Paul-Paull MS, 2: 88.

[818]   Congregational Church, Crown Point, N.Y., membership list.

[819]   Paul-Paull MS, 2: 88.

[820]   Hemenway, *Vermont Historical Gazetteer,* 5: 619.

[821]   Paul-Paull MS, 2: 88.

[822]   Vermont Vital Records; Louis W. Flanders, *Simon Ide, Yeoman, Freeman, Pioneer Printer: With a Genealogy of the Ide Family* (Rutland, Vt., 1931), 209.

[823]   Flanders, *Simon Ide,* 209; Vermont Vital Records (Mary's death).

[824]   Paul-Paull MS, 2: 88.

[825]   Ibid.

[826]   *Vital Records of Marblehead, Massachusetts to the end of the year 1849,* 2: 16, 332.

[827]   Ibid., 16, 408.

[828]   Essex Probate Records, no. 21748.

[829]   *Vital Records of Manchester, Massachusetts to the end of the year 1849* (Salem, Mass., 1903), 207, 217.

Children of Hardy and Mary (Stevens) (Ashton) Phippen, born at Marblehead:[830]

    i.   ELIZABETH[7] PHIPPEN, bp. 11 Oct. 1767; d. soon after.

   ii. SEETH ("LEAFY") PHIPPEN, bp. at Marblehead 22 Oct. 1769. She m. at Gloucester, Mass. 27 Nov. 1794, SAMUEL EDWARDS[831] (intentions filed at Manchester 15 Nov. 1794).[832] He was b. at Manchester 20 Aug. 1771, son of Samuel and Lydia (Allen) Edwards.[833] He died suddenly of a hemorrhage in Manchester 27 Sept. 1832, aged 61.[834]

  iii. ELIZABETH PHIPPEN, bp. at Marblehead 22 Sept. 1771; m. at Gloucester 7 Dec. 1791 (intentions 19 Aug. 1791), Capt. ABRAHAM STONE,[835] who was b. at Manchester 27 Oct. 1768, son of William and Anna (Woodberry) Stone.[836] He d. June 1825 in the West Indies of "disease of the climate" at the age of 56, along with his son, Abraham Stone Jr., aged 30.[837] Elizabeth d. in 1839, apparently in Manchester.[838]

41. JOSHUA[6] PHIPPEN (*Nathaniel*[5-4], *Samuel*[3], *Joseph*[2], *David*[1]) was born at Salem, Massachusetts 27 January 1742, son of Nathaniel and Seeth (Hardy) Phippen.[839] He died there 12 April 1811, aged 69 years.[840] The Rev. William Bentley noted in his diary for 12 April 1811, "This evening died Joshua Phippen aet. 70, he has large connections in Salem."[841] Administration of the estate of Joshua Phippen of Salem, cooper, was granted 21 October 1811 to Ursula Phippen, who gave bond with Joseph J. and Isaac Knapp.[842]

---

[830] Baptisms noted in *Vital Records of Marblehead, Massachusetts to the end of the year 1849,* 1: 396.

[831] *Vital Records of Manchester, Massachusetts to the end of the year 1849,* 162, 207; *Vital Records of Gloucester, Massachusetts to the end of the year 1849,* 2: 424.

[832] *Vital Records of Manchester, Massachusetts to the end of the year 1849,* 46, 207; *Vital Records of Gloucester, Massachusetts to the end of the year 1849,* 2: 193.

[833] *Vital Records of Manchester, Massachusetts to the end of the year 1849,* 46.

[834] Ibid., 252.

[835] Ibid., 207, 216; *Vital Records of Gloucester, Massachusetts to the end of the year 1849,* 2: 425, 527.

[836] *Vital Records of Manchester, Massachusetts to the end of the year 1849,* 113.

[837] Ibid., 289 (apparently of yellow fever).

[838] Ibid. The town record states "Mrs. Stone, w. Abraham rec. in 1839" (no given name cited).

[839] *Vital Records of Salem, Massachusetts to the end of the year 1849,* 2: 167.

[840] Ibid., 6: 138.

[841] *The Diary of William Bentley,* 4: 16.

[842] Essex Probate Records, no. 21756.

Joshua Phippen married, first, at Salem 3 October 1764, **HANNAH SIBLEY**,[843] who was born there 12 April 1741, daughter of Samuel and Meribah (Bartlett) Sibley.[844] She died 21 March 1801, aged 60 years, of consumption.[845] Joshua Phippen married, second, 25 October 1801, **URSULA (KNAPP) SYMONDS**,[846] who was baptized at Salem 28 December 1746, daughter of Ebenezer and Sarah (Butler) Knapp.[847] She was the widow of Jonathan Symonds, whom she had married 1 May 1771.[848] She survived her second husband, dying as Joshua Phippen's widow on 20 December 1818, aged 70 years, of consumption. William Bentley[849] wrote in his diary:

> 21 December 1818. Died Ursula, widow of Joshua Phippen. She was a d. of John Knapp whose estate lay in Becket street & sister to the father Samuel, of Capt. Joseph Knapp who now holds the estate of Capt John Hodges in Essex between Orange & Curtis street. His father was a remarkable pedestrian & could go without fatigue from Salem to Boston & return. Ursula married a Symonds & was his widow when she married Joshua Phippen. Joshua P's d. married as 2nd wife to G. Hodges. Ursula was 70 & died in North fields, upon a possession she held from her first husb. by whom she had two d's who srvive her. One has married a Webster & the other is single. She was interred in the old ground.[850]

Joshua Phippen was a cooper by trade, and in 1782 he built the house at 25 Hardy Street in Salem. He was a viewer and culler of staves and hoops in Salem in 1775, 1777–81, and 1783. He was also measurer

---

[843]   *Vital Records of Salem, Massachusetts to the end of the year 1849,* 4: 189, 307.

[844]   Ibid., 2: 286; J. S. Sibley, *The Sibley Family in America* (1972), 325–26.

[845]   *Vital Records of Salem, Massachusetts to the end of the year 1849,* 6: 137. *The Diary of William Bentley,* 2: 368, mentions her death.

[846]   *Vital Records of Salem, Massachusetts to the end of the year 1849,* 4: 371; *Columbian Centinel,* 31 Oct. 1801.

[847]   Arthur M. Knapp, *The Knapp Family in America: A Genealogy of the Descendants of William Knapp, Who Settled in Watertown, Massachusetts in 1630* (Boston, 1909), 13.

[848]   *Vital Records of Salem, Massachusetts to the end of the year 1849,* 3: 575, 4: 368. Ellery and Bowditch, *The Pickering Genealogy,* 1: 212, states that she was the daughter of of Isaac Knapp.

[849]   *Vital Records of Salem, Massachusetts to the end of the year 1849,* 6: 139.

[850]   *The Diary of William Bentley,* 4: 566.

of salt 1782–83.[851] While he was inspector of pork and beef (in 1801), he reported to the Rev. William Bentley that such a small amount of pork and beef was exported from Marblehead that nobody would apply for the job there—so he traveled to Marblehead on occasion.[852] In December 1793, his family suffered greatly from an epidemic of smallpox spread from a vessel that had come into the port of Salem.[853]

Joshua Phippen was listed in Salem in the 1790 census with a houshold consisting of five white males over 16, four white males under 16, and five white females.[854]

Children of Joshua and Hannah (Sibley) Phippen, born at Salem:[855]

63   i.   NATHANIEL[7] PHIPPEN, b. 28 Jan. 1765;[856] bp. 3 June 1770.

       ii.   JOSHUA PHIPPEN, b. 30 July 1767; bur. Salem 8 Oct. 1767.[857]

      iii.   SAMUEL PHIPPEN, b. 30 July 1767; d. 1 Jan. 1768.[858]

       iv.   HANNAH PHIPPEN, b. 26 Dec. 1768;[859] bp. 3 June 1770; m. at Salem
             25 March 1798, Capt. GEORGE HODGES,[860] who was b. at Salem 18
             July 1765, son of Capt. John and Mary (Manning) Hodges,[861] and
             d. 28 July 1827, aged 62 years, of enteritis.[862] On Sunday, 22 March
             1812, William Bentley wrote: "George Hodges & wife, d. of her
             Sister Wid. Mary Babbidge, pr. for her Br. at sea. Lois Phippen, d. of
             Sister in law Babbidge, & husb. & brother at sea. John Babbidge &
             wife, d. of his Sister in law Babbidge."[863] (See Mary, below.) Hannah
             d. at Salem 16 June 1837, the widow of George Hodges, Esq.[864]

---

[851]   Essex County, Massachusetts officers and committees 1755-1783 (Mss A 7772).
        R. Stanton Avery Special Collections, NEHGS, Boston.

[852]   *The Diary of William Bentley,* 2: 369.

[853]   Ibid., 276.

[854]   U.S. Bureau of the Census, *Heads of Families at the First Census of United States Taken
        in the Year 1790: Massachusetts* (Washington, D.C., 1908; reprint, Baltimore, 1973),
        97.

[855]   All information, other than the baptisms, if not otherwise cited, is noted in John
        Langdon Sibley, *A History of the Town of Union, Maine* (Boston, 1851), 500; all bap-
        tisms are noted in "Salem Baptisms," *Essex Institute Historical Collections* 22 [1885]:
        245.

[856]   *Vital Records of Salem, Massachusetts to the end of the year 1849,* 2: 168.

[857]   Sibley, *A History of the Town of Union, Maine,* 500.

[858]   Ibid.

[859]   *Vital Records of Salem, Massachusetts to the end of the year 1849,* 2: 166.

[860]   Ibid., 3: 506; *Columbian Centinel,* 28 March 1798.

[861]   *Vital Records of Salem, Massachusetts to the end of the year 1849,* 1: 439.

[862]   Ibid., 5: 335.

[863]   *The Diary of William Bentley,* 4: 90.

[864]   *Vital Records of Salem, Massachusetts to the end of the year 1849,* 5: 336.

    v. MARY ("POLLY") PHIPPEN, b. 12 Oct. 1770; d. of consumption 17 March 1812;[865] m. (int. dated 13 April 1793), BENJAMIN BABBIDGE of Portsmouth, N.H.,[866] who was b. in 1765, son of Benjamin and Elizabeth (Woodwell) Babbidge. He d. at sea in Oct. 1811. He had sailed as master of the brig *Nabby* from Turks Island and was never heard from again.[867] The Rev. William Bentley wrote, "Mrs. Babbidge buried this day [19 March 1812] was the widow of Capt. B. Babbidge who was lost at sea last year, & who was seduced by Col. Archer to endorse his Paper, by which the wretch & all who relied upon him were ungulphed [*sic*]. Strip[p]ed of property & of her husband & feeble frame she sank under accumulated ills."[868]

    vi. SARAH PHIPPEN, b. 8,[869] bp. 13 Dec. 1772; m. at Salem 26 July 1791, GEORGE DEAN,[870] son of Capt. Thomas and Mary (Cash) Dean. She d. as his widow at Salem 25 July 1801.[871] In his diary, the Rev. William Bentley noted (on 2 August 1801), "Joshua Phippen d. of dau. Dean pr for 2 sons at sea. Thurs one returned, Thomas Dean, d. of d. in law Dean."[872] George Dean d. of fever at Port-au-Prince, Hispaniola 14 Feb. 1792, aged 22.

64   vii. JOSHUA PHIPPEN, b. 2 July 1774; d. 30 April 1805, aged 31.[873]

    viii. EUNICE PHIPPEN, twin, b. 22,[874] bp. 24 Dec. 1775; d. 30 Oct. 1776.

    ix. MARGARET PHIPPEN, twin, b. 22 Dec. 1775; d. in a few days.

65   x. HARDY PHIPPEN, b. 6,[875] bp. 12 July 1778.

    xi. EUNICE PHIPPEN, b. 22 March 1780; d. of consumption at Salem 19 Dec. 1799, aged 20.[876] William Bentley noted in his diary (on 22 Dec. 1799), "Joshua Phippen, wife and children d. of D. Eunice pr for 2 sons at sea."[877] The *Salem Gazette* of 24 Dec. 1799 contained an obituary notice that praised her uncommon sweetness of disposition and modest deportment, and said that she was "greatly esteemed and beloved."[878]

66   xii. JOSEPH PHIPPEN, b. 14 March 1783.

---

[865] Ibid., 62.

[866] Ibid., 3: 67, 4: 190.

[867] Ibid., 5: 61.

[868] *The Diary of William Bentley*, 4: 90.

[869] *Vital Records of Salem, Massachusetts to the end of the year 1849*, 2: 169.

[870] Ibid., 3: 286, 4: 191.

[871] Ibid., 5: 199.

[872] *The Diary of William Bentley*, 2: 381.

[873] *Vital Records of Salem, Massachusetts to the end of the year 1849*, 6: 138.

[874] Ibid., 2: 166.

[875] Ibid.

[876] Ibid., 6: 137.

[877] *The Diary of William Bentley*, 2: 325.

[878] Ellery and Bowditch, *The Pickering Genealogy*, 2: 352.

42. SAMUEL[6] **P**HIPPEN (*David*[5], *Nathaniel*[4], *Samuel*[3], *Joseph*[2], *David*[1]) was born at Salem, Massachusetts 28 December 1745, son of David and Priscilla (Bickford) Phippen. He died at Salem 22 February 1798, aged 53 years,[879] and was buried there in the Charter Street Burial Ground.[880]

Samuel Phippen married at Salem 27 October 1782, **M**ARY **S**WAIN,[881] daughter of Joseph and Elizabeth (Chipman) (Warren) Swain. He lived near Union Wharf, where he was a cabinetmaker.[882]

A Martha Washington chair, ca. 1790, attributed to Samuel Phippen of Salem, was among the pieces of antique American furniture included in the White House's Diplomatic Reception Room when it was refurbished in the Kennedy years.[883] Samuel retired from his business in 1793. The following announcement appeared in the February 19, 1793 *Salem Gazette*:

> Samuel Phippen informs his customers and others
> that he is about leaving the Cabinet-making Business,
> and has ready made a Variety of Cabinet Work, which
> he will exchange for other Goods or Cash — viz.
> Mahogany Desks and Books-Cases, mahogany swelled
> Desks, mahogany plain Desks — black-walnut, cedar,
> birch and maple Desks — Loge-top black-walnut Cases
> of Draws, mahogany and birch Dining Tables, mahogany
> Bureau Tables, mahogany and birch Stand Tables,
> mahogany and birch Light Stands, mahogany high-
> post Bedsteads, common ditto with sacking bottoms,
> mahogany and birch Chairs — dining, bow-back and
> kitchen Chairs — Coopers Tools, Seamen's Chests, and
> a number of other Articles.[884]

The Phippens of Salem were noted craftsmen in the wood trades. One author described the "extraordinary continuity of five generations of craftsmen following the same trade," which "is unmatched in any other Salem family."[885]

---

[879]   *Vital Records of Salem, Massachusetts to the end of the year 1849,* 6: 139.

[880]   "Charter Street Burial-Ground," *Essex Institute Historical Collections 13* [1877]: 108.

[881]   *Vital Records of Salem, Massachusetts to the end of the year 1849,* 4: 191, 360.

[882]   Bjerkoe, *The Cabinetmakers of America,* 170.

[883]   Gloria Gould, "White House Heritage Enriched by Antique Furnishings," *The Boston Sunday Herald,* 12 November 1961, 13.

[884]   Henry Wyckoff Belknap, *Artists and Craftsmen of Essex County, Massachusetts* (Salem, Mass., 1927), 63-64.

[885]   Benno M. Forman, "Salem Tradesmen and Craftsmen Circa 1762: A Contemporary Document," *Essex Institute Historical Collections,* 107 [1971] 62-81, at 79.

After his death, Mrs. Phippen was living with her daughter, Mrs. Josiah Dow, in Wakefield, New Hampshire. She died at Brooklyn, New York, where her daughter and son-in-law were living. Samuel Phippen was a member of a volunteer company from Salem that participated in the unsuccessful expedition in 1778 to retake Rhode Island from the British forces.[886]

Children of Samuel and Mary (Swain) Phippen, born at Salem:[887]

    i. REBECCA MARIA[7] PHIPPEN, b. 7 Dec. 1783; m. at Salem 5 Jan. 1806, JOSIAH DOW of Boston, Mass. They lived in Wakefield.[888] They later moved to Brooklyn, N.Y., where he became a most prominent merchant.[889]

    ii. SAMUEL PHIPPEN, b. 23 April 1785; d. 2 Oct. 1804, aged 19, of "hectic";[890] bur. in Charter Street Burial Ground.[891]

43. EBENEZER[6] PHIPPEN (*David[5]*, *Nathaniel[4]*, *Samuel[3]*, *Joseph[2]*, *David[1]*) was born at Salem, Massachusetts 13 January 1750, son of David and Priscilla (Bickford) Phippen. He died at Salem 27 March 1792, aged 42 years.[892] He was a cabinetmaker in Salem.[893]

Ebenezer Phippen married at Salem 27 October 1772, **ELIZABETH SIMMES,**[894] daughter of Stephen and Sarah (Norris) Symmes. A notice of his death appeared in the *American Apollo* issue dated 6 April 1792.[895] The Rev. William Bentley of Salem recorded the death in his diary:

> 1 April 1792: Mr. [Ebenezer] Phippen died after long confinement. Since the war he paid little attention to business, tho a Carpenter. He was very much involved in his affairs, & acting for the Church there was an entire failure of his property. He has since disappeared

---

886   "Expedition to Rhode Island in 1778," *Essex Institute Historical Collections* 1 [1859]: 113.

887   *Vital Records of Salem, Massachusetts to the end of the year 1849*, 2: 168.

888   Ibid., 3: 310, 4: 190; *Columbian Centinel*, 8 Jan. 1806.

889   Robert P. Dow, *The Book of Dow, Genealogical Memoirs of the Descendants of Henry Dow 1637, etc.* (1929), 355.

890   *Vital Records of Salem, Massachusetts to the end of the year 1849*, 6: 139.

891   "Charter Street Burial Ground," *Essex Institute Historical Collections* 13 [1877]: 108.

892   *Vital Records of Salem, Massachusetts to the end of the year 1849*, 6: 137.

893   Bjerkoe, *Cabinetmakers of America*, 170.

894   *Vital Records of Salem, Massachusetts to the end of the year 1849*, 4: 189, 310.

895   "Death Notices, *American Apollo*, 1792," *Register* 140 [1986]: 64–71 at 69.

from public worship, & at length in extreme indigence, depending only on his friends, he had a very hard death. He has left a wife, very deaf & seven children, wholly unprovided for.[896]

Ebenezer's widow, Elizabeth, died in June 1826, aged 74 years.[897]

Children of Ebenezer and Elizabeth (Simmes) Phippen:

    i.   ELIZABETH[7] PHIPPEN, b. about 1773; m. at Salem 11 Oct. 1795, EDWARD ARCHER,[898] who was b. at Salem 28 March 1767, son of Capt. John and Elizabeth (Norris) Archer. Elizabeth (Phippen) Archer d. as his widow 25 May 1866, aged 93.[899]

67   ii. DAVID PHIPPEN, b. at Reading, Mass. 25 July 1775.

    iii. EBENEZER PHIPPEN, b. in 1777; a blockmaker, he served as an apprentice and a journeyman to Jonathan Smith. Ebenezer d. unm. of cholera morbus 14 Aug. 1813, aged 36.[900]

    iv. SAMUEL PHIPPEN, b. between 1777 and 1784; d. young.

    v. STEPHEN PHIPPEN, b. between 1777 and 1784; d. young.

    vi. LYDIA FISK PHIPPEN, b. between 1777 and 1784; d. unm.

    vii. SARAH NORRIS PHIPPEN, b. about 1784; d. before 2 April 1805 (when her death notice was published), aged 21 years.[901] Her death was noted by the Rev. William Bentley in his diary, and it was the cause of some friction. Bentley wrote that Rev. Worcester (minister at the Tabernacle Church) had "crept in upon us in the Phippen family. Upon the decease of the young girl the family invited me to the funeral services & the mother protested that the interference had not her consent."[902]

    viii. RUFUS PHIPPEN, bp. at Salem 7 Aug. 1785; [903]d. of worms at Salem 28 Feb. 1790, aged 5 years.[904]

---

[896] *The Diary of William Bentley,* 1: 358.

[897] *Vital Records of Salem, Massachusetts to the end of the year 1849,* 6: 137 (her death notice was published on 6 June 1826).

[898] Ibid., 3: 56, 4: 189.

[899] Massachusetts State Archives. Massachusetts Vital Records (1841–1915). Microfilm & Digitial series, NEHGS [hereafter Mass. VR], (1866) 192: 212.

[900] *The Diary of William Bentley,* 4: 188; *Vital Records of Salem, Massachusetts to the end of the year 1849,* 6: 137.

[901] Ibid., 139.

[902] *The Diary of William Bentley,* 3:145, 149, 150.

[903] "Salem Baptisms," *Essex Institute Historical Collections* 22 [1885]: 245.

[904] *Vital Records of Salem, Massachusetts to the end of the year 1849,* 6: 139.

ix. HARRY (or Henry) PHIPPEN, b. in Oct. 1788; bp. 27 Feb. 1790;[905] d. of consumption at Salem 2 March 1790, aged 18 months.[906]

x. NANCY PHIPPEN, bp. at Salem 27 Feb. 1790;[907] d. there 27 Jan. 1863, aged 73 years 5 months;[908] m. (1) at Salem 16 Sept. 1810, JOSEPH H. SMITH;[909] m. (2) at Salem 11 June 1832, Capt. JOHN HILL GLOVER.[910]

xi. MARIA (or MARY) PHIPPEN, bp. at Salem 16 March 1792;[911] d. of "atrophy" 7 Dec. 1792, aged 11 months.[912]

44. NATHANIEL[6] PHIPPEN (*David[5], Nathaniel[4], Samuel[3], Joseph[2], David[1]*) was born at Salem, Massachusetts 18 May 1758, son of David and Priscilla (Bickford) Phippen. He died at Salem 24 February 1815, aged 57 years, of consumption.[913] Nathaniel married at Salem 2 May 1779, **ABIGAIL HOOPER,**[914] daughter of James and Sarah (Blaney) Hooper. She died at Salem 13 May 1832, aged 70 years.[915]

During the Revolutionary War, Nathaniel became a carpenter's mate on the sloop *Tyrannicide,* which was commanded by his brother-in-law, Captain John Fiske.[916] In 1783, he was living on Essex Street, next to Captain Joseph Peabody and Captain Benjamin West.[917] He is listed as the master of the brigantine *Juno,* 113 tons, when it was registered on 16 September 1803.[918] He also was master of the schooner *Success* after 1805.[919] The Rev. William Bentley recorded on 5 March 1815:

He was the son of our Deacon David & possessed an athletic constitution. Not pursuing his labours at sea

---

[905] Ibid., 2: 166; "Salem Baptisms," *Essex Institute Historical Collections* 22 [1885]: 245.

[906] *Vital Records of Salem, Massachusetts to the end of the year 1849,* 6: 137.

[907] Ibid., 2: 168; "Salem Baptisms," *Essex Institute Historical Collections* 22 [1885]: 245.

[908] Mass.VR (1863), 165: 251.

[909] *Vital Records of Salem, Massachusetts to the end of the year 1849,* 4: 190, 324.

[910] Anna Glover, *Glover Memorials and Genealogies* (Boston, 1867), 405-06.

[911] *Vital Records of Salem, Massachusetts to the end of the year 1849,* 2: 167; "Salem Baptisms," *Essex Institute Historical Collections* 22 [1885]: 245.

[912] *Vital Records of Salem, Massachusetts to the end of the year 1849,* 6: 138.

[913] Ibid.

[914] Ibid., 3: 517, 4: 190.

[915] Ibid., 6: 136.

[916] *Mass. Soldiers and Sailors in the Revolutionary War,* 12: 339-40.

[917] Phillips, *Salem and the Indies,* 18.

[918] "Danvers Ships and Ship Masters," *Historical Collections of the Danvers Historical Society* 8 [1920]: 93.

[919] "Ship Registers of the District of Salem and Beverly, 1789-1900," *Essex Institute Historical Collections* 41 [1905]: 373.

he cultivated with great diligence & success a spot of ground near his house & in autumn went up to the turf ground on Forest River. Strangely he began to fail & eventually died. As usual to his employments & exposures his sufferings were imputed but he died at the age of his father & brethren as I have observed. They have one son a prisoner in England. A daughter wife of Joseph Knapp.[920]

The *Essex Institute Historical Collections* lists some of Captain Phippen's voyages from Salem newspaper notices: he arrived at Salem on the brig *Patty* from Cadiz 26 July 1787; he arrived on the same brig from Cadiz 25 December 1787. An advertisement on 1 January 1788 read as follows:

> Just imported from Cadiz, In the Brig Patty, Captain Phippen, By John Fisk and to be sold at his store on the long Wharf, Salem: Cask and Jar raisins, Fresh lemons, olives, sweet oil in jars, sherry Wine.

The *Essex Institute Historical Collections* mentions additional voyages: on 19 February 1788 Captain Phippen arrived from Cadiz; on 12 August 1788, aboard the schooner *Peggy*, from Spain; on 6 January 1789 from Malaga; and on 21 July 1789 from Cadiz.[921]

Children of Nathaniel and Abigail (Hooper) Phippen, born at Salem:

    i.   NATHANIEL[7] PHIPPEN, b. about 1779; drowned off Cape of Good Hope "from on board Capt. Chipman" 4 Jan. 1796, aged 17 years.[922]

    ii. ABIGAIL PHIPPEN, b. about 1781; d. suddenly at Salem 22 July 1827, aged 46;[923] m. at Salem 10 June 1798, JOSEPH JENKINS KNAPP.[924] He m. (2) LYDIA FISKE KING, daughter of William and Rebecca[6] (Phippen) King. She d. at Salem 21 July 1847, aged 74 years. After her death, in 1830, her sons Joseph Jenkins Knapp Jr. (bp. at Salem 2 Jan. 1803) and John Francis Knapp (bp. at Salem 29 Sept. 1811) were

---

[920] *The Diary of William Bentley,* 4: 318.

[921] James Duncan Phillips, "Salem Ocean Borne Commerce: From the Close of the Revolution to the Establishment of the Constitution, 1783-1789," *Essex Institute Historical Collections* 75 [1939]: 364, 371–73, 76 [1940]: 68, 75, 84.

[922] *Vital Records of Salem, Massachusetts to the end of the year 1849,* 6: 138.

[923] Ibid., 5: 380.

[924] Ibid., 3: 575, 4:188; Knapp, *The Knapp Family in America,* 33.

convicted and executed for their roles in the infamous murder of their wealthy uncle, Capt. Joseph White, a retired Salem merchant.[925]

iii. SAMUEL PHIPPEN, b. about 1782; d. of fever, apparently at sea ("with Capt. Taylor"), on 4 June 1799, aged 17.[926]

iv. SARAH/SALLY PHIPPEN, b. in 1785; d. unm. of "nervous fever" 12 Oct. 1806, aged 21 years;[927] she was to have married JOSHUA OAKES.

v. JOHN PHIPPEN bp. 23 Dec. 1787;[928] d. at sea.

45. THOMAS[6] **PHIPPEN** (*Thomas*[5], *Nathaniel*[4–3], *Joseph*[2], *David*[1]) was born at Salem, Massachusetts 25 December 1750, and baptized there 1 March 1752, son of Thomas and Margaret (Driver) Phippen. He died at Salem 24 December 1839, aged 89 years.[929] Thomas married at Salem, in the Episcopal Church, on 27 December 1774, **REBECCA WELLMAN,**[930] who was born at Salem 3 October 1755 and baptized there, as an adult, 8 October 1775, daughter of Timothy and Mary (Henderson) Wellman.[931] She died at Salem in May 1837, aged 81 years.[932]

Thomas Phippen served in the Revolutionary War as a private stationed at Salem for defense of the seacoast.[933] He was a mariner, and in August 1799 he was third in command of the ship *Henry*, a privateer owned by Elias Hasket Derby, merchant, of Salem.

Children of Thomas and Rebecca (Wellman) Phippen, born at Salem:[934]

i. MARGARET/PEGGY[7] PHIPPEN, b. 22, bp. 24 Oct. 1775; d. 13 Oct. 1777.[935]

---

[925] *Vital Records of Salem, Massachusetts to the end of the year 1849*, 1: 497 (baptisms of Joseph and John), 5: 380 (execution dates). See "The Tell-Tale Murder," *Smithsonian*, November 2010, 61–68.

[926] *Vital Records of Salem, Massachusetts to the end of the year 1849*, 6: 139.

[927] Ibid.

[928] Ibid., 2: 167; "Salem Baptisms," *Essex Institute Historical Collections* 22 [1885]: 245.

[929] *Vital Records of Salem, Massachusetts to the end of the year 1849*, 6: 139; J. W. Wellman, *Descendants of Thomas Wellman of Lynn, Massachusetts* [hereafter *Descendants of Thomas Wellman*] (Boston, 1918), 168, gives the date as 22 Dec. 1839.

[930] *Vital Records of Salem, Massachusetts to the end of the year 1849*, 4: 191, 450.

[931] Wellman, *Descendants of Thomas Wellman*, 168; "Salem Baptisms," *Essex Institute Historical Collections* 22 [1885]: 245.

[932] *Vital Records of Salem, Massachusetts to the end of the year 1849*, 6: 139.

[933] *Massachusetts Soldiers and Sailors of the Revolutionary War* (Boston, 1896-1908) 12 [1904]: 340.

[934] All baptisms in "Salem Baptisms," *Essex Institute Historical Collections* 22 [1885]: 245.

[935] Wellman, *Descendants of Thomas Wellman*, 168.

68   ii.   THOMAS PHIPPEN, b. 6 June 1778.[936]
69   iii. JOSEPH PHIPPEN, b. 23 Oct. 1779.[937]
70   iv.   ISRAEL PHIPPEN, b. 18 Sept. 1781;[938]
      v.   REBECCA PHIPPEN, b. 18 Feb. 1784;[939] bp. in Feb. 1784;[940] d. 10 June
            1786.[941]
      vi.   REBECCA PHIPPEN, b. 13 Sept. 1786; bp. in Sept. 1786; d. unm.[942]

46. WILLIAM[6] **PHIPPEN** (*Thomas*[5], *Nathaniel*[4], *Samuel*[3], *Joseph*[2], *David*[1])
was born at Salem, Massachusetts 27 February 1752/53 and baptized 1
March 1752[/53], son of Thomas and Margaret (Driver) Phippen.[943]
He died at Salem 28 May 1796, aged 44 years,[944] and was buried in the
Charter Street Burial Ground there.[945]

   William Phippen married, first, at Salem 22 November 1777, **LOIS
HITCHINGS**,[946] who was baptized at Salem 12 September 1779.[947] She
died at Salem 11 March 1794, aged 40 years,[948] and was buried in the
Charter Street Burial Ground.[949] William married, second, at Salem 6
August 1794, **ANNA (____) RING**.[950] She died at Salem 23 July 1815.[951]

   William Phippen was a trader; on 17 May 1786, he bought a shop
in Salem from General Amos Hovey.[952]

---

[936]   Wellman, *Descendants of Thomas Wellman*, 168.
[937]   Ibid.
[938]   Ibid.
[939]   Ibid.
[940]   "Salem Baptisms," *Essex Institute Historical Collections* 22 [1885]: 245, gives this date,
        but *Vital Records of Salem, Massachusetts to the end of the year 1849*, 2: 168, states that
        Rebecca, daughter of Thomas, was baptized in Sept. 1786.
[941]   Wellman, *Descendants of Thomas Wellman*, 168.
[942]   Ibid. *Vital Records of Salem, Massachusetts to the end of the year 1849*, 2: 168, gives year
        of baptism as 1786, while Wellman genealogy says she was born in 1787.
[943]   *Vital Records of Salem, Massachusetts to the end of the year 1849*, 2: 169.
[944]   Ibid., 6: 139.
[945]   "Charter Street Burial-Ground," *Essex Institute Historical Collections* 13 [1877]: 108.
[946]   *Vital Records of Salem, Massachusetts to the end of the year 1849*, 3: 502, 4: 191.
[947]   "Salem Baptisms," *Essex Institute Historical Collections* 22 [1885]: 245.
[948]   *Vital Records of Salem, Massachusetts to the end of the year 1849*, 6: 138.
[949]   "Charter Street Burial-Ground," *Essex Institute Historical Collections* 13 [1877]: 108.
[950]   *Vital Records of Salem, Massachusetts to the end of the year 1849*, 4: 191, 258.
[951]   Ibid., 6: 137.
[952]   Essex Deeds 144: 114; Daniel Hovey Association, *The Hovey Book* (Haverhill, Mass.,
        1913), 178.

Children of William and Lois (Hitchings) Phippen, born at Salem:[953]

71   i.   WILLIAM[7] PHIPPEN, b. about 1778.
     ii.   LOIS PHIPPEN, bp. 6 May 1780; m. at Salem 13 Dec. 1800, BENJAMIN BALCH.[954]
    iii.   JAMES PHIPPEN, bp. 6 May 1780; d. at sea Aug. 1795, aged 15.[955]
     iv.   MOSES HITCHINGS PHIPPEN, bp. in Nov. 1795; d. at Salem 14 Aug. 1808, aged 23; feltmaker.[956]
      v.   LYDIA PHIPPEN, bp. 30 Dec. 1786.
     vi.   MARY/POLLY PHIPPEN, b. about 1788; m. at Salem 19 April 1805, ELIJAH FULLER;[957] d. of consumption 13 Jan. 1828.[958]
72   vii.   GEORGE PHIPPEN, bp. in March 1790.
    viii.   LUCY PHIPPEN, bp. 26 Feb. 1792; d. unm. of heart disease 16 Sept. 1881.[959]

47. DAVID[6] PHIPPENEY (*Archibald[5], Benjamin[4], James[3], Benjamin[2], David[1]*) was born in 1762, son of Archibald and Charity (Stratton) Phippeney. He died at Hartford, Connecticut 15 May 1815. He married, before 1790, **RUTH ADAMS,** daughter of Ebenezer and Ruth (Merrill) Adams. She died 18 March 1862.

David Phippeney was a weaver. The family was probably the one enumerated in Farmington, Hartford County, Connecticut, in the 1810 census.[960] Ruth appears as head of household in Hartford in the 1820 census.

---

[953] Baptisms in "Salem Baptisms," *Essex Institute Historical Collections* 22 [1885]: 245; also *Vital Records of Salem, Massachusetts to the end of the year 1849,* 2: 165 (Lydia), 166 (George), 168 (Moses), 169 (Lucy).
[954] *Vital Records of Salem, Massachusetts to the end of the year 1849,* 3: 74, 4: 190; *Columbian Centinel,* 27 Dec. 1800.
[955] *Vital Records of Salem, Massachusetts to the end of the year 1849,* 6: 137.
[956] Ibid., 138.
[957] Ibid.,3: 391, 4: 190
[958] Ibid., 5: 265.
[959] Mass.VR (1881), 328: 294.
[960] 1810 U.S. Census, Farmington, Hartford Co., Conn., p. 409.

Children of David and Ruth (Adams) Phippeney, born at Hartford:[961]

    i.   HARRIET M.[7] PHIPPENEY, b. 12 Nov. 1790; m. (1) at Hartford 3 Nov. 1816, HENRY WHITMAN, son of William and Lucy (Steele) (Beech) Whitman; m. (2) at Hartford 29 Oct. 1850, EDWARD C. LEWIS of Bridgeport, Conn.

    ii. HENRY PHIPPENEY, b. 1 Sept. 1792. Likely the man listed as head of his own household in Hartford in the 1820 census; still living, in Hartford, alone in the 1870 census.

    iii. RUTH PHIPPENEY, b. 12 Feb. 1796; d. young.

73   iv. DAVID PHIPPENEY, b. 23 Nov. 1797.

74   v. WILLIAM ARCHIBALD PHIPPENEY, b. 12 July 1801.

    vi. RUTH PHIPPENEY, b. 23 Dec. 1803; m. at Hartford 26 March 1827, WILLIAM SMITH of Hartford.

    vii. CHARITY PHIPPENEY, b. 29 March 1807; m. (1) at Hartford 21 April 1835, JOSIAH H. BOWLES; m. (2) EDWARD NOBLE.

    viii. ALMIRA PHIPPENEY, b. 19 Jan. 1811; m. at Hartford 15 Nov. 1837, SAMUEL CASE of Hartford.

48. ASAHEL[6] PHIPPENEY (*Archibald[5]*, *Benjamin[4]*, *James[3]*, *Benjamin[2]*, *David[1]*) was born about 1772, son of Archibald and Charity (Stratton) Phippeney; he died at Waltham, Vermont 4 October 1818, aged 46.[962] His record in the 1800 and 1810 censuses for New Haven, Addison County, Vermont, suggests that he was married, but no children or further information has been found.[963]

The 1820 census for Waltham, Adison County, Vermont, lists an Amy Phippeney, who is most likely his widow. She appears to have been **AMY LANGWORTHY,** daughter of Joseph and Azubah (MacWithey) Langworthy, who was born about 1773. She married, second, **ROGER BROWN,** and died in December 1857 in Saint Lawrence County, New York.[964] It is likely that one or more subsequent unplaced Phippeney

961 Information about children from White, Lorraine Cook, ed. "Hartford 1635-1855," The Barbour Collection of Connecticut Town Vital Records, vol. 19 (Baltimore: Genealogical Publishing Co., 1999), 322.

962 Elizabeth Prather Ellsberry, comp., *Cemetery Records of Addison County, Vermont* (Chillicothe, Mo., ca. 1965), vol. 3 (online database at www.Ancestry.com).

963 1800 U.S. Census, New Haven, Addison Co., Vt., p. 109: one male 26–44 (Asahel); one female of the same; and one male and one female each aged 16–25.

964 William Franklin Langworthy, *The Langworthy Family: Some Descendants of Andrew and Rachel (Hubbard) Langworthy* (Rutland, Vt., 1940), 221.

lines emerging from Vermont in subsequent decades can be traced to Asahel and Amy (Langworthy) Phippeney, but the names of this couple's children are not known.

49. WILLIAM[6] **PHIPPENEY** (*Archibald*[5], *Benjamin*[4], *James*[3], *Benjamin*[2], *David*[1]) was born say 1780, son of Archibald and Charity (Stratton) Phippeney. In the 1800 census for New Haven, Addison County, Vermont, he may be the male aged 16 to 26 who was living with his brother Asahel Phippeney, each apparently with a female in the same age group. In the 1810 census for New Haven, William Phippeney is listed separately, aged 26 to 45, with a wife of the same age and two children (a boy and a girl) under 10.

He was married by 1810 to **MARY NEWMAN**.[965] There were at least two Newman families in New Haven, Vermont, at the time he would have married. He appears to have migrated shortly after 1810 to Pompey, Onondaga County, New York, where he is enumerated in the 1820 census. It is not known whether he died in Onondaga County or migrated farther after 1820.

Children of William and Mary (Newman) Phippeney include:

    i.   ELIZABETH[7] PHIPPENEY, b. in 1811; m. (1) in Onondaga Co. in 1829, FRANKLIN HAMMOND. Issue. Franklin Hammond d. in 1852. Elizabeth m. (2) AUGUSTUS STILES TORRANCE, who owned a wool factory in or around Gowanda, N.Y. They later went west. Elizabeth died in Kansas.[966]

75   ii.   CALVIN EVET PHIPPENEY, b. in Onondaga Co. 8 March 1819.

50. DAVID BENJAMIN[6] **PHIPPENEY** (*Benjamin*[5-4], *James*[3], *Benjamin*[2], *David*[1]) was enumerated in the 1800 census for West Haven, Rutland County, Vermont, next to Benjamin[5] "Fippeny." He is listed as a young adult, with wife and one younger male, who is possibly a son. In the 1820 census for West Haven, "D. B. Phippeny" is enumerated with a household that includes several children; "David B. Phippeny" is still listed there in 1840.

---

[965] Her maiden name was given on the license for their son Calvin E. Phippeney's second marriage in 1889; this information courtesy of descendant Kay Brett.

[966] Information from descendant Michael Smith.

51. JOEL⁶ **PHIPPANY** (*James*⁵⁻³, *Benjamin²*, *David¹*) was born at New Milford, Connecticut 7 August 1773, son of James and Rosannah (Brownson) Phippeney, and died at Sheldon, New York 8 April 1834. He was a farmer and shoemaker.⁹⁶⁷

Joel Phippany married at Hinesburgh, Vermont in 1798, **ELECTA GATES,** who was born at Ridgefield, Connecticut 11 April 1779, daughter of David and Jerusha (Whitney) Gates.⁹⁶⁸ They lived in Hinesburgh until 1815, when they removed to Sheldon. Electra (Gates) Phippany died at Sheldon 29 October 1816. Joel Phippany then married, as his second wife, **CHLOE MCWHORTER.**⁹⁶⁹

Children of Joel and Electa (Gates) Phippany, born at Hinesburgh:⁹⁷⁰

     i.   ROSANNA⁷ PHIPPANY m. CYRUS GROUT. Lived at Pembroke, N.Y.; d., childless, on 8 Feb. 1875.

    ii.   WALTER SCOTT PHIPPANY, b. about 1803; d. unm. at Pittsford, N.Y., about 1823, aged about 20.

76   iii.   HORACE PHIPPANY.

77   iv.   GEORGE JAMES PHIPPANY, b. 6 Dec. 1811.

52. PETER⁶ **PHIPPENEY** (*James*⁵⁻³, *Benjamin²,* *David¹*) was born at New Milford, Connecticut 31 January 1779, son of James and Rosannah (Brownson) Phippeney.⁹⁷¹ He married at New Milford 29 September 1808, **DORCAS FENN.**⁹⁷² Bridgewater, Connecticut, was incorporated as a town in May 1856. At the first town meeting, Peter was selected as a fence viewer.⁹⁷³ He was still living in Bridgewater, aged 81, at the time of the 1860 census, with his daughter Caroline and her husband Anson Beardsley.⁹⁷⁴

---

⁹⁶⁷ S. Whitney Phoenix, *The Whitney family of Connecticut, and its affiliations; being an attempt to trace the descendants . . . of Henry Whitney, from 1649 to 1878,* 3 vols. [hereafter *The Whitney Family of Connecticut*] (New York, 1878), 1: 190.

⁹⁶⁸ Ibid.

⁹⁶⁹ Ibid.

⁹⁷⁰ Information about children from Phoenix, *The Whitney family of Connecticut,* 1: 520.

⁹⁷¹ Orcutt, *History of Stratford,* 2: 1267–68.

⁹⁷² "New Milford 1712-1860," *The Barbour Collection of Connecticut Town Vital Records,* vol. 30, 167.

⁹⁷³ Samuel Orcutt, *History of the Towns of New Milford and Bridgewater, Connecticut, 1703–1882* (Hartford, 1882), 433.

⁹⁷⁴ 1860 U.S. Census, Bridgewater, Litchfield Co., Conn., p. 589.

Children of Peter and Dorcas (Fenn) Phippeney, born at New Milford:[975]

78   i. JAMES MADISON[7] PHIPPENEY, b. in 1810.

    ii. CAROLINE MATILDA PHIPPENEY, b. in 1812; m. 4 May 1830, ANSON BEARDSLEY.[976] She was living as a widow with her brother George Phippeney in 1880.[977]

    iii. SALLY MINERVA PHIPPENEY, b. in 1813; d. in 1847.

    iv. HENRY HARRISON PHIPPENEY, b. in 1815; unm. in 1844.

    v. OLIVER WOLCOTT PHIPPENEY, b. in 1817; living in 1850 in New Milford with wife ELMIRA (surname unknown), who was b. about 1820.[978] He d. in 1851.

    VI. STANLEY GRISWOLD PHIPPENEY, b. in 1819; d. in 1822.

79   vii. GEORGE EDGAR PHIPPENEY, b. in 1820.

    viii. HENRYETTA ELLEN PHIPPENEY, b. in 1823; d. in 1835.

    ix. MARQUIS LAFAYETTE PHIPPENEY, b. in 1825; d. in 1834.

    x. JULIA MARIA PHIPPENEY, b. in 1827; d. in 1858.

    xi. FREDERIC EARL PHIPPENEY, b. in 1830; d. in 1843.

80   xii. CHARLES LEE PHIPPENEY, b. in 1834.

    xiii. HORATIO GATES PHIPPENEY, b. in 1836. Living, single, as a stock herder near his brother Charles L. in Paradise Valley Twp., Humbolt Co., Nev., at the time of the 1870 census. In 1880 he was living in Red Bluff, Tehama Co., Calif.

---

[975] As reported in Orcutt, *History of Stratford,* 2: 1267–68.

[976] "New Milford 1712-1860." *The Barbour Collection of Connecticut Town Vital Records,* vol. 30, 167.

[977] 1880 U.S. Census, Monroe, Fairfield Co., Conn., p. 231B.

[978] 1850 U.S. Census, New Milford, Litchfield Co., Conn., p. 152.

CHAPTER 9

THE SEVENTH GENERATION

53. ASEPH[7] PHIPPEN (*Samuel*[6-3], *Joseph*[2], *David*[1]) was born at Westminster, Windham County, Vermont 21 August 1787, son of Samuel and Ruth (Lane) Phippen.[979] He married **SEBRINA SMEDLEY.** They were residing in Watertown, Jefferson County, New York, in 1820, and at Lyme, Jefferson County, in 1840.[980]

Children of Aseph and Sebrina (Smedley) Phippen, born in New York:

<blockquote>

i. JOHN[8] PHIPPEN, m. MAHALY ____. Probably the John Phippin who was living at Cicero, Onondaga Co., N.Y., at the time of the 1840 census.

81   ii. HIRAM PHIPPEN, b. about 1819.

iii. SAMUEL V. PHIPPEN.

iv. SEBRINA PHIPPEN m. HIRAM SAGE, who was b. at Stewartsville, Minn. in 1813, son of Amos Sage.[981]

v. GEORGE PHIPPEN.

vi. AMASA PHIPPEN.

vii. RICHARD PHIPPEN of Edwards, N.Y.

viii. AMELIA PHIPPEN m. ____ MATTICE.

ix. ELECTRA PHIPPEN m. ____ POWERS.

x. LUCINDA PHIPPEN m. ____ HENDRICH.

xi. LOVINA PHIPPEN m. ____ FULLER.

</blockquote>

---

[979] The information on Aseph Phippen and his family was provided by descendant Mary Margaret (Pappa) Schwerzmann in 1977.

[980] 1820 U.S. census, Watertown, Jefferson Co., New York, roll M33_72, p. 486; 1840 U.S. census, Lyme, Jefferson Co., New York, roll 292, p. 644.

[981] Elisha L. Sage, *Genealogical Record of the Descendants of David Sage . . .* (Batavia, N.Y., 1919), 50.

54. HORATIO[7] **PHIPPEN** (*Samuel*[6-3], *Joseph*[2], *David*[1]) was born at Westminster, Vermont 8 September 1797, son of Samuel and Ruth (Lane) Phippen, and died at Watertown, Jefferson County, New York 20 May 1861.[982] He married, on 15 February 1837, **ELVIRA TUTTLE,** daughter of Joseph and Rhoda (Rockwell) Tuttle, who was born 13 August 1815.[983] They resided at Watertown, New York.[984] She died, a widow, at Watertown 11 February 1893, in her 78th year.[985]

Horatio was a farmer; he farmed a tract of land in Watertown with his brother Chester, who is listed as a farmer in Horatio's household in both the 1850 and 1860 censuses.

Children of Horatio and Elvira (Tuttle) Phippen, born at Watertown: [986]

82   i. HOMER W.[8] PHIPPEN, b. 22 Dec. 1837.

     ii. WILLIAM PENN PHIPPEN, b. 15 July 1839; d. 11 Aug. 1870.

    iii. GEORGE T. PHIPPEN, b. and d. 19 June 1843.

    iv. ROCKWELL C. PHIPPEN, b. 24 Jan. 1845; according to census records, he resided in Rochester, Minn. in 1880; High Forest, Minn. in 1900; and Stewartville, Minn. in 1910.

83   v. CHAUNCEY WALTER PHIPPEN, b. 19 Nov. 1849.

55. JOSEPH[7] **PHIPPEN** (*Joseph*[6], *Samuel*[5-3,] *Joseph*[2], *David*[1]) was born at Westminster, Vermont 29 April 1780, son of Joseph and Silence (Paul) Phippen.[987] He married at Athens, Vermont 20 April 1802, **SUBMIT ("MITTY") HOOKER,** who was born at Westminster 9 July 1786.[988]

Between 1807 and 1810, Joseph Phippen and his family settled in Angelica Township, Allegany County, New York, where he is enumerated in subsequent censuses. Joseph Phippen died there, intestate, by 26 May 1845, when petition was filed for letters of administration, which

---

982   George Tuttle, *The Descendants of William and Elizabeth Tuttle* (Rutland Vt., 1883), 508

983   Ibid.

984   Ibid. Horatio and his family are listed in the 1850 and 1860 census in Watertown; widow Elvira is listed in the 1870 and 1880 census in Watertown. In 1880, Elvira was living with her son Homer and his family.

985   *The Watertown Herald,* 18 Feb. 1893 (news2.nnyln.net/watertown-herald/search. html).

986   Unless noted otherwise, information about their children is from Tuttle, *The Descendants of William and Elizabeth Tuttle,* 509.

987   Paul-Paull MS, 2: 78.

988   Submit Hooker's birth and marriage date communicated by Kenneth[12] Phippen.

were subsequently granted to his widow, Mitty Phippen. Of the net estate of about $110, one third was granted to his widow; the rest was divided in equal shares among seven surviving children, listed below. [989] Widow Mitty Phippen, of Angelica, wrote her will 17 June 1851. The will, which was proved 8 May 1873, left all her property already in his possession, plus four cows, to her son Henry Phippen of Angelica.

Children of Joseph and Submit (Hooker) Phippen surviving in 1845:[990]

	i.	SILENCE/LILA[8] PHIPPEN, b. at Westminster 5 Oct. 1802;[991] m., before 1845, ENOS SHAW.
84	ii.	DANIEL PHIPPEN, b. in Vt. about 1803.
	iii.	AMY PHIPPEN, b. in Vt. about 1807; m., before 1845, DAVID JENNINGS; issue.
	iv.	JOHN PHIPPEN, b. in N.Y. about 1812; living, single, with his mother Mitty, in 1860.
85	v.	ORLANDO/ORA PHIPPEN, b. at Angelica 3 Aug. 1815.
	vi.	DIANA PHIPPEN, b. at Angelica about 1819; m. before 1845, ADAM RENWICH.
86	vii.	HENRY PHIPPEN, b. at Angelica about 1827.

56. BENJAMIN[7] PHIPPEN (*Joseph*[6], *Samuel*[5–3,] *Joseph*[2], *David*[1]) was born at Westminster, Vermont 6 October 1781, son of Joseph and Silence (Paul) Phippen,[992] and died at Westminster 31 November 1836.[993] He married at Athens, Vermont, in December 1823, **SARAH ATCHERSON** of Rockingham, Vermont, who was born at Greenfield, Massachusetts 2 October 1784, daughter of Thomas and Agnes (Simpson) Atcherson.[994] She died at Rockingham 28 March 1861.

Benjamin Phippen was a farmer in Westminster.[995]

---

[989] Allegany County, N.Y., Probate Book E, p. 160; Administration, Book E, p. 338; Settlement, Book 7, p. 316. Communicated by Kenneth Phippen. Paul-Paull MS, 2:78, lists his death date as 26 Dec. 1845, but this must be an error.

[990] Unless noted otherwise, information about children is from 1860 U.S. Census, Allegany Co., N.Y., pp. 375, 378.

[991] Vermont Vital Records (as Lila).

[992] Paul-Paull MS, 2: 78.

[993] Ibid. A Benjamin Phippen who died 20 May 1830, aged 52, is buried near Joseph and Silence (Paul) Phippen in Westminster, Vt. Vermont Vital Records says Benjamin died 20 Nov. 1836 (buried at West Parish in Westminster).

[994] Paul-Paull MS, 2: 79.

[995] Ibid.

Children of Benjamin and Sarah (Atcherson) Phippen, born at Westminster:[996]

    i.   JANE AUGUSTA[8] PHIPPEN, b. 29 July 1828; m. 4 July 1850, DAVID A. ABBOTT of Putney, Vt.[997] They settled at Brattleboro, Vt. Children (surname *Abbott*): 1. *Ada More,* b. at Hinsdale, N. H., 8 April 1852, d. at Putney 31 Aug. 1863; 2. *Jennie Lena,* b. at Putney 24 Jan. 1857; m. *George Asa Eels.*

   ii.   MARY ZILPHA PHIPPEN, b. 15 Oct. 1832; m. 20 April 1862, GEORGE W. FULLER of Bellows Falls, Vt., son of Washington and Lucinda (Constantino) Fuller of Brattleboro. Children (surname *Fuller*), all born at Brattleboro: 1. *Walter G.,* b. 6 Sept. 1863, living in Boston in 1885; 2. *Albert A. H.,* b. 4 Sept. 1866, living at Effingham, Ill., in 1885; 3. *Abbie E.,* b. in 1873.

57. JONATHAN[7] **PHIPPEN** (*Joseph*[6], *Samuel*[5–3,] *Joseph*[2], *David*[1]) was born at Westminster, Vermont 11 July 1783, son of Joseph and Silence (Paul) Phippen. He married **VINA PARMETER.** No further record.[998]

Children of Jonathan and Vina (Parmeter) Phippen:

    i.   ACHSAH[8] PHIPPEN.
   ii.   ORPHA PHIPPEN.
  iii.   LAURA PHIPPEN.

58. ISAAC[7] **PHIPPEN** (*Joseph*[6], *Samuel*[5–3,] *Joseph*[2], *David*[1]) was born at Rockingham, Vermont 15 February 1793, son of Joseph and Silence (Paul) Phippen.[999] He died at Salt Lake City, Utah 2 May 1875. He was a farmer, wagon maker, carpenter, and shoemaker.

As a young man, Isaac Phippen moved from Vermont to Allegany County, New York, where his oldest brother lived. A few years later, he moved to Springfield, Ohio.[1000] He married there, in September 1818, **ADAH STEWART,** daughter of Luther and Esther (Smith) Stewart, who was born at Neversink, New York 19 July 1795.[1001] Adah died at Salt Lake City 14 April 1870, after fifty-two years of marriage and pioneering.

---

[996] Information about children is from Paul-Paull MS, 2: 79, 81.

[997] Paul-Paull MS says her name was Jane.

[998] Paul-Paull MS, 2: 78–79.

[999] Ibid., 2: 80.

[1000] Ibid.

[1001] Ibid.

Isaac and Adah moved back to Vermont from Ohio in 1823, and then made a further move to Chatauqua County, New York, in 1825. In the late 1830s they became early members of the Mormon Church, Isaac Phippen attaining the rank of high priest by 1848.[1002] They moved to Commerce, Illinois (later called Nauvoo), in 1839.[1003] During the brief period between the completion of the Nauvoo temple in December 1845 and its abandonment in February 1846, Isaac and Adah (Stewart) Phippen, with their two eldest sons and daughters-in-law, were among the group of Mormon faithful who underwent sacramental endowment there.[1004] They left Nauvoo with the Mormon exodus in 1846; settled on the Missouri River, north of Omaha, Nebraska, in 1847; moved north across the river into the newly formed Pottawattamie County, Iowa, by 1848; and finally migrated to Utah in 1852.[1005] They resided in Grantsville and Coalville, Utah, and then settled with their son, James Worthington Phippen, in Salt Lake City.[1006] Adah (Stewart) Phippen was one of the first of about one thousand early members of the Mormon Female Relief Society at Nauvoo between 1842 and 1844.[1007]

Isaac Phippen's youngest daughter, Ada Loiza (Phippen) Walker, when in her seventies, wrote the following remarkable memoir of her family's experiences as early members of the Mormon community, for the Daughters of the Utah Pioneers:[1008]

My Grandfather Joseph Phippen was born in Massachusetts in 1762. His wife's name was Silva Paul. They moved from Vermont, where my father, Isaac, was born in 1792 in the town of Westminster, Winden County, the seventh child of a family of 13 children. He

---

[1002] On 2 January 1848, Isaac "Phippin" was one of the thirteen high priests at Allred, Pottawattamie Co., Iowa. See Lyman D. Platt, "Early Branches of the Church of Jesus Christ of Latter-Day Saints, 1830–1850," *Nauvoo Journal* 3 [1991]: 3–50 at 3.

[1003] Isaac Phippen is listed in the 1842 Hancock Co. (Ill.) Tax Records: Lyman D. Platt, "1842 Hancock County Tax Records" [Index], *Nauvoo Journal* 2 [1990]: 24–52 at 44.

[1004] H. Michael Marquardt, "Nauvoo Temple Endowment Index," data from the Nauvoo Temple records of the Church of Jesus Christ of Latter-day Saints, <*http://www.xmission.com/~research/family/familypage.htm*>.

[1005] The migration path is as given in Paul-Paull MS, 2: 80.

[1006] Ibid.

[1007] Maurine Carr Ward, "'This Institution Is a Good One': The Female Relief Society of Nauvoo, 17 March 1842 to 16 March 1844," *Mormon Historical Studies* 3 [2002]: 86–203 at 170.

[1008] This text was taken from an electronic version, posted in a WorldConnect database in 2000 by Phippen descendant Susan Marie (Phippen) Stewart of Bountiful, Utah.

lived there as a boy working on a farm and going to school in the winter months where he secured a fair education. When he was about 25 years old, a cousin of his sent for him to come to Ohio and learn the carpenter trade. He went and learned the carpenter's and builder's trade. He also learned to make all kinds of furniture which came in very handy in later years. After he had been in Ohio some time when he met the girl that became my mother. Her name was Ada Stewart. She was one of a large family. My mother was born 19 July 1798 in a western county of the state of New York. Her father and family removed to the state of Ohio, in Clark Co. My father and mother were married 18 October 1818 in Ohio. They lived there some years and my mother had two children and they were doing well, but about that time my father's mother died and his father wanted him to come home and take charge of his farm, as his older brothers had married and left the state. So they removed to Vermont and lived there some years. My mother had two more children—three boys and a girl. After awhile my grandfather married again and things became unpleasant. So my father removed his family to Chatugua Co, New York, where they lived many years and became well fixed financially and enjoyed life. My brothers and sister grew up with the advantages of good schools and plenty to live on.

In 1833 they heard the Gospel and joined the Church of Jesus Christ, but did not move to any of the places where the Mormon people had settled. They were counseled to stay and keep a place for the missionaries to stay as they traveled through. So they stayed until 1839. Then my father sold everything and removed his family to Commerce, later called Nauvoo. My two oldest brothers and my sister were baptized soon after their parents. The name was soon changed to Nauvoo. They were all sick with the ague but my father and his oldest brother. So my father secured a piece of land near the city and built a house where they lived a while. In 1841 my mother lost her young child; it was a great trial to them. Soon after my father got a lot in Nauvoo and built a good house where I was born in 1842.

Before I was very old the people not of our faith
began to have trouble with the Mormons. They wanted
to drive them from their homes as they had done so many
times before. Things got worse and worse and when I was
a year and 10 months old the Prophet and his brother
Hyrum were martyred. I have heard my mother tell what
a time of sorrow it was, and times were hard and many
of the people were poor but they continued to work on
the temple and finally got it finished so that many went
through and were endowed and felt repaid for all their
hardships.

In 1845 times were very bad in Nauvoo. They had
to stand guard around the city and my brother was on
guard and was shot accidentally and died a few hours
later. In 1846 we had to leave our homes with hundreds
of others. There was much suffering among the people
and many were sick. We had two wagons for our family
and my brother's family. So we left everything, almost,
and crossed the Mississippi River and came to Winter
Quarters where we stayed until after the Mormon
Battalion boys had gone. Also after the first company had
gone to Utah. In the summer of 1847 my father planted
some corn and other vegetables and raised considerable
stuff that helped us through the winter. In the summer
of 1848 we crossed the Missouri River into the state of
Iowa. My father secured a large farm where he raised a
hundred bushels of corn that he sold to the gold seekers
to get money to go to Utah. He also made wagons for
people to cross the plains. My mother spun and made
cloth for clothing and every effort was made to get fit out
to cross the plains. With hard work and economy they
got a good outfit together, but as there were some poor
that had to be helped to cross the plains, my father had a
widow and three children in one of his wagons. On June
28, 1852, we were ready to start to Utah again. My father
and mother left everything only that which they could
put in the two wagons. Left their farm and never got
one cent for it. Their house and nearly everything that
was in them. Only a small stove and a chair for two, not
even a table, but we had plenty of provisions and clothes
and had no regrets for what we left. The only thought

was to get to Zion, the valley of the Mormons. We had quite a time getting started. The cows decided they did not want to go to Utah but with much persuasion and some other things, we got to the Missouri River. There were hundreds of wagons waiting their turn to cross the river. I think we stayed two nights before we could cross as there was only one boat and two wagons with teams could cross at a time. Then there were all the loose stock to cross after Father had gotten all his things over. They with a hundred other wagons, traveled several miles to a large flat where we camped, and the companies were organized into fifties with a captain over each fifty families and a captain over each ten. Our company was the 12th and our captain was Harmon Cutler. Two other companies were organized at the same time; the 10th and the 11th. We traveled together for several hundred miles for mutual protection. We saw lots of buffalo and lots of Indian scares. If there were wood and grass, and water for the teams, our captain always camped over for Sunday and held meetings and we generally had meetings Thursday nights. There they sang the songs [of] Zion and rejoiced to think they were going to the Valley. No one grumbled over their hardships. We went on and on and had dances. We stopped and dried buffalo meat and washed our clothes when we stopped for a day or two. The women would take their stoves out and wash the clothes and bake up a lot of bread and cakes. When we milked the cows, Mother would put the milk in the churn and when we camped at noon the butter would be churned and we ate the milk with our bread and mush. They never cooked at noon. That was a time to rest. When we got to a place called Ash Hollow the Indians stole all our horses. So the captain had to have oxen draw his carriage the rest of the way to the Valley. When we got to Independence Rock we had a wedding. Lots of the young folks went through the Devil's Gate. I wanted to go but Mother would not let me. She said I was too little. Our captain was awful slow and some of the company got dissatisfied and said that the snow would catch us before we got to the Valley. So they divided the company and put my father in as Captain and we went along fine but had some snow in

South Pass. We were all glad when we saw the valley of the Great Salt Lake. It surely looked beautiful to us. We beat the other part of the company 15 days.

Before we had been in the city a week my father bought a lot with a small house on it, in the 10th ward. And we were glad to have a roof over our heads once more. At the next spring conference, 1853, they laid the corner stone for the temple. Being a child I watched everything they did very carefully and never will forget the impression I had at the time. It made a mark that has never left me and never will while life lasts. I was 10 years old at the time.

In 1854 my father moved his family to Grantsville where we lived several years. The Indians were very troublesome for some years, so we lived in a fort all the time we lived in Grantsville. My father engaged in farming and stock raising, helping to build the fort walls, and standing guard at times when the Indians were worse. My mother was a fine nurse so she had plenty of calls. At other times she spun and made cloth for our clothes. She made a great deal of butter and cheese, made molasses out of beets, out of parsnips, and anything that had sugar in it.

In 1850 we moved back to Salt Lake City. We stayed there about two years. Then Father thought he had to have a place for his stock. So in 1861 Father got land in Coalville, Summit County, and still we moved. We lived there some years. In 1867 the Indians became very bad in Summit County and we had to move into Coalville. We had been living one mile and a half from the settlement, and it was no longer safe for a few families to stay out so far. My parents moved back to Salt Lake City and lived in our old home, where they both died. My mother died on April 14, 1870, aged 72. My father died May 2, 1875, aged 86. They were buried in the City Cemetery in Salt Lake City.

Children of Isaac and Adah (Stewart) Phippen:[1009]

87   i.   JAMES WORTHINGTON[8] PHIPPEN, b. at Springfield, Ohio 12 Oct. 1819.
88   ii. JOSEPH FREEMAN PHIPPEN, b. at Springfield 20 Sept. 1822.
        iii. ESTHER PARMELIA PHIPPEN, b. at Rockingham,Vt. 6 Sept. 1824; d. at Springville, Utah 3 May 1913; m. at Nauvoo 27 Oct. 1844, NOAH PACKARD,[1010] who was b. at Plainfield, Mass. 24 April 1821, son of Noah and Sophia (Bundy) Packard; he died at Springville 26 Jan. 1900. Children (surname *Packard*): 1. *Noah Romanzo*; 2. *Adah Loanda*; 3. *James Willis*; 4. *Charles Isaac*; 5. *Orrin Smith*; 6. *Lillian May*.
        iv. ISAAC CLARK PHIPPEN, b. at Charlotte, N.Y. 17 Dec. 1828; d. at Nauvoo 18 Sept. 1845 (accidentally shot while standing guard during the troubles of 1845).
        v.   ASA STEWART PHIPPEN, b. at Charlotte 30 April 1832; d. of fever at Nauvoo 7 Jan. 1843; bur. there 15 Jan. 1843, aged 10.[1011]
89   vi. SYLVESTER SMITH PHIPPEN, b. at Charlotte 20 May 1834.
        vii. ALMON SHERMAN PHIPPEN, b. at Charlotte 6 Feb. 1837; d. at Hancock, Ill. 2 Sept. 1841.
        viii. ADAH LOIZA PHIPPEN, b. at Nauvoo 2 Sept. 1842; d. at Salt Lake City 31 Dec. 1933; m. (1) at Salt Lake City 14 March 1857, AROET LUCIUS LITTLE HALE; (2) at Coalville, Utah 17 May 1863, JEREMIAH MAHONEY; (3) at Salt Lake City 1 Aug. 1870, WILLIAM HENRY WALKER. She had children by all three husbands.

59. CALVIN[7] **PHIPPEN** (*Joseph*[6], *Samuel*[5-3,] *Joseph*[2], *David*[1]) was born at Westminster, Vermont 4 May 1799, son of Joseph and Silence (Paul) Phippen. He died at Tioga, Pennsylvania 22 March 1876. Calvin married at Westminster 4 July 1824, **JERUSHA GOODELL,** who was born at Westminster 6 August 1802, daughter of Levi and Olive (____) Goodell.[1012] Jerusha died 31 May 1891.They had lived in Mount Holly, Vermont, then settled in Tioga County, Pennsylvania, in 1831.[1013]

[1009] Unless noted otherwise, information about children is from Paul-Paull MS, 2: 80, 81, 83.

[1010] Also mentioned in Charles Packard Wight, *Descendants of Samuel Packard* (North Auburn, Maine, 1956), 82 (typescript in the collection of the Maine Historical Society).

[1011] Fred E. Woods, "The Cemetery Record of William D. Huntington, Nauvoo Sexton," *Mormon Historical Studies* 3.1 [2002]: 131–63 at 137.

[1012] Paul-Paull MS, 2: 81; Clarence W. Bowen, *The History of Woodstock, Connecticut* (Norwood, Mass., 1926-43), 5: 637.

[1013] *History of Tioga County, Pennsylvania* (New York, 1883), 313–26.

Calvin and Jerusha (Goodell) Phippen are buried together with their son Joseph Phippen at the Lawrenceville Cemetery in Tioga.[1014]

Children of Calvin and Jerusha (Goodell) Phippen:[1015]

i. JOSEPH[8] PHIPPEN, b. at Westminster 7 April 1825; d. at Tioga 16 Nov. 1904. He moved with his father to Mount Holly, and then to Tioga Co. He was a postmaster and merchant in that county in 1885. He never married and was living with his mother in 1885.

ii. FREEMAN PHIPPEN, b. at Mt. Holly 28 Oct. 1826. He m. OPHELIA ____,[1016] and settled at Lawrenceville, Tioga Co., where he became a contractor and builder. He was living there in 1885.

iii. ORVILLA PHIPPEN, b. at Plymouth, Vt. 15 Dec. 1828; m. JUDSON BEEMAN.

iv. MARY M. PHIPPEN, b. at Westminster 25 April 1831; m. BENJAMIN MEADE.

v. CURTIS R. PHIPPEN, b. at Lawrenceville 3 Feb. 1835. He enlisted in the 86th New York Regiment and saw three years of service during the Civil War. He was a carpenter and builder, and d. about 1886.

vi. JANE ADALINE PHIPPEN, b. at Lawrenceville 16 May 1838; m. 10 Dec. 1863, JOSHUA HOBART WEBB of Rockingham, Vt., who was b. 9 Dec. 1837.[1017] She was living at Bellows Falls, Vt., in 1885. Child (surname *Webb*): *Blanch,* b. at Lawrenceville 30 July 1878.

vii. HORACE A. PHIPPEN, b. at Lawrenceville 19 Aug. 1841; d. about 1886. He fought in the 86th New York Regiment during the Civil War and was wounded at the Battle of Bull Run. He was a carpenter and builder.

viii. ELIZA A. PHIPPEN, b. at Lawrenceville 12 Nov. 1844; m. WILLIAM WOOD.

90   ix. LOREN D. PHIPPEN, b. 20 July 1848.

x. CHILD, d. in infancy.

[1014] Transcription of Lawrenceville Cemetery records, Lawrenceville Borough, Tioga Co., Pennsylvania, by M. Lucille Stage et al., 2002. At "Tri-Counties Genealogy & History by Joyce M. Tice" <*www.RootsWeb.com/~srgp/cemt/lawrd04.htm*>.

[1015] Unless noted otherwise, information about children is from Paul-Paull MS, 2: 81, 84.

[1016] 1880 U.S. Census, Lawrenceville, Tioga Co., Pa.; they had no children living with them at that time.

[1017] Lyman S. Hayes, *History of the town of Rockingham, Vermont* (Bellows Falls Vt., 1907), 779.

60. CLARK[7] **PHIPPEN** (*Jonathan*[6], *Samuel*[5–3,] *Joseph*[2], *David*[1]) was born at Westminster, Vermont 24 January 1789, son of Jonathan Atwater and Mary (Averill) Phippen. He died in 1859.[1018] Clark Phippen married at Westminster 24 December 1810, **BETSEY WRIGHT,**[1019] daughter of Elihu and Betsey (Wheeler) Wright. She died 14 August 1869, aged 80, and was buried at Crown Point, New York.[1020]

They lived first at Westminster. In 1818, Clark appears on the Assessor's Roll for the Town of Crown Point.[1021] Later he lived in Stockholm, New York.

Children of Clark and Betsey (Wright) Phippen:[1022]

91   i.   SAMUEL[8] PHIPPEN, b. about 1816.

        ii. ADALINE PHIPPEN, b. about 1820; d. 18 Feb. 1844, aged 24.

        iii. TILER PHIPPEN, b. in 1822; d. 2 Feb. 1823, aged 10 months.

92   iv. AMBROSE PHIPPEN, b. about 1824.

93   v.   AMASA B. PHIPPEN, b. at Crown Point 9 Feb. 1826.

94   vi. WARREN T. PHIPPEN, b. 1 Dec. 1827.

        vii. MARTHA PHIPPEN, b. in Dec. 1830; m. JUDSON WOLCOTT. She was on the membership list of the Congregational Church of Crown Point in 1869. Martha d. 2 March 1877, aged 47. Her husband d. 9 Feb. 1878, aged 54.

        viii. JANE PHIPPEN (called "ADALINE" in marriage record), b. at Stockholm, St. Lawrence Co., N.Y. 23 May 1832; d. 5 July 1919, aged 87; m. at Crown Point, as his second wife, 3 July 1851, ALMON COLTON FARR, son of Abijah and Rocksel (Hasting) Farr, who was b. at Crown Point in 1818. He d. at Shoreham, Vt. 19 Jan. 1889, aged 71 years. Children (surname *Farr*): 1. *Belle Jane,* m. *William Howard Birchard;* 2. *Winifred,* spinster.

61. DAVID ATWATER or **AVERILL**[7] **PHIPPEN** (*Jonathan Atwater*[6], *Samuel*[5–3], *Joseph*[2], *David*[1]) was born at Westminster, Vermont 2 January 1798, son of Jonathan Atwater and Mary (Averill) Phippen. He died 1 June 1865 aged 67 and is buried in the New East Parish Cemetery in Westminster.[1023]

[1018] Correspondence with G. Birchard, Springfield, Mass., 28 March 1977.

[1019] Ibid.

[1020] Cemetery marker, White Church Cemetery, Crown Point, N.Y.

[1021] H. P. Smith, *History of Essex County* [New York] (Syracuse, N.Y., 1885), 335.

[1022] Unless noted otherwise, information about children comes from correspondence with G. Birchard, Springfield, Mass., 28 March 1977.

[1023] Cemetery marker, New Cemetery, Westminster, Vt.

David A. Phippen married at Putney, Vermont 12 April 1822, HANNAH SARGENT, who was born at Putney 8 August 1796, daughter of Samuel and Mary (Washburn) Sargent.[1024] She died 4 September 1864.[1025] They lived on Phippen Hill, where his father had settled.

Children of David A. and Hannah (Sargent) Phippen, born at Westminster:[1026]

  i. ANNE[8] PHIPPEN, b. 28 Dec. 1822; m. 16 May 1847, A.V.D. UNDERWOOD.

  ii MARY PHIPPEN, b. 24 Aug. 1824; m. 25 Dec. 1850, JOSEPH IDE.

95 iii. RODNEY ATWATER PHIPPEN, b. 26 Oct. 1826.

  iv. NARCISSE BELINDE PHIPPEN, b. 27 April 1828; d. unm. 5 July 1863.[1027]

  v. ELECTRA RICHARDSON PHIPPEN, b. 23 April 1830; m. (1) 4 Dec. 1851, JOHN M. PROUTY, who was b. at Royalston, Vt. 15 June 1819, son of Isaac and Sally (Clement) Prouty.[1028] John Prouty d. 6 July 1859. Electra m. (2) at Putney 1 Jan. 1868, DANIEL LYMAN ALDRICH. Electra d. 3 Oct. 1868.[1029]

  vi. RUTH HANNAH PHIPPEN, b. 1 Sept. 1833;[1030] m. at Brattleboro, Vt. 20 Aug. 1863, ALBERT SIDNEY SPENCER.

  vii. SARAH ISABEL PHIPPEN, b. April 30 1835;[1031] m. 17 April 1866, JOHN LOOMIS COLLINS; d. in 1909.[1032]

  viii. MARGARET LUCY PHIPPEN, b. 21 Jan. 1838; d. 7 Aug. 1843.[1033]

62. SAMUEL[7] PHIPPEN (*Jonathan Atwater[6]*, *Samuel[5-3]*, *Joseph[2]*, *David[1]*) was born at Westminster, Vermont 7 October 1799, son of Jonathan Atwater and Mary (Averill) Phippen. He died at Lyndon, Vermont 8 December 1887, aged 88 years, 2 months, 1 day.[1034] Samuel married

---

[1024] Christopher C. Denny, *Genealogy of the Denny Family in England and America* (Leicester, Mass., 1886), 96.

[1025] Cemetery marker, New Cemetery, Westminster, Vt.

[1026] Unless noted otherwise, information about children is from the Vermont Vital Records and/or Denny, *Genealogy of the Denny Family*, 120–21.

[1027] Cemetery marker, New Cemetery, Westminster, Vt.

[1028] *Vital Records of Royalston, Massachusetts to the end of the year 1849* (Worcester, Mass., 1906), 60.

[1029] Charles Henry Pope, *Prouty (Proute) Genealogy* (Boston, 1910), 133.

[1030] Paul-Paull MS, 2: 89.

[1031] Ibid.

[1032] Correspondence with E. Thornton Clark, 1977.

[1033] Cemetery marker, New Cemetery, Westminster, Vt.

[1034] Vermont Vital Records.

at Lyndon, Vermont 6 November 1825, **BETSEY DREW,** who was born at Gilmanton, New Hampshire in August 1800, daughter of Theo and Betsey (____) Drew of Burke, Vermont;[1035] Betsey died at Lyndon 9 September 1883, aged 83 years 29 days. Samuel lived in Lyndon and was a farmer.

Children of Samuel and Betsey (Drew) Phippen:[1036]

96   i.   LUCIUS A.[8] PHIPPEN, b. 28 Oct. 1828.

       ii. DELIA G. PHIPPEN, b. about 1828; m. at Lyndon 9 March 1858, LYMAN J. RANDALL.[1037]

       iii. FANNY PHIPPEN, m. 21 Oct. 1850, DAVID GILSON, who was b. at East Burke, Vt. 30 April 1824, son of Leonard and Abigail (Brigham) Gilson; d. 21 Dec. 1897.[1038]

       iv. MARY PHIPPEN, b. about 1830.

97   v.   ELMORE PHIPPEN, b. at Lyndon 27 Oct. 1834.

       vi. MELISSA B. PHIPPEN, b. about 1837; m. at Lyndon 15 May 1859, MELVIN WHITE.

98   vii. AMASA R. PHIPPEN, b. 4 July 1840.

       viii. MYRON A. PHIPPEN, b. 1 Oct. 1845; d. of yellow fever at New Berne, N. C. 14 Sept. 1864, "aged 29[19] years 11 months 14 days; a farmer in Lyndon."[1039]

63. NATHANIEL[7] PHIPPEN (*Joshua[6]*, *Nathaniel[5-4]*, *Samuel[3]*, *Joseph[2]*, *David[1]*) was born at Salem, Massachusetts 28 January 1765, son of Joshua and Hannah (Sibley) Phippen;[1040] he was baptized there 3 June 1770.[1041] He died at Salem 9 March 1809, aged 44 years, of consumption.[1042] Nathaniel married at Salem 4 September 1786, **ANNA PICKETT** of Beverly, Massachusetts.[1043] Anna died at Salem 22 December 1834, aged 70.[1044]

[1035] Vermont Vital Records.

[1036] Unless otherwise noted, information on the children is from the Vermont and New Hampshire Vital Records.

[1037] Ibid.

[1038] Willard Brigham, *The History of the Brigham Family* (New York: The Grafton Press), 494.

[1039] Vermont Vital Records.

[1040] *Vital Records of Salem, Massachusetts to the end of the year 1849,* 2: 168.

[1041] Ibid. (baptism record refers to him as "Nathan").

[1042] Ibid., 6: 138.

[1043] Ibid., 4: 190, 194.

[1044] *Vital Records of Salem, Massachusetts to the end of the year 1849,* 6: 137, states that "Anna, w. of Nathaniel b. July 22, 1769, d. Dec. 22, 1834, a. 70 y." The next entry shows, under deaths in Salem, "Anna, July 23, 1815." Perley states her death date

Nathaniel was a cooper; after their marriage, the family lived in Portsmouth, New Hampshire (where Nathaniel was enumerated in the 1790 census[1045]) but returned to Salem, where he lived on Derby Street.[1046]

Children of Nathaniel and Anna (Pickett) Phippen:[1047]

99   i.   SAMUEL[8] PHIPPEN b. at Salem 5 Feb. 1787.

100   ii.   BENJAMIN PHIPPEN, b. at Portsmouth 25 Oct. 1788.

101   iii.   NATHANIEL PHIPPEN, b. at Portsmouth 19 Feb. 1791.

102   iv.   JOSHUA PHIPPEN, b. at Salem 15 Nov. 1793.

       v.   EUNICE PHIPPEN, b. at Salem 26 Feb., bp. there 10 July 1796; d. unm. at Salem 19 Nov. 1863.[1048]

      vi.   ANN PHIPPEN, b. at Salem 20 July 1798; d. unm. at Chelsea, Mass. 10 Dec. 1882.[1049] The will of Ann Phippen, single woman of Gloucester, Mass., named Nathaniel Phippen of Salem, nephew; Joseph Phippen of Salem, nephew; William T. Phippen of Boston, nephew; John P. Phippen of Boston, nephew; Joshua Phippen of Salem, nephew; Mary Dustin Phippen of Salem, niece; Charlote Lane, widow, of Annisquam, sister; and others.[1050]

    vii.   CHARLOTTE PHIPPEN, b. at Salem 13 Aug. 1800;[1051] m. there 10 Dec. 1822, Captain OLIVER GRIFFIN LANE,[1052] who was b. at Gloucester, Massachusetts 25 Nov. 1798, son of Gideon and Hannah (Griffin)

---

as 23 July 1815 (*The History of Salem, Massachusetts,* 2: 330). The later death date seems more acceptable because the record names Anna's husband as Nathaniel. The authors have assigned the Anna who died 23 July 1815 as the wife of William[6] Phippen (*Thomas[5], Nathaniel[4], Samuel[3], Joseph[2], David[1]*).

[1045] 1790 Census, Portsmouth, Rockingham County, New Hampshire, Roll: M637_5; p. 209.

[1046] Ellery and Bowditch, *The Pickering Genealogy,* 2: 350. Nathaniel returned to Salem before 1800; he is listed in Salem in the 1800 census. *See* 1800 Census, Salem, Essex County, Massachusetts, Roll: 14; Page: 421; Image: 220.

[1047] Unless noted otherwise, births records are from *Vital Records of Salem, Massachusetts to the end of the year 1849,* 2: 165 (Benjamin, Ann), 166 (Eunice), 167 (Joshua), and 168 (Samuel, Nathaniel). Ellery and Bowditch, *The Pickering Genealogy,* 2: 566–67, states that Benjamin and Nathaniel were born in Portsmouth, N.H.

[1048] Perley, *The History of Salem, Massachusetts,* 2: 330.

[1049] Mass. VR (1882) 339: 347; Essex County, Massachusetts Probate Records, file no. 59305 (will of Ann Phippen of Gloucester).

[1050] Essex County, Massachusetts Probate Records, file no. 59305.

[1051] *Vital Records of Gloucester, Massachusetts to the end of the year 1849,* 1: 539; *Vital Records of Salem, Massachusetts to the end of the year 1849,* 2: 165.

[1052] *Vital Records of Salem, Massachusetts to the end of the year 1849,* 3: 586, 4: 189.

Lane.[1053] He d. at Gloucester 17 Jan. 1867. Charlotte d. there 21
Sept. 1886, aged 86 years, 1 month, and 8 days. They had seven
children.[1054] The following tribute to Charlotte appears in the *Lane
Genealogies:*

Mrs. Charlotte (Phippen) Lane belonged to one of the staid
families peculiar to ancient Salem. She accompanied her husband
on several voyages, sailing to Europe, South America, and around
Cape Horn to California. She was closely identified with the
Universalist church at Annisquam, and when the Sunday School
was organized she was among its earliest teachers. She possessed a
very remarkable memory, which she retained to the last, and would
give facts and recall dates when others were in doubt. 'A kind
friend and neighbor, of generous heart and worthy motives.'

64. JOSHUA[7] **PHIPPEN** (*Joshua*[6], *Nathaniel*[5–4], *Samuel*[3], *Joseph*[2], *David*[1]) was
born at Salem, Massachusetts 2 July 1774, son of Joshua and Hannah
(Sibley) Phippen.[1055] He died at Salem 28 April 1805, aged 31.[1056] He
was a cooper.

Joshua Phippen married at Salem 18 March 1799, **SUSANNA ("ANNA"**
or **"NANCY") TRASK** of Beverly, Massachusetts;[1057] intentions were filed
at Beverly 3 February 1799.[1058] Susanna Trask was born at Beverly 17
August 1774, daughter of Ebenezer and Betsey (___) Trask.[1059] Susanna
(Trask) Phippen died at Beverly 23 (or 24) October 1823, aged 49.[1060]

Children of Joshua and Susannah (Trask) Phippen, born at Salem:[1061]

    i. ANN/NANCY[8] PHIPPEN, b. about 1800; d. of consumption at Beverly
        25 Nov. 1840, aged 40;[1062] m. at Beverly 28 May 1820, DENNISON

[1053] *Vital Records of Gloucester, Massachusetts to the end of the year 1849,* 1: 418.
[1054] James Hill Fitts, *Lane Genealogies,* 3 vols. (Exeter, N.H., 1891–1902), 3: 312–16.
[1055] Sibley, *A History of the Town of Union, Maine,* 500; see also Sibley, The Sibley Family
in America, 1: 576.
[1056] Sibley, *A History of the Town of Union, Maine,* 500; *Vital Records of Salem, Massachusetts
to the end of the year 1849,* 6: 138 (buried 30 April 1805).
[1057] *Vital Records of Salem, Massachusetts to the end of the year 1849,* 4: 189, 397; *Vital
Records of Beverly, Massachusetts to the end of the year 1849,* 2: 238, 311.
[1058] *Vital Records of Beverly, Massachusetts to the end of the year 1849,* 2: 238, 311.
[1059] Ibid., 1: 331.
[1060] Ibid., 2: 526.
[1061] Ellery and Bowditch, *The Pickering Genealogy,* 2: 569.
[1062] *Vital Records of Beverly, Massachusetts to the end of the year 1849,* 2: 387.

WALLIS BROWN,[1063] who was b. there 17 Feb. 1797, son of Wallis and Hannah (Cole) Brown of Beverly.[1064] Dennison Wallis d. at Beverly 12 Oct. 1823.[1065]

ii. HANNAH PHIPPEN m. at Beverly 27 May 1821, TRISTRAM WOODBURY,[1066] who was b. there 11 Sept. 1796, son of Andrew Woodbury.[1067]

65. HARDY[7] **PHIPPEN** (*Joshua*[6], *Nathaniel*[5-4], *Samuel*[3], *Joseph*[2], *David*[1]) was born at Salem, Massachusetts 6 and baptized there 12 July 1778, son of Joshua and Hannah (Sibley) Phippen.[1068] He died of dropsy at Salem 9 October 1868.[1069] Hardy Phippen married at Salem 18 March 1804, his stepsister **URSULA KNAPP SYMONDS,**[1070] daughter of Jonathan and Ursula (Knapp) Symonds.[1071] Ursula died at Salem 17 February 1859.[1072]

Hardy was a master mariner.[1073] He was the mate on the ill-fated voyage of the brigantine *Nabby,* captained by Nathaniel Hathorne on its 1808 trip to Surinam. Captain Hathorne, along with six others of the crew, died of disease, and the ship had to be sailed back to Salem under Hardy's captaincy.[1074] On 6 July 1809, along with Benjamin Babbidge, he was listed as owner and master of the 103-ton schooner *Minerva,*[1075] and on 29 March 1809 as the master of the 154-ton brig *Falmouth*. On 9 December 1809 William Bentley reported:

> Last night the brig Minerva, H. Phippen, after high tide entering our harbour ran into the cove on the south side of Abbot's point after having passed the dangerous ledges

---

[1063] Ibid., 45, 238.

[1064] Ibid., 1: 54. He was baptized at Beverly 6 July 1806. *See also* Ellery and Bowditch, *The Pickering Genealogy,* 2: 569.

[1065] *Vital Records of Beverly, Massachusetts to the end of the year 1849,* 2: 385.

[1066] Ibid., 238, 351.

[1067] Ibid., 1: 385.

[1068] Ellery and Bowditch, *The Pickering Genealogy,* 2: 352.

[1069] Mass.VR (1868) 211: 248.

[1070] *Vital Records of Salem, Massachusetts to the end of the year 1849,* 4: 189, 371.

[1071] Ellery and Bowditch, *The Pickering Genealogy,* 2: 352.

[1072] Mass.VR (1859) 129: 171.

[1073] Perley, *The History of Salem, Massachusetts,* 2: 330.

[1074] Hubert H. Hoeltje, "Captain Nathaniel Hathorne: Father of the Famous Salem Novelist," *Essex Institute Historical Collections* 89 [1953]: 352–53.

[1075] "Ship Registers," *Essex Institute Historical Collections* 41 [1905]: 151–52.

at that point. She was gotten off without much damage next tide.[1076]

He served as a private in Captain N. Blood's Company, Lieut. Colonel J.White's Regiment, from 17 September to 10 October 1814 at Salem for the purpose of military instruction during the War of 1812.[1077]

The obituary notice for Captain Phippen, printed in the *Salem Register* on 12 October 1868, stated "that before he retired from the sea, he had filled all stations, from boy to captain; that he had traversed all oceans, and visited all parts within the reach of maritime adventure; that he was an active and worthy citizen from the beginning to the end, and that his faculties, intellectually and physically, were wonderfully preserved to the last. He followed the sea about twenty-five years, commanding the ships of the most prominent merchants of Salem. He afterwards engaged in the grocery business in Salem."[1078]

Children of Hardy and Ursula Knapp (Symonds) Phippen, born at Salem:[1079]

103   i.   JOSEPH HARDY[8] Phippen, b. 10 June 1807.
       ii.   URSULA SYMONDS PHIPPEN, b. 21 Sept. 1809; m. at Salem 10 March 1840, ISAAC NEEDHAM CHAPMAN.[1080]
104   iii. JOSHUA PHIPPEN, b. 13 Dec. 1812.
105   iv.   GEORGE DEAN PHIPPEN, b. 13 April 1815.

66. JOSEPH[7] PHIPPEN (*Joshua[6]*, *Nathaniel[5-4]*, *Samuel[3]*, *Joseph[2]*, *David[1]*) was born at Salem, Massachusetts 14 March 1783, son of Joshua and Hannah (Sibley) Phippen[1081]. He was lost at sea on 31 August 1818.[1082] He married at Salem 1 March 1807, **LOIS FAIRFIELD,**[1083] daughter of

---

[1076] *The Diary of William Bentley,* 3: 483.

[1077] Massachusetts Adjutant General's Office, *Records of the Massachusetts Volunteer Militia Called Out by the Governor of Massachusetts to Suppress a Threatened Invasion During the War of 1812–14* (Boston, 1913), 138.

[1078] Ellery and Bowditch, *The Pickering Genealogy,* 2: 352.

[1079] Births are recorded in *Vital Records of Salem, Massachusetts to the end of the year 1849,* 2: 166 (George), 167 (Joseph, Joshua), 169 (Ursula).

[1080] *Vital Records of Salem, Massachusetts to the end of the year 1849,* 3: 202, 4: 191; *Columbian Centinel,* 14 March 1840.

[1081] Sibley, *A History of the Town of Union, Maine,* 500–1. The information in this volume was provided to the author by George D. Phippen. Ibid., 507.

[1082] Ibid., 501.

[1083] *Vital Records of Salem, Massachusetts to the end of the year 1849,* 3: 345, 4: 190.

William and Rebecca (Becket) Fairfield of Salem.[1084] He was called Joseph Phippen Jr. to distinguish him from Joseph[7], son of Thomas.[1085]

Joseph Phippen was a mariner. He served aboard the *Grand Turk*, a famous privateer, during the War of 1812. Captain Green of the *Grand Turk* placed Joseph Phippen in charge of the captured British brig Acorn and had him sail it back to Salem.[1086]

Joseph was captain of the ship *Albatros* and was washed overboard on 31 August 1818. Felt's *Annals of Salem* has the following entry:

> Aug. 31 [1818] The Albatros, full of sea skins and oil, from Faulkland Islands, is wrecked in a severe gale, loses her captain, Joseph Phippen, and five men. The mate and four others are taken off three days after the calamity. They left five of their company at the Islands, with a sloop, to collect a similar cargo.[1087]

The Rev. William Bentley also noted the loss of Captain Phippen:

> [4 April 1819] Lois Phippen has lately lost her husband, was Capt of the Albatross, & washed overboard. Three of the Crew escaped & returned. Married in 1807.[1088]

Jonathan Archer was named administrator of his estate on 5 January 1819.[1089] Widow Lois Phippen petitioned the Essex Probate Court on 6 April 1819 to be named guardian of daughter Louisa, then 9 years of age. She gave her bond with George Hodges, merchant, and Hardy Phippen, trader. William Fairfield (1824) and Hardy Phippen (1825) were subsequently named as Louisa's guardian.[1090]

Lois (Fairfield) Phippen married second, **JOSIAH CLARK** of Hillsborough, New Hampshire (intentions filed at Salem 23 October 1824), and appears to have settled in Hillsborough with her daughter.[1091]

[1084] Ellery and Bowditch, *The Pickering Genealogy*, 2: 352.

[1085] *Vital Records of Salem, Massachusetts to the end of the year 1849*, 4: 190.

[1086] Edgar Stanton MacLay, *A History of American Privateers* (New York, 1899), 399-400.

[1087] Felt, *Annals of Salem*, 2nd ed., 2: 344.

[1088] *The Diary of William Bentley*, 4: 585; *see* also entry for 25 Oct. 1818 at 4: 555.

[1089] Essex PR, no. 21754.

[1090] Essex PR, no. 21757.

[1091] *Vital Records of Salem, Massachusetts to the end of the year 1849*, 3: 215, 4: 190 (the Salem record shows her name as "Mrs. Louis" Phippen).

Child of Joseph and Lois (Fairfield) Phippen:

i. LOUISA SARAH FAIRFIELD[8] PHIPPEN, b. at Salem 16 Oct. 1809;[1092] m.
(1) at Hillsborough 11 Dec. 1827, ANDREW JAMESON,[1093] who was
b. at Antrim, N.H. 6 Feb. 1793, son of Thomas and Mary (Steele)
Jameson. Andrew Jameson was a hotel keeper in Hillsborough. They
also lived in Lowell, Mass., and Cincinnati, Ohio. He d. at Cincinnati
20 March 1839.[1094] Louisa m. (2) at Salem 31 July 1848, PETER EATON
WEBSTER.[1095] They resided in Salem. He d. 17 April 1850. Louisa
(Phippen) (Jameson) Webster d. 11 Oct. 1870.[1096] No children.

67. DAVID[7] **PHIPPEN** (*Ebenezer*[6], *David*[5], *Nathaniel*[4], *Samuel*[3], *Joseph*[2],
David[1]) was born at Reading, Massachusetts 25 July 1775, son of Ebenezer
and Elizabeth (Simmes) Phippen.[1097] He died at Salem, Massachusetts
14 January 1849, aged 73 years, of consumption.[1098] David married at
Salem 17 February 1799, **NANCY ("ANNE," "ANSTISS") COOK,**[1099]
who was born at Salem 2 August 1778,[1100] daughter of Benjamin and
Anna (Clough) Cook. She died 24 October 1815, aged 37 years, of
fever.[1101]

David Phippen was a ropemaker, housewright, and mariner.[1102] His
gravestone is located in the Charter Street Burial Ground in Salem.[1103]
The inscription reads: "MR. DAVID PHIPPEN, Died Jan. 14, 1849: Aged 73. /
Asleep in Jesus, blessed sleep / From which none ever wakes to weep."[1104]

[1092] E. O. Jameson, *The Jamesons in America, 1647–1900* (Boston, 1901), 446.

[1093] New Hampshire Vital Records.

[1094] Jameson, *The Jamesons in America*, 446.

[1095] *Vital Records of Salem, Massachusetts to the end of the year 1849*, 3: 542.

[1096] Jameson, *The Jamesons in America*, 446.

[1097] *Vital Records of Salem, Massachusetts to the end of the year 1849*, 2: 166. His death
record states that he was born in Reading, Mass. Ibid., 6: 137.

[1098] *Vital Records of Salem, Massachusetts to the end of the year 1849*, 6: 137. See also Mass.
VR (1849) 39: 230.

[1099] *Vital Records of Salem, Massachusetts to the end of the year 1849*, 3: 242, 4: 189.

[1100] Ibid., 2:168. *See also Vital Records of Salem, Massachusetts to the end of the year 1849*, 1:
201 (Anne Cook, d. of Benjamin and Anne, bp. 9 Aug. 1778).

[1101] *Vital Records of Salem, Massachusetts to the end of the year 1849*, 6: 138.

[1102] Perley, *The History of Salem, Massachusetts*, 2: 330.

[1103] "Charter Street Burial-Ground Inscriptions," *Essex Institute Historical Collections* 13
[1877]: 108.

[1104] Jeanne Stella, "Charter Street Cemetery Inscriptions, Salem, Massachusetts," *The
Essex Genealogist* 28 [2008]: 137.

Children of David and Nancy (Cook) Phippen, born at Salem:[1105]

  i. DAVID[8] PHIPPEN, b. 11 Nov. 1799; lived at Danvers, Mass.; d. unm. 26 Sept. 1887, aged 87 years, 10 months and 10 days ("choked while eating").[1106] He was a farmer.

  ii. ANNA KENNEDY/NANCY/ANN PHIPPEN, b. 2 Feb., bp. 9 Aug. 1801;[1107] d. unm. 16 April 1875.[1108]

106 iii. EBENEZER PHIPPEN, b. 16 Nov. 1802.[1109]

  iv. SUSAN KENNEDY PHIPPEN, b. 5 Aug. 1805; d. young.

107 v. BENJAMIN COOK PHIPPEN, b. 11 Feb. 1807.

  vi. SUSAN KENNEDY PHIPPEN, b. 16 Sept. 1808; d. unm. at Salem 21 Feb. 1901, aged 92;[1110] bur. in Harmony Grove Cemetery in Salem. In her will, dated 1 March 1898 and proved 18 March 1901, she named her brother Stephen Phippen of New Boston, N.H.; niece Anna M. Jowders of New Ipswich, N.H.; cousin Rufus Archer of Salem; Mrs. Emma J. Knight, daughter of her cousin Mrs. Sarah Mathews; Grace Knight, daughter of Mrs. Emma Knight; Mrs. Ellen Pratt, daughter of her cousin Mrs. Sarah Matthews; Miss Minnie Kennedy; and her friend Mrs. Susan E. Choate. The executor was David Choate of Salem.[1111]

108 vii. STEPHEN SIMS PHIPPEN, b. 30 March 1813.

68. THOMAS[7] **PHIPPEN** (*Thomas*[6–5], *Nathaniel*[4], *Samuel*[3], *Joseph*[2], *David*[1]) was born at Salem, Massachusetts 6 June 1778, son of Thomas and Rebecca (Wellman) Phippen.[1112] He died at Salem 25 October 1813, aged 34 years, a suicide.[1113] Thomas married at Salem 8 August 1801,

---

[1105] Births are recorded in *Vital Records of Salem, Massachusetts to the end of the year 1849*, 2:165 (Benjamin), 166 (David, Ebenezer), 168 (Nancy), 169 (Susan, Susan, Stephen).

[1106] Mass.VR (1887) 382: 199.

[1107] *Vital Records of Salem, Massachusetts to the end of the year 1849*, 2: 165.

[1108] Mass.VR (1875) 274: 272.

[1109] Cranberry Isles town records give the date as 13 Nov. 1803. *Records of Cranberry Isle: Birth & Deaths 1763-1890* (Maine State Archives), 17.

[1110] Mass.VR (1901) 516: 637.

[1111] Essex PR, no. 87852.

[1112] Wellman, *Descendants of Thomas Wellman, 168; Vital Records of Salem, Massachusetts to the end of the year 1849*, 2: 169 (bp. 7 June 1778).

[1113] *The Diary of William Bentley*, 4: 209; *Vital Records of Salem, Massachusetts to the end of the year 1849*, 6: 139 (bur. 26 Oct. 1813); *Essex Register*, 27 Oct. 1813 ("Mr. Thomas Phippen, jr., aged 34, by suicide.")

SARAH ("SALLY") LUFKIN,[1114] who was baptized at Salem 30 June 1786, daughter of Solomon and Mary (____) Lufkin.[1115] Widow Sally Phippen married, second, at Salem 21 March 1824, WILLIAM HALL.[1116] Sarah (Lufkin) (Phippen) Hall died at Salem, where she was buried on 28 July 1835.[1117]

The suicide of Thomas Phippen is described in the diary of William Bentley:

> [25 Oct. 1813] As I passed in my morning walk I was called into a house in which a young head of a family had cut his throat. He had been Master of a Vessel & was aged 34. This intemperate had destroyed his prospects & violated all his duties, & he had entered in the service of the Navy. The officer had visited him that morning to call him to his duty & he retired to a loft & with a jack knife cut his throat from ear to ear. No man was in the house. I found that he was prostrate & the artery cut off & he expired soon after I entered. He is from one of our antient families & a strange excentricity is in many branches of it. He was not in my charge & therefore as soon as succor was given I retired.[1118]

Children of Thomas and Sarah (Lufkin) Phippen, born at Salem:[1119]

    i.   REBECCA[8] PHIPPEN, bp. 29 Dec. 1804; d. young.

    ii.   SALLY PHIPPEN, b. 23 March,[1120] bp. 10 April 1806; m. at Cambridge, Mass. 30 Nov. 1831, EDMUND BOARDMAN of Meredith, N.H.[1121] He was a soap maker in Cambridgeport, Mass., and a farmer in Alexandria, N.H. They moved to Bristol, N.H. about 1874. She d. at Bristol 1 Dec. 1875, aged 69 years. He d. at Bristol 16 Oct. 1888, aged 82 years.[1122]

[1114] *Vital Records of Salem, Massachusetts to the end of the year 1849,* 3: 620, 4: 191.

[1115] Ibid., 1: 532.

[1116] Ibid., 3: 459, 4: 191.

[1117] Ibid., 5: 306. The age at death in the death record—43 years of age—is an error; she was probably at least 49 years old at the time of her death.

[1118] *The Diary of William Bentley,* 4: 209.

[1119] Unless noted otherwise, births and baptisms are from *Vital Records of Salem, Massachusetts to the end of the year 1849,* 2: 165 (baptism of Charles), 168 (baptism of Rebecca and Rebecca, baptism of Sally), and 169 (baptism of Thomas).

[1120] Richard W. Musgrove, *History of the Town of Bristol, Grafton County, New Hampshire,* 2 vols. (Bristol, N.H., 1904), 2: 47.

[1121] *Vital Records of Cambridge, Massachusetts to the end of the year 1850,* 2: 40, 308.

[1122] Musgove, *History of the Town of Bristol, New Hampshire,* 2: 47.

  iii. THOMAS PHIPPEN, bp. 9 July 1807; said to have been washed overboard from the schooner *Juno* near Cape Cod, 8 Jan. 1822, aged 15.[1123]

  iv. CHARLES PHIPPEN, bp. 28 Dec. 1812; d. with his brother Thomas, on 8 Jan. 1822, aged 13.[1124]

  v. REBECCA PHIPPEN, bp. 28 Dec. 1812.

109 vi. GEORGE PHIPPEN, b. ca. Aug. 1813 (calculated from death record).[1125]

69. JOSEPH[7] **PHIPPEN** (*Thomas*[6-5], *Nathaniel*[4], *Samuel*[3], *Joseph*[2], *David*[1]) was born at Salem, Massachusetts, 23 October 1779, son of Thomas and Rebecca (Wellman) Phippen.[1126] He married at Salem 27 November 1803, **ABIGAIL ("NABBY") DANE,**[1127] who was born about 1777 and baptized in Salem 12 March 1786, at the age of 9 years, daughter of Joseph and Mary (Wellman) Dane.[1128]

 Joseph Phippen died before June 1816, when guardianship of his children—Abigail D., aged 11; Mary Eliza, 10; Rebecca, 8; Joseph, 7; and Margaret, 3—was granted to his widow Abigail Phippen.[1129] Abigail died at Salem, a widow, in March 1834, aged 56 years.[1130]

 Children of Joseph and Abigail (Dane) Phippen, born at Salem:

  i. ABIGAIL DANE[8] PHIPPEN, bp. 29 Oct. 1804;[1131] d. unm. at Salem 25 Dec. 1844, aged 40, of consumption.[1132]

  ii. MARY ELIZA PHIPPEN, bp. 26 May 1806;[1133] d. unm. at Salem 18 March 1889.[1134]

[1123] *Vital Records of Salem, Massachusetts to the end of the year 1849,* 6: 139.

[1124] Ibid., 137.

[1125] Mass. VR (1890) 410: 330.

[1126] Wellman, *Descendants of Thomas Wellman,* 168.

[1127] *Vital Records of Salem, Massachusetts to the end of the year 1849,* 3: 275, 4: 190; *Columbian Centinel,* 10 Dec. 1803.

[1128] *Vital Records of Salem, Massachusetts to the end of the year 1849,* 1: 231. Joseph and Abigail were first cousins; their mothers, Rebecca (Wellman) Phippen and Mary (Wellman) Dane, were sisters. See Wellman, *Descendants of Thomas Wellman,* 168.

[1129] Essex PR, no. 21738.

[1130] *Vital Records of Salem, Massachusetts to the end of the year 1849,* 6: 138 (death notice published 1 April 1834); *Columbian Centinel,* 2 April 1834.

[1131] *Vital Records of Salem, Massachusetts to the end of the year 1849,* 2: 165.

[1132] Ibid., 6: 137.

[1133] Ibid., 2: 167.

[1134] Mass. VR (1889) 400: 354.

    iii. REBECCA PHIPPEN, bp. 29 Feb. 1808;[1135] d. unm. at Salem 18 Sept. 1898, at 90 years, 7 months, and 8 days.[1136]

    iv. JOSEPH D. PHIPPEN, b. in 1809; d. 18 Oct. 1827, aged 18, of consumption.[1137]

    v. MARGARET PHIPPEN, b. in 1813; d. 24 Sept. 1848, aged 35, of consumption.[1138]

70. ISRAEL[7] **PHIPPEN** (*Thomas*[6–5], *Nathaniel*[4], *Samuel*[3], *Joseph*[2], *David*[1]) was born at Salem, Massachusetts 18 September 1781, son of Thomas and Rebecca (Wellman) Phippen.[1139] He died at Salem, 23 February 1859, age 79 years, 6 months.[1140] Israel married at Salem 24 July 1808, **SARAH HUTSON**,[1141] who was baptized 30 September 1781, daughter of John and Hannah (Harmson) Hutson of Marblehead, Massachusetts.[1142] Sarah died at Salem 1 November 1855, at age 75.[1143]

    Israel was a mariner and was imprisoned in the infamous Dartmoor Prison in England during the War of 1812.[1144]

    Children of Israel and Sarah (Hutson) Phippen, born at Salem:[1145]

    i. SALLY[8] PHIPPEN, b. 18 Oct. 1809; d. 23 May 1826, aged 16, of peritonitis.[1146]

    ii. ISRAEL PHIPPEN, b. 12 Jan. 1812. No further record.

    iii. MARY A. PHIPPEN, b. 1 Aug. 1814; d. at Boston, Mass. 10 March 1887.[1147]

[1135] *Vital Records of Salem, Massachusetts to the end of the year 1849*, 2: 168.

[1136] Mass.VR (1898) 481: 594.

[1137] *Vital Records of Salem, Massachusetts to the end of the year 1849*, 6: 138 (year of birth from age at death).

[1138] Ibid., 6: 138 (year of birth from age at death).

[1139] Wellman, *Descendants of Thomas Wellman, 168; Vital Records of Salem, Massachusetts to the end of the year 1849*, 2: 166 (bp. after June 1781).

[1140] Mass.VR (1859) 129: 171; Perley, *The History of Salem, Massachusetts*, 2: 330.

[1141] *Vital Records of Salem, Massachusetts to the end of the year 1849*, 3: 534, 4: 189.

[1142] *Vital Records of Marblehead, Massachusetts to the end of the year 1849*, 1: 286.

[1143] Mass.VR (1855) 83: 174; Perley, *The History of Salem, Massachusetts*, 2: 330.

[1144] Benjamin F. Browne, "Dartmoor Prisoners," *Essex Institute Historical Collections* 5 [1863]: 235.

[1145] Births are recorded in *Vital Records of Salem, Massachusetts to the end of the year 1849*, 2: 165 (Ann Maria), 166 (Israel, Esther), 167 (Mary, Martha), 168 (Sally).

[1146] Ibid., 6: 139.

[1147] Mass.VR (1887) 384: 69.

iv. MARTHA PHIPPEN, b. 14 Feb. 1817; m. at Salem 11 Sept. 1838, WILLIAM EDWARDS,[1148] who was b. at Salem 11 July 1814, son of Joseph and Sally (Lang) Edwards.[1149] She d. at Salem 22 Dec. 1878.[1150]

v. ESTHER ADAMS PHIPPEN, b. 23 April 1820; m. at Salem 7 Sept. 1852, JOHN B. TEST, JR.[1151]

vi. ANN MARIA PHIPPEN, b. 14 Nov. 1823; m. at Salem 9 Aug. 1853, FRED B. BARTLETT.[1152]

71. WILLIAM[7] **PHIPPEN** (*William*[6], *Thomas*[5], *Nathaniel*[4], *Samuel*[3], *Joseph*[2], *David*[1]) was born at Salem, Massachusetts about 1778, son of William and Lois (Hitchings) Phippen. He died about 1841.[1153] He married at Salem 27 June 1797, **SARAH E. HATHORNE**,[1154] who was baptized at Salem, 25 July 1773, daughter of Joseph and Elizabeth (Sanders) Hathorne.[1155] She died 21 January 1847, aged 73, of consumption.[1156] William was a tobacconist.[1157]

Children of William and Sarah (Hathorne) Phippen, presumably born at Salem:[1158]

i. WILLIAM[8] PHIPPEN, b. in 1799; washed overboard at sea from schooner Union, on passage to Martinique, in 1823, aged 24.[1159]

ii. JOSEPH H. PHIPPEN, b. 9 Sept. 1800; d. at Salem 23 Sept. 1875, of "paralysis;"[1160] m. 20 Feb. 1828, ELIZABETH GAVET,[1161] who was b. at Salem 30 Jan. 1797, daughter of John and Susannah (Hill) Gavet.[1162] Elizabeth ("Betsey") died at Salem 21 Nov. 1862, of asthma.[1163] [Elizabeth (Gavet) Phippen's older sister, Abigail Gavet, m. Robert[2]

[1148] *Vital Records of Salem, Massachusetts to the end of the year 1849*, 3: 328, 4: 190.

[1149] Ibid., 1: 274.

[1150] Mass.VR (1878) 301: 272.

[1151] Mass.VR (1852) 60: 201; Perley, *The History of Salem, Massachusetts*, 2: 330.

[1152] Mass.VR (1853) 69: 283.

[1153] Perley, *The History of Salem, Massachusetts*, 2: 330.

[1154] *Vital Records of Salem, Massachusetts to the end of the year 1849*, 4: 191.

[1155] Ibid., 1: 412.

[1156] Ibid., 6: 139.

[1157] Perley, *The History of Salem, Massachusetts*, 2: 330.

[1158] Ibid.

[1159] *Vital Records of Salem, Massachusetts to the end of the year 1849*, 6: 140.

[1160] Mass. VR (1875) 274: 279 (birthdate calculated from age at death); Perley, *The History of Salem, Massachusetts*, 2: 330.

[1161] *Vital Records of Salem, Massachusetts to the end of the year 1849*, 3: 408, 4: 191.

[1162] Joseph Gavit, "Philip Gavet of Salem, Mass., and Some of His Descendants," *Register* 77 [1923]: 34–58 at 41.

[1163] Mass.VR (1862) 156: 271.

Phippen (*Robert*[1]) of the *other* Salem Phippen family.] Joseph was a cordwainer.[1164]

72. GEORGE[7] **PHIPPEN** (*William*[6], *Thomas*[5], *Nathaniel*[4], *Samuel*[3], *Joseph*[2], *David*[1]) was born in Salem, Massachusetts 2 February 1790,[1165] the son of William and Lois (Hitchings) Phippen. He was baptized at the North Church in Salem in March 1790.[1166] He died at Chicago, Illinois 15 April 1873.[1167]

George Phippen married, first, at Middletown, Connecticut in September 1812, **SARAH "SALLY" SAVAGE**.[1168] She died at Lynn, Massachusetts in September 1817, aged 22.[1169] George Phippen married, second, at Lynn 5 November 1818, **ELIZA RHODES**,[1170] who was born at Lynn 11 December 1796, daughter of Amos and Elizabeth (Parsons) Rhodes.[1171] She died at Lee, Massachusetts 18 August 1844, aged 48.[1172] George married, third, at Tyringham, Massachusetts 26 November 1846, **ABIGAIL BUELL**,[1173] who was born at Sandisfield, Massachusetts, 28 March 1798, daughter of Joseph and Lucy (Pickett) Buell.[1174] Abigail (Buell) Phippen died at Norwalk, Ohio 3 December 1868, aged 70.[1175]

On 7 January 1810, the Rev. William Bentley mentioned George Phippen in his diary: "a Charity Scholar, one Phippen of Providence College, gave [his] generous assistance" to the Baptist service.[1176] He

---

[1164] Perley, *The History of Salem, Massachusetts,* 2: 330.

[1165] William Cathcart, *The Baptist Encyclopaedia,* 3 vols. (Philadelphia, 1881), 2: 920.

[1166] *Vital Records of Salem, Massachusetts to the end of the year 1849,* 2: 166.

[1167] *The Chicago Daily Tribune,* 17 April 1873, 8; *The Historical Catalogue of Brown University 1764-1934* (Providence, 1936), 115.

[1168] *Columbian Centinel,* 16 Sept. 1812.

[1169] Ibid., 13 Sept. 1817.

[1170] *Vital Records of Lynn, Massachusetts to the end of the year 1849* (Salem, Mass., 1905), 2: 302; *Columbian Centinel,* 11 Nov. 1818.

[1171] *Vital Records of Lynn, Massachusetts to the end of the year 1849* (Salem, 1905), 1: 347.

[1172] *Vital Records of Lee, Massachusetts, to the Year 1850* (Boston: New England Historic Genealogical Society, 220.

[1173] *Vital Records of Tyringham, Massachusetts to the end of the year 1849,* 71, 81.

[1174] *Vital Records of Tyringham, Massachusetts to the end of the year 1849,* 71. However, the *Buell Genealogy* states birth was at Great Barrington; see Albert Welles, *History of the Buell Family in England . . . and in America . . .* (New York, 1881), 123.

[1175] Welles, *History of the Buell Family,* 344. Mass.VR (1868) 211:61 has her death on the same date, but at Tyringham, Mass.

[1176] *The Diary of William Bentley,* 3: 489.

attended Brown University and received his degree in 1811.[1177] He was ordained a Baptist minister at Middletown on 11 June 1812.[1178]

The Reverend George Phippen had a pastorate at Lynn, where the Baptist Society was incorporated on 15 April 1816, and he was settled as their first minister on 15 September 1816. He remained there until 1820.[1179] He also had pastorates at Canton, Connecticut, and West Troy and Newburgh, New York. He was at the Lee Baptist Church from April 1844 to April 1846.[1180]

He was living in Cortlandt, New York, in 1850 and in Canton in 1860. He was living in Chicago (age 80) with his daughter Eliza and her family at the time of the 1870 census.[1181]

Children of the Rev. George and Sally (Savage) Phippen:

     i. SARAH ANN[8] PHIPPEN m. at Canton in May 1836, THOMAS HOTCHKISS of New York.[1182]

110   ii. GEORGE PHIPPEN.[1183]

Children of Rev. George and Eliza (Rhodes) Phippen:

    iii. AMOS R. PHIPPEN, b. in 1825; d. 17 Feb. 1859, aged 34; bur. at Canton.[1184]

    iv. MARY LUMMUS PHIPPEN, b. at Lynn 23 April 1828;[1185] m. THADDEUS HAMPTON of Michigan.[1186]

    v. ELIZA RHODES PHIPPEN, b. at Canton ca. 1830; m. (by her father) at Peekskill, N.Y., on 11 Oct. 1850 to JARED WINTHROP MILLS,[1187]

[1177] *The Historical Catalogue of Brown University,* 115.

[1178] *The Baptist Encyclopaedia,* 2: 920; *The Diary of William Bentley,* 4: 102. (Bentley incorrectly states the location as Middleborough, Mass.)

[1179] Alonzo Lewis and James R. Newhall, *History of Lynn, Essex County, Massachusetts, 1629-1864* (Lynn, 1890), 379, 584.

[1180] Rev. Amory Gale, *History of the town of Lee, Mass.: a lecture delivered before the Young Men's Association of Lee, Mass.* (Lee, Mass., 1854), 40. *See also The Baptist Encyclopaedia,* 2: 920.

[1181] 1860 U.S. census, Canton, Hartford Co., Conn., roll M653_79, p. 494' 1870 U.S. census, Chicago, Cook Co., Ill., roll M593_199, p. 466B.

[1182] *Columbian Centinel,* 21 May 1836.

[1183] *Vital Records of Lee, Massachusetts, to the Year 1850,* 78, 220.

[1184] Lucius Barnes Barbour, "Inscriptions from Gravestones at Canton, Conn.," *Register* 81 [1927]: 275–92 at 291.

[1185] *Vital Records of Lynn, Massachusetts to the end of the year 1849,* 325.

[1186] Charles A. Flagg, *An Index of Pioneers From Massachusetts to the West* (Salem, Mass., 1915), 58.

[1187] Mass. VR (1850), 45: 34a.

who was b. at Canton 19 Aug. 1823, son of Norman and Charlotte (Laflin) Mills. Eliza d. at Chicago, Ill., on 12 March 1915. Jared Mills d. there 26 Feb. 1889.[1188]

vi. JAMES H. PHIPPEN, b. in 1834; d. 7 April 1836, aged 2 years, 8 months; bur. at Canton.[1189]

vii. LUCIUS R. PHIPPEN, d. 14 July 1841 and buried at the Old Town Cemetery in Newburgh.[1190]

73. DAVID[7] PHIPPANY (*David[6], Archibald[5], Benjamin[4], James[3]*, Benjamin[2], *David[1]*) was born at Hartford, Connecticut 23 November 1797, son of David and Ruth (Adams) Phippany. He married **MARIA SQUIRES,** who was born 19 July 1805 and died 25 July 1884, daughter of Elisha and Chloe Squires. In the 1850 census, they were living in Hartford, and he was described as a printer. Both were alive, with none of their children in their household, in the 1870 and 1880 censuses.[1191]

Children of David and Maria (Squires) Phippany, listed in the 1850 census:[1192]

i. DAVID G. or S.[8] PHIPPANY, b. about 1828.

ii. WILLIAM W. PHIPPANY, b. 25 Dec. 1830; d. 3 June 1838.

iii. HENRY C. PHIPPANY, b. 29 Jan. 1832; d. 22 April 1873. Likely the Henry Phippany who, with wife FANNY (b. about 1835), is listed in New Haven, Conn., in the 1860 census.[1193] Fanny moved to New York City after her husband's death; Frances Phippany, widow of Henry, was living at 1560 Broadway in 1886.[1194] "Miss Fanny Phippany" ran a brothel at 36 West 15th Street in New York City, which was listed in the 1870 *Gentlemen's Directory*, a pocket-sized Manhattan brothel guide. Fanny was described as "of a very selfish disposition," and the servants were described as "very disagreeable to visitors."[1195] The 1870 Census lists Fanny's profession as

---

[1188] Alfred L. Holman and Louis E. Laflin, *Laflin Genealogy* (Chicago, 1930), 76.

[1189] Barbour, "Inscriptions from Gravestones at Canton, Conn.," Register 81 [1927]: 291.

[1190] *A Record of the Inscriptions in the Old Town Burying Ground of Newburgh, N.Y.* (1898) (accessed at www.oldtowncemetery.org).

[1191] 1880 U.S. Census, Hartford, Hartford Co., Conn., E.D. 17, p. 4, surname "Phippay."

[1192] 1850 U.S. Census, Hartford, Hartford Co., Conn., p. 138. See also Mackenzie, *Colonial Families of America*, 3: 398–403.

[1193] 1860 U.S. Census, New Haven, New Haven Co., Conn., Roll M653_86, Page 272.

[1194] *Trow's New York City Directory for the Year Ending May 1, 1886.*

[1195] [Unknown Author], *Gentleman's Directory,* (New York 1870) (available at www.

"Assignation House," (i.e., a brothel).[1196]

    iv. HARRIET MARIA PHIPPANY, b. 27 Feb. 1834; m. EDWARD CUFFIN LEWIS.

    v. CHARLES M. PHIPPANY, b. 14 April 1836; d. 8 July 1838.

111 vi. CHARLES W. PHIPPANY, b. 25 Dec. 1838.

    vii. ANDREW J. PHIPPANY, b. 13 May 1841; d. 3 June 1843.

    viii. GEORGE A. PHIPPANY, b. 17 Aug. 1843; d. 24 May 1852.

    ix. JAMES E. PHIPPANY, b. 10 Dec. 1846; d. 28 May 1852.

    x. ALICE B. PHIPPANY, b. 31 July 1849; d. 27 June 1851.

74. WILLIAM ARCHIBALD[7] PHIPPENEY (*David[6], Archibald[5], Benjamin[4], James[3], Benjamin[2], David[1]*) was born in Connecticut 12 July 1801, son of David and Ruth (Adams) Phippeney.[1197] He married, first, **EMILY STARKWEATHER,** daughter of Roger and Martha (Flint) Starkweather. She died at Wolcottville (part of Torrington, Litchfield County, Connecticut) at age 42, as reported in the *Hartford Daily Times*.[1198] It is also likely that he was the William Phippeney, aged 59, a tailor, who was living in Torrington at the time of the 1860 census with a second wife, **ALMIRA** (aged 57 in this census; surname unknown), and one child Harriet.[1199]

Children of William Archibald and Emily (Starkweather) Phippeney include:[1200]

    i. HARRIET ADAMS[8] PHIPPENEY, b. 14 Dec. 1827; m. 19 July 1866, Samuel Morse, son of Orville and Charity (Thompson) Morse. Harriet d. 13 March 1880.

    ii. MARIA LOUISA PHIPPENEY, b. 23 Nov. 1830; d. 6 Dec. 1854.

112 iii. WILLIAM ROGER PHIPPENEY Jr., b. about 1833.

NewYorkTimes.com <<http://documents.nytimes.com/a-vest-pocket-guide-to-brothels-in-19th-century-new-york-for-gentlemen-on-the-go>>), at 32-33.

[1196] 1870 Census, NewYork Ward 18 District 1, NewYork, NewYork; Roll: M593_1001; Page: 6A; Image: 258947.

[1197] Mackenzie, *Colonial Families of America,* 3: 403.

[1198] *Hartford Daily Times,* 16 May 1848.

[1199] 1880 U.S. Census, Torrington, Litchfield Co., Conn., Roll M653_81, Page 457.

[1200] 1860 U.S. Census, Torrington, Litchfield Co., Conn., p. 138. See also Mackenzie, *Colonial Families of America,* 3: 403.

75. CALVIN EVET⁷ PHIPPENEY (*William⁶, Archibald⁵, Benjamin⁴, James³, Benjamin², David¹*) was born at Pompey, Onondaga County, New York 8 March 1819, son of William and Mary (Newman) Phippeney. He died in Nemaha County, Nebraska 16 February 1894. Calvin married, first, 17 February 1842, **MARY PHILLIPS,** who died in 1888. He married, second, in Nemaha County 7 March 1889, **BELINDA (MILES) PHILLIPS** (widow of Erwin Phillips, brother of his first wife). She survived him and was living in Custer, Oklahoma, at the time of the 1910 census.[1201]

At the time of the 1850 and 1860 censuses, Calvin E. Phippeney and family were living in Wright, Hillsdale County, Michigan. They subsequently settled in Nemaha County. A biographical history of Nebraska published in 1882 contains this sketch:

> C. E. PHIPPENNEY, farmer, P. O. Peru [Nemaha County], born in 1820 in Pompey, N.Y. He has been a lifelong farmer. In 1841, he became a pioneer settler of Michigan, and just twenty years later he located in Nebraska, buying the farm on which he now lives, when it was in a state of nature. The rude cottonwood shanty that sheltered during the toilsome days of "war times" was supplanted, in 1871 by a commodious and tasteful brick farmhouse, environing which he has groves and orchard and suitable farm buildings, all done by himself and sons in the past twenty years. His wife was Mary Phillips, of St. Lawrence County, N.Y. They are members of the Baptist church of Highland, and have four children -- Henrietta (Mrs. A. K. Farnham), Lydia (Mrs. W. W. Bush), Orville (who married Jennie McKnight), and Rosalind (now Mrs. J. Good). A. P. Phippenney, a son of C. E. Phippenney, removed to Pueblo, Colo., and while serving as an officer of the law was fatally shot by a rough, whom he was trying to apprehend. He left five motherless children, four of whom are now with the grandparents.[1202]

Calvin Phippeney's death was recorded in a book of reminiscences by a local newspaper editor:[1203]

[1201] 1910 U.S. Census, Grant Township, Custer Co., Oklahoma, E.D. 123, sheet 2B, line 74.

[1202] A. T. Andreas, *History of the State of Nebraska* (Chicago, 1882), Nemaha County, part 20, "Other Towns," Biographical Sketches.

[1203] John H. Dundas, *Nemaha County* (Auburn, Neb., 1902), 195.

On the 16th [of February, 1894] Calvin E. Phippenney dropped dead while at work feeding his stock about the barn, but as there was no suspicion of foul play no inquest was held.

Children of Calvin E. and Mary (Phillips) Phippeney:[1204]

      i. HENRIETTA[8] PHIPPENNEY, b. in Ohio about 1843.

113   ii. ALVIN P. PHIPPENNEY, b. in Ohio about 1848.

114   ii. ORVILLE EARL PHIPPENNEY, b. in Michigan 7 June 1850.

     iv. LYDIA PHIPPENNEY, b. in Michigan about 1852.

      v. ROSALIND PHIPPENNEY, b. in Michigan about 1859.

76. HORACE[7] **PHIPPANY** (*Joel*[6], *James*[5-3], *Benjamin*[2], *David*[1]) was born at Hinesburgh, Vermont, son of Joel and Electra (Gates) Phippany. He died at Lyndonville, New York, in October 1850. He married **ELIZABETH BLANCHARD,**[1205] who was born in New Hampshire about 1804. In the 1840 census, they resided at Yates, Orleans County, New York. At the time of the 1860 census, his widow was living at Yates.

Children of Horace and Elizabeth (Blanchard) Phippany:[1206]

      i. ARTHUR H.[8] PHIPPANY, b. in Nov. 1834. Living with his sister Mary, both unm., in 1900.

115   ii. ALBERT HOLLAR PHIPPANY, b. about 1837.

     iii. MARY ELECTRA PHIPPANY, b. in March 1838. Living, unm., with her brother Arthur in 1900. She appears to have been briefly married to _____ SMITH between 1870 and 1880, as she is listed with that surname in the 1880 census.

     iv. EUGENE PHIPPANY, b. about 1843.

      v. CATHERINE PHIPPANY, b. about 1844.

116   vi. CARROLL L. PHIPPANY, b. in July 1844.

[1204] 1850 U.S. Census, Wright, Hillsdale Co., Michigan, p. 353; 1860 U.S. Census, Medina, Lenawee Co., Michigan, p. 683; 1870 U.S. Census, Glenrock, Nemaha Co., Nebraska, p. 300.

[1205] Phoenix, *The Whitney family of Connecticut,* 1: 520.

[1206] Ibid., 2: 1217; augmented by the 1860 U.S. Census, Yates, Orleans Co., N.Y., p. 33.

77. GEORGE JAMES[7] **PHIPPANY** (*Joel*[6], *James*[5-3], *Benjamin*[2], *David*[1]) was born at Hinesburgh,Vermont 6 December 1811,son of Joel and Electra (Gates) Phippany.[1207] He married at Bennington, Wyoming County, New York 16 October 1836, **CHARITY MARIA CRANE,** who was born at Batavia, New York 28 November 1816, daughter of Amherst and Polly (Brooks) Crane of Batavia.[1208] George was a merchant.They lived in Ellington, Chautauqua County, New York, until 1 March 1853, when they moved to Albion, Calhoun County, Michigan. They were still living there in 1874. Charity died there 27 January 1875.[1209] George was still living in 1900.

Children of George James and Charity (Crane) Phippany, born at Ellington: [1210]

117 i. WALTER SCOTT[8] PHIPPANY, b.15 Sept. 1837.

  ii. HENRY CLAY PHIPPANY, b. 17 July 1842; living in Albion in 1880.[1211]

78. JAMES MADISON[7] **PHIPPANY** (*Peter*[6], *James*[5-3], *Benjamin*[2], *David*[1]) was born in Connecticut in 1810, son of Peter and Dorcas (Fenn) Phippeney. He married at Bridgewater, Litchfield County, Connecticut 6 January 1836, **HARRIET RUGGLES,**[1212] who was born in Connecticut about 1816. In the 1860 census, James was living in Bridgewater with his wife. He was sealer of weights and measures in Bridgewater in 1856.[1213] James Madison Phippany died in 1873.

Children of James Madison and Harriett (Ruggles) Phippany include:[1214]

  i. IDA[8] PHIPPANY, aged 1 month at the time of 1860 census enumeration.

79. GEORGE EDGAR[7] **PHIPPANY** (*Peter*[6], *James*[5-3], *Benjamin*[2], *David*[1]) was born in Connecticut about 1820 or 1821, son of Peter and

---

[1207] Phoenix, *The Whitney family of Connecticut,* 1: 520.

[1208] Ibid.

[1209] Ibid.

[1210] Ibid., 2: 1218.

[1211] Ibid.

[1212] "New Milford 1712-1860," *The Barbour Collection of Connecticut Town Vital Records,* vol. 30, 167.

[1213] Orcutt, *History of the Towns of New Milford and Bridgewater, Connecticut, 1703–1882,* 433.

[1214] 1860 U.S. Census, Bridgewater, Litchfield Co., Conn., p. 611.

Dorcas (Fenn) Phippeney. He married **MARY A. RUGGLES,** who was born in Connecticut about 1821 or 1822, and lived in New Milford, Connecticut. For the 1870 and 1880 censuses, he was enumerated in Bridgewater, Litchfield County, Connecticut, and in Monroe, Fairfield County, Connecticut, respectively. In 1880 he was living with wife Mary, but in 1870, he was listed with his widowed sister, Caroline (Phippeney) Beardsley.

Child of George E. and Mary A. (Ruggles) Phippany:[1215]

    i.   SARAH EDDY[8] PHIPPANY, b. in Connecticut about 1847.

80. CHARLES LEE[7] PHIPPANY (*Peter[6], James[5-3], Benjamin[2], David[1]*) was born in Connecticut about 1834, son of Peter and Dorcas (Fenn) Phippeney. He married **LUCY J.** _____, who was born in New York State about 1836.

In the 1870 census, he was living in Paradise Valley Township, Humboldt County, Nevada, single, near his brother Horatio Gates Phippeney. In the 1880 census, he is listed as a teamster, in Prescott, Yavapai County, Arizona, with his wife and four children.

Children of Charles Lee and Lucy J. (_____) Phippany, living in 1880:[1216]

        i.   DORCAS B.[8] PHIPPANY, b. in California about 1870.
118   ii. OLIVER LEE PHIPPANY, B. IN NEVADA ABOUT 1872.
119   III. LYMAN OSCAR PHIPPANY, b. in Nevada 21 Oct. 1873.
     iv. GEORGE S. or A. PHIPPANY, b. in Nevada about 1876; m. **ALICE** _____. Living in Thompson Valley, Yavapai Co., Ariz., in the 1910 census; he was enumerated in Prescott, Ariz., with his wife in 1920.

[1215] 1850 U.S. Census, New Milford, Litchfield Co., Conn., p. 152.
[1216] 1880 U.S. Census, Prescott, Yavapai Co., Ariz., p. 24.

CHAPTER 10

THE EIGHTH GENERATION

81. HIRAM[8] **PHIPPEN** (*Aseph*[7], *Samuel*[6-3], *Joseph*[2], *David*[1]) was born at Watertown, Jefferson County, New York about 1819, son of Aseph and Sebrina (Smedley) Phippen. At the time of the 1880 census, he was living at Elbridge, Onondaga County, New York, with his wife **HELLEN** _____, and their youngest child, Alice. In 1870, his wife is called Ellen.

Children of Hiram and Hellen/Ellen (_____) Phippen include:[1217]

    i.   FRANK[9] PHIPPEN, b. at Jordan, N.Y. 27 April 1856; d. at Syracuse, N.Y. in Jan. 1945.

    ii. FLORENCE PHIPPEN m. CLINT HENDRICKS.

    iii. ALICE PHIPPEN, b. in New York State about 1866.

82. HOMER W.[8] **PHIPPEN** (*Horatio*[7], *Samuel*[6-3], *Joseph*[2], *David*[1]) was born at Watertown, New York 22 December 1837, son of Horatio and Elvira (Tuttle) Phippen. He married 11 February 1862, **JENNIE E. WARE.**[1218]

Children of Homer and Jennie (Ware) Phippen:

    i.   CORA[9] PHIPPEN, b. at Watertown 3 June 1865; d. there in 1866.

120   ii. WALTER PHIPPEN, b., presumably at Watertown, N.Y., on 31 May 1868.

    iii. GERTRUDE PHIPPEN, b. 18 May 1871.

    iv. CASSIUS EDWARD PHIPPEN, b. at Lewiston, N.Y. 19 Sept. 1877; d. at Watertown in 1880.

[1217] 1870 U.S. Census, Jordan, Onondaga Co., New York, p. 2; 1880 U.S. Census, Elbridge, Onondaga Co., New York, E.D. 169, p. 41. Information also provided by Mary Margaret Schwerzmann

[1218] Tuttle, *The Descendants of William and Elizabeth Tuttle,* 509.

83. CHAUNCEY WALTER[8] PHIPPEN (*Horatio*[7], *Samuel*[6-3], *Joseph*[2], *David*[1]) was born on the family homestead at Watertown, New York 19 November 1849, son of Horatio and Elvira (Tuttle) Phippen.[1219] He married at Brownsville, New York 1 October 1874, ALZADA ALICE CLEVELAND.[1220] In 1890 he lived at 75 Arsenal Street in Watertown.[1221] Alzada died 26 July 1938.[1222]

Chauncey Phippen was a farmer for a few years, and then he set up as a carpenter and joiner, a trade in which he was engaged for over twenty years before turning to market gardening.

Children of Chauncey Walter and Alzada Alice (Cleveland) Phippen, born at Watertown:[1223]

    i.   WALTER MONTRAVILLE[9] PHIPPEN, b. 19 March 1877.

    ii. EMOGENE ALVARIA PHIPPEN, b. 24 Oct. 1880.

84. DANIEL[8] PHIPPEN (*Joseph*[7], *Joseph*[6], *Samuel*[5-3], *Joseph*[2], *David*[1]) was born in Vermont about 1803, but raised in Angelica Township, Allegany County, New York, son of Joseph and Submit (Hooker) Phippen. He married, before 1835, LYDIA _____. They stayed in Angelica and raised a family there.

Children of Daniel and Lydia (____) Phippen, listed in the 1860 census[1224] :

    i.   ARAUNAH[9] PHIPPEN, b. about 1836; living unm. with her mother in the 1880 census.

    ii. DIANA PHIPPEN, b. about 1838.

    iii. DANIEL PHIPPEN, b. about 1839.

    iv. MALVINA PHIPPEN, b. about 1844.

    v. SARAH PHIPPEN, b. about 1850.

[1219] Edgar C. Emerson, *Our County and Its People: A Descriptive Work on Jefferson County, New York* (Boston History Co., 1898), 181.

[1220] Edmund J. Cleveland, *The Genealogy of the Cleveland and Cleaveland Families* (Hartford, 1899), 1965.

[1221] Hamilton Child, *Geographical Gazetteer of Jefferson County, New York, 1684–1890* (Syracuse, 1890), 230.

[1222] New York D.A.R., *Unpublished Bible, Family, and Miscellaneous Records* 80 [1952]: 3 (Family Bible of Emogene Cleveland Atwood).

[1223] From Cleveland, *The Genealogy of the Cleveland and Cleaveland Families*, 1965; Tuttle, *The Descendants of William and Elizabeth Tuttle*, 509.

[1224] 1860 U.S. Census, Angelica, Allegany Co., N.Y., p. 378.

85. ORLANDO⁸ ("ORA" OR "ORY") PHIPPEN (*Joseph⁷, Joseph⁶, Samuel⁵⁻³, Joseph², David¹*) was born in Angelica Township, Allegany County, New York 3 August 1815, son of Joseph and Submit (Hooker) Phippen. He married in 1839, **ELIZABETH A. BENSON**, who was born at Apple River, Jo Daviess County, Illinois in 1815, daughter of Didymus and Elizabeth (Fish) Benson. Elizabeth died at Apple River in 1880.

Ory Phippen had settled in Apple River by 1838, and his family was enumerated there in the 1870 census.

Children of Orlando and Elizabeth (Benson) Phippen, born in Illinois:

    i.   ORLANDO⁹ PHIPPEN, b. about 1842. He served in the Civil War, enlisting in 1862 in Company E, 96th Regiment of Illinois Volunteer Infantry; discharged at the close of the war.[1225]

    ii. LUCINDA PHIPPEN, b. about 1849.

    iii. ALBERT CLARK PHIPPEN, b. about 1850.

121   iv. EDWIN DIDYMUS PHIPPEN, b. about 1852.

86. HENRY⁸ PHIPPEN (*Joseph⁷, Joseph⁶, Samuel⁵⁻³, Joseph², David¹*) was born at Angelica, Allegany County, New York about 1827, son of Joseph and Submit (Hooker) Phippen. He married before 1850, **ROXALANA** ———.

In the 1860 census, Henry Phippen is listed with his wife and two children.

Children of Henry and Roxalana (———) Phippen:[1226]

    i.   JOSEPH C.⁹ PHIPPEN, b. about 1850.

    ii. EMMA A. PHIPPEN, b. about 1858.

87. JAMES WORTHINGTON⁸ PHIPPEN (*Isaac⁷, Joseph⁶, Samuel⁵⁻³, Joseph², David¹*) was born at Springfield, Clark County, Ohio 12 October 1819, son of Isaac and Ada (Stewart) Phippen.[1227] He married at Newstead, Erie County, New York 9 August 1845, **JULIA ADELIA PRATT,** who was born at Newstead 31 October 1825, daughter of Silas and Silence⁷ (Phippen) (Crowell) Pratt. Silence was the daughter of Joseph⁶ and Silence (Paul) Phippen (*see No. 38*).[1228]

[1225] From an online abstract drawn from the *History of Jo Daviess County, Illinois* (Chicago: H. F. Kett, 1878).

[1226] 1860 U.S. Census, Angelica, Allegany Co., N.Y., p. 90.

[1227] Paul-Paull MS, 2: 82.

[1228] Ibid.

James and Julia headed for Nauvoo, Illinois, two days after their marriage and arrived just as trouble was beginning there. They returned to Newstead, where they remained until 1852, when they started west again. They met James's father at Council Bluffs, Iowa, and journeyed together to Salt Lake City, arriving 28 September 1852. They were living there in 1885. James had been in the saddlery and harness business.[1229]

In the 1900 census, James W. Phippen was living with his daughter Elna L. (Phippen) Stanford in Little Wood River Precinct, Blaine County, Idaho, near the family of his nephew Almon Marcellus Phippen.[1230]

Children of James Worthington and Julia Adelia (Pratt) Phippen:[1231]

122   i.   SILAS LUCIAN[9] PHIPPEN, b. at Newstead 5 Dec. 1846.

      ii.   LEONARD PHIPPEN, b. 28 Nov. 1853; d. at Salt Lake City, Utah 24 March 1854.

     iii.   ROSABEL ADELIA PHIPPEN, b. at Salt Lake City 4 Nov. 1855; m. there 7 Dec. 1874, WILLIAM F. BRIM. They were living at Albion, Cassia Co., Idaho, in 1885. They had no children.[1232]

     iv.   WORTHINGTON ELMER PHIPPEN, b. 10 Jan. 1858; d. at Salt Lake City 17 Oct. 1858.

      v.   ELNA LODENA PHIPPEN, b. at Salt Lake City 21 May 1861; d. at Logan, Cache Co., Utah, 11 June 1945; m. 22 Dec. 1881, CYRUS J. STANFORD, who was b. at East Cambridge, Mass. 31 Jan. 1857, son of Stephen and Louisa (Foreman) Stanford. He d. at Logan 15 June 1949. Their children, b. in Utah, were (surname *Stanford*): 1. *Elna Pearl*, b. 10 Dec. 1883; 2. *Julia Myrtle*, b. 7 Nov. 1886; 3. *Cyrus Rollo*, b. 5 July 1890, d. 11 Aug. 1890; 4. *Joseph Sedley*, b. 14 July 1891; [1233] 5. *Vernal L.*, b. May 1895. In 1900 this family was living in Little Wood River Pct., Blaine Co., Idaho.

     vi.   FRANK EUGENE PHIPPEN, b. 7 March 1864; d. at Salt Lake City 24 March 1864.

    vii.   JULIA PERMELIA PHIPPEN, b. 18 Sept. 1865; d. at Salt Lake City 5 March 1866.

   viii.   SILA PEARL PHIPPEN, b. 3 Sept. 1871; d. at Salt Lake City 17 Oct. 1872.

[1229] Paul-Paull MS, 2: 82.
[1230] 1900 U.S. Census, Little Wood River Pct., Blaine Co., Idaho, p. 160.
[1231] Paul-Paull MS, 2: 83.
[1232] Ibid., 85.
[1233] Ibid.

88. JOSEPH FREEMAN[8] PHIPPEN (*Isaac[7], Joseph[6], Samuel[5-3], Joseph[2], David[1]*) was born at Springfield, Clark County, Ohio 20 September 1822, son of Isaac and Ada (Stewart) Phippen.[1234] He was a sawyer and engineer by trade, and for a good many years was engaged in the operation and building of sawmills. He died at Albion, Cassia County, Idaho 25 November 1912. Joseph Phippen married, first, at Nauvoo, Hancock County, Illinois 11 February 1844, **ANN DAYTON,** who was born 5 August 1826, daughter of Hirum and Permelia (Bandy) Dayton.[1235] They settled in Pottawattamie County, Iowa, in 1847 and in 1852 moved to Salt Lake City, Utah. Ann died at Salt Lake City 11 April 1859.[1236] After his first wife's death, Joseph married, second, at Salt Lake City 12 September 1866, **ELIZA JANE HUDSON,** who was born in Illinois in January 1844, daughter of Wilford and Julia Ann (Graybill) Hudson.[1237] They moved to Cassia County, Idaho, in 1884.[1238]

Children of Joseph Freeman and Ann (Dayton) Phippen:[1239]

123   i.   JOSEPH HYRUM[9] PHIPPEN, b. at Nauvoo 8 Dec. 1844.

       ii.   ISAAC FREEMAN PHIPPEN, b. at Nauvoo in Nov. 1845; d. 1 Jan. 1848.

      iii.   JULIA ANN PHIPPEN, b. at Pottawattamie Co. 2 July 1848; m. in 1864, HYRUM ELDRIDGE.

      iv.   ADA IRENE PHIPPEN, b. at Pottawattamie Co. 16 Dec. 1850; m. 29 Feb 1868, GEORGE BRIM.

       v.   PARMELIA FRANCELA PHIPPEN, b. at Salt Lake City 31 Aug. 1854; m. 25 July 1871, CHARLES BASSETT.

      vi.   ELLEN MARIA PHIPPEN, b. at Salt Lake City 7 May 1855; d. there in 1873.

124 vii.   ALMON MARCELLUS PHIPPEN, b. at Salt Lake City 6 Feb. 1856.

    viii.   WILLIAM CLARENCE PHIPPEN, b. at Salt Lake City 4 Feb. 1858; m. JENNIE HOWARD. They had no children.

Children of Joseph Freeman and Eliza Jane (Hudson) Phippen:[1240]

      ix.   CELIA ANN[9] PHIPPEN b. 30 June 1867.

125   x.   WILFORD FREEMAN PHIPPEN, b. in Utah 8 Nov. 1869.

[1234] Ibid., 83.

[1235] Ibid. Her birthdate is from H. Michael Marquardt, "Nauvoo Temple Endowment Index," online at <*http://www.xmission.com/~research/family/familypage.htm*>.

[1236] Paul-Paull MS, 2: 83.

[1237] Ibid., 85.

[1238] Ibid., 83.

[1239] Unless indicated otherwise, information about children is from ibid.

[1240] Paul-Paull MS, 2: 85.

xi. MARY JANE PHIPPEN, b. 8 Jan. 1873.

xii. EMMA AMANDA PHIPPEN, b. 20 Sept. 1875.

xiii. EDNA CLARE PHIPPEN b. 23 May 1878.

xiv. BERTHA LOANDA PHIPPEN, b. 3 May 1882.

89. SYLVESTER SMITH[8] PHIPPEN (*Isaac[7]*, *Joseph[6]*, *Samuel[5-3]*, *Joseph[2]*, *David[1]*) was born at Chautauquaa County, New York 20 May 1834, son of Isaac and Ada (Stewart) Phippen.[1241] He settled with his father in Salt Lake City, Utah, in 1852 and married there 5 April 1855, **MARY JANE BRIM,** born 28 June 1838, daughter of Alexander and Anna M. (Bishop) Brim.[1242]

For a time Sylvester and Mary Jane lived at Genoa, Carson Valley [now Douglas County], Nevada; they returned to Salt Lake City in 1857. They removed to Coalville, Summit County, Utah, in 1860, but once again, in 1870, returned to Salt Lake City. Sylvester was a justice of the peace, assessor, and collector of taxes. He also owned and operated various mills in Utah and Idaho.[1243]

Children of Sylvester and Mary Jane (Brim) Phippen:[1244]

i. FRANKLIN SYLVESTER[9] PHIPPEN, b. at Genoa 27 Oct. 1856; d. at Salt Lake City 11 Nov. 1860.

126 ii. ADELBERT SMITH PHIPPEN, b. at Salt Lake City 1 April 1858.

iii. ANNA LOUISA PHIPPEN, b. at Salt Lake City 4 March 1860; d. there 15 Sept. 1943; m. there 11 Dec. 1878, JOSEPH MORONI PETTIGREW, son of David and Caroline (Cope) Pettigrew. Child (surname *Pettigrew*): *Neomia Mabel,* b. 15 Dec. 1879.

iv. MARY ADAH PHIPPEN, b. at Salt Lake City 13 July 1862; m. there 11 Dec. 1883, HUGH PINNOCK. Child (surname *Pinnock*): *Mary Alice,* b. 28 April 1885.

v. CLARA LOVENIA PHIPPEN, b. at Coalville, Utah 6 June 1864; d. at Salt Lake City 4 May 1879.

vi. CHARLES EDGAR PHIPPEN, b. at Coalville 18 Oct. 1866; d. there 18 June 1868.

vii. FLORENCE MAY PHIPPEN, b. at Coalville 22 Oct. 1869; d. there 9 Aug. 1870.

[1241] Paul-Paull MS, 2: 84.

[1242] Ibid.

[1243] Ibid.

[1244] Information about children is from Paul-Paull MS, 2: 84, 86.

    viii. FRED WORTHINGTON PHIPPEN, b. at Salt Lake City 2 July 1872; d. there 8 Sept. 1877.

    ix. EFFIE ADELIA PHIPPEN, b. at Salt Lake City 16 Sept. 1874.

    x. MABEL JANE PHIPPEN, twin, b. at Salt Lake City 27 May 1879; d. there 19 June 1880.

127   xi. EDWARD BERT PHIPPEN, twin, b. at Salt Lake City 27 May 1879.

90. LOREN D.[8] **PHIPPEN** (*Calvin*[7], *Joseph*[6], *Samuel*[5-3], *Joseph*[2], *David*[1]) was born at Lawrenceville, Pennsylvania 20 July 1848, son of Calvin and Jerusha (Goodell) Phippen. He married, first, before 1865, **DASSIE BUFFINGTON,** who was born about 1849 and died in 1875. He married, second, **SOPHIA SUSAN BOYDEN,** who was born 16 November 1855, daughter of Addison Boyden (1805–1899) and Sophia (Colvin) Boyden. Sophia died at Wellsboro, Pennsylvania 22 October 1921.[1245]

    Child of Loren D. and Dassie (Buffington) Phippen:

    i. GUY[9] PHIPPEN, b. 1865; m. at Delmar, Pa. 25 Nov. 1878, _____.

    Children of Loren D. and Sophia (Boyden) Phippen:

    ii. NORAH JEANETTE PHIPPEN, b. 18 March 1881; m. SEYMOUR BOWERS, who was b. in 1878 and d. in 1974.

128   iii. ROSS ALONZO PHIPPEN, b. at Wellsboro 5 March 1885.

    iv. LOREN FREEMAN PHIPPEN, b. 15 Aug. 1891; d. 18 April 1963; m. ELSIE SPENCER.

91. SAMUEL[8] **PHIPPEN** (*Clark*[7], *Jonathan*[6], *Samuel*[5-3], *Joseph*[2], *David*[1]) was born in New York State about 1816. He is *probably* the son of Clark Phippen of Stockholm, St. Lawrence County, New York. With wife **ROBA** or **ROBY,** born about 1818, he appears in the 1860 and 1880 censuses with his family in Stockholm, St. Lawrence County. A teenage girl, Electa Phippen, aged 17 in 1860 and living in nearby Hermon, St. Lawrence County, could be their daughter.

    Children of Samuel and Roba (____) Phippen:

    i. BETSY JANE[9] PHIPPEN, b. about 1851; m., before 1880, OLIVER HARDY.

    ii. KING S. PHIPPEN, b. about 1862.

[1245] Information about Loren D. Phippen's family was supplied by Jessie Brabham, daughter of Margaret Eudora Phippen Brooks, from information compiled by Maude Ethel (Russell) Phippen in an unpublished family history. See also Paul-Paull MS and W.H.H. Stowell, *The Stowell Genealogy* (Rutland, Vt., 1922), 685.

92. AMBROSE⁸ PHIPPEN (*Clark⁷, Jonathan⁶, Samuel⁵⁻³, Joseph², David¹*) was born in New York about 1824. He is *probably* the son of Clark Phippen of Stockholm, St. Lawrence County, New York. With wife **ADALINE**, born about 1827, he appears in the 1860 and 1880 censuses with his family in Stockholm.

Children of Ambrose and Adaline (_____) Phippen:[1246]

    i.   Ellen H.⁹ PHIPPEN, b. about 1852.

    ii. GEORGE A. PHIPPEN, b. about 1853.

    iii. MARY ANN PHIPPEN, b. about 1856.

    iv. FREDERICK H. PHIPPEN, b. about 1858.

    v. ADDIE PHIPPEN, b. about 1864.

    vi. KATIE PHIPPEN, b. about 1867.

    vii. CLARK F. PHIPPEN, b. about 1869.

93. AMASA B.⁸ PHIPPEN (*Clark⁷, Jonathan⁶, Samuel⁵⁻³, Joseph², David¹*) was born at Crown Point, New York 9 February 1826, son of Clark and Betsey (Wright) Phippen. He died at Stockholm, New York 28 September 1878. Amasa married 17 September 1854, **SAREPTHA CONVERSE**.[1247]

Children of Amasa B. and Sareptha (Converse) Phippen:[1248]

    i.   HERBERT⁹ PHIPPEN, b. about 1859. He was a farmer in Stockholm, listed there through the 1940 census.

    ii. FLORA PHIPPEN, b. about 1861.

    iii. HOMER PHIPPEN, b. about 1863.

94. WARREN T.⁸ PHIPPEN (*Clark⁷, Jonathan⁶, Samuel⁵⁻³, Joseph², David¹*) was born 1 December 1827, son of Clark and Betsey (Wright) Phippen. He married in 1854, **MARY E. FLOYD,** who was born about 1832. She died in 1870; Warren died in Michigan in 1913.[1249]

[1246] 1860 and 1880 U.S. censuses, Stockholm, St. Lawrence Co., N.Y., p. 21 (1860) and p. 17 (1880). Children i–iv are listed in the 1860 census and ii and iv–vii in the 1880 census.

[1247] Correspondence with G. Birchard, Springfield, Mass., 28 March 1977.

[1248] 1880 U.S. Census, Stockholm, St. Lawrence Co., N.Y., p. 19.

[1249] Birchard correspondence, 1977.

Children of Warren T. and Mary (Floyd) Phippen:[1250]

   i. MARY A.[9] PHIPPEN, b. about 1855.

   ii. BETSY I. PHIPPEN, b. about 1859.

   iii. MINNETTE S. PHIPPEN, b. about 1865.

   iv. EMMA E. PHIPPEN, b. about 1867.

95. RODNEY ATWATER[8] PHIPPEN (*David A.[7], Jonathan Atwater[6], Samuel[5-3], Joseph[2,] David[1]*) was born at Westminster, Vermont 26 October 1826, son of David A. and Hannah (Sargent) Phippen. He married, first, 18 December 1851, **ANNE MEHITABLE EDDY,**[1251] who was born at Royalston, Massachusetts 23 October 1827, daughter of William and Hannah (Knight) Eddy.[1252] She died at Royalston July 13 1864.[1253] Rodney Atwater Phippen married, second, 15 April 1866, his sister-in-law **HANNAH MARIE MASON EDDY,**[1254] who was born at Royalston 2 July 1825.[1255] Rodney and Hannah left no children. Rodney Phippen died at Gardner, Massachusetts in 1913.[1256] The couple resided in Gardner.[1257]

96. LUCIUS A.[8] PHIPPEN (*Samuel[7], Jonathan[6], Samuel[5-3], Joseph[2], David[1]*) was born in Vermont 28 October 1828, son of Samuel and Betsey (Drew) Phippen. He died at Burke, Vermont 13 January 1891, aged 62 years, 2 months, 16 days.[1258] He married at Burke 23 March 1858, **ELINOR HADLEY SMITH.**[1259] He was a joiner and a farmer.

Children of Lucius A. and Elinor Hadley (Smith) Phippen, born at Burke:[1260]

   i. MAE A.[9] PHIPPEN, b. about 1869; m. at Lyndon, Vt. 12 Dec. 1890, ALBION L. HOWE.

   ii. EMILY PHIPPEN, b. 10 Aug. 1867; d. at Burke 15 Sept. 1868.

   iii. EMILY PHIPPEN, b. 29 Oct. 1869.

[1250] 1860 and 1880 U.S. censuses, Stockholm, St. Lawrence Co., N.Y., p. 51 (1860), p. 13 (1880). Children i and ii are listed in the 1860 census, i–iv in the 1880 census.

[1251] Mass. VR (1851) 56: 237.

[1252] *Vital Records of Royalston, Massachusetts to the end of the year 1849,* 29.

[1253] Denny, *Genealogy of the Denny Family,* 120.

[1254] Mass. VR (1866) 191: 253.

[1255] *Vital Records of Royalston, Massachusetts to the end of the year 1849,* 29.

[1256] Mass. VR (1913) 44: 479.

[1257] Correspondence with E. Thornton Clark, 1977.

[1258] Vermont Vital Records. (Date of birth calculated from age at death.)

[1259] Ibid.

[1260] Ibid.

97. ELMORE[8] PHIPPEN (*Samuel[7], Jonathan[6], Samuel[5–3], Joseph[2], David[1]*) was born at Lyndon, Vermont 27 October 1834, son of Samuel and Betsey (Drew) Phippen.[1261] He died at Burke, Vermont 13 May 1905, aged 70 years, 6 months, 19 days.[1262] Elmore married at Burke 5 March 1861, **KERON DUSTIN JENKINS,** who was born at Brighton, Vermont 2 August 1835, daughter of Loren and Betsey (Blinn) Jenkins.[1263] Elmore Phippen was a farmer in Burke.[1264]

Child of Elmore and Keron Dustin (Jenkins), born at Burke:[1265]

129   i.   FRANK ELMORE[9] PHIPPEN, b. 15 March 1862.

98. AMASA R.[8] PHIPPEN (*Samuel[7], Jonathan[6], Samuel[5–3], Joseph[2], David[1]*) was born in Vermont 4 July 1840, son of Samuel and Betsey (Drew) Phippen. He died at Goffstown, New Hampshire 14 November 1924, aged 84 years. 4 months. 10 days.[1266] He married, first, 10 August 1862, **HARRIET L. WELLS.** Amasa was of Lyndon, Vermont, and a carpenter and farmer at the time of his marriage.[1267] He married, second, at Manchester, New Hampshire 30 November 1895, **ABBIE J. COOKE.**[1268]

Child of Amasa R. and Harriet (Wells) Phippen:[1269]

i.   DELIA A.[9] PHIPPEN, b. 10 Nov. 1863.

99. SAMUEL[8] PHIPPEN (*Nathaniel[7], Joshua[6], Nathaniel[5–4], Samuel[3], Joseph[2], David[1]*) was born at Salem, Massachusetts 5[1270] and baptized there 18 February 1787,[1271] son of Nathaniel and Anna (Pickett) Phippen. He married at Salem 2 December 1810, **SARAH "SALLY" BURNS,**[1272] who was baptized at Salem 23 November 1788, daughter of Edward and Sally (____) Burns.[1273]

[1261] Vermont Vital Records.
[1262] Ibid.
[1263] Roland Rowell, *Biographical Sketch of Samuel Rowell and notice of some of his descendants, with genealogy for seven generations, 1754-1898* (Manchester, N.H., 1898), 128.
[1264] Ibid.
[1265] Vermont Vital Records.
[1266] Ibid.
[1267] Vermont Vital Records.
[1268] N.H. Vital Records.
[1269] Vermont Vital Records.
[1270] *Vital Records of Salem, Massachusetts to the end of the year 1849,* 2: 168.
[1271] "Salem Baptisms," *Essex Institute Historical Collections* 22 [1885]: 245.
[1272] *Vital Records of Salem, Massachusetts to the end of the year 1849,* 3: 170, 4: 191.
[1273] Ibid., 1: 140 (as Sally Burn).

Samuel was a cooper. He died at Salem 25 June 1821, aged 35 years, of "intemperance."[1274] Sally (Burns) Phippen married second at Salem, 21 March 1824, **WILLIAM HALL**.[1275]

100. BENJAMIN[8] PHIPPEN (*Nathaniel[7], Joshua[6], Nathaniel[5-4], Samuel[3], Joseph[2], David[1]*) was born at Portsmouth, New Hampshire 25 October 1788, son of Nathaniel and Anna (Pickett) Phippen, and baptized 10 July 1796.[1276] He died 24 February 1862.[1277] Benjamin married 15 January 1829, **MARY MASSEY WELLS**.[1278]

Benjamin was a cooper in Salem, Massachusetts. Mary survived him.[1279]

Children of Benjamin and Mary Massey (Wells) Phippen, born at Salem:[1280]

      i. BENJAMIN FRANKLIN[9] PHIPPEN, b. 15 June 1830; cooper; d. unm. at Salem 5 May 1871.[1281]

130   ii. NATHANIEL PHIPPEN, b. 26 Jan. 1832.

131   iii. JOSEPH E. PHIPPEN, b. 11 Dec. 1833.

    iv. MARTHA PHIPPEN, b. 31 Oct. 1835; d. March 1837. [1282]

    v. MARTHA CLARK PHIPPEN, b. 12 Jan. 1838; m. at Salem 6 July 1859, SAMUEL A. LORD,[1283] who was b. about 1835.[1284]

    vi. JOHN PRINCE PHIPPEN, b. 2 Oct. 1840; of Boston, Mass., in 1863.[1285]

132 vii. WILLIAM TRUMBULL PHIPPEN, b. 25 Sept. 1842.

101. NATHANIEL[8] PHIPPEN (*Nathaniel[7], Joshua[6], Nathaniel[5-4], Samuel[3], Joseph[2], David[1]*) was born at Portsmouth, New Hampshire 19 February 1791, son of Nathaniel and Anna (Pickett) Phippen.[1286] Nathaniel

---

[1274] *Vital Records of Salem, Massachusetts to the end of the year 1849*, 6: 139.

[1275] Ibid., 4: 191.

[1276] Ibid., 2: 165.

[1277] Perley, *The History of Salem, Massachusetts*, 2: 330; Mass.VR (1862) 156: 265.

[1278] *Vital Records of Salem, Massachusetts to the end of the year 1849*, 4: 189, 451.

[1279] Perley, *The History of Salem, Massachusetts*, 2: 330.

[1280] Unless noted otherwise, information about children is from *Vital Records of Salem, Massachusetts to the end of the year 1849*, 2: 165, 167, 168, 169.

[1281] Perley, *The History of Salem, Massachusetts*, 2: 331; Mass.VR (1871) 248: 254.

[1282] *Vital Records of Salem, Massachusetts to the end of the year 1849*, 6: 138.

[1283] Perley, *The History of Salem, Massachusetts*, 2: 331; Mass.VR (1859) 126: 223.

[1284] Birth year calculated from age at marriage.

[1285] Perley, *The History of Salem, Massachusetts*, 2: 331.

[1286] *Vital Records of Salem, Massachusetts to the end of the year 1849*, 2: 168.

Phippen was a cooper in Salem, Massachusetts;[1287] he died there 22 May 1864.[1288] He married at Salem 24 December 1820, **MARTHA C. CLARK,**[1289] daughter of Isaac and Alice Clark.[1290] She died as his widow 9 May 1883, aged 80 years, 7 months, 11 days, of "exhaustion."[1291]

During the War of 1812, Nathaniel was imprisoned in the infamous Dartmoor Prison in Devon, England.[1292]

Children of Nathaniel and Martha (Clark) Phippen, born at Salem:[1293]

> i.   MARTHA ANN[9] PHIPPEN, bp. 2 July 1826; m. at Salem 30 Sept. 1845, WILLIAM A. FRYE.[1294] They were living in Athol, Mass., in 1874 and 1883.[1295]
>
> ii. CHARLOTTE LANE PHIPPEN, bp. 2 July 1826; m. at Salem 25 April 1843, WILLIAM HENRY ARCHER,[1296] who was b. there 27 July 1816, son of William and Elizabeth (Daniels) Archer.[1297]
>
> iii. BENJAMIN HOWARD PHIPPEN, bp. 5 Aug. 1827; clerk; m. at Salem 14 Feb. 1854, SARAH E. LARRABEE.[1298] Benjamin Phippen d. at Salem 9 May 1857; Sarah survived him.[1299]
>
> 133 iv. JOSHUA B. PHIPPEN, b. 7 Feb., bp. at Salem 5 Sept. 1830.
>
> v.   MARY DUSTIN PHIPPEN, bp. 21 Sept. 1834; d. unm. 31 March 1883.[1300]

102. JOSHUA[8] **PHIPPEN** (*Nathaniel*[7], *Joshua*[6], *Nathaniel*[5-4], *Samuel*[3], *Joseph*[2], *David*[1]) was born at Salem, Massachusetts 15 November 1793[1301] and

---

[1287] Perley, *The History of Salem, Massachusetts*, 2: 331.

[1288] Mass. VR (1864) 174: 261.

[1289] *Vital Records of Salem, Massachusetts to the end of the year 1849*, 3: 215, 4: 190.

[1290] Perley, *The History of Salem, Massachusetts*, 2: 331.

[1291] Mass. VR (1883) 346: 290.

[1292] Browne, "Dartmoor Prisoners," *Essex Institute Historical Collections* 5 [1863]: 235.

[1293] *Vital Records of Salem, Massachusetts to the end of the year 1849*, 2: 165 (baptism of Benjamin), 166 (baptism of Charlotte), 167 (baptism of Martha Ann, birth and baptism of Joshua, baptism of Mary).

[1294] Ibid., 3: 391, 4: 190.

[1295] Perley, *The History of Salem, Massachusetts*, 2: 331.

[1296] *Vital Records of Salem, Massachusetts to the end of the year 1849*, 3: 59, 4: 189.

[1297] Ibid., 1: 49.

[1298] Perley, *The History of Salem, Massachusetts*, 2: 331.

[1299] Ibid.

[1300] Ibid.; Mass. VR (1883) 346: 289.

[1301] *Vital Records of Salem, Massachusetts to the end of the year 1849*, 2: 167.

baptized 10 July 1796,[1302] son of Nathaniel and Anna (Pickett) Phippen. He died at Roxbury, Massachusetts 20 August 1833, aged 40 years, of delirium tremens.[1303] He is buried in the Granary Burial Ground in Boston.[1304] He married at the Second Baptist Church, Boston, Massachusetts 9 April 1820, **ELIZA H. HOWARD.**[1305] She was likely the Mrs. Phippen, living in Roxbury in February 1841, who was a petitioner with six others for the town of Brookline to annex land in Roxbury.[1306]

103. JOSEPH HARDY⁸ PHIPPEN (*Hardy⁷, Joshua⁶, Nathaniel⁵⁻⁴, Samuel³, Joseph², David¹*) was born at Salem, Massachusetts 10 June 1807, son of Captain Hardy and Ursula Knapp (Symonds) Phippen.[1307] He married, first, at Salem 26 March 1840, **SUSAN HARRIS LORD,**[1308] daughter of David and Lucy (Harris) Lord. She died at Beverly, Massachusetts, 3 February 1882.[1309] He married, second, 26 November 1883, her sister **EMELINE LORD,**[1310] who died 6 December 1906. [1311]

Joseph Hardy was a bank cashier. He died 15 October 1898, aged 91 years.[1312] At the time of his death, he was Salem's "oldest son."[1313] He had no issue.

104. JOSHUA⁸ PHIPPEN (*Hardy⁷, Joshua⁶, Nathaniel⁵⁻⁴, Samuel³, Joseph², David¹*) was born at Salem, Massachusetts 13 December 1812, son of Captain Hardy and Ursula Knapp (Symonds) Phippen.[1314] He died at Salem 8 October 1890.[1315]

[1302] "Salem Baptisms," *Essex Institute Historical Collections* 22 [1885]: 245.

[1303] *Vital Records of Roxbury, Massachusetts to the End of the Year 1849,* 2 vols. (Salem, Mass., 1925), 1: 614. His death is also listed in Brookline vital records (*Vital Records of Brookline, Massachusetts to the end of the year 1849* [Salem, 1929], 221).

[1304] Robert J. Dunkle and Ann S. Lainhart, *Inscriptions and Records of the Old Cemeteries of Boston* (Boston, 2000), 465. His gravestone states that he was from Brookline.

[1305] "Marriage Records of the Rev. Thomas Baldwin, Pastor of the Second Baptist Church, Boston, Massachusetts," *Register* 126 [1972]: 141–45 et seq., at 142.

[1306] Brookline Town Records, Meeting March 1, 1841, p. 36.

[1307] *Vital Records of Salem, Massachusetts to the end of the year 1849,* 2: 167.

[1308] Ibid., 4: 189.

[1309] Mass.VR (1882) 337: 286.

[1310] Mass.VR (1883) 343: 366.

[1311] Mass.VR (1906) 78:185.

[1312] MassVR (1898) 481: 595.

[1313] Obituary, *Salem Evening News,* 17 Oct. 1898.

[1314] *Vital Records of Salem, Massachusetts to the end of the year 1849,* 2: 167.

[1315] Perley, *The History of Salem, Massachusetts,* 2: 331; Mass.VR (1890) 409: 396.

Joshua married, first, 22 April 1841, **BETSEY BARR HOLMAN,**[1316] who was born 6 September 1817, daughter of Jonathan and Betsey (Barr) Holman.[1317] She died 9 April 1854.[1318] He married, second, at South Danvers, Massachusetts 27 May 1856, **EUNICE LOUISE DANIELS,**[1319] who was born about 1830,[1320] daughter of David Daniels. She died as Joshua's widow 20 September 1914.[1321]

Joshua Phippen was a gas fitter and merchant.[1322]

Child of Joshua and Betsey (Holman) Phippen, born at Salem:[1323]

    i.   MARY ELIZABETH[9] PHIPPEN, b. 20 May 1842;[1324] m. 5 Nov. 1864, RICHARD PRICE,[1325] who was b. at Salem 23 Jan. 1841,[1326] son of Ebenezer and Hannah (____) Price.

Children of Joshua and Eunice (Daniels) Phippen, born at Salem:[1327]

134   ii.   JOSHUA H. PHIPPEN, b. about 1858.

135   iii.   EDWARD AUGUSTUS PHIPPEN, b. 12 Oct. 1859.[1328]

    iv.   HARDY PHIPPEN, b. 3 Nov. 1862; physician.[1329] He graduated with an A.B. from Harvard College in 1884, and from Harvard Medical School in 1889. He trained in surgery at Massachusetts General Hospital and then Boston Lying-in-Hospital. He also studied for a year in Vienna, Austria. Dr. Hardy Phippen practiced medicine in Salem.[1330] He died there in 1954.[1331]

[1316] *Vital Records of Salem, Massachusetts to the end of the year 1849,* 4: 189.

[1317] Perley, *The History of Salem, Massachusetts,* 2: 331.

[1318] Ibid.

[1319] Ibid.; Mass.VR (1856) 99: 231.

[1320] The 1860 U.S. Census (Salem, Essex Co., Mass.) states her age as 30 years.

[1321] Perley, *The History of Salem, Massachusetts,* 2: 331.

[1322] Ibid.

[1323] "Materials for a History of the Ropes Family," *Essex Institute Historical Collections* 7 [1865]: 160.

[1324] *Vital Records of Salem, Massachusetts to the end of the year 1849,* 2: 167.

[1325] Perley, *The History of Salem, Massachusetts,* 2: 331; Mass.VR (1864) 171: 245.

[1326] *Vital Records of Salem, Massachusetts to the end of the year 1849,* 2: 196.

[1327] Perley, *The History of Salem, Massachusetts,* 2: 331; 1860 and 1870 U.S. censuses, Salem, Essex Co., Mass., p. 262 (1860), p. 42 (1870).

[1328] Mass.VR (1859) 123: 272.

[1329] Mass.VR (1862) 150: 283; correspondence with Hardy[11] Phippen, 18 Oct. 1975.

[1330] Scott H. Paradise, comp., *The Story of Essex County,* 4 vols. (New York, [1935]), 3: 123–24.

[1331] Correspondence with Hardy Phippen (1975).

105. GEORGE DEAN⁸ PHIPPEN (*Hardy⁷, Joshua⁶, Nathaniel⁵⁻⁴, Samuel³, Joseph², David¹*) was born at Salem, Massachusetts 13 April 1815, son of Captain Hardy and Ursula (Symonds) Phippen.[1332] He died at Salem 26 December 1895.[1333] George married at Salem 13 April 1840, **MARGARET BARTON,**[1334] who was born there 23 July 1815, daughter of John and Mary (Webb) Barton.[1335] Margaret (Barton) Phippen died 1 December 1896.[1336]

George was the cashier at the Salem National Bank in Salem for 37 years, from 1858 until his death.[1337] In his obituary, he was described as "a man of rare business ability and perspicuity."[1338] He was also an avid antiquarian and botanist. He was one of the 17 members of the first board of officers of the Essex Institute (founded in 1848) and its first librarian.[1339] He was the genealogist who published the first compiled Phippen genealogy, in 1868, with a facsimile of the Phippen chart of 1808.[1340] His obituary also described his gardening interests:

> He had been a great lover of flowers for years, and an authority on botany. His garden was one of the finest in Salem, and was one of the points of interest to be visited by all who were being shown the sights of Salem.

Children of George Dean and Margaret (Barton) Phippen, born at Salem:[1341]

136 i. GEORGE BARTON⁹ PHIPPEN, b. 12 Feb. 1841.

   ii. SAMUEL WEBB PHIPPEN, b. 13 Oct. 1846; d. at Salem 22 June 1847, of lung fever, aged 8 months.[1342]

137 iii. ARTHUR HENRY PHIPPEN, b. 7 Sept. 1849.

138 iv. CHARLES ENDECOTT PHIPPEN b. 20 Jan. 1856.[1343]

[1332] *Vital Records of Salem, Massachusetts to the end of the year 1849,* 2: 166.

[1333] Perley, *The History of Salem, Massachusetts,* 2: 331; Mass.VR (1895) 454: 573.

[1334] *Vital Records of Salem, Massachusetts to the end of the year 1849,* 4: 189.

[1335] Ibid., 1: 73.

[1336] Perley, *The History of Salem, Massachusetts,* 2:331.

[1337] Ibid.

[1338] Obituary, George D. Phippen, *Salem Evening News,* 27 Dec. 1895, 1.

[1339] "Remarks of George D. Phippen," *Essex Institute Historical Collections* 30 [1893]: 148–54 at 148.

[1340] Phippen, "Fitzpen or Phippen, and Allied Families," *The Heraldic Journal* 4 [1868]: 1–20.

[1341] Unless noted otherwise, information about children is from *Vital Records of Salem, Massachusetts to the end of the year 1849,* 2: 165, 166, 168.

[1342] Ibid., 6: 139.

[1343] Perley, *The History of Salem, Massachusetts,* 2: 331.

106. Ebenezer⁸ Phippen (*David⁷, Ebenezer⁶, David⁵, Nathaniel⁴, Samuel³, Joseph², David¹*) was born at Salem, Massachusetts 16 November 1802, son of David and Nancy (Cook) Phippen.[1344] He died at Eden, Maine 3 April 1863.[1345] He married **Hannah Cousins,** who was born 7 February 1806,[1346] daughter of Elisha and Thankful (Hopkins) Cousins. Hannah died at Eden 7 December 1881, aged 75 years, 10 months.[1347]

Ebenezer Phippen was a seaman and resided at Eden (now Bar Harbor).

Children of Ebenezer and Hannah (Cousins) Phippen:[1348]

    i.   Susan Ann⁹ Phippen, b. 16 Nov. 1830; d. at Cranberry Isles, Maine 20 Dec. 1830.

    ii. Mary Ann C. Phippen, b. 30 Jan. 1834; d. at Cranberry Isles 10 April 1837.

   iii. Hannah Emeline S. Phippen, b. at Eden 22 Dec. 1836;[1349] d. there unm. 24 Aug. 1894, of apoplexy.[1350]

139   iv. Samuel C. Phippen, b. at Eden 20 Aug. 1842.[1351]

140   v. Charles D. Phippen, b. at Eden 14 Nov. 1845.[1352]

107. Benjamin Cook⁸ Phippen (*David⁷, Ebenezer⁶, David⁵, Nathaniel⁴, Samuel³, Joseph², David¹*) was born at Salem, Massachusetts 11 February 1807, son of David and Nancy (Cook) Phippen.[1353] He died at Salem 20 August 1866.[1354] He was a baker.[1355] Benjamin Phippen married at Marblehead, Massachusetts 20 April 1830, **Ann Bowditch Melzard,**[1356] who was baptized at Marblehead 30 May 1813, daughter

---

[1344] *Vital Records of Salem, Massachusetts to the end of the year 1849,* 2: 166. According to Records of Cranberry Isles, Births & Deaths 1763–1890, he was born 13 Nov. 1803.

[1345] Records of Cranberry Isles, Births & Deaths 1763¬–1890.

[1346] Ibid.

[1347] Ibid.

[1348] Unless noted otherwise, information about children is from Records of Cranberry Isles, Births & Deaths 1763–1890.

[1349] She is listed as the first child in the record.

[1350] Maine Vital Records.

[1351] In Records of Cranberry Isles, he is listed as the second child, with a birthdate of 22 Aug. 1843.

[1352] In Records of Cranberry Isles, he is listed as the third child.

[1353] *Vital Records of Salem, Massachusetts to the end of the year 1849,* 2: 165.

[1354] Mass. VR (1866) 192: 214.

[1355] Perley, *The History of Salem, Massachusetts,* 2: 331.

[1356] *Vital Records of Marblehead, Massachusetts to the end of the year 1849,* 2: 288, 332.

of Thomas and Sarah (Trefry) Melzard of Marblehead.[1357] She died 1 November 1865.[1358]

The 1840 Census of Salem shows the "B. Phippen" household with one male 30–40 (Benjamin), one male under 5, one female 20–30 (his wife Ann), one daughter 10–15, and one daughter 5–10. His two younger children, Annie and David, appear with Benjamin and his wife in the 1850 census, and their parents' names are confirmed on their death records. Their oldest daughter is almost certainly Susan Kennedy Phippen, named after Benjamin's sister.[1359]

Children of Benjamin Cook and Ann Bowditch (Melzard) Phippen:

    i. SUSAN KENNEDY[9] PHIPPEN, b. Marblehead ca. 1830; m. at Salem 6 Jan. 1848 (intentions dated 18 Dec. 1847 at Hamilton), PETER H. JOWDERS of Hamilton. Peter was b. at Beverly, Mass. ca. 1825. Children (surname *Jowders*): 1. *Hervey*, d. at Hamilton 3 May 1848, aged 1 month, 15 days; 2. *Lydia A.*, b. ca. 1850; 3. *Sarah Jane*, b. at Hamilton 8 Oct. 1851; 4. *Ora Haskel*, b. at Hamilton 22 July 1853; 5. *David Hervy*, b. at Hamilton 23 June 1855; 6. *Benjamin F.*, b. ca. 1858; 7. *Emily Lincoln*, b. 19 June 1862.[1360]

    ii. ANNIE M. PHIPPEN b. at Salem 15 April 1836; d. at Rindge, N.H. 10 Jan. 1916; m. at Salem 24 Nov. 1853, ALEXANDER JOWDERS of Lynn, Mass. At least six children[1361]

141   iii. DAVID PHIPPEN, b. at Salem 7 May 1838.[1362]

108. STEPHEN SIMS[8] PHIPPEN (*David[7], Ebenezer[6], David[5], Nathaniel[4], Samuel[3], Joseph[2], David[1]*) was born at Salem, Massachusetts 30 March 1813, son of David and Nancy (Cook) Phippen.[1363] Stephen died at

[1357] Ibid., 1: 345.

[1358] Perley, *The History of Salem, Massachusetts,* 2: 331.

[1359] 1840 and 1850 U.S. censuses, Salem, Essex Co., Mass., p. 258 (1840), p. 222 (1850).

[1360] *Vital Records of Salem, Massachusetts to the end of the year 1849,* 3: 555, 4: 191 (marriage); *Vital Records of Hamilton, Massachusetts to the end of the year 1849,* 59, 68 (intentions); Mass. VR (1848–49) 39: 171 (Hervey); 1850 U.S. Census, Hamilton, Essex Co., Mass., p. 20 (Lydia); Mass. VR (1851) 51: 162 (Sarah Jane); Ibid. (1853), 72: 177 (Ora); Ibid. (1855), 90: 170 (David); Ibid. (1883), 343: 360 (Benjamin, via his marriage record); Ibid. (1862), 150: 199 (Emily).

[1361] N.H. Vital Records (death); Mass. VR (1853) 69: 286 (marriage); 1870 and 1880 U.S. censuses, New Ipswich, Hillsborough Co., N.H. (Alexander Jowders household), p. 226 (1870), p. 16 (1880).

[1362] Perley, *The History of Salem, Massachusetts,* 2: 331.

[1363] *Vital Records of Salem, Massachusetts to the end of the year 1849,* 2: 169.

Concord, New Hampshire 3 May 1907, aged 93 years, 1 month, 3 days, at his son Clarence Fipphen's house on Fayette Street.[1364] Stephen Phippen married, first, at Weare, New Hampshire 18 April 1837, SUSAN CHASE, daughter of Captain. Amos and Nancy (Tuttle) Chase.[1365] By 1840 the couple had settled at New Boston, New Hampshire, where they are enumerated in the census. After the death of Susan (Chase) Phippen (after the 1850 census), Stephen married, second, 11 April 1854, ADALINE AUGUSTINA DAILEY,[1366] originally of Philadelphia, Pennsylvania. She died at New Boston 27 December 1891, aged 57 years 8 months 26 days.[1367] Stephen was a farmer and lived in New Boston—on the road to Weare and close to the Weare line—until 1892, when he went to live with his son in Concord, New Hampshire.[1368]

The undated will of Stephen Phippen is as follows:[1369]

> Be it known that I Stephen Phippen of New Boston in the county of Hillsborough and State of New Hampshire, being mindful of the end of life but of sound and perfect mind and memory, do make publish and declare this my last will and testament.
>
> 1st: I give, devise and bequeath to my son Harvey H. Phippen the sum of one dollar.
>
> 2nd: I give devise and bequeath to my son Leroy Phippen the sum of one dollar.
>
> 3rd: I give, devise and bequeath to my son George Phippen the sum of one dollar.
>
> 4th: I give, devise and bequeath to my son Clarence F. Phippen the sum of one dollar.
>
> 5th: I give, devise and bequeath to my beloved wife Adaline Phippen all the rest, residue and remainder of my estate, real, personal, or mixed whereever situated, provided she survive me, and to use the same to maintain and support herself during her natural life without any

---

[1364] N.H. Vital Records; obituary, *Concord Monitor,* 3 May 1907.

[1365] N.H. Vital Records; John C. Chase and George W. Chamberlain, *Seven Generations of the Descendants of Aquila and Thomas Chase* (Derry, N.H., 1928), 152–53.

[1366] Handwritten marriage certificate in possession of Richard Fipphen.

[1367] Death record (Town Clerk, New Boston, N.H.) states birthplace but no parentage.

[1368] "Vigorous at 92: Stephen Fipphen of Concord, N.H., Takes Great Interest in Current Events," *Boston Sunday Globe,* 20 May 1906, 49. The profile includes a picture of Stephen.

[1369] Merrimack County, N.H., Probate Records.

hindrance or question by any of my children, and after her decease or if she should pass away before I do the followings

6th: I give, and devise to my son Leroy Phippen in addition what I have given him in section two of this my will, twenty four dollars.

7th: I give and devise to my son George Phippen in addition what I have given him in section three of this my will, twenty four dollars.

8th: I give and devise to my son Clarence F. Phippen, all the rest and remainder of my estate after the decease of my wife Adaline Phippen or if she die before me then after my decease.

9th: I appoint my son Clarence F. Phippen and Thomas O. Knowlton executor of this my will.

10th: I order and direct a lot to be secured in the New Boston Cemetery and at my decease that my first wifes remains be removed and interred there and that our graves be marked with suitable monuments and that this be done by my said executors before the payment of any legacy.

Signed, sealed and declared by said Stephen Phippen to be his last will in our presence and each of us signed in the presence of each other unto and of said Stephen Phippen

Signed Thomas O. Knowlton, William Eaton, and Emma R Knowlton

On 28 May 1907, Clarence F. Fipphen of Concord as principal, Nellie E. Knee, and Norris A. Dunklee were bound in the amount of $1,600 in the matter of the estate of Stephen Phippen of Concord.[1370]

It is not clear why the spelling of the surname in this line of the family changed to "Fipphen." (Family legend had it that Stephen was illiterate but knew that an *h* followed a *p*.) In the 1860 census for New Boston, the name was listed as "Fipping." Stephen signed his will, an undated instrument, "Phippen." His son Clarence, as the administrator of his estate, spelled Stephen's name "Phippen" and signed his own name as "Fipphen." Clarence erected the memorial stones in the New Boston cemetery in memory of Susan Chase, Adaline Dailey, and

---

[1370] On the same document, Phippen is also spelled "Fipphen."

Stephen Phippen, where the the surname is spelled "Phippen." Oddly, Stephen's obituary and death certificate use the "Fipphen" spelling.

Children of Stephen and Susan (Chase) Phippen, born at New Boston:[1371]

142   i.   HARVEY H.[9] FIPPHEN, b. 1840.
143   ii. LEROY AUGUSTUS PHIPPEN, b. 18 July 1846.[1372] Called "Augustus" in the 1850 census.

Children of Stephen and Adaline (Dailey) Phippen, born at New Boston:[1373]

       iii. GEORGE F.[9] FIPPHEN, b. 11 July 1856; m. (1) at Goffstown, N.H. 6 May 1879, IANZA (JENNIE) OSBURNE, b. 29 Nov. 1861, daughter of Daniel B. and Mary A. (Follansbee) Osburne. Ianza d. at South Weare, N.H. 20 Sept. 1883, aged 21 years, 9 months, 20 days. George was a laborer. He was listed as a taxpayer in 1880 in Weare, N.H.[1374] He was listed in Amherst, N.H., in the 1900 census. He m. (2), after the 1900 census, MARY L. HEBERT. He d. at Amherst 27 May 1905. After his death, Mary m. (2) at Milford, N.H. 25 January 1906, CHARLES E. RICH. *Child:* FRANK EDWARD[10] FIPPHEN, b. at Amherst abt. 1904. Frank E. Fipphen is listed in the 1910 census with his mother, step-father and half-siblings. He subsequently took his step-father's surname. He m., as FRANK EDWARD RICH, at Hancock, N.H. 20 October 1923, GLADYS ROSE WEBB.[1375] They were living in Athol, Mass. in 1930.
       iv. SUSAN E. FIPPHEN, b. 1 Feb. 1858; d. young, after the 1860 census.
144   v.   CLARENCE FRED FIPPHEN, b. 2 Dec. 1861.[1376]

[1371] 1850 U.S. Census, New Boston, Hillsborough Co., N.H., p. 336.

[1372] Gravestone of Leroy A. Phippin, Weare, N.H., cemetery.

[1373] 1860 U.S. Census, New Boston, Hillsborough Co., N.H., p. 135; 1870 U.S. Census, New Boston, Hillsborough Co., N.H., p. 8; NH Vital Records (birth and death of George, marriage of George and Ianza, death of Ianza, birth of Susan).

[1374] William Little, *The History of Weare, New Hampshire, 1735–1888* (Lowell, Mass., 1888), 619.

[1375] N.H. Vital Records (marriage of Mary (Hebert) Fipphen, marriage of Frank E. Rich); 1910 U.S. Census, Weare, Hillsborough Co., N.H., roll T624_864, p. 9A.

[1376] The 1860 census for Stephen's family shows "Clarance F. Fipping" aged 1 or 10 months. Since the census is supposedly dated 11 and 12 July 1860, either the census date is incorrect, Clarence is older than he claims in later years, or his parents had an earlier Clarence who died young.

109. GEORGE⁸ PHIPPEN (*Thomas⁷⁻⁵, Nathaniel⁴, Samuel³, Joseph², David¹*) was born at Salem, Massachusetts about August 1813, based upon his age at death, son of Thomas and Sarah (Lufkin) Phippen. He died at Brookline, Massachusetts 28 April 1890, aged 76 years, 8 months.[1377] George married, first, **LUCY ANN ALLEN (OR BAIN OR BACON),** who was born at Boston, Massachusetts about 1817, daughter of William and Lucy A. (____) Allen. Lucy died of dropsy at Boston 5 July 1852.[1378]

George married, second, by 1870, **ISABELLA (DIAS) STONE** of Boston. Isabella, daughter of James and Ann (____) Dias, was born at New Hampshire around June 1821 and died at Boston 14 November 1887. Isabella had previously been married to Marshall Spring Stone. Two of her daughters by this marriage were listed with the name "Phippen" with their mother and stepfather George in the 1870 census of Boston. It is likely Marshall and Isabella divorced; he died at Melrose, Massachusetts 25 August 1896.[1379]

In 1850, George Phippen's family was living in Boston; in 1860, George, wife Lucy (although this is in error since she was clearly dead), and daughter Mary were living in Charlestown.[1380] George Phippen was listed as a barber in 1850 and a clerk in 1860.

George and Lucy Ann (Allen) Phippen are buried in Woodlawn Cemetery, Chelsea, Massachusetts.

Children of George and Lucy Ann (Allen) Phippen:[1381]

    i. SARAH A.⁹ PHIPPEN, b. about 1834; m. at Boston 7 April 1853, JUSTIN L. GUNN. Two children (surname *Gunn*): 1. *Henry Justin*, b. at Boston 26 March 1856; 2. *Melvin Brooks*, b. at Boston 2 Nov. 1858.[1382]

        Sarah (Phippen) Gunn died after 1860 and her husband remarried. Justin L. Gunn died at Bridgewater, Mass. 25 Sept. 1879, age 52.

[1377] Mass.VR (1890) 410: 330.

[1378] Ibid. (1852) 68: 37 (Lucy's death). Lucy's death record shows her father as William Bain, her cemetery record shows her maiden name as Allen, and her son George's marriage record identifies her maiden name as Bacon.

[1379] Mass.VR (1887) 384: 355 (death of Isabella, birth calculated from death record); J. Gardner Bartlett, Simon Stone Genealogy (Boston, 1926), 250 (information on Marshall Stone and Isabella; this genealogy claims her maiden name is "Dyer," although her death record and marriage records of her children show Dias or Diaz); 1870 U.S. Census, Boston, Ward 6, Suffolk Co., Mass., p. 21.

[1380] 1850 U.S. Census, Boston, Ward 11, Suffolk Co., Mass.; 1860 U.S. Census, Charlestown, Middlesex Co., Mass. Note, this census does say Lucy.

[1381] 1850 U.S. Census, Boston, Ward 11, Suffolk Co., Mass., p. 25.

[1382] Mass.VR (1856) 98: 78 (Henry); ibid, (1858), 116: 110 (Melvin).

The cause of his death is listed as "violence, murder."[1383] A story on his death was featured on the front page of the *Boston Globe* of 29 Sept. 1879. Justin Gunn was murdered with a hatchet. His wife immediately suspected her stepson Henry of the crime. Henry Gunn stole some of his father's items and was a fugitive until he was apprehended 14 Oct. 1879 in Boston, during which he stayed briefly with Henry Noyes, his Phippen uncle by marriage, who encouraged him to turn himself in. He was arraigned for murder at Brockton and pleaded not guilty. His trial began at Plymouth 19 Feb. 1880.

The murder was described as one of the most horrible instances of parricide ever chronicled in southeastern Massachusetts. Henry J. Gunn was found guilty of second-degree murder on 20 May 1880 and was sentenced to life in prison.

On 25 Oct. 1894, a request for executive clemency by Henry J. Gunn was granted by Governor Frederic T. Greenhalge, and he was released from Charlestown prison after serving fourteen years. Fifteen months later, on 23 Feb. 1896, Henry J. Gunn committed suicide in Jersey City, N.J.[1384]

145   ii.   GEORGE PHIPPEN JR., b. 28 Jan. 1836.
       iii. CHARLES EDWARD PHIPPEN, b. at Boston about Dec. 1837; d. unmarried at Charlestown, Mass. 24 April 1859.[1385]
       iv.   CORDELIA G. PHIPPEN, b. at South Kingstown, R.I. about 1840; m. at Boston 24 Nov. 1859, HENRY NOYES.[1386]
       v.   MARY FRANCIS ALLEN PHIPPEN, b. 9 July 1846; d. at Moultonboro, N.H. 25 Jan. 1912; m. (1) ROBERT Y. FOSTER; m. (2) ALFRED G. SANBORN.[1387]

110. GEORGE[8] PHIPPEN (*George[7]*, *William[6]*, *Thomas[5]*, *Nathaniel[4]*, *Samuel[3]*, *Joseph[2]*, *David[1]*) was the son of the Rev. George and Sally (Savage) Phippen. He married at Richmond, Virginia 11 September 1837, **HANNAH P. LOWNES.**[1388]

[1383] Mass.VR (1879), 311: 263.

[1384] Articles covering "The Bridgewater Parricide" and Henry Justin Gunn include *Boston Daily Globe,* 29 Sept. 1879, 1; 16 Oct. 1879, 4; 18 Oct. 1879, 4; 20 Feb. 1880, 1; 18 May 1880, 2; 19 May 1880, 2; 21 May 1880, 2; 26 Oct. 1894, 1; 26 Feb. 1896, 3; and New York Times, 27 Sept. 1879, 2; 16 Oct. 1879, 1 (confession).

[1385] Mass.VR (1859), 130: 60.

[1386] Ibid. (1859), 128:30.

[1387] Cemetery marker, Lee Cemetery, Moultonboro, N.H.

[1388] Family database of Samuel Alsup on RootsWeb WorldConnect.

Children of George and Hannah (Lownes) Phippen:

    i.   ELIZA RHODES PHIPPEN, b. at Lee, Mass. 19 Nov. 1840; d. there 23 or 25 Sept. 1846.[1389]

    ii. ANN LOWNES PHIPPEN, b. at Richmond, Va. ca. Jan. 1843; d. at Lee 6 Dec. 1847, aged 4 years, 11 months.[1390]

    iii. ELIZA ANN PHIPPEN, b. at Lee 25 Oct. 1847.[1391]

111. CHARLES W.[8] **PHIPPANY** (*David*[7–6], *Archibald*[5], *Benamin*[4], *James*[3], *Benjamin*[2], *David*[1]), was born in Connecticut 25 December 1838, son of David and Maria (Squires) Phippany. He married **ABBY** ____, who was born in 1838. (According to one record, Abby was born in England, but the birthplace of their sons' mother is shown as Ireland in the 1900 census). In the 1880 census, Charles was living in Hartford, Connecticut, with his wife and two children. In 1900, widowed, he was living in Torrington, Connecticut, with sons David and Daniel (both single).

Children of Charles W. and Abby (____) Phippany, born in Connecticut:[1392]

    i.   CHARLES[9] PHIPPANY, b. about 1874.

    ii. DANIEL PHIPPANY, b. in Dec. 1875; living in 1920 in Oregon City, Lucas Co., Ore.

    iii. DAVID PHIPPANY, b. in Oct. 1877.

    iv. JENNIE PHIPPANY, b. in 1879.

112. WILLIAM ROGER[8] **PHIPPENEY** (*William Archibald*[7], *David*[6], *Archibald*[5], *Benjamin*[4], *James*[3], *Benjamin*[2], *David*[1]) was born in Connecticut about 1833, son of William Archibald and Emily (Starkweather) Phippeney. He married at West Warren, Pennsylvania 17 September 1854, **ORPAH ANN ROGERS,** who was born in Pennsylvania 26 March 1835, daughter of James Dickerson and Sarah Fenton (Dare) Rogers.

At the time of the 1860 census, William was living in Wolcottville (Torrington), Litchfield County, Connecticut, next door to his (apparent) parents and unmarried sister. He and Orpah had two children listed in the 1860 census. In 1870, the family was in Meriden, New Haven County, Connecticut. Orpah was living in Torrington in 1910.

[1389] *Vital Records of Lee, Massachusetts to the year 1850* (Boston, 1903), 78, 220.

[1390] Ibid., 220.

[1391] Ibid., 78, 220.

[1392] 1880 U.S. Census, Torrington, Litchfield Co., Conn., p. 235A.

William saw service in the Civil War in Company A, Twenty-Fifth Regiment, Connecticut Volunteers. He died at West Warren, Pennsylvania 27 November 1895.

Children of William and Orpah Ann (Rogers) Phippeney:[1393]

  i. FRANCIS EUGENE[9] PHIPPENEY, b. 6 March 1856; living with his mother in Torrington in 1880 and 1900.[1394]

  ii. MARGARET DWYER PHIPPENEY, b. about 1859.

146 iii. WILLIAM ARCHIBALD PHIPPENEY, b. 19 June 1861.

  iv. EMMA LOUISE PHIPPENEY, b. 6 Oct. 1867; m., 14 Sept. 1899, FREDERICK SOLYMON BROWN, son of Lucius Edgar and Susan (Taylor) Brown.

113. ALVIN P.[8] PHIPPENNEY (_Calvin Evet[7], William[6], Archibald[5], Benjamin[4], James[3], Benjamin[2], David[1]_) was born in Ohio about 1848, son of Calvin E. and Mary (Phillips) Phippenney. He lived in Kansas for awhile before settling in Pueblo, Colorado, where he was a police officer. On 30 June 1879, Alvin Phippenney was shot and killed by drunken cattle drovers while keeping the peace in a Pueblo saloon. The COLORADO CHIEFTAIN for 3 July 1879 carries a lengthy, serialized news story on the murder and its aftermath, excerpted here:

> MURDER MOST FOUL: A POLICEMAN SHOT
> WHILE IN THE DISCHARGE OF HIS DUTY
>
> During the past two or three days a number of cattle men from the round up, which have reached this neighborhood, have been in the city enjoying themselves. On Saturday and Sunday the boys indulged in a good deal of harmless hilarity somewhat noisy but no one was injured in any way. Yesterday morning a number of them collected in the Arkansas Hall saloon, on Santa Fe avenue, and the party was joined by John Baxter, a farmer, who lives on Mrs. Steele's ranch about nine or ten miles up the Fontaine. The party were all somewhat under the influence of liquor, and Baxter became quarrelsome. Some of the cow men knew that Baxter was a dangerous

---

[1393] 1860 U.S. Census, Torrington, Litchfield Co., Conn., p. 457; 1870 U.S. Census, Meriden, New Haven Co., Conn., p. 178.

[1394] 1900 U.S. Census, Torrington, Litchfield Co., Conn., E.D. 257, p. 9B.

man when under the influence of liquor, and cautioned their comrades about him, fearing that trouble would come. No attention was paid to the warning, and about noon the party became exceedingly noisy. About half past twelve Policeman Alvin Phippenny went into the saloon and attempted, as we are informed, to arrest some of the parties. He clinched with Baxter, and one shot was fired inside the saloon. The men came out into the street where four shots were fired. They again rolled into the saloon, when another shot was heard. The policeman fell in front of the bar, a ball having entered his back under the shoulder blade and passing through his body, lodged directly under the nipple. Baxter was shot directly through the stomach. Phippeny died in about fifteen minutes after the shooting.

Drs. Cortright and Owen were called in immediately, but nothing could be done to save the wounded man's life. He asked Dr. Owen if he was going to die, and being answered in the affirmative, said: "Well, good bye, I did my duty as well as I could." In answer to an inquiry as to who did the shooting, he replied that Baxter and another man both shot him. Policeman Bilby then came to him, and the dying man told him that he had received his death wound in the discharge of his duty. He asked to be allowed to get all the fresh air possible, and died calmly and perfectly conscious until the last. Policeman Phippenny has been a resident of Pueblo for the past two or three years. He came here from Nebraska, was about thirty two or three years of age, and was a widower with three or four small children dependent upon him. He was a brave and faithful officer and died, as he said, in the discharge of his duty. ... Mr. Phippeny, we are informed, was to have been married on the evening of the day upon which he was killed. . . .

At four o'clock yesterday afternoon the funeral of the murdered policeman took place. . . . The funeral was one of the largest ever seen in the city, there being some thirty vehicles in the procession all well filled. All of the learned professions were represented and many ladies were present. During the funeral many of the business houses of the city were closed in accordance with the request of the city council. It is the intention of the city authorities to have a neat railing placed around the lot in the cemetery and a tombstone erected over the dead officer's grave, with a suitable inscription describing the manner of his death. A subscription has been commenced to raise a fund for the benefit of the orphan children of the deceased.[1395]

Children of Alvin P. Phippenney, listed with their grandparents in Nebraska in the 1880 census:[1396]

147   i.   HERBERT CALVIN[9] PHIPPENNEY, b. in Kansas about 1869.
148   ii. ACEL PHIPPENNEY, b. in Kansas about 1871.
        iii. GRACE ADEL PHIPPENNEY, b. in Nebraska about 1873; m. in Otoe Co., Neb. 5 Nov. 1894, HARRY TRUMAN RATLIFF. They had at least six children and lived most of their lives in Bushnell, Kimball Co., Neb., where they are buried. Grace was raised by her uncle, Orville Earl Phippenney, q.v.
        iv. IDA MAY PHIPPENNEY, b. in Nebraska about 1875; m. in Otoe Co. 26 Sept. 1893, SAMUEL BEE EDWARDS. They had at least three children.

114. ORVILLE EARL[8] PHIPPENNEY (*Calvin Evet[7]*, *William[6]*, *Archibald[5]*, *Benjamin[4]*, *James[3]*, *Benjamin[2]*, *David[1]*) was born in Michigan 7 June 1850, son of Calvin E. and Mary (Phillips) Phippenney. He married **JENNIE McKNIGHT**. In the 1880 census he was living near his parents in Nemaha County, Nebraska, with his wife, a son, and Grace Adel, orphaned daughter of his brother Alvin P. Phippenney, *q.v.,* as his "adopted daughter." They were still living in Nebraska (Auburn, Nemaha County) in 1920.

Children of Orville E. and Jennie (_____) Phippenney, all born in Nebraska:[1397]

        i.   J. C.[9] PHIPPENNEY, b. about 1878.
        ii. ROBERTA PHIPPENNEY, b. about 1887.

115. ALBERT HOLLAR[8] PHIPPANY (*Horace[7]*, *Joel[6]*, *James[5-3]*, *Benjamin[2]*, *David[1]*) was born about 1837 in Yates, Orleans County, New York, son of Horace and Elizabeth (Blanchard) Phippany. He married **FRANCES _____**, born in New York about 1850. In 1880 he was living in Yates with his wife.

[1395] *Colorado Chieftain,* 3 July 1879; newspaper courtesy of descendant Kay Brett.
[1396] 1880 U.S. Census, Glen Rock, Nemaha Co., Neb., p. 15.
[1397] Ibid., p. 12.

Children of Albert Hollar and Frances (____) Phippany in 1880:[1398]

149   i.   HORACE[9] PHIPPANY, b. May 1869.
       ii. MARY E. PHIPPANY, b. about 1872; m. GEORGE AUSTIN, who was b.
            in Ireland in Feb. 1869. Children (surname *Austin*): 1. *Alice,* b. in
            April 1896; 2. *Frances,* b. about 1899. In 1900 Mary was living with
            her husband, a cooper; sister, Bertha; and daughter in Royalton,
            Niagara Co., N.Y.; in 1910 she was with her husband and two
            daughters in Royalton.
       iii. BERTHA PHIPPANY, b. in Oct. 1875. Living with her sister's family in
            Royalton in 1900.
       iv. WILLIAM PHIPPANY, b. about 1879.

116. CARROLL L.[8] PHIPPANY (*Horace[7], Joel[6], James[5-3], Benjamin[2], David[1]*)
was born in Yates, Orleans County, New York in July 1844, son of
Horace and Elizabeth (Blanchard) Phippany. He married **SAPHRONIA**
____, who was born in New York State in July 1848. In 1880 he was
living in Tuscarora, Cheboygan County, Michigan, with his wife and
children.

Children of Carroll L. and Saphronia (____) Phippany in 1880:[1399]

       i.   FLOYD[9] PHIPPANY, b. in New York State in , May 1872. Floyd and his
            sister Lela were living together in the 1930 census, in Yates, Orleans
            Co., N.Y.
       ii. MABEL PHIPPANY, b. in New York State about 1873.
       iii. LELA PHIPPANY, b. in New York State in Nov. 1876.

117. WALTER SCOTT[8] PHIPPANY (*George[7], Joel[6], James[5-3], Benjamin[2],
David[1]*) was born at Ellington, New York, 15 September 1837, son of
George James and Charity (Crane) Phippany; he died between 1874
and 1880, probably in Albion, Michigan. He lived at Brockport, New
York, from 1859 to August 1861. He was a private in Company C,
3rd Regiment, New York Volunteer Cavalry, from 3 August to 21
December 1861. He served as a clerk in the U.S. Army's Quartermaster
department at Memphis, Tennessee, from February 1862 to April 1863,
and as chief clerk in the same department, at Nashville, Tennesee, from
January 1864 to April 1865. Walter married at Jonesville, Michigan
20 April 1865, **GENEVIEVE BLANCHARD,** who was born at Albion,

---

[1398] 1880 U.S. Census, Yates, Orleans Co., N.Y., p. 316C.
[1399] 1880 U.S. Census, Tuscarora, Cheboygan Co., Mich., E.D. 36, p. 137.

Michigan 19 September 1846, daughter of Charles and Maria (Crane) Blanchard.[1400] Walter settled briefly in Laporte, Indiana; on returning to Albion, he engaged in business until 6 September 1870, when he and his wife relocated to Chicago, Illinois. They were living there in 1874 at 566 South Dearborn Street.[1401] In the 1880 census (Albion, Michigan), Walter's wife and daughter were living with her parents;[1402] he, on the other hand, was living in Loveland, Larimer County, Colorado, in a boarding house, enumerated as an insurance agent.[1403]

Child of Walter S. and Genevieve (Blanchard) Phippany, born at Albion:

    i.   JESSIE MARIA[9] PHIPPANY, b. 28 Feb. 1866.

118. OLIVER LEE[8] PHIPPENY (*Charles Lee*[7], *Peter*[6], *James*[5-3], *Benjamin*[2], *David*[1]) was born in Nevada about 1872, son of Charles Lee and Lucy J. (____) Phippany. He married at Congress, Yavapai County, Arizona, 14 April 1897, **ROSA LEE GIBSON**.[1404]

Child of Oliver Lee and Rosa (Gibson) Phippany, born at Phoenix, Arizona:[1405]

150   i   CHARLES WILLIAM[9] PHIPPENY, b. 23 July 1899.

119. LYMAN OSCAR[8] PHIPPENY (*Charles Lee*[7], *Peter*[6], *James*[5-3], *Benjamin*[2], *David*[1]) was born in Nevada 21 October 1873, son of Charles Lee and Lucy J. (____) Phippany. He was married, perhaps briefly, to **ANNIE** ____, who is listed in the 1900 census in Martinez, Yavapai County, Arizona, with their young son Ernest. In 1920, Ernest was living with his father, described as a widower.[1406]

Child of Lyman Oscar and Annie (____) Phippeny:[1407]

    i.   ERNEST ROBERT[9] PHIPPENY, b. in Arizona 22 May 1900.

[1400] Michigan Marriages, 1851–1875 (online at *Ancestry.com*) as "Walter S. Phipany" and "Jennie Blanchard."

[1401] Phoenix, *The Whitney family of Connecticut*, 2:1218.

[1402] 1800 U.S. Census, Albion, Calhoun Co., Mich., p. 373D.

[1403] 1880 U.S. Census, Loveland, Larimer Co., Colo., p. 39.

[1404] Arizona Marriages, 1864–1982 (online at *Ancestry.com*), citing Yavapai County Marriages, vol. 2, p. 216 (County Courthouse, Yavapai Co., Ariz.).

[1405] 1900 U.S. Census, Buckeye, Maricopa Co., Ariz., E.D. 33, p. 319A

[1406] 1920 U.S. Census, Prescott, Yavapai Co., Ariz., E.D. 119, p. 6B; had son *Ernest Robert Phippany*, age 19, b. Ariz., mother b. Kans.

[1407] Full name and birthdate listed on 1917 draft registration card, Yavapai Co., Ariz.; accessed via *Ancestry.com*.

CHAPTER 11

THE NINTH GENERATION

120. WALTER[9] **PHIPPEN** (*Homer*[8], *Horatio*[7], *Samuel*[6-3], *Joseph*[2], *David*[1]) was born in New York State 31 May 1868, son of Homer W. and Jennie E. (Ware) Phippen. He married **JULIA** ____.

Children of Walter and Julia (____) Phippen:

    i.   ROBERT[10] PHIPPEN, b. 24 April 1915.
    ii. MILDRED PHIPPEN, b. 11 May 1919.
    iii. ROSS PHIPPEN, twin, b. 2 March 1922.
    iv. ROY PHIPPEN, twin, b. 2 March 1922.

121. EDWIN DIDYMUS[9] **PHIPPEN** (*Orlando*[8], *Joseph*[7], *Joseph*[6], *Samuel*[5-3], *Joseph*[2], *David*[1]) was born at Apple River, Jo Daviess County, Illinois about 1852, son of Orlando and Elizabeth (Benson) Phippen. He died at Charles City, Iowa in 1931. He married **ELIZA ELLEN POWER,** who was born at Apple River.

Children of Edwin Didymus and Eliza Ellen (Power) Phippen:

       i.   MARY ELIZA[10] PHIPPEN, b. at Apple River 4 Jan. 1876; d. at Charles City 27 March 1955; m. there 13 Nov. 1895, JESSE ROWLEY. Issue.
151 ii. JOSEPH ALBERT PHIPPEN, b. at Apple River 1 March 1878; d. at Grand Junction, Colo. 13 March 1960.
      iii. MABEL EDNA PHIPPEN, b. 9 June 1881; m. LEO MURPHEY.
      iv. ORY ABSALOM PHIPPEN, b. 10 Aug. 1884.

122. SILAS LUCIAN[9] **PHIPPEN** (*James Worthington*[8], *Isaac*[7], *Joseph*[6], *Samuel*[5-3], *Joseph*[2], *David*[1]) was born at Newstead, Erie County, New York 5 December 1848, son of James Worthington and Julia (Pratt) Phippen. He married at Salt Lake City, Utah 29 March 1869, **MARTHA MITCHELL,** daughter of Benjamin S. and Lovina (Buckwater) Mitchell. She died at Albion, Cassia County, Idaho 29 January 1878. He died at Salt Lake City 19 June 1886.

Children of Silas Lucian and Martha (Mitchell) Phippen:

    i.   JULIA LAVONIA[10] PHIPPEN, b. 17 Feb. 1870; d. 17 Dec. 1940; m. at Salt Lake City 17 March 1897, FRANCIS MURPHY. Issue.[1408]

    ii. SILAS LUCIAN PHIPPEN, b. in June 1872.

152   iii. FRANK WORTHINGTON PHIPPEN, b. at Salt Lake City 4 Feb. 1874.

    iv. MARTHA ROSABEL PHIPPEN, b. at Salt Lake City 16 Oct. 1876.

    v. ELLA IRENE PHIPPEN, b. at Albion 8 Jan. 1878.

123. JOSEPH HYRUM[9] PHIPPEN *(Joseph Freeman[8], Isaac[7], Joseph[6], Samuel[5-3], Joseph[2], David[1])* was born at Nauvoo, Illinois 8 December 1844, son of Joseph Freeman and Ann (Dayton) Phippen. He died at North Hollywood, California 26 July 1931. Joseph married at Salt Lake City, Utah 10 May 1870, **MARY SOPHIA DRUCE**, daughter of John and Julia Ann (Jinks) Druce. He was living at Tikura, Alturas County, Idaho, in 1885.

Children of Joseph Hyrum and Mary Sophia (Druce) Phippen:[1409]

    i.   HYRUM CLARENCE[10] PHIPPEN, b. at Salt Lake City 2 Oct. 1871; m. 20 June 1901, ROSE HANNAH BENNETT.

    ii. KATIE ADELIA PHIPPEN , b. in Toole Co., Utah 6 Nov. 1874; m. EVERETT FARMER DIX.

153   iii. ERNEST DRUCE PHIPPEN, b. in Blaine Co., Idaho 10 April 1884.

124. ALMON MARCELLUS[9] PHIPPEN, *(Joseph Freeman[8], Isaac[7], Joseph[6], Samuel[5-3], Joseph[2], David[1])* was born at Big Cottonwood Canyon, Utah 4 February 1858, son of Joseph and Ann (Dayton) Phippen.[1410] He died at Carey, Blaine County, Idaho 18 June 1942. He married, 25 December 1882, **NONA ALFRETTA BRIM,** who was born in Coalville, Summit County, Utah 27 December 1866, daughter of Joseph Henry and Rhuhamah (Fisher) Brim.[1411]

[1408] FamilySearch Ancestral File, v4.19, at *www.FamilySearch.org* [hereafter Ancestral File]. Information in these files comes from a number of sources with varying levels of accuracy. Information about early LDS pioneers, however, tends to be more reliable. In this instance, for example, the information is generally consistent with the Paul-Paull MS.

[1409] Ibid.

[1410] Correspondence with Ernest D. Phippen, 1977.

[1411] Ancestral File at *www.FamilySearch.org.*

In 1900, the family was living in Little Wood River Precinct in Blaine County; in 1910, they were in Carey in the same county.[1412]

Children of Almon Marcellus and Nona Alfretta (Brim) Phippen, born in Idaho:[1413]

i. CARL MARCELLUS[10] PHIPPEN, b. 9 Oct. 1883; m. 1 Nov. 1910, FLORENCE KELSEY.

ii. NORA ELLA or ELLEN PHIPPEN, b. 29 June 1886; m. JOHN D. BAIRD.

iii. WILLIAM FREDERICK PHIPPEN, b. 17 June 1888; d. 6 Sept. 1889.

iv. CHAUNCY FREEMAN PHIPPEN, b. 18 July 1890; m. 6 June 1918, ANNE MARIE KIRBY.

v. LENA BLANCHE PHIPPEN, b. 23 Dec. 1892; m. 22 Dec. 1915, JOHN THOMAS BENNETT.

vi. MELVIN ARNOLD PHIPPEN, b. 2 May 1895; m. 3 July 1939, RUTH FRANCES DAGGETT.

vii. JOSEPH CECIL PHIPPEN, b. at Carey, Idaho 4 Dec. 1897; d. in 1898.

vii. GOLDMAN WARNER PHIPPEN, b. 27 July 1899; m. 3 July 1921, MARGARET GEISE MONTAGUE.

viii. WINNIE MAY PHIPPEN, b. 6 Dec. 1901; d. 2 Oct. 1956; m. 3 July 1921, LYLE MERRILL MONTAGUE.

ix. MILDRED PEARL PHIPPEN, twin, b. at Carey 7 April 1905; m. 22 Dec. 1929, ROLLY LAWRENCE KNOWEL.

x. MILFORD EARL PHIPPEN, twin, b. at Carey 7 April 1905; m. 25 Dec. 1936, DOROTHY ALICE TAYLOR.

125. WILFORD FREEMAN[9] PHIPPEN (*Joseph Freeman[8]*, *Isaac[7]*, *Joseph[6]*, *Samuel[5-3]*, *Joseph[2]*, *David[1]*) was born in Utah 8 November 1869, son of Joseph Freeman and Eliza Jane (Hudson) Phippen. In 1900, he was living in Albion Precinct, Cassia County, Idaho, with his wife and one son. He married at Logan, Utah 23 June 1892, **EMMA LOUISE WILLIAMS,** who was born at Brigham City, Utah 2 August 1870, daughter of Lemuel Lewis and Emma (Wardle) Williams.

[1412] 1900 U.S. Census, Little Wood River Precinct, Blaine Co., Idaho, p. 160; 1910 U.S. Census, Carey Precinct, Blaine Co., Idaho, p. 164.

[1413] Ancestral File, verified from U.S. censuses only through 1930, at *www.FamilySearch. org.*

Children of Wilford Freeman and Emma Louise (Williams) Phippen, born in Idaho:[1414]

    i.   EARL M.[10] PHIPPEN, b. in April 1893.

    ii. CORA E. PHIPPEN, b. in July 1895.

    iii. WILFORD K. PHIPPEN, b. in May 1897.

126. ADELBERT SMITH[9] PHIPPEN (*Sylvester Smith[8], Isaac[7], Joseph[6], Samuel[5-3], Joseph[2], David[1]*) was born at Salt Lake City, Utah 1 April 1858, son of Sylvester Smith and Mary Jane (Brim) Phippen.[1415] He married at Salt Lake City 29 January 1880, **SUSAN ACENATH LUFKIN,** who was born there 11 November 1860, daughter of George Washington and Martha Ann (Townsend) Lufkin.[1416]

Adelbert was a farmer.[1417] He died at Salt Lake City 14 August 1943.[1418] Susan died at Bountiful, Davis County, Utah 1 November 1936.[1419]

Children of Adelbert and Susan Acenath (Lufkin) Phippen:[1420]

    i.   GEORGE ADELBERT[10] PHIPPEN, b. at Salt Lake City 17 Dec. 1880; m. 18 Dec. 1907, BARBARA ABIGAIL WILLIAMS. Issue.

    ii. GUY TOWNSEND PHIPPEN, b. at Salt Lake City 3 Oct. 1885; d. 5 April 1952; m. 26 June 1907, EUNICE ELIZABETH CHIDESTER. Issue.

    iii. AUSTIN SLOANE PHIPPEN, b. at Logan, Utah, 22 Sept. 1888; d. there 10 Oct. 1888.

    iv. MARTHA LUFKIN PHIPPEN, b. at Logan 9 Nov. 1892; m. 19 Dec. 1912, HORACE BROUGH.

127. EDWARD BERT[9] PHIPPEN (*Sylvester Smith[8], Isaac[7], Joseph[6], Samuel[5-3], Joseph[2], David[1]*) was born at Salt Lake City, Utah 27 May 1879, son of Sylvester Smith and Mary Jane (Brim) Phippen. He married at Salt Lake City 26 September 1906, **LIZZIE ATKINSON,** who was born at Scarborough, Yorkshire, England 28 September 1874, daughter of Jacob and Sarah (Drewery) Atkinson. In 1920 they were living in Salt Lake City with two children.

[1414] Ancestral File at *www.FamilySearch.org.*

[1415] Paul-Paull MS, 2: 86; records of Martha Lufkin Phippen Brough.

[1416] Records of Martha Lufkin Phippen Brough.

[1417] Paul-Paull MS, 2: 86.

[1418] Records of Martha Lufkin Phippen Brough.

[1419] Ibid.

[1420] Paul-Paull MS, 2: 86; records of Martha Lufkin Phippen Brough.

Children of Edward Bert and Lizzie (Atkinson) Phippen include:[1421]

 i. DORA MABLE[10] PHIPPEN, b. at Salt Lake City 21 Sept. 1907; d 18 Oct. 1998; m. at Salt Lake City 11 Oct. 1928, WILFORD DAVID GYGI.

 ii. ARTHUR EDWARD PHIPPEN, b. at Salt Lake City 18 Oct. 1908; died 11 Dec. 1994; m. at Salt Lake City 28 August 1935, VIRGINIA MARIE COULAM.

128. ROSS ALONZO[9] PHIPPEN (*Loren*[8], *Calvin*[7], *Joseph*[6], *Samuel*[5-3], *Joseph*[2], *David*[1]) was born at Delmar, Pennsylvania 5 March 1885, son of Loren D. and Sophia (Boyden) Phippen. He died at Wellsboro, Pennsylvania 7 December 1928. He married there 21 September 1914, **MAUDE ETHEL RUSSELL**, who was born at Wellsboro 29 July 1893, daughter of Lucius Lester Russell, Jr. (1863–1910), and Dora Adell (Stowell) Russell (1859–1913). Maude died at Wellsboro 8 November 1970.[1422]

Children of Ross Alonzo and Maude Ethel (Russell) Phippen, born at Wellsboro:

154 i. FLOYD RUSSELL[10] PHIPPEN, b. 29 Dec. 1916; d. 20 July 1946.

 ii. MARGARET EUDORA PHIPPEN, b. 29 Oct. 1918; d. at Wellsboro 18 March 1980; m. there 6 Feb. 1935, JESSE ROBERT BROOKS, who was b. at Wellsboro 11 March 1915, son of Joseph and Mary Gwendolyn (Hall) Brooks, and d. at Alachua, Fla. 22 Aug. 1988.

 iii. HILDA RUTH PHIPPEN, b. 4 Jan. 1925; m. F. WILBUR WILSON, who was b. in 1905 and d. in 1983. She d. at Lansing, N.Y. 3 Aug. 2007.[1423]

129. FRANK ELMORE[9] PHIPPEN (*Elmore*[8], *Samuel*[7], *Jonathan*[6], *Samuel*[5-3], *Joseph*[2], *David*[1]) was born at Burke, Vermont 15 March 1862.[1424] He worked for awhile in a store in Burke before moving to Connecticut. He married at Hartford, Connecticut 2 October 1891, **IVA FORBES**, daughter of A. L. Forbes.[1425] Frank later moved to Worcester, Massachusetts; he died there 23 April 1893.[1426] His widow went to live in New York, New York.

[1421] International Genealogical Index (Dora); Ancestral File (Arthur), at *www.FamilySearch.org.*

[1422] Information about Ross Alonzo Phippen was supplied by Jessie Brabham, daughter of Margaret Eudora Phippen Brooks, from information compiled by Maude Ethel (Russell) Phippen in an unpublished family history.

[1423] Social Security Death Index.

[1424] Rowell, *Biographical Sketch of Samuel Rowell,* 184.

[1425] Ibid.

[1426] Ibid.

Child of Frank Elmore and Iva (Forbes) Phippen:[1427]

    i.   ETHEL[10] PHIPPEN, b. at Burke,Vt., 23 Sept. 1892.

130. NATHANIEL[9] PHIPPEN (*Benjamin*[8], *Nathaniel*[7], *Joshua*[6], *Nathaniel*[5–4], *Samuel*[3], *Joseph*[2], *David*[1]) was born at Salem, Massachusetts 26 January 1832, son of Benjamin and Mary Massey (Wells) Phippen.[1428] He died 19 January 1914.[1429] Nathaniel married 28 February 1866, **ABBIE M. ELLIS,** who was born about 1847.[1430] Nathaniel was a cooper in Salem and was listed in the city directories as living at 25 Hardy Street and then at 22 Forest Street from 1869 to 1872.[1431]

Children of Nathaniel and Abbie (Ellis) Phippen, born at Salem:

    i.   ABBIE L.[10] PHIPPEN, b. 27 June 1867;[1432] m. at Salem 16 Sept. 1896, CALEB H. MORSE, who was b. about 1869, son of Caleb and Susan J. (____) Morse.[1433]

    ii. ANNA MAUD PHIPPEN, b. 21 July 1874;[1434] m. 8 April 1903, CHARLES E. EBSEN.[1435]

131. JOSEPH E.[9] PHIPPEN (*Benjamin*[8], *Nathaniel*[7], *Joshua*[6], *Nathaniel*[5–4], *Samuel*[3], *Joseph*[2], *David*[1]) was born at Salem, Massachusetts 11 December 1833, son of Benjamin and Mary Massey (Wells) Phippen.[1436] He married there 19 September 1855, **ABBIE B. PERRY,**[1437] who was born at Salem 14 December 1836, daughter of Ittai Perry, Jr. and Abigail (Hinman) Perry.[1438] Joseph Phippen died at Salem 27 November 1902; Abby B. (Perry) Phippen died 12 June 1910.[1439]

Joseph was a cooper in Salem, and was listed in the city directories as living at 59 Derby Street in 1866 and at 5 Mall Street from 1874 to 1896.[1440]

[1427] Rowell, *Biographical Sketch of Samuel Rowell*, 185.

[1428] *Vital Records of Salem, Massachusetts to the end of the year 1849*, 2: 168.

[1429] Perley, *The History of Salem, Massachusetts*, 2: 331.

[1430] Mass.VR (1866) 189: 269.

[1431] Salem City Directories, 1869–1872.

[1432] Ibid.; Mass.VR (1867) 196: 266 (record reads "female").

[1433] Mass.VR (1896), 460:530.

[1434] Mass.VR (1874), 259: 321.

[1435] Perley, *The History of Salem, Massachusetts*, 2: 331.

[1436] Ibid.; *Vital Records of Salem, Massachusetts to the end of the year 1849*, 2: 167.

[1437] Perley, *The History of Salem, Massachusetts*, 2: 331.

[1438] Fitts, *Lane Genealogies*, 3: 285.

[1439] Perley *The History of Salem, Massachusetts*, 2: 331.

[1440] Salem Directories, 1866, 1874–1896.

Child of Joseph and Abbie (Perry) Phippen, born at Salem:[1441]

    i.   Mercy E.[10] Phippen, b. 22 July 1860; d. 10 March 1861, aged 7 months, 18 days.

132. William Trumbull[9] Phippen (*Benjamin[8], Nathaniel[7], Joshua[6], Nathaniel[5-4], Samuel[3], Joseph[2], David[1]*) was born at Salem, Massachusetts 25 September 1842, son of Benjamin and Mary Massey (Wells) Phippen.[1442] He died at Medford, Massachusetts 8 November 1910.[1443] He married at Salem 12 April 1863, **Sarah Addie Dix**,[1444] who was born at Bucksport, Maine in 1843, daughter of Daniel and Eliza Ann (Crosby) Dix. She died at Medford 10 July 1904.[1445]

William Phippen was an artist and a photographer.[1446] In 1866, he and Sarah were listed as living at 4 Hardy Street in Salem; in 1869, at 25 Hardy Street; and in 1872, at 31 Hardy Street. William's name does not appear in later Salem directories; he was apparently living in Somerville, Massachusetts, after approximately 1872.[1447]

Children of William Trumbull and Sarah Addie (Dix) Phippen:

    i.   Mary Eliza[10] Phippen, b. at Salem 18 Feb. 1866.[1448]

   ii. Carrie Lillian Phippen, b. at Salem 1 Dec. 1867.[1449]

  iii. Irene Phippen, b. at Somerville, Mass. 20 March 1875; d. there 11 May 1875.[1450]

133. Joshua B.[9] Phippen (*Nathaniel[8-7], Joshua[6], Nathaniel[5-4], Samuel[3], Joseph[2], David[1]*) was born at Salem, Massachusetts, 7 February and baptized there 5 September 1830, son of Nathaniel and Martha (Clark) Phippen.[1451] Joshua married at Salem, 20 March 1854, **Mary R. Dakin**,[1452] who was born 3 February 1836, daughter of Timothy and

[1441] Mass.VR (1860) 147: 280; Perley, *The History of Salem, Massachusetts,* 2: 331.

[1442] *Vital Records of Salem, Massachusetts to the end of the year 1849,* 2: 169; Perley 2:331.

[1443] Perley, *The History of Salem, Massachusetts,* 2: 331, Mass.VR (1910), 70:11 (death).

[1444] Mass.VR (1863), 162: 202; Perley, *The History of Salem, Massachusetts,* 2: 331.

[1445] Mass.VR (1904), 65: 338.

[1446] Perley, *The History of Salem, Massachusetts,* 2: 331.

[1447] Salem City Directories, 1869; Somerville City Directories, 1874.

[1448] Perley, *The History of Salem, Massachusetts,* 2: 331; Mass.VR (1862) 186: 261.

[1449] Perley, *The History of Salem, Massachusetts,* 2: 331.

[1450] Mass.VR (1875) 269: 187, (1875) 275: 184.

[1451] *Vital Records of Salem, Massachusetts to the end of the year 1849,* 2: 167.

[1452] Mass.VR (1854) 78: 227.

Sarah A. (____) Dakin.[1453] She died 18 December 1886.[1454] He died 17 December 1904.[1455]

Joshua served in the Civil War: he mustered into the 1st Battalion, Massachusetts Volunteer Heavy Artillery, on 17 January 1863, age 33, employed as a gas fitter; he mustered out 29 June 1865.[1456]

Children of Joshua B. and Mary R. (Dakin) Phippen:

    i.   ELLA or MARY ELLA[10] PHIPPEN, b. about 1855 ("Ella" in 1860 census; "Mary E." in 1880 census).

    ii. JOSHUA H. PHIPPEN, b. at Salem 31 May 1857;[1457] d. there 16 May 1865.[1458]

134. JOSHUA H.[9] PHIPPEN (*Joshua*[8], *Hardy*[7], *Joshua*[6], *Nathaniel*[5-4], *Samuel*[3], *Joseph*[2], *David*[1]) was born at Salem, Massachusetts about 1858, son of Joshua and Eunice (Daniels) Phippen.[1459] He was a musician and lived in Winchester, Massachusetts. He married at Winchester 16 June 1891, **ADDIE ELIZABETH GREELEY,**[1460] who was born at Charlestown, Massachusetts 19 November 1860, daughter of William P. and Elizabeth J. (McClary) Greeley.[1461]

Children of Joshua H. and Addie Elizabeth (Greeley) Phippen, born at Winchester:[1462]

       i.   RUTH G.[10] PHIPPEN, b. 14 Oct. 1894.

155   ii. WILLIAM SAFFORD PHIPPEN, b. 8 Dec. 1897.

135. EDWARD AUGUSTUS[9] PHIPPEN (*Joshua*[8], *Hardy*[7], *Joshua*[6], *Nathaniel*[5-4], *Samuel*[3], *Joseph*[2], *David*[1]) was born at Salem, Massachusetts 12 October 1859, son of Joshua and Eunice (Daniels) Phippen. He died at Salem 21 March 1948. He was a bank teller and a businessman.[1463]

[1453] Perley, *The History of Salem, Massachusetts,* 2: 331.

[1454] Mass.VR (1886) 373:304.

[1455] Mass.VR (1904) 1904/82:473.

[1456] *Massachusetts Soldiers, Sailors, and Marines in the Civil War,* 6: 98.

[1457] Mass.VR (1857) 105: 329.

[1458] Mass.VR (1865) 183: 254.

[1459] Perley, *The History of Salem, Massachusetts,* 2: 331.

[1460] Mass.VR (1891) 416: 394.

[1461] George H. Greely, *Genealogy of the Greely-Greeley Family* (Boston, 1905), 535, 847–48.

[1462] Mass.VR (1894), 440: 451 (Ruth's birth), (1897), 467: 486 (William's birth).

[1463] Correspondence with Hardy Phippen, 18 Oct. 1975.

Edward Phippen married at Concord, Massachusetts 8 October 1884, MARY LOUISE DARLING, who was born at Charlestown, Massachusetts 23 February 1861, daughter of Elijah S. and Abbie (Lowd) Darling. Mary Louise died at Salem 8 July 1934.[1464]

Children of Edward Augustus and Mary Louise (Darling) Phippen:

156   i.   CLEMENT LOWELL[10] PHIPPEN, b. at Boston, Mass. 16 Oct. 1885.[1465]

      ii.   HARDY PHIPPEN, b. at Newton, Mass. 14 April 1887; d. at Newtonville 28 Oct. 1902.[1466]

157   iii.   EDWARD WILLARD PHIPPEN, b. at Newtonville 4 April 1891.

      iv.   MILDRED DARLING PHIPPEN, b. at Newton in June 1896 and d. there 8 June 1932.[1467]

136. GEORGE BARTON[9] PHIPPEN (*George[8], Hardy[7], Joshua[6], Nathaniel[5-4], Samuel[3], Joseph[2], David[1]*) was born at Salem, Massachusetts 12 February 1841, son of George and Margaret (Barton) Phippen.[1468] He married 30 November 1865, **MARY ELIZA STODDER,**[1469] who was born 8 March 1841, daughter of Simon and Hannah (____) Stodder.[1470]

George was treasurer of the New York and New England Railroad Company,[1471] and also a broker. He moved to Boston, Massachusetts, about 1894.[1472]

Children of George Barton and Mary Eliza (Stodder) Phippen, born at Salem:[1473]

      i.   GEORGE STODDER[10] PHIPPEN, b. 3 July 1868; he m. at Salem 19 Oct. 1893, ANNIE E. HATHAWAY.[1474]

      ii.   CAROLINE BARTON PHIPPEN, b. 2 Dec. 1876.

[1464] Ibid.

[1465] Mass.VR (1885) 360: 121.

[1466] Mass.VR (1887) 386: 233 (birth), (1902) 529: 670 (death).

[1467] Mass.VR (1896) 83: 379 (amended record).

[1468] *Vital Records of Salem, Massachusetts to the end of the year 1849,* 2: 166.

[1469] Perley, *The History of Salem, Massachusetts,* 2: 331; Mass.VR (1865) 180: 262.

[1470] *Vital Records of Salem, Massachusetts to the end of the year 1849,* 2: 325.

[1471] Perley, *The History of Salem, Massachusetts,* 2: 331.

[1472] Ibid.

[1473] Ibid.; Mass.VR (1868) 205: 281 (George; record reads "Stoddard"), (1876) 277: 297 (Caroline).

[1474] Mass.VR (1893) 435: 248.

137. ARTHUR HENRY⁹ PHIPPEN (*George⁸, Hardy⁷, Joshua⁶, Nathaniel⁵⁻⁴, Samuel³, Joseph², David¹*) was born at Salem, Massachusetts 7 September 1849, son of George and Margaret (Barton) Phippen.[1475] Arthur married, first, at Salem 18 December 1873, **MARY ELIZABETH CHAMBERLAIN,**[1476] who was born there 11 May 1849, daughter of James and Elizabeth (Sinclair) (Gray) Chamberlain.[1477] Mary died at Salem 27 August 1879.[1478] Arthur married, second, at Salem 6 October 1881, **ELIZABETH M. SANBORN,** who was born in 1851, daughter of Osgood and Elizabeth M. (West) Sanborn.[1479] She died 10 September 1917.[1480] Arthur Phippen was a bank clerk.[1481]

Children of Arthur and Mary (Chamberlain) Phippen, born at Salem:[1482]

      i. MARGARET CHAMBERLAIN¹⁰ PHIPPEN, b. 15 and d. 17 Feb. 1875.

158   ii. WALTER GRAY PHIPPEN, b. 25 Dec. 1876.

     iii. ELIZABETH CHAMBERLAIN PHIPPEN, b. 7 July and d. 5 Aug. 1879.

Children of Arthur and Elizabeth (Sanborn) Phippen, born at Salem:[1483]

     iv. ELIZABETH RUSSELL PHIPPEN, b. 30 April 1884; m. at Salem 9 Oct. 1912, WALTER EVERETT POOR.

159   v. HENRY OSGOOD PHIPPEN, b. 2 Sept. 1885.

160   vi. ARTHUR PHIPPEN, b. 19 May 1887.

138. CHARLES ENDECOTT⁹ PHIPPEN (*George⁸, Hardy⁷, Joshua⁶, Nathaniel⁵⁻⁴, Samuel³, Joseph², David¹*) was born at Salem, Massachusetts 20 January 1856, son of George and Margaret (Barton) Phippen.[1484] He was a bookkeeper and a director of several banks in Salem. He married at Beverly, Massachusetts 11 October 1880, **HARRIET ELLEN GIFFORD,**

[1475] *Vital Records of Salem, Massachusetts to the end of the year 1849,* 2: 165.

[1476] Perley, *The History of Salem, Massachusetts,* 2: 331; Mass.VR (1870) 253: 327.

[1477] Perley, *The History of Salem, Massachusetts,* 2: 331.

[1478] Ibid.

[1479] Ibid.; Mass.VR (1881) 325: 333.

[1480] Perley, *The History of Salem, Massachusetts,* 2: 331.

[1481] Ibid.

[1482] Ibid.; Mass.VR (1875) 274: 270 (Margaret), (1876) 277: 297 (Walter).

[1483] All information about children is found in Perley, *The History of Salem, Massachusetts,* 2: 331, and also Mass.VR (1912) 310: 278 (marriage of Elizabeth), (1884) 349: 342 (birth of Elizabeth), (1885) 358: 349 (birth of Henry).

[1484] Perley, *The History of Salem, Massachusetts,* 2: 331; Mass.VR (1856) 96: 254b.

daughter of Thomas J. and Harriet M. (____) Gifford.[1485] He died at Boston, Massachusetts 20 March 1930.[1486]

Children of Charles Endecott and Harriet Ellen (Gifford) Phippen:[1487]

    i.   MARGARET BARTON[10] PHIPPEN, b. 27 Aug. 1883.

    ii. ELEANOR GIFFORD PHIPPEN, b. 16 May 1891; m. 11 Nov. 1915, DANIEL GORDON TOWER of Indiana.

139. SAMUEL C.[9] PHIPPEN (*Ebenezer*[8], *David*[7], *Ebenezer*[6], *David*[5], *Nathaniel*[4], *Samuel*[3], *Joseph*[2], *David*[1]) was born at Eden, Maine 20 August 1842, son of Ebenezer and Hannah (Cousins) Phippen.[1488] He married (intentions filed 6 July 1866), **FANNY GRAY,** who was born in England 11 February 1846, daughter of Mark Gray.[1489] She was of Mount Desert, Maine, and he was of Eden at the time of their marriage.

Samuel Phippen was a fisherman and resided at Cranberry Isles.[1490] He was paid $21 for labor on the highways of Isleford in 1908 and was road commissioner in 1910–11.[1491] He was listed on the voters list at Isleford for the years 1909–29.[1492] He died 31 January 1932, aged 89 years, 5 months, 11 days.[1493] Fanny Phippen died at Cranberry Isles 15 March 1924, aged 78 years, 1 month, 4 days.[1494]

Children of Samuel and Fanny (Gray) Phippen:[1495]

161   i.   JOHN DANA[10] PHIPPEN, b. at Eden 25 Dec. 1867.

162   ii. FRED W. PHIPPEN, b. at Cranberry Isles 26 May 1870.

163   iii. HARRY VERNON PHIPPEN, b. at Cranberry Isles 19 Oct. 1871.

    iv. FLORA EMMA PHIPPEN, b. at Cranberry Isles 18 June 1879; m. there 2 Nov. 1901, FRANCIS W. BUNKER of Cranberry Isles.[1496]

[1485] Perley, *The History of Salem, Massachusetts,* 2: 331; Mass.VR (1880) 316: 312.

[1486] Obituary, *New York Times,* 21 March 1930.

[1487] Information about children is found in Perley, *The History of Salem, Massachusetts,* 2: 331.

[1488] Records of Cranberry Isles, Births & Deaths 1763–1890.

[1489] Ibid.

[1490] Cranberry Isles Directory, 1928, 160.

[1491] Isleford Town Reports, 1908, 1910–11.

[1492] Ibid., 1909–29.

[1493] Maine Vital Records.

[1494] Ibid.

[1495] Unless noted otherwise, information about children is from Records of Cranberry Isles, Birth & Deaths 1763–1890, 114.

[1496] Maine Vital Records.

140. CHARLES D.[9] **PHIPPEN** (*Ebenezer*[8], *David*[7], *Ebenezer*[6], *David*[5], *Nathaniel*[4], *Samuel*[3], *Joseph*[2], *David*[1]) was born at Eden, Maine 14 November 1845, son of Ebenezer and Hannah (Cousins) Phippen. He died at Hermon, Maine 6 February 1913, aged 69 years, 2 months, 23 days.[1497] Charles married, first, at Bar Harbor, Maine 28 August 1871, **PRISCILLA MAYO,** who was born about March 1839, daughter of Ambrose and Pamelia (Hopkins) Mayo. Priscilla died at Eden 8 December 1892, aged 53 years, 9 months.[1498] Charles married, second, at Eden 23 April 1904, **FLORA E. (LADD) COUSINS,** who was born at Eden 30 October 1856, daughter of Daniel and Martha (Southard) Ladd, and widow of Wellington Cousins.[1499] She died at Hermon 26 July 1913.[1500]

Charles Phippen lived at Eden and Hermon, Maine, and was a sailor and farmer.

Children of Charles and Priscilla (Mayo) Phippen, born at Eden:[1501]

> i. LEONA ARDELL[10] PHIPPEN, b. 9 July 1872;[1502] d. at Eden 1 Sept. 1899.
>
> 164 ii. FRANK ZEMRO PHIPPEN, b. 10 Sept. 1873.
>
> 165 iii. CHESTER MITCHELL PHIPPEN, b. 14 Nov. 1875.
>
> iv. EUGENE N. PHIPPEN, b. 22 Dec. 1878; d. unm. at Eden 18 Nov. 1896.

141. DAVID[9] **PHIPPEN** (*Benjamin*[8], *David*[7], *Ebenezer*[6], *David*[5], *Nathaniel*[4], *Samuel*[3], *Joseph*[2], *David*[1]) was born at Salem, Massachusetts 7 May 1838, son of Benjamin Cook and Ann Bowditch (Melzard) Phippen.[1503] David married first, at Salem 19 April 1857, **LUCRETIA HUTCHINGS,**[1504] who was born at Provincetown, Massachusetts in 1837, daughter of Joseph Benjamin and Mary Sarah (Fuller) Hutchings. She died at Charlestown, Massachusetts 19 May 1859, aged 23 years, 7 months, 21 days.[1505]

[1497] Maine Vital Records.

[1498] Ibid.

[1499] Ibid.

[1500] Ibid.

[1501] Unless noted otherwise, information about children is from the vital records of Eden, Maine.

[1502] Records of Cranberry Isles, Birth & Deaths 1763–1890.

[1503] Perley, *The History of Salem, Massachusetts,* 2: 331.

[1504] Mass. VR (1857) 108: 287.

[1505] Mass. VR (1859) 130: 54.

David Phippen enlisted for the Civil War 17 November 1861, in the 4th Battery of Massachusetts Light Artillery. He slipped on a gangplank while disembarking guns at Baton Rouge, Louisiana on 12 July 1862. Owing to the injury he sustained from this incident, he was discharged 25 September 1862.[1506]

David married, second, at Salem 1 December 1863, JULIA CASEY,[1507] who was born in 1843, daughter of Daniel and Ellen (____) Casey. He was listed on the certificate as a farmer. After he returned from service, he was able to work only intermittently. He died at Salem 9 May 1872,[1508] aged 34 years, 2 days, of consumption and chronic diarrhea—the result of his Civil War service.[1509] Julia died at Salem 14 August 1923.[1510]

Child of David and Julia (Casey) Phippen, born at Stockbridge, Vermont:

    i. ANNIE M.[10] PHIPPEN, b. 20 Feb. 1866; m. at Salem 27 July 1887, CHARLES R. BARTLETT, who was born at Marblehead, Mass. 22 April 1858, son of Charles Wesley and Hannah C. (Martin) Bartlett. Annie d. 30 March 1890, aged 24 years, 1 month, 10 days. One daughter (surname *Barlett): Mabel Lane*, b. at Salem 13 Oct. 1888.[1511]

142. HARVEY H.[9] FIPPHEN (*Stephen Sims[8], David[7], Ebenezer[6], David[5], Nathaniel[4], Samuel[3], Joseph[2], David[1]*) was born at New Boston, New Hampshire in 1842, son of Stephen Sims and Susan (Chase) Phippen/Fipphen. He died at Manchester, New Hampshire 9 January 1917, aged 80 years. He married at Weare, New Hampshire 5 September 1870, **SARAH (MILLS) BULLOCK** of Hopkinton, New Hampshire, daughter of Joseph and Celinda (Clough) Mills. She died at South Weare 1 May 1903.[1512] They had no children.

Harvey was a farmer. He and his wife lived at South Weare. He was listed as a taxpayer in Weare in 1880 and appeared (age 49) in the 1887 Weare census. Sarah was listed as 41 in the same census.

[1506] *Mass. Soldiers, Sailors, and Marines,* 5: 393.

[1507] Mass. VR (1863) 162: 209.

[1508] Perley, The History of Salem, Massachusetts, 2: 331.

[1509] Mass. VR (1872) 247: 307.

[1510] Mass. VR (1923) 73: 70.

[1511] Mass. VR (1887) 379: 373 (marriage), (1858) 114: 244 (Charles' birth), (1890) 409: 386 (Annie's death, birth calculated from age at death), (1888) 385: 378 (Mabel's birth).

[1512] N.H. Vital Records.

143. Leroy Augustus[9] Phippen (*Stephen Sims[8], David[7], Ebenezer[6], David[5], Nathaniel[4], Samuel[3], Joseph[2], David[1]*) was born at New Boston, New Hampshire 18 July 1846, son of Stephen Sims and Susan (Chase) Phippen. He died at Weare, New Hampshire 6 September 1893, aged 47 years, 1 month, 19 days.[1513] He married at Hopkinton, New Hampshire 1 March 1874, **Delcena L. Purinton** of Weare, daughter of John S. and Sarah J. Purinton.[1514] Leroy was 27 at the time of his marriage, and Delcena (born in Pembroke, New Hampshire) was 17.[1515] She married second, at Francestown, New Hampshire 16 July 1902, **Eugene G. Gale**.[1516]

They lived at North Weare, New Hampshire. Leroy was listed as age 40, a laborer, and Delcina as 39, in the 1887 Weare census.

Children of Leroy and Delcena (Purinton) Phippen:

     i.   Charles A.[10] Phippen, b. in 1872;[1517] listed as 11 in the 1887 Weare census; d. at Boston, Mass. 8 Jan. 1904 in a railroad accident.[1518]

    ii.   Susie E. Fipphen, b. 23 April 1878;[1519] listed as 9 in 1887 Weare census; m. 3 July 1892, Frederick Foote, who was b. at Francestown, N.H. 6 April 1866, son of Isaac Foote.[1520] She d. at Francestown 25 Dec. 1933.[1521]

144. Clarence Fred[9] Fipphen (*Stephen Sims[8], David[7], Ebenezer[6], David[5], Nathaniel[4], Samuel[3], Joseph[2], David[1]*) was born at New Boston, New Hampshire 2 December 1861, son of Stephen Sims and Adaline (Dailey) Phippen.[1522] He died at Concord, New Hampshire 3 March 1929, aged 67 years, 3 months, 1 day.[1523] He married at Manchester, New Hampshire 26 November 1891, **Lillian Mae Wyman,** who was born at Manchester 12 July 1872, daughter of George and Mary (Parmenter) Wyman. She died at Concord 28 March 1923.[1524]

[1513] N.H. Vital Records.

[1514] Ibid.

[1515] Ibid.

[1516] Ibid.

[1517] Little, *History of Weare*, 850.

[1518] Mass.VR (1904) 5: 256.

[1519] N.H. Vital Records.

[1520] W. R. Cochrane, *History of Francestown, N.H.* (Nashua, 1895), 710; N.H. Vital Records.

[1521] N.H. Vital Records.

[1522] N.H. Vital Records (birthdate calculated from age at death).

[1523] Ibid.; Obituary, *Concord Daily Monitor,* 4 March 1929.

[1524] N.H. Vital Records.

Clarence was a bricklayer and construction contractor in Weare and Concord.[1525]

Children of Clarence Fred and Lillian Mae (Wyman) Fipphen:

166   i.   CLARENCE WYMAN[10] FIPPHEN, b. at North Weare, N.H. 12 April 1894.[1526]
       ii. EARL EDWARD FIPPHEN, b. at Concord 16 Oct. 1898; m. HARRIET E. SMALL, who was born at Eastport, Maine 14 April 1902, dau. of Hayden L. and Augusta (Thayer) Small. Earl Fipphen died at Worcester, Mass. 10 May 1959.[1527] No issue. She m. (2) J. WALTER JOHNSON. She died in Jacksonville, Fla. 24 Feb. 1994 at the age of 91.[1528] Earl Fipphen was a physician with a practice in Worcester.[1529]

145. GEORGE[9] PHIPPEN (*George[8]*, *Thomas[7-5]*, *Nathaniel[4]*, *Samuel[3]*, *Joseph[2]*, *David[1]*) was born 28 January 1836, son of George and Lucy Ann (Allen) Phippen. He married, first, **ELLEN M. SMITH**, who was born 29 October 1834, daughter of John and Mary C. (_____) Smith of Boston, Massachusetts. In the 1860 census, they were living at Boston, in the household of Ellen (Smith) Phippen's mother, Mary A. Smith. Ellen M. (Smith) Phippen died 27 May 1861 aged 26, of dropsy.[1530]

George Phippen married, second, at Taunton, Massachusetts 6 February 1868, his late wife's younger sister, **MARY E. SMITH**, who was born 7 April 1839.[1531] They continued to live in Mrs Smith's house. George is likely the Phippen whose death is listed at Boston in 1892.[1532] Mary E. (Smith) Phippen died, a widow, at Boston 29 July 1897.[1533]

George Phippen Jr. was listed as a bank clerk in the census records. He is buried with his two wives in Woodlawn Cemetery in Chelsea, Massachusetts.

[1525] Concord, N.H., City Directory, 1913, 728.
[1526] N.H. Vital Records.
[1527] Death Certificate for Earl E. Fipphen, 10 May 1959, Mass. Registry of Vital Records and Statistics, Boston, Mass.
[1528] Obituary, *Worcester Telegram & Gazette,* 1 March 1994; Social Security Death Index.
[1529] Letter from Harriet Small Fipphen to John S. Fipphen, 1979.
[1530] Mass. VR (1861) 149: 68.
[1531] Mass. VR (1868) 208: 134.
[1532] Mass. VR (1892) 429: 342.
[1533] Mass. VR (1897) 474: 304.

Child of George and Ellen M. (Smith) Phippen:[1534]

  i. ANNA LOUISE[10] PHIPPEN, b. 15 April 1858.

146. WILLIAM ARCHIBALD[9] PHIPPENY (*William Roger[8], William Archibald[7], David[6], Archibald[5], Benjamin[4], James[3], Benjamin[2], David[1]*) was born at Torrington, Connecticut 19 June 1861. He married **MARION E. ROBBINS,** who was born 9 February 1865, daughter of Edward W. and Elizabeth (Stanley) Robbins. In 1900, they were living at Waterbury, New Haven County, Connecticut, with five children.

Children of William Archibald and Marion (Robbins) Phippeny:[1535]

  i. ELIZABETH WILLO[10] PHIPPENY, b. 29 Sept. 1883; m. 30 March 1907, HENRY W. WYMAN.
167 ii. WILLIAM EDWARD PHIPPENY, b. at Waterbury 20 Dec. 1887.
  iii. LIZZIE STANLEY PHIPPENY, b. 31 Aug. 1889.
  iv. SARAH ADAIR PHIPPENY, b. 20 March 1891; m. FREDERICK A. HOTCHKISS, son of Charles and Nettie (Seely) Hotchkiss.
  v. MARION ROBBINS PHIPPENY, b. 28 Feb. 1898.

147. HERBERT CALVIN[9] PHIPPENNEY (*Alvin P.[8], Calvin Evet[7], William[6], Archibald[5], Benjamin[4], James[3], Benjamin[2], David[1]*) was born in Kansas about 1869, son of Alvin P. and _____ Phippenney. He married in Otoe County, Nebraska 13 February 1893, **AMANDA "MANDY" GILLISPIE.** Herbert died between 1910 and 1920 at a hospital for the insane at Fort Supply, Oklahoma.[1536] Amanda was living apart in 1910, at Swan Lake Township, Caddo County, Oklahoma. In the 1920 census, she was living at Johnson, Kimball County, Nebraska.

148. ACEL[9] PHIPPENNEY (*Alvin P.[8], Calvin Evet[7], William[6], Archibald[5], Benjamin[4], James[3], Benjamin[2], David[1]*) was born in Nebraska about 1871, son of Alvin P. and _____. He married, first, in Nemaha County, Nebraska 18 March 1894, **FRANCES WHITE,** who was born in Tennessee about

---

[1534] Mass. VR (1858) 116: 27.
[1535] 1900 U.S. Census, Waterbury, New Haven Co., Conn., p. 91.
[1536] From Kay Brett: "He is listed as a patient there in the 1910 Federal Census and his name is listed in the burial records there, but no date. I have not found him in the 1920 Census." Herbert's widow, Mandy Phippenney, lived next door to Herbert's sister Grace Ratliff in Kimball Co., Neb., in the 1920 census.

1875, daughter of John M. and Martha J. (____) White. Acel and Frances are listed in the 1900 census in Lebanon, Laclede County, Missouri, with their eldest son. Acel and Frances divorced.

Acel married, second, around 1906, **MAY G. McMILLEN,** who was born in Mississippi about 1876. In 1910 Acel and his new wife were living with Acel's oldest son John and May's brother William P. McMillen in Lebanon, while Frances (White) Phippenney is living with her parents and her daughters, Bernice and Roberta, in Neodosha, Kansas. In 1920, Frances (White) Phippenney was listed with her three children in Manhattan, Kansas. Acel Phippany, however, was still living in Lebanon with his second wife[1537]

Children of Acel and Frances (White) Phippenney:[1538]

  i. JOHN HERBERT[10] PHIPPENNEY, b. in Mo. 11 Oct. 1899. In the 1920 census, he is enumerated twice: once with his mother in Manhattan, Kans., and once alone in Saint Louis, Mo. He d. at San Francisco, Calif. 26 March 1953.[1539]

  ii. BERNICE J. PHIPPENNEY, b. in Mo. about 1902.

  iii. ROBERTA J. PHIPPENNEY, b. in Kans. about 1904.

149. HORACE[9] **PHIPPANY** (*Albert Hollar*[8], *Horace*[7], *Joel*[6], *James*[5-3], *Benjamin*[2], *David*[1]) was born, probably in Orleans County, New York, in May 1869, son of Albert Hollar and Frances (____) Phippany. He married **NELLE M_____,** who was born in September 1874.

In the 1900 census, he was a salesman, living with Nelle and his brother William in Rochester, Monroe County, New York. In the 1910, 1920, and 1930 censuses in Rochester, he was a pharmacist, living with his wife, also a pharmacist; in 1920, his father, Hollar, lived with them.[1540]

[1537] From Kay Brett: "They had at least three children and the marriage ended in divorce. I don't know what happened to Acel. Frances moved in with her father in Manhattan, Kansas."

[1538] 1910 U.S. Census, Lebanon, Laclede Co., Mo., roll T624_793, p. 1A; 1910 U.S. Census, Neodosha, Wilson Co., Kans., E.D. 220, sh. 9A.

[1539] California Death Index, 1940–1997 (accessible at *www.Ancestry.com*).

[1540] 1900, 1910, 1920, and 1930 U.S. censuses, Rochester, Monroe Co., New York, E.D. 120, sh. 2A (1900), E.D. 204, sh. 11B (1910); E.D. 242, sh. 12A (1920); E.D. 28-149, sh. 44B (1930).

150. CHARLES WILLIAM[9] PHIPPENY (*Oliver Lee*[8], *Charles Lee*[7], *Peter*[6], *James*[5-3], *Benjamin*[2], *David*[1]) was born in Arizona 23 July 1899, son of Oliver Lee and Rosa (Gibson) Phippeny. He married **BELLE MARGARET TIPTON,** who was born at Phoenix, Maricopa County, Arizona 9 September 1900, daughter of James Daniel and Dora MaryJane (Nail) Tipton.

In the 1930 census, he was an electrician living at Phoenix with his father-in-law, wife, and son. Charles William Phippeny died at Scottsdale, Arizona in August 1970; his widow died at Scottsdale in July 1978.[1541]

Children of Charles W. and Belle (Tipton) Phippeny include:

    i.   CHARLES LEE[10] PHIPPENY, b. in Arizona 15 Oct. 1929; d. 22 March
         1978; m. _____ WALT, who was b. in Ariz., daughter of Walter Lee
         and Ruby Alma (Dossey) Walt. *Children:* three daughters and a son,
         Charles Lee[11] *Phippeny.*[1542]

[1541] World War I Draft Registration Card (birth date); 1930 U.S. Census, Phoenix, Maricopa Co., Ariz., ED 7-20, p. 8B; Social Security Death Index; Robyn Peterson, RootsWeb WorldConnect database at *www.RootsWeb.com.*

[1542] Social Security Death Index; One World Tree at *www.Ancestry.com* (compiler not listed).

CHAPTER 12

THE TENTH GENERATION

151. JOSEPH ALBERT[10] **PHIPPEN** (*Edwin Didymus*[9], *Orlando*[8], *Joseph*[7], *Joseph*[6], *Samuel*[5–3], *Joseph*[2], *David*[1]) was born at Apple River, Jo Daviess County, Illinois 1 March 1878, son of Edwin Didymus and Eliza Ellen (Power) Phippen. He died at Grand Junction, Colorado 13 March 1960. Joseph married at Burlington, Kansas 24 July 1907, **PEARL BELL BREESE,** who was born at Westphalia, Kansas 13 April 1883. She died at Mapleton, Kansas, 20 November 1947.

Children of Joseph Albert and Pearl Bell (Breese) Phippen:[1543]

- i. OLIVIA[11] PHIPPEN, b. 8 June 1908; d. 13 Dec. 1969; m. (1) VON W. HOOD; m. (2) ____ BURKE.
- ii. LETHA MAY PHIPPEN, b. 16 Nov. 1909; m. VINCENT JOSEPH BRUNIN; lived at Saint Mary's, Kans.
- iii. CLAUDE JOSEPH PHIPPEN, b. 13 July 1911; d. in Plumas Co., Calif. m. (1) JESSIE ____, who was b. in 1894 and d. in 1975; m. (2) EVELYN ____, who was b. 3 Sept. 1914 and d. at Yuba City, Calif. 1 Nov. 2000.[1544]
- iv. HAROLD CLARK PHIPPEN, b. 25 April 1913; m. VESTA ____; lived at Fort Riley, Kans.
- 168 v. GEORGE ALBERT PHIPPEN, b. at Charles City, Iowa 11 July 1915.
- vi. EARL PHIPPEN, b. in June 1917; d. 21 June 1921; bur. at Mayette, Kans.
- vii. JUANITA PEARL PHIPPEN, b. at Emmett, Pottawatamie Co., Kans. 20 Aug. 1921; d. at Topeka, Kans. 6 Oct. 1991; m. (1) BENNY CIANCURULLA; m. (2) at Westmoreland, Pottawamie Co. 7 Sept. 1937, CLAUDE SMITH, who was b. at Ratcliff, Ark. 30 Nov. 1913 and d. at Topeka 21 Feb. 1974.

[1543] Based on information supplied in January 2006 by descendant Kenneth Wade 13 Phippen.

[1544] California Death Index, 1940–1997 (accessible at *www.Ancestry.com*) (Claude's death); Blaine Co. Marriage Records, 1: 282 (marriage); Social Security Death Index; Kenneth Wade Phippen (Evelyn's death).

viii. HARRY CLAUDE PHIPPEN, b. at Emmett 18 July 1923; d. at Topeka; m. (1) HATTIE ____, who was b. 10 Dec. 1902 and d. at Atwater, Merced Co., Calif. in July 1974; m. (2) BETTY ____; m. (3) ANNA ____.

169   ix. LOREN DEWAYNE PHIPPEN, b. at Havensville, Kans. 5 March 1927.

152. FRANK WORTHINGTON[10] **PHIPPEN** (*Silas Lucian*[9], *James Worthington*[8], *Isaac*[7], *Joseph*[6], *Samuel*[5-3], *Joseph*[2], *David*[1]) was born at Salt Lake City, Utah 4 February 1874, son of Silas Lucian and Martha (Mitchell) Phippen. He died in Union County, Oregon 21 August 1930. Frank married at Carey, Blain County, Idaho 8 September 1903, **SARAH PEARL FORD,** who was born in Georgia about 1874 and died in Union County 12 September 1948.[1545]

Children of Frank Worthington and Sarah Pearl (Ford) Phippen, b. Idaho:[1546]

i. ROBERT A.[11] PHIPPEN, b. ca. 1904; d. in Union Co. 8 Jan. 1956; m. MAUDIE ____.[1547]

ii. FRANK MIL PHIPPEN, b. 20 June 1905; d. in Umatilla Co., Ore. 17 Sept. 1978; m. CLARA ____.[1548]

iii. CALVIN LUCEEN PHIPPEN, b. 26 Sept. 1907; d. in Union Co.; m. LULA ___; d. 20 July 1994.[1549]

iv. EMMA P. PHIPPEN, b. ca. 1909.

v. IDA F. PHIPPEN, b. ca. 1911.

vi. ELLA M. PHIPPEN, b. ca. 1913.

vii. CHARLES DOYLE PHIPPEN, b. 13 March 1916; d. in Feb. 1987; last residence Coeur d'Alene, Kootenai Co., Idaho.[1550]

153. ERNEST DRUCE[10] **PHIPPEN** (*Joseph Hyrum*[9], *Joseph Freeman*[8], *Isaac*[7], *Joseph*[6], *Samuel*[5-3], *Joseph*[2], *David*[1]) was born at Bellevue, Blaine County, Idaho 10 April 1884, son of Joseph Hyrum and Mary Sophia (Druce) Phippen. He died in Riverside County, California 22 August 1979. He married at Salt Lake City, Utah 10 April 1909, **FREDONIA OPHELIA RICHARDS,** who was born at Ogden, Utah 27 January 1885, daughter

---

[1545] Ore. Death Certificate nos. 115 (Frank's death), 10484 (Sarah's death).

[1546] 1910 and 1920 U.S. censuses, Carey, Blaine Co., Idaho, E.D. 62, sh. 5A (1910), E.D. 85, sh. 4A (1920); 1930 U.S. Census, Elgin, Union Co., Ore., E.D. 31-11, sh. 2B.

[1547] Ore. Death Certificate no.1130.

[1548] Social Security Death Index; Ore. Death Certificate no. 78-15412.

[1549] Ibid., Death Certificate no. 94-15593.

[1550] Social Security Death Index.

of Samuel Parker Richards. She died at Glendale, California, 17 October 1962.[1551]

Children of Ernest Druce and Fredonia (Richards) Phippen:[1552]

    i. ELLIS LAMONT[11] PHIPPEN, b. at Tooele, Utah 23 July 1910.

    ii. RHEA IANTHA PHIPPEN, b. at Carey, Idaho 14 Sept. 1911; d. at Pocatello, Idaho 30 Dec. 1915.

    iii. MELVA PHIPPEN, b. at Boise, Idaho 24 March 1918; m. WILLISTON JENNINGS STEVENS.

    iv. JOSEPH RICHARD PHIPPEN, b. at Los Angeles, Calif. 24 July 1921; m. VIRGINIA JEAN GUTHRIE.

    v. ARTHUR ERNEST PHIPPEN, b. at Los Angeles 27 April 1924; m. 18 April 1948, MARY LOU GARRETT.

154. FLOYD RUSSELL[10] PHIPPEN (*Ross Alonzo[9], Loren[8], Calvin[7], Joseph[6], Samuel[5-3], Joseph[2], David[1]*) was born at Wellsboro, Pennsylvania 29 December 1916, son of Ross Alonzo and Maude Ethel (Russell) Phippen. He died at Wellsboro 20 July 1946. He married **MURIEL CLEVELAND**, who was born in 1921 and died in 1978.[1553]

Children of Floyd Russell and Muriel (Cleveland) Phippen:

170   i. RONALD FLOYD[11] PHIPPEN, b. 29 Jan. 1941.

    ii. KENNETH ROBERT PHIPPEN, b. 22 Oct. 1942; m. BARBARA JANE ROWE.

    iii. MARSHA ANN PHIPPEN, b. 18 May 1945; m. (1) 1 Sept. 1960, JAMES MILLER, divorced; m. (2) 3 Aug. 1967, MIKE MISCHKE.

155. WILLIAM SAFFORD[10] PHIPPEN (*Joshua H.[9], Joshua[8], Hardy[7], Joshua[6], Nathaniel[5-4], Samuel[3], Joseph[2], David[1]*) was born at Winchester, Massachusetts 8 December 1897,[1554] son of Joshua H. and Addie

---

[1551] Calif. Death Index, 1940–97 (accessible at *www.Ancestry.com*) (Ernest and Fredonia's birth and death); Calif. Passengers Lists, Sept. 1950, List 121 (at *www.Ancestry.com*) (birthplaces of Ernest and Fredonia).

[1552] 1930 U.S. Census, Los Angeles, Los Angeles Co. Calif., E.D. 19-613, sh. 8A; Calif. Birth Index, 1905–1995 (Joseph and Arthur).

[1553] Information about Floyd Russell Phippen was supplied by Jessie Brabham, daughter of Margaret Eudora Phippen Brooks, from information compiled by Maude Ethel (Russell) Phippen in an unpublished family history.

[1554] Mass.VR (1897) 467: 486. Information on the family of William Safford Phippen was provided by sons William Greeley[11] Phippen, Charles Gilman[11] Phippen, and granddaughter Pamela Safford[12] Phippen.

Elizabeth (Greeley) Phippen. He married at Chicago, Illinois 18 April 1923, KATHERINE MARIE MURPHY, who was born at Woburn, Massachusetts 23 May 1899, daughter of Francis James and Katherine Elizabeth (McDermott) Murphy.[1555] He lived in Reston, Virginia, where he died 6 August 1979.[1556]

Children of William Safford and Katherine Marie (Murphy) Phippen:

171 i. WILLIAM GREELEY[11] PHIPPEN, b. at Rockford, Ill. 14 Feb. 1924.

  ii. GEORGE ROBERT PHIPPEN, b. at Rockford 10 June 1925; m. 12 July 1952, MARY GILDERSLEEVE; living in McLean, Virginia in 1975. She d. 26 June 2011.[1557]

  iii. CHARLES GILMAN PHIPPEN, b. at Boston, Mass. 12 Jan. 1931; m. at Winchester 7 March 1953, CYNTHIA MORSE, who was born at Winchester 12 Jan. 1933. He d. at Westmoreland, N.H, 17 April 2011.[1558] Children: 1. *Cathryn May Phippen,* b. at Chelsea, Mass. 17 Sept. 1954; m. 2 August 1975, *Paul Mark Thompson;* living in Deerfield, Ill. in 1975; 2. *Cynthia Louise Phippen,* b. at Hartford, Conn. 16 Nov. 1957; 3. *David Charles Phippen,* b. at Hartford 27 Jan. 1960; 4. *Cheryl Ann Phippen,* b. at Hartford 1 Oct. 1961; 5. *Cristyn Joy Phippen,* b. at Hartford 20 Feb. 1968.

  iv. RICHARD SAFFORD PHIPPEN, b. at Winchester 16 Feb. 1934; d. at Plymouth, Mass. 22 August 2010. Children: 1. *Dawn M. Phippen;* 2. *Penelope A. Phippen;* and 3. *Richard Safford Phippen, Jr.*[1559]

156. CLEMENT LOWELL[10] PHIPPEN (*Edward Augustus*[9], *Joshua*[8], *Hardy*[7], *Joshua*[6], *Nathaniel*[5–4], *Samuel*[3], *Joseph*[2], *David*[1]) was born at Boston, Massachusetts 16 October 1885, son of Edward Augustus and Mary Louise (Darling) Phippen.[1560] He died at Cambridge, Massachusetts 4 January 1944. He married at Belmont, Massachusetts in September 1912, GRACE RICHARDSON, who was born at Belmont 22 July 1885, daughter of J. Howard and Emma (Hill) Richardson. She died at Belmont 9 September 1969.

[1555] Mass.VR (1899) 485: 679 (listed as Catherine on birth record).

[1556] Obituary, *The Washington Post,* 9 Aug. 1979.

[1557] Obituary, *The Winchester Star,* 29 June 2011.

[1558] Obituary, *The Hartford Courant,* 19 April 2011.

[1559] Obituary, *Old Colony Memorial,* 26 Aug. 2010.

[1560] Information about Clement Lowell Phippen is from correspondence with Hardy Phippen, 18 Oct. 1975; Mass.VR (1885) 360: 121 (birth).

For many years Clement Phippen was employed in the oil business; in particular, he was department head of the New England Accounting and Auditing Division of Socony Oil Company.

Children of Clement Lowell and Grace (Richardson) Phippen:[1561]

    i.   CLEMENT RICHARDSON[11] PHIPPEN, b. at Brooklyn, N.Y., 5 July 1914; d. at Albany, N.Y. in July 1939.

172   ii. HARDY PHIPPEN, b. at Brooklyn 4 Aug. 1917.

   iii. LYDIA PHIPPEN, b. at Cambridge 7 Aug. 1921; m. in June 1947, JOHN D. OGILBY.

157. EDWARD WILLARD[10] PHIPPEN (*Edward Augustus⁹, Joshua⁸, Hardy⁷, Joshua⁶, Nathaniel⁵⁻⁴, Samuel³, Joseph², David¹*) was born at Newtonville, Massachusetts 4 April 1891, son of Edward Augustus and Mary Louise (Darling) Phippen.[1562] He died at Stoneham, Massachusetts 6 February 1976. He married, first, at Watertown, Massachusetts in 1925, **GLADYS MILTON POOR,** from whom he was subsequently divorced. He married, second, at Belmont, Massachusetts 23 February 1936, **INA (THOMAS) MORRISON,** who was born at St. Stephen, New Brunswick, and who died at Boston, Massachusetts 26 October 1965.[1563]

E. Willard Phippen was a banker; for many years he was associated with the Cambridge Trust Company in Cambridge, Massachusetts.

158. WALTER GRAY[10] PHIPPEN (*Arthur⁹, George⁸, Hardy⁷, Joshua⁶, Nathaniel⁵⁻⁴, Samuel³, Joseph², David¹*) was born at Salem, Massachusetts 25 December 1876, son of Arthur Henry and Mary Elizabeth (Chamberlain) Phippen.[1564] He died at Salem 23 September 1967.[1565] He married at Buffalo, New York 16 April 1906, **ETHEL ARNOLD PATCH,**[1566] who was born 15 January 1881, daughter of Maurice Byron and Emily Isabella (White) Patch.[1567]

[1561] Ibid.

[1562] Mass.VR (1891) 413: 294.

[1563] Mass. Death Record no. 020765 (death of Edward), Mass.VR (1925) 58: 116 (marriage of Edward and Gladys), (1936) 4: 457 (marriage of Edward and Ina).

[1564] Mass.VR (1876) 277: 297; Perley, *The History of Salem, Massachusetts,* 2: 331.

[1565] Obituary, *Salem Evening News,* 23 Sept. 1967, p. 2; obituary, *New England J. Med.,* 277:1149, 23 Nov. 1967.

[1566] Perley, *The History of Salem, Massachusetts,* 2: 331; Mass.VR (1906) 562: 643.

[1567] Frank Edson Shedd, *Daniel Shed Genealogy; Ancestry and Descendants of Daniel Shed of Braintree, Massachusetts, 1327–1920* (Boston, 1921), 382.

Walter received his A.B. from Harvard College in 1900 and his M.D. from Harvard University in 1904. He lived in Salem most of his life and also practiced surgery there for almost 60 years. He lived at 31 Chestnut Street, in a brick house built by Pickering Dodge in 1828 or 1829. The Allen family had lived there until 1912. Dr. Phippen occupied the house from 1914 until at least 1939. He was president of the Salem Hospital Medical Staff from 1935 to 1953, when he was elected president emeritus. He was chief of the hospital's surgical service for many years, and was president of the Massachusetts Medical Society from 1939 to 1941.[1568]

Joining his medical knowledge with an interest in history, Dr. Walter Phippen authored a paper on the Salem Hospital that the Essex Institute published in 1966.[1569]

Children of Walter Gray and Ethel Arnold (Patch) Phippen:[1570]

    i.   ROBERT JORDAINE PHIPPEN, b. 31 Aug. 1916;[1571] adopted December 1916; d. at Hull 16 July 1984.[1572]

    ii. BARBARA EMILY[11] PHIPPEN, b. 7 Dec. 1920; m. SAMUEL HOWARD DONNELL.

159. HENRY OSGOOD[10] PHIPPEN (*Arthur*[9], *George*[8], *Hardy*[7], *Joshua*[6], *Nathaniel*[5-4], *Samuel*[3], *Joseph*[2], *David*[1]) was born at Salem, Massachusetts 2 September 1885, son of Arthur and Elizabeth (Sanborn) Phippen. He was a clerk. He moved to Hamilton, Massachusetts, and married, 5 October 1910, **EDITH WHIPPLE DANE,** daughter of Ephraim and Annie (Knowlton) Dane.[1573]

Children of Henry Osgood and Edith (Dane) Phippen:[1574]

173   i.   HENRY OSGOOD[11] PHIPPEN, b. 15 March 1912.

    ii. JOAN ALMIRA PHIPPEN, b. 18 June 1915; she m. at Hamilton

---

[1568] "Presidents of the Massachusetts Medical Society," available at www.massmed.org.

[1569] Walter G. Phippen, *From Charter Street to the Lookout; the Salem Hospital–a brief history* (Salem, Mass., 1966).

[1570] *Harvard College, Class of 1900, 25th Reunion Report,* 549–50; *Harvard College, Class of 1900, 50th Reunion Report,* 501–3; *The National Cyclopedia of American Biography* (New York, 1971), 53: 417–18.

[1571] Essex County Probate Records, file no. 125616.

[1572] Obituary of Robert Phippen, *The Boston Globe,* 17 July 1984.

[1573] Perley, *The History of Salem, Massachusetts,* 2: 331; MassVR (1910) 594: 689.

[1574] Information about children is from Perley, *The History of Salem, Massachusetts,* 2: 331–32.

5 October 1935, FRANCIS MARSH II of Dedham, Mass.;[1575] she d. at Westwood, Mass. 6 April 2004.[1576]

174   iii.   RICHARD DANE PHIPPEN, b. 1 July 1918.

       iv.   GERALDINE PHIPPEN, b. 4 July 1925.

160. ARTHUR[10] **PHIPPEN** (*Arthur*[9], *George*[8], *Hardy*[7], *Joshua*[6], *Nathaniel*[5-4], *Samuel*[3], *Joseph*[2], *David*[1]) was born at Salem, Massachusetts 19 May 1887, son of Arthur Henry and Elizabeth (Sanborn) Phippen. He was a bank clerk. He married 24 February 1915, **ALICE DAVENPORT BOWDEN** of Marblehead, Massachusetts.[1577]

Children of Arthur and Alice (Bowden) Phippen:[1578]

       i.   MARY ELIZABETH[11] PHIPPEN, b. 11 July 1915.

       ii.   JANE WEST PHIPPEN, b. 23 May 1918.

       iii.   ARTHUR PHIPPEN, b. 13 Jan. 1923.

161. JOHN DANA[10] **PHIPPEN** (*Samuel*[9], *Ebenezer*[8], *David*[7], *Ebenezer*[6], *David*[5], *Nathaniel*[4], *Samuel*[3], *Joseph*[2], *David*[1]) was born at Eden, Maine 25 December 1867, son of Samuel C. and Fanny (Gray) Phippen.[1579] He married at Cranberry Isles, Maine 23 July 1892, **VIOLA OBER,** who was born in 1874, daughter of William and Ellen K. (_____) Ober of Tremont, Maine.[1580]

John Phippen lived at Cranberry Isles; he was a surfman and fisherman. He is listed on the voting list for Isleford, Maine, for 1909–29, and he served on the New School Building Committee in 1913.[1581] He died at Cranberry Isles 13 May 1935, aged 67 years 4 months 18 days.[1582] Viola Phippen died 15 July 1967.[1583]

Children of John Dana and Viola (Ober) Phippen:[1584]

       i.   RALPH OBER[11] PHIPPEN, b. at Tremont, Maine 13 Jan. 1900; d. 25 July 1980; m. in 1947, VIRGINIA DOROTHY VERGE, who was b.

[1575] "Miss Joan Phippen A Bay State Bride," *The New York Times,* 6 Oct. 1935.

[1576] Obituary of Joan (Phippen) Marsh, *The Boston Globe,* 7 April 2004.

[1577] Perley, *The History of Salem, Massachusetts,* 2: 332.

[1578] Ibid.

[1579] Records of Cranberry Isles.

[1580] Ibid.

[1581] Isleford town reports.

[1582] Records of Cranberry Isles.

[1583] Maine VR.

[1584] Unless noted otherwise, information about children is from Maine VR.

at Malden, Mass. 18 Dec. 1917, daughter of Joseph Warren and Virginia Dorothy (Walbruel) Verge. Virginia d. at Ellsworth, Maine, 5 Sept. 2003. Ralph was a lobsterman. No issue.[1585]

ii. HAROLD D. PHIPPEN, b. at Cranberry Isles 5 May 1907; d. 31 March 1932, aged 24 years, 10 months, 26 days.

iii. LAURENCE O. PHIPPEN, b. at Cranberry Isles 13 Aug. 1908; d. at Malden, Mass. 31 July 1974.[1586]

162. FRED W.[10] **PHIPPEN** (*Samuel*[9], *Ebenezer*[8], *David*[7], *Ebenezer*[6], *David*[5], *Nathaniel*[4], *Samuel*[3], *Joseph*[2], *David*[1]) was born at Cranberry Isles, Maine 26 May 1870, son of Samuel C. and Fanny (Gray) Phippen. He married 30 March 1895, **INEZ STANLEY,** who was born about 1868.[1587]

Fred is listed in the town report for Isleford as being on the school committee and as truant officer in 1908.[1588] He is listed as of Isleford in the Cranberry Isles census for 1909, and he was a voter in the years 1909, 1910, 1911, 1913, 1917, and 1921–29.[1589] Fred was a fisherman and lived at Cranberry Isles.[1590] He died at Mount Desert, Maine, by drowning, 11 October 1930, aged 60 years, 4 months, 15 days.[1591] Inez (Stanley) Phippen died 29 May 1957, aged 88 years, 6 months.[1592]

Children of Fred W. and Inez (Stanley) Phippen, born at Cranberry Isles:

i. MILTON AUGUSTUS[11] PHIPPEN, b. 29 Sept. 1895.[1593] He d. at Togus, Maine 18 Jan. 1958, aged 63 years, 3 months, 19 days.

175   ii. LESLIE R. PHIPPEN, b. 21 July 1899.[1594]

163. HARRY VERNON[10] **PHIPPEN** (*Samuel*[9], *Ebenezer*[8], *David*[7], *Ebenezer*[6], *David*[5], *Nathaniel*[4], *Samuel*[3], *Joseph*[2], *David*[1]) was born at Cranberry Isles, Maine 17 October 1871, son of Samuel C. and Fanny (Gray)

[1585] Obituary, *Bangor Daily News,* 5 Sept. 2003.

[1586] Ancestry.com, *Massachusetts Death Index, 1970-2003* [database on-line].

[1587] Maine VR.

[1588] Isleford, Maine, Town Report for 1908.

[1589] Isleford Town Reports for indicated years.

[1590] Cranberry Isles directory, 1928, 160.

[1591] Maine VR.

[1592] Ibid.

[1593] Information about Milton is from Maine VR.

[1594] Cranberry Isles records.

Phippen.[1595] He died at Cranberry Isles 16 December 1913, aged 42 years, 1 month, 27 days, of cancer of the liver.[1596] He married 12 November 1896, **AGNES MAY STANLEY,** who was born 11 September 1877.[1597] Agnes Phippen died at Waterville, Maine 6 September 1948, aged 70 years, 11 months, 25 days.[1598]

Harry Phippen was a fisherman and lived at Cranberry Isles. He does not appear on the voting list for Isleford, Maine, after 1914, although Agnes is on the list through 1929.

Children of Harry V. and Agnes (Stanley) Phippen, born at Cranberry Isles:

> i. WINFIELD E.[11] PHIPPEN, b. 25 May 1898; d. 9 Oct. 1898, aged 4 months, 14 days.[1599]
>
> ii. FANNIE MAY PHIPPEN, b. 18 April 1906;[1600] m. at Waterville, Maine 14 Jan. 1928, HAROLD FINNEMORE; d. at Fallston, Md. 16 April 1979.

164. FRANK ZEMRO[10] PHIPPEN (*Charles[9], Ebenezer[8], David[7], Ebenezer[6], David[5], Nathaniel[4], Samuel[3], Joseph[2], David[1]*) was born at Eden, Maine 10 September 1873, son of Charles D. and Priscilla (Mayo) Phippen.[1601] He died 9 August 1916, aged 41 years, 10 days. He was a carpenter.

Frank married at Eden 20 February 1904, **NETTIE M. PIERCE,** who was born about 1886, daughter of Walden and Nellie (___) Pierce. After Frank's death, Nettie (Pierce) Phippen married second, 30 April 1917, **HAROLD DOW** of Hancock, Maine.

Children of Frank Z. and Nettie M. (Pierce) Phippen:[1602]

> i. THELMA BEATRICE[11] PHIPPEN, b. 1 Oct. 1904; d. 19 Feb. 1967; m. at Hancock, Maine 1 June 1940, LEROY MELVIN NASON. No issue.
>
> 176 ii. FRANCIS EUGENE PHIPPEN, b. 10 Oct. 1907.
>
> iii. NELLIE F. PHIPPEN, b. 27 July 1910; d. 25 Feb. 1974; m. 17 Sept. 1930, ALLEN BRENTON, a carpenter, aged 29 years. Children (surname

---

[1595] Ibid.

[1596] Ibid.

[1597] Maine VR.

[1598] Ibid.

[1599] Cranberry Isles records.

[1600] All information about Fannie May is from Maine VR.

[1601] Information about Frank Zemro Phippen is from Maine VR. (The calculated birth date disagrees with the recorded birth date.)

[1602] Ibid.

Brenton): 1. *Barbara Ann,* b. at Hancock, Maine 21 April 1931, d. at Dover, N.H. 27 Jan. 1976, aged 44; m. ____ *Danzinger;* 2. *Clarence Allen,* b. at Hancock 6 May 1932; 3. *Stephen Dean,* b. at Hancock 23 Sept. 1944; 4. *David Francis,* b. at Hancock 18 Feb. 1947; 5. *Thomas Michael,* b. at Bangor, Maine 23 April 1953.

177 iv. CHARLES RUSSELL, b. at Seal Harbor, Maine, 24 Sept. 1912.[1603]

165. **CHESTER MITCHELL[10] PHIPPEN** (*Charles[9], Ebenezer[8], David[7], Ebenezer[6], David[5], Nathaniel[4], Samuel[3], Joseph[2], David[1]*) was born at Eden, Maine 14 November 1875, son of Charles D. and Priscilla (Mayo) Phippen. He married 5 October 1918, **ADELIA (____) (REED) LURVEY.**[1604] They lived on Town Hill Road at Bar Harbor, Maine.

Chester died at Bar Harbor 28 July 1942, aged 66 years 9 months 14 days. Adelia died there 7 August 1929.[1605]

Child of Chester and Adelia (____) (Reed) (Lurvey) Phippen:

178 i. JOHN WINTHROP[11] PHIPPEN, b. at Town Hill, Maine 27 Dec. 1919.[1606]

166. **CLARENCE WYMAN[10] FIPPHEN** (*Clarence[9], Stephen[8], David[7], Ebenezer[6], David[5], Nathaniel[4], Samuel[3], Joseph[2], David[1]*) was born at North Weare, New Hampshire 12 April 1894, son of Clarence Fred and Lillian Mae (Wyman) Fipphen.[1607] He died at Shrewsbury, Massachusetts 7 May 1933.[1608] He married at Concord, New Hampshire 2 October 1920, **ETHEL DOLE,**[1609] who was born at Concord 18 October 1895, daughter of Walter and Cora (Chesley) Dole.[1610] After Clarence's death, Ethel worked as a home economics teacher in the Shrewsbury school system. She married, second, at Shrewsbury 5 May 1953, **ELROY B. DEAN** of Shrewsbury. She died at Shrewsbury 29 June 1984.[1611]

Clarence Fipphen graduated from Dartmouth College in the class of 1916 and Harvard Medical School in the class of 1919. He served as a private in Company K, Harvard Unit S.A.T.C. of the U.S. Army

---

[1603] He is unnamed in the birth record; name supplied by Carol Phippen Silsby.
[1604] Information about Chester Mitchell Phippen is from Maine VR.
[1605] Maine VR.
[1606] Maine VR.
[1607] N.H. VR.
[1608] Mass. VR (1933) 76: 118.
[1609] N.H. VR.
[1610] Ibid.
[1611] Mass. VR (1984), certificate no. 033485.

during World War 1. His army discharge papers list him as having blue eyes and light brown hair, and being 5 feet 8 inches tall.[1612] He practiced medicine in Shrewsbury.

Children of Clarence Wyman and Ethel (Dole) Fipphen:

    i.   RICHARD DOLE[11] FIPPHEN, b. at Shrewsbury 17 Aug. 1923; d. at Berlingsen, Germany, in the service of his country, on 8 April 1945.[1613]

    ii.   DONALD WYMAN FIPPHEN, b. at Worcester, Mass. 25 Oct. 1924; d. at Shrewsbury 20 May 1927.[1614]

179   iii. JOHN STANLEY FIPPHEN, b. at Worcester 12 Dec. 1927.[1615]

167. WILLIAM EDWARD[10] PHIPPENEY (*William Archibald[9]*, *William Roger[8]*, *William Archibald[7]*, *David[6]*, *Archibald[5]*, *Benjamin[4]*, *James[3]*, *Benjamin[2]*, *David[1]*) was born at Waterbury, New Haven County, Connecticut 20 December 1887, son of William Archibald and Marion (Robbins) Phippeney. He was living in 1920 in Waterbury with wife **ETHEL D. CALLENDAR** and several children. By 1930, Ethel (Callendar) Phippeney had married **BENJAMIN R. BEVIER,** who was born in New York 1 August 1874; Phippeney children Robert and Ruth were living with her, the only Phippeneys found in the 1930 census in Connecticut— the original state of the Phippeney ancestors.[1616]

Children of William Edward and Ethel (Callendar) Phippeney, born in Connecticut:[1617]

    i.   BERTHA MARION[11] PHIPPENEY, b. 19 Dec. 1908.

    ii.   WILLIAM ROGERS PHIPPENEY, b. 10 Aug. 1910.

   iii. ROBERT EDWARD PHIPPENEY, b. 20 Nov. 1911; d. 12 March 1998; last residence Rio Rancho, Sandoval Co., N.M.[1618]

   iv. RUTH PHIPPENEY, b. about 1917.

    v. ETHEL PHIPPENEY, b. about 1919.

[1612] Discharge papers from the U.S. Army.

[1613] Mass. VR (1923) 110: 69 (birth); telegram from U.S. Dept. of War, 16 April 1945 (death).

[1614] Mass. VR (1924) 153: 211 (birth), (1927) 66: 381 (death).

[1615] Mass. VR (1927), 104: 460.

[1616] 1930 U.S. Census, East Hartford, Hartford Co., Conn; World War I Draft Registration Cards for William Edward Phippeney and Benjamin R. Bevier.

[1617] 1920 U.S. Census, Waterbury, New Haven Co., Conn., roll T625_195, p. 6A.

[1618] Social Security Death Index.

CHAPTER 13

THE ELEVENTH GENERATION

168. GEORGE ALBERT[11] **PHIPPEN** (*Joseph Albert*[10], *Edwin Didymus*[9], *Orlando*[8], *Joseph*[7], *Joseph*[6], *Samuel*[5–3], *Joseph*[2], *David*[1]) was born at Charles City, Iowa 11 July 1915, son of Joseph Albert and Pearl Belle (Breese) Phippen. He died at Skull Valley, Arizona 13 April 1966.[1619] George married **LOUISE G. GOBLE,** who was born 28 April 1924 and died at Skull Valley 9 January 2001.[1620]

George Phippen became a celebrated painter of the American West. He was one of the founders of the Cowboy Artists of America, which was established in 1965 to encourage the creation and collection of western art in the tradition of Charles Russell and Frederic Remington. He was the group's first president. His legacy can be seen in the collections of the Phippen Museum of Western Art in Prescott, Arizona.[1621]

Children of George Albert and Louise (Goble) Phippen:

    i.   ERNIE[12] PHIPPEN.
   ii.   LYNN EDWIN PHIPPEN.
  iii.   LOREN PHIPPEN.
  iv.   DARRELL PHIPPEN, b. in 1955.
   v.   WINONA LOUISE PHIPPEN.

169. LOREN DEWAYNE[11] **PHIPPEN** (*Joseph Albert*[10], *Edwin Didymus*[9], *Orlando*[8], *Joseph*[7], *Joseph*[6], *Samuel*[5–3], *Joseph*[2], *David*[1]) was born at Havensville, Kansas 5 March 1927, son of Joseph Albert and Pearl Bell (Breese) Phippen. Loren married, first, **BERTHA MARIA HARTMANN,** from whom he was subsequently divorced. He married, second, at

---

[1619] "Cowboy Artist George Phippen, Dead," *Reno Evening Gazette,* 15 April 1966 (accessible at Ancestry.com); Social Security Death Index.

[1620] Information on George Phippen and his family was obtained from the genealogical website of Albert D. Hart, Jr., downloaded 15 Aug. 2010.

[1621] Ibid.; see also *"George Phippen Retrospective,"* at phippenartmuseum.org.

Houston, Texas 25 July 1953, **PATSY ANN NIXON,** who was born at
Snyder, Arkansas, 6 June 1929. Issue.

170. RONALD FLOYD[11] **PHIPPEN** (*Floyd Russell*[10], *Ross Alonzo*[9], *Loren*[8],
Calvin[7], *Joseph*[6], *Samuel*[5-3], *Joseph*[2], *David*[1]) was born 29 January 1941,
son of Floyd Russell and Muriel (Cleveland) Phippen. He married 19
July 1961, **JOYCE CARNWRIGHT,** who was born 17 August 1942.[1622]

Children of Ronald Floyd and Joyce (Carnwright) Phippen:

    i.   FLOYD WILLIAM[12] PHIPPEN, b. 26 July 1962.
    ii. RONALD FLOYD PHIPPEN, Jr., b. 10 Nov. 1963.

171. WILLIAM GREELEY[11] **PHIPPEN** (*William Safford*[10], *Joshua H.*[9],
Joshua[8], *Hardy*[7], *Joshua*[6], *Nathaniel*[5-4], *Samuel*[3], *Joseph*[2], *David*[1]) was born
at Rockford, Illinois 14 February 1924, son of William Safford and
Katherine Marie (Murphy) Phippen. He married at Syracuse, New York
6 July 1949, **DORIS LUCILLE PARKER,** who was born at Philadelphia,
Pennyslvania 22 August 1927, the daughter of William Elmer and
Lucille E. (Waybright) Parker. William G. Phippen was a physician.

Children of William Greeley and Doris (Parker) Phippen:[1623]

    i.   PAMELA SAFFORD[12] PHIPPEN, b. at West Point, N.Y. 19 Aug. 1950; m.
        19 April 1974, MARK WILLIAM COULTER.
    ii. WILLIAM GREELEY PHIPPEN, Jr., b. at San Antonio, Texas 20 Sept.
        1952.
    iii. ELIZABETH MARIE PHIPPEN, b. at San Antonio 1 Dec. 1953.
    iv. DAVID PARKER PHIPPEN, b. at Phoenixville, Pa. 26 March 1958.

172. HARDY[11] **PHIPPEN** (*Clement Lowell*[10], *Edward Augustus*[9], *Joshua*[8],
Hardy[7], *Joshua*[6], *Nathaniel*[5-4], *Samuel*[3], *Joseph*[2], *David*[1]) was born at
Brooklyn, New York 4 August 1917, son of Clement Lowell and
Grace (Richardson) Phippen.[1624] He died at Bridgeport, Connecticut
7 November 2004.[1625]

[1622] Information about Ronald Floyd Phippen was supplied by Jessie Brabham, daughter
of Margaret Eudora Phippen Brooks, from information compiled by Maude Ethel
(Russell) Phippen in an unpublished family history.
[1623] Information provided by William Greeley Phippen and his daughter Pamela Safford
Phippen (1975-1977).
[1624] Information provided by Hardy Phippen and Hardy Phippen Jr. in 1975.
[1625] Obituary, *Connecticut Post* [Bridgeport, Conn.], 10 Nov. 2004.

Hardy Phippen was raised on the family homestead in Belmont, Massachusetts. He graduated from Harvard University in 1939. In World War II, he served in Italy in the U.S. Army Air Corps as a DC-3 transport plane pilot, achieving the rank of first lieutenant. A stockbroker for much of his career, he lived in Bridgeport, Fairfield, and Easton, Connecticut.[1626]

Hardy Phippen married, first, at Brookline, Massachusetts 9 March 1944, **CLEMENTINE HOBBS,** who was born at Brookline 18 October 1918, daughter of Walter Lawrence and Bertha Melora (Smith) Hobbs. This marriage ended in divorce in August 1972. Hardy Phippen married, second, at Stamford, Connecticut 8 October 1972, **RUTH DEIXEL.**[1627] She died at Bridgeport, Connecticut 16 February 1983.[1628] Hardy married, third, **DALE NAVEKEN ALBRIGHT.**

Children of Hardy and Clementine (Hobbs) Phippen, born at Chicago, Illinois:[1629]

    i.   HARDY[12] PHIPPEN, JR., b. 9 July 1946. He lives in Manhattan. An actor, he had a part in the 1998 movie *Meet Joe Black.*[1630]

    ii.   HELEN PHIPPEN, b. 29 June 1948.

    iii.   LAWRENCE PHIPPEN, b. 17 Nov. 1949.

173. HENRY OSGOOD[11] PHIPPEN (*Henry Osgood*[10,] *Arthur*[9], *George*[8], *Hardy*[7], *Joshua*[6], *Nathaniel*[5-4], *Samuel*[3], *Joseph*[2], *David*[1]) was born at Hamilton, Massachusetts 15 March 1912, the son of Henry Osgood and Edith Whipple (Dane) Phippen.[1631] He died at Salem, Massachusetts 26 September 1998.[1632] Henry married at Stockbridge, Massachusetts 20 June 1936, **BETSEY LOUISE DUNN,**[1633] who was born at New York, New York 4 January 1914, daughter of Douglas and Bertha Vaughn (Clark) Dunn,[1634] She died at Salem 9 February 1989.[1635]

[1626] Ibid.

[1627] Information provided by Hardy Phippen. *Social Security Death Index* (Ruth Phippen).

[1628] Ancestry.com, *Connecticut Death Index, 1949-2001; Social Security Death Index* (Ruth Phippen).

[1629] Information provided by Hardy Phippen.

[1630] Internet Movie Database.

[1631] Perley, *The History of Salem, Massachusetts,* 2: 331; information provided by Clark12 Phippen in 1975.

[1632] Obituary, *Boston Globe,* 2 Oct. 1998; Ancestry.com. Massachusetts Death Index, 1970-2003.

[1633] "Phippen-Dunn" marriage announcement, *The New York Times,* 21 June 1936.

[1634] Information provided by Clark12 Phippen.

[1635] Ancestry.com. *Massachusetts Death Index, 1970-2003.*

He earned a bachelor's degree and a master's degree in economics at Trinity College in Hartford. He taught at Episcopal Academy in Merion, Pennsylvania, and Governor Dummer Academy in Byfield, Massachusetts, before joining the Boston investment firm N. W. Rice Co. in 1936. After he retired in 1977, he served as tax assessor for the Town of Wenham, Massachusetts.[1636]

Children of Henry Osgood and Betsey Louise (Dunn) Phippen:

      i.   Sandra Edith[12] Phippen, b. 18 Jan. 1937; m. 14 July 1956, Donald A. Klein; living in Fort Collins, Colo. in 1998.

180   ii.   Clark Phippen, b. at Salem 24 Feb. 1939.

174. Richard Dane[11] Phippen (*Henry Osgood[10,] Arthur[9], George[8], Hardy[7], Joshua[6], Nathaniel[5-4], Samuel[3], Joseph[2], David[1]*) was born 1 July 1918, son of Henry Osgood and Edith Whipple (Dane) Phippen.[1637] He married in 1951,[1638] **Susanne LaCroix,** daughter of Morris and Esther (Paine) LaCroix. She died at Wenham, Massachusetts 28 April 2015.[1639] He died at Wenham 7 October 2016 at the age of 98.[1640]

Children of Richard Dane and Susanne (LaCroix) Phippen:

      i.   William LaCroix[12] Phippen.

     ii.   Peter Dane Phippen.

   iii.   Edith Morris Phippen.

   iv.   David Osgood Phippen.

     v.   Anne ward phippen.

   vi.   Henry Paine Phippen.

  vii.   Joanna Lee Phippen.

175. Leslie R.[11] Phippen (*Fred W.[10], Samuel[9], Ebenezer[8], David[7], Ebenezer[6], David[5], Nathaniel[4], Samuel[3], Joseph[2], David[1]*) was born at Cranberry Isles, Maine 21 July 1899, son of Fred and Inez (Stanley) Phippen.[1641] He married 12 October 1921, **Marjorie E. Bulger,**[1642] who was born at Cranberry Isles 15 July 1904, daughter of Oscar and Millie (Harding) Bulger.[1643]

[1636] Obituary, *Boston Globe,* 2 Oct. 1998.

[1637] Perley, *The History of Salem, Massachusetts,* 2: 332.

[1638] Massachusetts Marriage Index, 1901–1955, 1966–1970 (accessed at *www.ancestry.com*).

[1639] Obituary, Boston Globe, 5 May 2015.

[1640] Obituary of Richard D. Phippen, *Hamilton Chronicle,* 14 October 2016.

[1641] Maine VR.

[1642] Ibid.; Index to Maine Marriages 1892–1966, 1977–1996.

[1643] Obituary, *Bangor Daily News,* 25 March 2002.

Leslie Phippen was a fisherman on the Cranberry Isles and died there 12 June 1986.[1644] Marjorie died at Bar Harbor, Maine, 20 March 2002, aged 97.[1645]

Children of Leslie R. and Marjorie (Bulger) Phippen:[1646]

    i.   SHIRLEY MOORE[12] PHIPPEN, b. at Great Cranberry Island, Me. 12 March 1922; d. at Ellsworth, Maine 6 July 1999;[1647] m. 21 Nov. 1946, LUCY DAY ROBINSON of Southwest Harbor, Maine, who was b. about 1920. Shirley Phippen was a veteran of World War II and a lobster fisherman. Child: *Yvonne Marie ("Bonnie") Phippen* b. at Bar Harbor 23 March 1951, m. in Aug. 1969, *John Goodwin Jr.*

   ii. WENONAH JEAN PHIPPEN, b. at Cranberry Isles 16 May 1925; m. (1) 5 May 1943, LESLIE F. WHITE Jr.; m. (2) 23 Oct. 1948, HORACE NATHAN BOYINGTON of Southwest Harbor. Wenonah was a telephone operator at the time of her second marriage. Wenonah d. before July 1999.[1648]

181   iii. PAUL ADELBERT PHIPPEN, b. at Cranberry Isles 3 Dec. 1926.

   iv. SHEILA LOUISE PHIPPEN, b. at St. Augustine, Fla.[1649] 5 Feb. 1930; m. (1) 16 Nov. 1948, JOHN R. HEBRON Jr., of Southwest Harbor, Maine;[1650] m. (2) CROSBY MILLS.[1651] She d. 4 Nov. 1955.[1652]

    v. LESLIE RICHARD PHIPPEN, b. at Southwest Harbor 19 July 1937; m. 10 Feb. 1957, GWENDOLYN FAYE MORRILL, dau. of Leslie William Morrill. He d. at Bangor, Maine 1 Feb. 2015. He was a lobster fisherman in Bass Harbor, Maine. Children: 1. *Cynthia J. Phippen* m. 27 May 1989, *Joseph A. Hunt;* 2. *Deborah Phippen;* 3. *Mickey Phippen;* 4. *Donald Phippen;* and 5. *Patrick Phippen.* [1653]

[1644] Maine Death Index, 1960–1997.

[1645] Obituary, *Bangor Daily News,* 25 March 2002.

[1646] Unless noted otherwise, information about children is from Maine VR. *See also* U.S. Census, *1930, Cranberry Isles, Hancock, Maine;* Roll 833; Page: 1B; Enumeration District: *11;* Image: *132.0.*

[1647] Obituary, *Ellsworth American,* July 1999.

[1648] Not mentioned in the obituary of her brother Shirley.

[1649] Information provided by Carol Phippen Silsby. The 1930 census gives her place of birth as Florida.

[1650] Index to Maine Marriages 1892–1966, 1977–1996.

[1651] Obituary (Shirley M. Phippen), *The Ellsworth American,* July 1999.

[1652] Social Security Death Index (Sheila L. Mills)(dates of birth and death)

[1653] Obituary, *Bangor Daily News,* 2 Feb. 2015.

176. FRANCIS EUGENE[11] PHIPPEN (*Frank Z.*[10], *Charles*[9], *Ebenezer*[8], *David*[7], *Ebenezer*[6], *David*[5], *Nathaniel*[4], *Samuel*[3], *Joseph*[2], *David*[1]) was born at Seal Harbor, Maine 10 October 1907, son of Frank Z. and Nettie (Pierce) Phippen.[1654] He married at Lamoine, Maine 2 July 1934, **ELIZABETH M. CLARKE**,[1655] who was born at Hancock, Maine 21 September 1915, the daughter of Walter Perkins and Etta (Jellison) Clarke.[1656] He lived in Hancock and died at Allendale, South Carolina 5 March 1970.[1657] She died at Hancock 1 December 2008.[1658]

Child (adopted) of Francis Eugene and Elizabeth (Clarke) Phippen:

>   i. SANFORD EDWIN ("SANDY") PHIPPEN. Sandy Phippen is a widely known and highly acclaimed educator, author, editor, humorist and TV host.[1659] He was born in White Plains, N.Y. 19 June 1942.[1660] He grew up in Hancock Point, Maine, and graduated from the University of Maine in 1964. He received a master's degree from Syracuse University in 1971 and taught high school English in New Hartford and Syracuse, New York, from 1964 to 1979, before returning home to his beloved Maine in 1979. He taught English at Orono High School from 1979 to 2004, and was subsequently on the faculty of the English Department of the University of Maine at Orono.
>
>   Sandy is the author of many books: *A History of The Town of Hancock* (1978); *The Police Know Everything* (1982); *People Trying to be Good* (1988); *Cheap Gossip: The Letters from Liverpool* (1989; collected columns from the *Tuesday Weekly* of Ellsworth, Maine); *Kitchen Boy* (1996, a novel); *The Messiah in the Memorial Gym and Other Writings 1973–1998* (1998); *The Sun Never Sets on Hancock Point* (2001); *Standing Just Outside the Door and Two Other Plays*

[1654] Maine VR; information supplied by Sanford E. Phippen.

[1655] Ibid.; Index to Maine Marriages 1892–1966, 1977–1996.

[1656] Information provided by Sanford E. Phippen; Obituary, *The Ellsworth American*, 4 Dec. 2008.

[1657] Maine VR.

[1658] Obituary, *The Ellsworth American*, 4 Dec. 2008; Social Security Death Index.

[1659] Information provided by Sanford E. Phippen; *see also* Faculty Profile—Sanford Phippen, http://english.umaine.edu/faculty/sanford-phippen/; Waterboro, Maine Public Library, *Maine Writers Index,* www.waterborolibrary.org/MWI_home.php (accessed 28 Aug. 2010); "Sanford Phippen to speak at UMM graduation," *Bangor Daily News,* 2 April 2005; David E. Philips, "In Search of the 'Real Maine,'" *Down East,* Feb. 1985, 21–24.

[1660] Correspondence with Sanford E. Phippen, September 1977 (birth and adoption).

(2003). He also contributed to *Inside Vacationland* (1984); *Maine Speaks* (1989); and *The Quotable Moose* (1994).

Kitchen Boy was included on the list of 100 Distinguished Maine Books compiled by the Baxter Society in 2000.[1661] His essay "Missing from the Books: My Maine" was originally published in 1980 in *Maine Life* and *Puckerbrush Review*.[1662]

As an editor, he produced the collection The Best Maine Stories: *The Marvelous Mystery* (1986; with Charles Waugh and Martin Harry Greenberg) and the nonfiction *High Clouds Soaring, Storms Driving Low: The Letters of Ruth Moore* (1993).

Sandy has been a columnist for *Maine Times, Tuesday Weekly* (Ellsworth), *Maine Life,* and *Ellsworth Weekly.* He has also written for *The New York Times, Down East* magazine, the *Bangor Daily News* and other periodicals. He is also the editor of the literary magazine *Puckerbrush Review.*

He hosted (1999–2004) the Maine PBS television show *A Good Read,* on which he was also featured as a writer. He also hosted (1997–1998) the Maine PBS series *RFD Maine,* which was nominated for a regional Emmy Award.

Sandy has won a number of awards for his teaching and writing, including Maine Teacher of the Year Finalist in 2004 and Teacher of the Year in Orono in 2003–2004.

Sandy lives in his hometown of Hancock. He was the founder of the Historical Society of the Town of Hancock and served (1978–1988) as librarian of Hancock Point Library for 11 summers. He was chosen as Hancock's Citizen of the Year in 2001. He has also served on the Maine Humanities Council (1984–1990) and the literature panel of the Maine Arts Commission (1990–1994).

177. Charles Russell[11] Phippen (*Frank Z.*[10], *Charles*[9], *Ebenezer*[8], *David*[7], *Ebenezer*[6], *David*[5], *Nathaniel*[4], *Samuel*[3], *Joseph*[2], *David*[1]) was born at Seal Harbor, Maine 24 September 1912, son of Frank Z. and Nettie (Pierce) Phippen.[1663] Charles married at Ellsworth, Maine 12 August

---

[1661] University of Maine Press and the Baxter Society, "The Mirror of Maine: One Hundred Distinguished Books That Reveal The History Of The State And The Life Of Its People," (2000), reprinted at www.library.scarborough.me.us/programs/mirrorofmaine.html (accessed on 28 Aug. 2010).

[1662] The essay can be read at http://dll.umaine.edu/welcome/wom/missing.htm.

[1663] Obituary, *Bangor Daily News,* 27 Oct. 2001.

1942, **FLORENCE E. MOON,**[1664] who was born at Hancock, Maine 7 August 1922, daughter of Leroy and Flora (Martin) Moon.[1665] She died at Bangor, Maine 12 August 1992.[1666] He died at Ellsworth, Maine 25 October 2001.[1667]

Charles moved to Hancock as a child and lived there until his death. During World War II, he served in the U.S. Navy aboard the U.S.S. *Mervine* and the U.S.S. *Fall River.*[1668]

Children of Charles Russell and Florence (Moon) Phippen:[1669]

    i.   CHARLES RUSSELL[12] PHIPPEN JR., b. at Bangor, Maine 13 Aug. 1943; m. at New Britain, Conn. 8 Aug. 1970, JEAN PRESTASH, born at New Britain 22 Sept. 1947, dau. of Walter and Sophie (Halun) Prestash. They live in Kensington, Conn.[1670] Children: 1. *Michael Phippen;* 2. *Amy Phippen.*[1671]

182   ii.   RICHARD LEROY PHIPPEN, b. at Bangor 6 Jan. 1946.

    iii.   CAROL ANN PHIPPEN, b. at Bar Harbor 6 Sept. 1961; m. 23 May 1982, JAMES ALLAN SILSBY Jr. Children (surname *Silsby*): 1. *James Allan III,* b. at Bangor 20 July 1984; 2. *Charles Raymond,* b. at Bangor 6 Sept. 1988.

178. JOHN WINTHROP[11] **PHIPPEN** (*Chester Mitchell*[10], *Charles*[9], *Ebenezer*[8], *David*[7], *Ebenezer*[6], *David*[5], *Nathaniel*[4], *Samuel*[3], *Joseph*[2], *David*[1]) was born at Town Hill (Bar Harbor), Maine 27 December 1919, son of Chester and Adelia (Reed) (Lurvey) Phippen.[1672] He married 8 November 1941, **ALTHEA MAXINE MURPHY,**[1673] who was born at West Tremont, Maine 16 June 1924,[1674] daughter of Pearl E. and Addie Belle (Pomroy) Murphy. She died at Bar Harbor, Maine 20 March 2003.[1675] John died

---

[1664] Index to Maine Marriages 1892–1966, 1977–1996.

[1665] Information provided by Charles R. Phippen Jr.; Social Security Death Index; Index to Maine Marriages 1892–1966, 1977–1996.

[1666] Index to Maine Deaths 1960–1996.

[1667] Obituary, *Bangor Daily News,* 27 Oct. 2001.

[1668] Ibid.

[1669] Unless noted otherwise, information about the children is from Maine VR.

[1670] Information provided by Charles R. Phippen Jr. and Carol Phippen Silsby.

[1671] Obituary, *Bangor Daily News,* 27 Oct. 2001.

[1672] Maine VR.

[1673] Maine VR; Index to Maine Marriages 1892–1966, 1977–1996.

[1674] Ibid.; Obituary, *Bangor Daily News,* 21 March 2003.

[1675] Ibid.; Social Security Death Index.

28 April 2007.[1676] John served in the U.S. Army in World War II. He worked as a mechanic for almost 60 years.[1677]

Children of John Winthrop and Althea Maxine (Murphy) Phippen:

    i.   PEARLE ADDIE[12] PHIPPEN, b. 24 Aug. 1945;[1678] m. (1) in Maine 1 June 1963, LESLIE B. THURSTON;[1679] m. (2) _____ MITCHELL;[1680] Pearle d. 11 Aug. 2002; her last residence was Ellsworth, Hancock Co., Maine.[1681]

    ii. JOHN WINTHROP PHIPPEN, Jr., b. 27 Jan. 1953; m. (1) in March 1971, SANDRA BEACHEMIN (divorced 16 June 1982); m. (2) in Maine 13 May 1983, DEBORAH J. SWANSON.[1682] He lived in Town Hill (Bar Harbor). He was a popular stock car racer and d. at Bangor 11 Sept. 2010.[1683]

   iii. NANCY ALTHEA PHIPPEN, b. at Bar Harbor 30 Nov. 1954;[1684] m. FRED GREENLAW.

   iv. THERESA PHIPPEN m. MICHAEL EDWARDS.

    v. RUTH PHIPPEN m. JAMES TRACY.

179. JOHN STANLEY[11] FIPPHEN (*Clarence[10–9]*, *Stephen[8]*, *David[7]*, *Ebenezer[6]*, *David[5]*, *Nathaniel[4]*, *Samuel[3]*, *Joseph[2]*, *David[1]*) was born at Worcester, Massachusetts 12 December 1927, son of Clarence Wyman and Ethel (Dole) Fipphen.[1685] He married at Boston, Massachusetts 12 October 1956, **CHRISTINE LOIS CHURCHILL,**[1686] who was born at Fort Fairfield, Maine 6 September 1927, daughter of William Leigh and Blanche

---

[1676] Obituary, *The Ellsworth American,* 3 May 2007 (accessible at Ancestry.com); Social Security Death Index.

[1677] Obituary, *The Ellsworth American,* 3 May 2007.

[1678] Maine VR.

[1679] Index to Maine Marriages 1892–1966, 1977–1996.

[1680] Obituary (John W. Phippen Sr.), *The Ellsworth American,* 3 May 2007.

[1681] Social Security Death Index, accessible at *www.Ancestry.com.*

[1682] Information about John Winthrop Phippen Jr. from Maine VR. *See also* Index to Maine Marriages 1892–1966, 1977–1996.

[1683] Obituary (John W. Phippen, Jr.), *Bangor Daily News,* 14 Sept. 2010.

[1684] Maine VR.

[1685] Birth Certificate of John Stanley Fipphen, 12 Dec. 1927, Mass. Registry of Vital Records and Statistics, Boston, Mass.

[1686] Marriage Certificate of John S. Fipphen and Christine L. Churchill, 12 Oct. 1956, Mass. Registry of Vital Records and Statistics, Boston, Mass.

Edith (Currier) Churchill of Fort Fairfield and Portland, Maine.[1687] He died at Lebanon, New Hampshire 29 January 2010, at the age of 82.[1688]

John Fipphen grew up in Shrewsbury, Massachusetts, where he graduated from Shrewsbury High School in 1945. He earned his bachelor's degree in physics from Clark University in Worcester in 1949, and was a spectroscopist for a Worcester-based forging company. John and Chris raised their family in Northborough, Massachusetts, where they lived for almost 30 years. They were both very active at the Trinity Church of Northborough and the Northborough Historical Society. After his retirement in 1987, John and Chris moved to Wolfeboro, New Hampshire.

John and his wife Chris were avid genealogists, researching their family history for nearly thirty years. John was an active member of several genealogical organizations, and was the co-author of this geneaology as well as the author of *Cemetery Inscriptions, Wolfeboro, New Hampshire* (1993) and *1798 Direct Tax New Hampshire District #13* (1989). Driven by their interest in genealogy and history, John and Chris made several trips to England, which trips were the highlight of their retirement years.[1689]

Children of John S. and Christine L. (Churchill) Fipphen, born at Worcester: [1690]

183   i.   RICHARD CHURCHILL[12] FIPPHEN, b. 16 January 1959.
184   ii. PETER JOHN FIPPHEN, b. 9 June 1960.

[1687] Birth Certificate of Christine Lois Churchill, 6 Sept. 1927, Town Clerk's Office, Fort Fairfield, Maine.

[1688] Death Certificate for John S. Fipphen, 29 Jan. 2010, N.H. Registry of Vital Records, Concord, N.H.

[1689] Obituary, *Granite State News,* 4 Feb. 2010, A10.

[1690] Mass. VR.

CHAPTER 14

THE TWELFTH GENERATION

180. CLARK[12] **PHIPPEN** (*Henry Osgood*[11-10], *Arthur*[9], *George*[8], *Hardy*[7], *Joshua*[6], *Nathaniel*[5-4], *Samuel*[3], *Joseph*[2], *David*[1]) was born at Salem, Massachusetts 24 February 1939, son of Henry Osgood and Betsey Louise (Dunn) Phippen. He married at Princeton, New Jersey 30 November 1963, **LOUISE EDITH BRICKLEY,** who was born 15 April 1940.[1691]

Clark Phippen worked with Continental Oil Company and was living in Weston, Connecticut, in 1975.

Children of Clark and Louise Edith (Brickley) Phippen, born at Bronxville, New York:

    i.   OLIVER DANE[13] PHIPPEN, b. 15 Aug. 1967.
   ii.   WINTHROP BRICKLEY PHIPPEN, b. 1 Feb. 1969.
  iii.   CHARLES HENRY PHIPPEN, b. 31 July 1973.

181. PAUL ADELBERT[12] **PHIPPEN** (*Leslie*[11], *Fred W.*[10], *Samuel*[9], *Ebenezer*[8], *David*[7], *Ebenezer*[6], *David*[5], *Nathaniel*[4], *Samuel*[3], *Joseph*[2], *David*[1]) was born at Cranberry Isles, Maine 3 December 1926, son of Leslie R. and Marjorie (Bulger) Phippen.[1692] He married, first, 24 December 1950, **ANNE WOSTER HERRICK** of Southwest Harbor, Maine, who was born about 1933; they were divorced on 22 September 1956. He married, second, in Maine 1 May 1965, **NANCY A. GINN.**[1693]

Paul Phippen was a lobster fisherman.[1694] He died at Chelsea, Massachusetts 15 April 1985.[1695]

[1691] All information on Clark Phippen and his children is from a questionnaire completed by Clark Phippen, Nov. 1975.

[1692] Maine VR.

[1693] Ibid.; Index to Maine Marriages 1892–1966, 1977–1996.

[1694] Maine VR.

[1695] *Massachusetts Death Index,* 1970-2003 [Ancestry.com database], Certificate no. 027536.

Children of Paul Adelbert and Anne (Herrick) Phippen, born at Bar Harbor, Maine:[1696]

    i. JOAN ELIZABETH[13] PHIPPEN, b. 24 Aug. 1951.

    ii. PAUL DANIEL PHIPPEN, b. 6 Feb. 1955.

182. RICHARD LEROY[12] PHIPPEN (*Charles Russell[11], Frank[10], Charles[9], Ebenezer[8], David[7], Ebenezer[6], David[5], Nathaniel[4], Samuel[3], Joseph[2], David[1]*) was born at Bangor, Maine 6 January 1946, son of Charles Russell and Florence (Moon) Phippen.[1697] He married at Manhasset, New York 2 January 1965, **PENELOPE FOSS,** who was born at Mineola, New York 31 January 1947, daughter of Edward L. and Susan (Lord) Foss.[1698] They divorced in 1984.[1699]

Richard L. Phippen was a state police officer for the State of Maine for 27 years, retiring in 1995.[1700] He resides in Vassalboro, Maine.

Children of Richard Leroy and Penelope (Foss) Phippen:

    i. KATHLEEN[13] PHIPPEN, b. at Mineola 25 April 1965; d. at Pittsburgh, Pa. 7 May 2001.[1701]

    ii. JASON RICHARD PHIPPEN, b. at Augusta, Maine 29 March 1970.[1702]

183. RICHARD CHURCHILL[12] FIPPHEN (*John[11], Clarence[10–9], Stephen[8], David[7], Ebenezer[6], David[5], Nathaniel[4], Samuel[3], Joseph[2], David[1]*) was born at Worcester, Massachusetts 16 January 1959, son of John Stanley and Christine L. (Churchill) Fipphen.[1703] He attended public schools in Northborough, Massachusetts, and earned his bachelor's degree from Bates College, Lewiston, Maine, in 1981. He received his law degree from Cornell University, Ithaca, New York, in 1984. He is an attorney in New York City.

He married at Glenwood Landing, New York 13 October 1985, **JANET BETH ROSENBLUM,**[1704] who was born at New York, New York

---

[1696] Maine VR.

[1697] Maine VR; correspondence with Richard Leroy Phippen, 29 Aug. 1977.

[1698] Correspondence with Richard Leroy Phippen, 29 Aug. 1977.

[1699] Maine VR.

[1700] "Department announces retirement of troopers," *Bangor Daily News,* 30 Jan. 1995.

[1701] Obituary, *Bangor Daily News,* 10 May 2001.

[1702] Correspondence with Richard Leroy Phippen, 29 Aug. 1977.

[1703] Birth Certificate for Richard Churchill Fipphen, 16 Jan. 1959, Mass. Registry of Vital Records and Statistics, Boston, Mass. *See also* Birth Announcement, *The Evening Gazette,* (Worcester, Mass.), 17 Jan. 1959, 6.

[1704] Marriage Certificate for Richard Churchill Fipphen and Janet Beth Rosenblum, 13 Oct. 1985, File No. 022860, City of New York, Office of the City Clerk, Marriage License Bureau, New York, New York. *See also* "Richard Fipphen Married to Janet Beth Rosenblum," *The New York Times,* 14 Oct. 1985, D12.

12 May 1957, daughter of Albert and Ruth (Karp) Rosenblum of Great Neck, New York.[1705] Richard and his family resided in Fairfield, Connecticut.

Children of Richard Churchill and Janet (Rosenblum) Fipphen, born at Stamford, Connecticut:[1706]

    i. DANIEL SETH[13] FIPPHEN, b. 5 May 1989.

   ii. EMILY VICTORIA FIPPHEN, b. 19 April 1992.

184. **PETER JOHN**[12] **FIPPHEN,** (*John*[11], *Clarence*[10-9], *Stephen*[8], *David*[7], *Ebenezer*[6], *David*[5], *Nathaniel*[4], *Samuel*[3], *Joseph*[2], *David*[1]) was born at Worcester, Massachusetts 9 June 1960, son of John Stanley and Christine L. (Churchill) Fipphen.[1707] He attended public schools in Northborough, Massachusetts, and earned his bachelor's degree in accounting and master's degree in taxation from Bentley College in Waltham, Massachusetts. He has pursued a career in taxation and finance.

Peter Fipphen married at Needham, Massachusetts 10 October 1987, **HOLLY BETH HAMMER,**[1708] who was born at LeMars, Iowa 5 December 1957, daughter of Richard Edward and Bonny Yvonne (Wick) Hammer of LeMars.[1709] Peter and his family reside in Chelmsford, Massachusetts.

Children of Peter John and Holly (Hammer) Fipphen, born at Boston, Massachusetts:[1710]

    i. ELIZABETH ANNE[13] FIPPHEN, b. 17 Oct. 1990.

   ii. REBECCA BRAY FIPPHEN, b. 8 Oct. 1993.

[1705] Birth Certificate for Janet Beth Rosenblum, 12 May 1957, Certif. No. 156-57-118432, City of New York, Department of Health, Bureau of Vital Records, New York, New York.

[1706] Birth Certificate for Daniel Seth Fipphen, 5 May 1989, File No. H078741-8 and Birth Certificate for Emily Victoria Fipphen, 19 April 1992, File No. K046168-7, Town Clerk's Office, Stamford, Connecticut.

[1707] Birth Certificate for Peter John Fipphen, 9 June 1960, Mass. Registry of Vital Records and Statistics, Boston, Mass.

[1708] Marriage Certificate for Peter John Fipphen and Holly Beth Hammer, 10 Oct. 1987, Town Clerk's Office, Brookline, Mass.

[1709] Birth Certificate for Holly Beth Hammer, 5 Dec. 1957, State of Iowa, Plymouth County Clerk's Office, Book 12, Page 48.

[1710] Birth Certificate for Elizabeth Anne Fipphen, 17 Oct. 1990, registered no. 15806, and Birth Certificate for Rebecca Bray Fipphen, 8 Oct. 1993, registered no. 14174, Mass. Registry of Vital Records and Statistics, Boston, Mass.

THE DESCENDANTS OF
ROBERT¹ PHIPPEN OF SALEM, MASSACHUSETTS

In assembling the information for the descendants of David¹ Phippen, the following account of Robert Phippen's descendants was developed. Given that this information is not available as a collection of related data elsewhere, this appendix presents a unique history of Robert Phippen's family.

Robert¹ Phippen was known by contemporaries in Salem as a foreigner or Englishman. He may well have been a distant relative of the numerous David¹ Phippen descendants in Salem, or perhaps the surname was assumed when he arrived in Salem. We have no information about his forebears.

A1. ROBERT¹ PHIPPEN, perhaps of Waterford, Ireland, was born about 1764. He apparently arrived at Salem, Massachusetts, as a young man some time before his marriage there. He died at sea in the West Indies, aged 29, before 3 November 1793.[1711] He is probably the man who (listed as Robert Maxwell) married at Salem 27 October 1782, **LYDIA VALPY,**[1712] who was born about 1765, daughter of Abraham and Lydia (Clough) Valpy of Salem.

[1711] Date calculated from age at time of death; see *Vital Records of Salem, Massachusetts to the end of the year 1849,* 6: 139, and William Bentley, "Parish List of Deaths Begun 1785," *Essex Institute Historical Collections* 14 [1878]: 224.

[1712] *Vital Records of Salem, Massachusetts to the end of the year 1849* record a marriage, on 27 Oct. 1782, of Robert Maxwell and Lydia Valpy, drawn (according to the original manuscripts of town vital records, copied in 1815) from the Record Book of the Episcopal Church of Salem (Salem town vital records, original manuscripts, vol. 5, page 13; FHL film 0761,210). The name Maxwell does not appear anywhere else in Vital Records of Salem, Massachusetts to the end of the year 1849, however. It is possible that this is the Phippen–Valpy marriage, and that the original church record recorded the groom's surname in error, or that the town clerk misread it in 1815, or even perhaps that Robert Maxwell was his original name and he subsequently changed his name to Robert Phippen because of the established family in the town.

News of Robert Phippen's death was received in Salem by 1 November 1793.[1713] In his diary entry for 3 November 1793, the Rev. William Bentley notes his concern for Lydia Phippen and her children following the death of her husband abroad. On 6 November he writes more fully that "the sickness in the West Indies has deprived us of two young men . . . [including] Mr. Phippen who has left a destitute family.[1714]. . ." Lydia (Valpy) Phippen died at Salem 23 December 1797, aged 32.[1715] William Bentley's death register records her death:

> Dec. 23 [1797]. Consumption, aet 32. Nine years married. She was a Valpy and grand-daughter of our former sexton Clough; left three children, two sons. Her husband died in the Southern States four years ago, ae 31. He was a foreigner, English, and died a mate on board of R. Derby's ship. Both not of our Society.[1716]

In his diary for 24 December, Bentley wrote further: "In the evening Lydia Phippen, alias Valpy was buried. She belonged to Eng. Church & from the business of Christmas fell into my hands."[1717]

Robert Phippen appears in the 1790 census. The entry for his household lists 1 male 16 years and over, 2 white males under 16 years, and 4 white females.[1718]

Children of Robert and Lydia (Valpy) Phippen, born at Salem:

i.   SON[2], bur. 4 April 1783.[1719]

A2   ii. ROBERT PHIPPEN, b. about 1784.

iii. LYDIA PHIPPEN, b. 27, bp. at St. Peter's Episcopal Church, Salem 30 Dec. 1786; m. at Salem 27 Nov. 1808, her second cousin ANDRUS CLOUGH, who was b. at Salem 13 Aug. 1781, son of Peter and Sarah (Gray) (Pease) Clough.[1720]

A3   iv. ABRAHAM PHIPPEN, b. about 1789.

[1713] *Vital Records of Salem, Massachusetts to the end of the year 1849,* 6: 139.

[1714] *The Diary of William Bentley,* 2: 72.

[1715] *Vital Records of Salem, Massachusetts to the end of the year 1849,* 6: 138.

[1716] Bentley, "Parish List of Deaths Begun 1785," *Essex Institute Historical Collections* 14 [1878]: 295–96. The last comment refers to their religious affiliation.

[1717] *The Diary of William Bentley,* 2: 251. On 31 Dec. 1797, he recorded writing condolences to Lydia Valpy Phippen's mother, Lydia, and sister Elizabeth.

[1718] *Heads of Families at the First Census of United States Taken in the Year 1790: Massachusetts* (Baltimore, 1973), 97.

[1719] *Vital Records of Salem, Massachusetts to the end of the year 1849,* 6: 140.

[1720] Ibid., 2: 167, 3: 361, 4: 190. The birth record in the *Vital Records of Salem, Massachusetts to the end of the year 1849,* showing her birth in 1784, may be an error, given the date of her baptism.

SECOND GENERATION

A2. ROBERT² PHIPPEN (*Robert¹*) was born at Salem, Massachusetts, probably in 1784, son of Robert and Lydia (Valpy) Phippen. He married at Salem 5 February 1809, **ABIGAIL GAVET,**[1721] who was born 1 September 1787, daughter of John and Susannah (Hill) Gavet.[1722] Abigail's youngest sister, Elizabeth, born 30 January 1798, married Joseph H.⁸ Phippen (*William⁷⁻⁶, Thomas⁵, Nathaniel⁴, Samuel³, Joseph², David¹*) (*q.v.*). This marriage brought the two Salem Phippen families together as in-laws.

In 1814 Robert Phippen was one of several men who served as privates in Capt. Benjamin Morgan's Company, Lieut. Col. J. White's regiment. This service at Salem was for the purpose of military instruction only, and lasted from two to ten days.[1723] Robert Phippen died at Salem 20 May 1842 of consumption, at the age of 58.[1724] The death record indicates his occupation as laborer. His widow, Abigail, died at Salem 4 April 1844, of apoplexy. The records disagree on her age at death; the state vital records give her age as 58 years, while the Salem record shows her as 57.[1725]

Children of Robert and Abigail (Gavet) Phippen, born at Salem except v:

A4 i. ROBERT H.³ PHIPPEN, b. ca. 1809 (calculated from age at death; see below).

A5 ii. EDWARD A. PHIPPEN, b. about 30 Dec. 1810 (calculated from age at death; see below).

A6 iii. NILES T. PHIPPEN, b. 10 Jan. 1812.[1726]

A7 iv. ABRAHAM W. PHIPPEN, b. 25 June 1813.

A8 v. GERMAN S. PHIPPEN, b. at Exeter, N.H. about 15 March 1815 (calculated from age at death; see below).

A9 vi. JONATHAN PHIPPEN, b. in Jan. 1818.[1727]

    vii. ABIGAIL PHIPPEN m. at Salem 20 Oct. 1840, ANDREW NICHOLS

[1721] *Vital Records of Salem, Massachusetts to the end of the year 1849,* 3: 407, 4: 190.

[1722] Gavit, "Philip Gavet of Salem Mass and Some of His Descendants," *Register* 77 [1923]: 34–58 at 41.

[1723] Gardner W. Pearson, *Massachusetts Volunteer Militia in the War of 1812* (Boston, 1913), 137.

[1724] *Vital Records of Salem, Massachusetts to the end of the year 1849,* 6: 139.

[1725] Ibid., 136.

[1726] Ibid., 2: 168.

[1727] Calculated from age at death; see below.

HAZELTON,[1728] who was b. 4 Jan. 1818, son of John and Lucy (Marshall) Hazelton. He served in the Civil War and d. 12 Sept. 1877. Abigail d. at Salem 5 May 1897.[1729]

A3. ABRAHAM[2] **PHIPPEN** (*Robert*[1]) was born at Salem, Massachusetts about 1789, son of Robert and Lydia (Valpy) Phippen. He died at Salem 5 December 1857, of lung fever, at the age of 68 years. The death record erroneously lists his parents as Abraham and Elizabeth Phippen.[1730] Abraham Phippen married, first, at Salem 6 July 1817, **SARAH TIPLADY,**[1731] who was baptized at Salem 30 May 1790, daughter of Thomas and Elizabeth (Giffords) Tiplady.[1732] Sarah died of consumption at Salem 16 July 1825.[1733] Abraham married, second, at Salem 6 November 1825, **SARAH ELIZABETH FLETCHER,**[1734] who was born at Salem 15 November 1805, daughter of John and Sarah (Doliver) Fletcher.[1735] Sarah (Fletcher) Phippen died at Salem 12 February 1851 at the age of 46, in childbirth.[1736] Abraham married, third, at Salem, 13 October 1853, his nephew Robert's widow **LYDIA ANN (MARSTON) PHIPPEN** (see below).[1737] Lydia died in childbirth at Salem 2 May 1854 at the age of 42 years, 4 months, 2 days.[1738]

Children of Abraham and Sarah (Tiplady) Phippen, born at Salem:[1739]

    i. SARAH A.[3] PHIPPEN, b. about 1820 and d. unm. at Salem 14 Oct. 1872, aged 52, of consumption.

    ii. DAUGHTER, b. in June 1823; d. 14 Feb. 1824, age 8 months.

    iii. MARY ELIZABETH PHIPPEN, b. 12 Sept. 1825; m. at Salem 16 Sept. 1844, CHARLES P. COTTLE. She d. at Boston, Mass., 20 June 1877, aged 51 years, 9 months, 8 days.

[1728] *Vital Records of Salem, Massachusetts to the end of the year 1849,* 3: 482, 4: 188.

[1729] Mass.VR (1897) 472: 602.

[1730] Mass.VR (1857) 111: 253.

[1731] *Vital Records of Salem, Massachusetts to the end of the year 1849,* 4: 188, 386.

[1732] Ibid., 2: 354.

[1733] Ibid., 6: 139.

[1734] Ibid., 3: 365, 4: 188.

[1735] Ibid., 1: 305.

[1736] Mass.VR (1851) 57: 156.

[1737] Mass.VR (1853) 69: 286.

[1738] Mass.VR (1854) 84: 171.

[1739] Mass.VR (1872) 247: 314 (Sarah), (1877) 294: 118 (Mary).

Children of Abraham and Sarah (Fletcher) Phippen, born at Salem:[1740]

iv. LYDIA C.[3] PHIPPEN, b. 4 June 1829; m. at Salem 28 Aug. 1853, CHARLES R. LEWIS, who was b. at Townsend, Mass. about 1828 and d. at Salem 10 May 1854, aged 25 years, 4 months, son of Alexander and Abigail (Robinson) Lewis. Her marriage record says she was the daughter of William and Lydia, although this age fits, and in 1860, Lydia C. Lewis is living with Charles and William, who would have been her brothers.[1741]

A10 v. ABRAHAM PHIPPEN, b. about 1831.

A11 vi. WILLIAM H. PHIPPEN, b. about 19 April 1833 (calculated from age at death).

vii. CHARLES F. PHIPPEN, b. about 12 Nov. 1836 (calculated). He may be the man who m. MARY A. TUCK, daughter of Philip H. Tuck; this man d. at Salem 28 Sept. 1878, aged 41 years 10 months 16 days, of typhoid fever.[1742] However, the marriage record says the groom was b. in 1834, son of Stephen Phippen. His identity has not been confirmed.

A12 viii. ROBERT C. PHIPPEN, b. 17 Jan. 1839.[1743]

ix. MARTHA W. PHIPPEN, b. about 1840.

x. GEORGE E. PHIPPEN, b. in 1843 and d. 4 Oct. 1844, aged 1 year.[1744]

xi. REBECCA B. PHIPPEN, b. in March 1847;[1745] m. at Salem 3 May 1869, JAMES H. ARNOLD, who was b. about 1845, son of James E. and Mary (___) Arnold.[1746]

THIRD GENERATION

A4. ROBERT H.[3] PHIPPEN (*Robert*[2–1]) was born at Salem, Massachusetts, about 1809, son of Robert and Abigail (Gavet) Phippen. Robert H. Phippen died of consumption in Salem 10 December 1849, at the age

---

[1740] 1850 U.S. Census, Salem, Essex Co., Mass., p. 396.

[1741] Mass. VR, (1853) 69: 286 (marriage), (1854) 84: 172 (Charles's death); 1860 U.S. Census, Salem, Essex Co., Mass., p. 224.

[1742] Mass. VR (1878) 301: 269.

[1743] *Vital Records of Salem, Massachusetts to the end of the year 1849*, 2: 168.

[1744] Ibid., 6: 137.

[1745] Ibid., 2: 168.

[1746] Mass. VR (1869) 217: 271.

of 40.[1747] He married at Salem 5 March 1832, **LYDIA ANN MARSTON,**[1748] who was born at Salem about 31 December 1811, daughter of William and Lydia A. (Mungrell) Marston. Lydia married, second, at Salem, 13 October 1853, her late husband's uncle **ABRAHAM**[2] **PHIPPEN** (see above).[1749] Lydia Ann (Marston) (Phippen) Phippen died in childbirth at Salem 2 May 1854 at the age of 42 years, 4 months, 2 days.[1750] Robert H. Phippen was a farmer.

Children of Robert H. and Lydia Ann (Marston) Phippen, born at Salem:[1751]

A13   i.   ROBERT A.[4] PHIPPEN, b. 19 April 1832.
          ii.   CHARLES HENRY PHIPPEN, b. about Sept. 1836 (calculated); d. at Salem 10 Jan. 1837, aged 5 months.[1752]
          iii.   LYDIA ALLEN PHIPPEN, b. 11 Aug. and d. 25 Aug. 1840, of whooping cough.[1753]
          iv.   LYDIA ALLEN PHIPPEN, b. 2 March and d. 23 March 1843.[1754]
          v.   LYDIA ALLEN PHIPPEN, b. in Aug. and d. 23 Dec. 1844.[1755]
A14   v.   CHARLES HENRY PHIPPEN, b. about 1845.
          vi.   HARRIET M. PHIPPEN, b. about March and d. 17 Aug. 1846, aged 5 months.[1756]

A5. EDWARD A.[3] **PHIPPEN** (*Robert*[2–1]) was born at Salem, Massachusetts 30 December 1810, son of Robert and Abigail (Gavet) Phippen. Edward Phippen married, first, at Salem 25 July 1834, **HARRIET WELLINGTON,** daughter of Thadeus and Sarah (_____) Wellington. Harriet died at Salem 31 July 1846, of consumption.[1757] Edward married, second, at Salem

---

[1747] Mass.VR (1849) 39: 239; *Vital Records of Salem, Massachusetts to the end of the year 1849,* 6: 139.

[1748] *Vital Records of Salem, Massachusetts to the end of the year 1849,* 4: 66, 190.

[1749] Mass.VR (1853) 69: 286.

[1750] Mass.VR (1854) 84: 171.

[1751] 1850 U.S. Census, Salem, Essex Co., Mass., p. 222, living in the household of Benjamin Cook[8] Phippen (*David*[7], *Ebenezer*[6], *David*[5], *Nathaniel*[4], *Samuel*[3], *Joseph*[2], *David*[1]).

[1752] *Vital Records of Salem, Massachusetts to the end of the year 1849,* 6: 137.

[1753] Mass.VR (1840) 14: 102.

[1754] *Vital Records of Salem, Massachusetts to the end of the year 1849,* 6: 138.

[1755] Mass.VR (1844) 14: 102.

[1756] Mass.VR (1846) 26: 121.

[1757] *Vital Records of Salem, Massachusetts to the end of the year 1849,* 6: 137.

5 September 1847, **MARY ANN HENLEY** of Eastport, Maine.[1758] She was born about 1821, calculated from her age (29) in the 1850 census. Edward died a widower 13 March 1868 at Charlestown, Massachusetts, at the age of 57 years, 2 months, 15 days, of consumption.[1759] The 1850 census gives his birthplace as Ireland, while the 1860 census gives Massachusetts.[1760]

Children of Edward A. and Harriet (Wellington) Phippen:

A15   i.   EDWARD A.[4] PHIPPEN, b. about 1836.[1761]
      ii. NANCY R. PHIPPEN, b. about 1844.
      iii. HARRIET E. PHIPPEN, b. about 1844; d. at Danvers, Mass. 12 Oct. 1890, aged 46.[1762] Perhaps she was the Harriet Phippen who m. at Concord, N.H. 2 June 1866, JOHN T. TENNEY.

Child of Edward A. and Mary Ann (Henley) Phippen:

      iv. JULIA A. PHIPPEN, b. 16 Aug. 1848; d. Salem 8 Nov. 1902; m. there 11 Feb. 1867, EDWARD H. BUXTON.[1763]

A6. NILES T.[3] PHIPPEN (*Robert*[2–1]) was born at Salem, Massachusetts 10 January 1812, son of Robert and Abigail (Gavet) Phippen.[1764] He died at Salem 20 October 1857, at the age of 42 years, 9 months 11 days, of consumption. Niles was listed as a laborer on his death record.[1765] Niles Phippen married at Salem 3 April 1839, **MARY JANE GROVER,**[1766] who was born at Bowden, Maine 24 April 1822. Mary (Grover) Phippen removed to Cincinnati, Ohio, according to the 1886–87 Salem Street directory.

Children of Niles T. and Mary Jane (Grover) Phippen:

      i.   NILES[4] PHIPPEN, d. 28 May 1843, aged 3 years.
      ii. SOPHIA B. PHIPPEN, b. about 1842; m. at North Reading, Mass. 10 July 1862, GEORGE E. MCINTIRE, who was b. about 1841,

[1758] Mass.VR (1847) 4: 189.
[1759] Mass.VR (1868) 212: 111.
[1760] 1850 and 1860 Federal censuses for Salem, Essex Co., Mass.
[1761] Mass.VR (1861) 145: 68, 136 (from age on marriage record).
[1762] Mass.VR (1890) 409: 258.
[1763] *Vital Records of Salem, Massachusetts to the end of the year 1849,* 2: 167 (birth); Mass. VR (1902) 528: 672 (death), (1867) 199: 268.
[1764] *Vital Records of Salem, Massachusetts to the end of the year 1849,* 2:168.
[1765] Mass.VR (1857) 111: 251.
[1766] *Vital Records of Salem, Massachusetts to the end of the year 1849,* 3: 452, 4: 190.

           son of Ernest and Rebecca (_____) McIntire.[1767]

    iii. NILES T. PHIPPEN, b. at Salem in 1844; drowned there 13 April 1850, aged 6 years.[1768]

    iv. MARTHA E. PHIPPEN, b. at Salem June 1846.[1769]

    v. DELIA B. PHIPPEN, b. at Salem 28 March 1846; d. there unm. 13 Sept. 1880, aged 34 years, 5 months, 15 days.[1770]

    vi. HENRY O. W. PHIPPEN, b. at Salem 29 Nov. 1848.[1771]

A16 vii. ROBERT H. PHIPPEN, b. at Salem 9 Sept. 1850.

    viii. NILES T. PHIPPEN, b. at Salem 9 Aug. 1852; d. there 31 Aug. 1854, aged 2 years, 22 days.[1772]

A17 ix. GEORGE LINCOLN PHIPPEN, b. at Salem 16 April 1855.[1773]

A7. ABRAHAM W.[3] PHIPPEN (*Robert*[2–1]) was born at Salem, Massachusetts 25 June 1813,[1774] son of Robert and Abigail (Gavet) Phippen. He died at Salem 13 July 1859, aged 46 years, 18 days. Abraham married at Salem 20 November 1836, **JANE "IRENA" GROVER,**[1775] who was born about 1820.

    Children of Abraham W. and Jane (Grover) Phippen, born in Salem:

    i. LYDIA A.[4] PHIPPEN, b. 20 Nov. 1838; m. (1) ABRAHAM[3] PHIPPEN JR. (see family A10);[1776] m. (2) at Salem, 24 Feb. 1866, James Bulger.[1777]

    ii. IRENE PHIPPEN, b. about 1840; m. (1) at Salem 22 April 1860, ALBERT L. FOSTER;[1778] m. (2) at Beverly, Mass. 24 March 1861, JOHANNES LUND, who was b. at Copenhagen, Denmark in 1820.[1779]

[1767] Mass.VR (1862) 154: 186.

[1768] Mass.VR (1850) 48:142.

[1769] *Vital Records of Salem, Massachusetts to the end of the year 1849,* 2: 167.

[1770] Mass.VR (1880) 319: 291.

[1771] *Vital Records of Salem, Massachusetts to the end of the year 1849,* 2: 166.

[1772] Mass.VR (1854) 84: 175; *Vital Records of Salem, Massachusetts to the end of the year 1849,* 2: 166.

[1773] Mass.VR (1855) 90: 240.

[1774] Mass.VR (1859) 129: 175; date of birth calculated from age at death.

[1775] *Vital Records of Salem, Massachusetts to the end of the year 1849,* 3: 451, 4: 188.

[1776] 1860 U.S. Census, Salem, Ward 2, Essex Co., Mass., p. 30.

[1777] Mass.VR (1866) 189: 269.

[1778] Mass.VR (1860) 135: 241.

[1779] Mass.VR (1861) 144: 129.

A18 iii. GEORGE P. PHIPPEN, b. 5 Jan. 1841.

A19 iv. OLIVER H. PHIPPEN, b. about 1844.

    v. ABBIE A. PHIPPEN, b. 1846; m. at Beverly 27 Sept. 1864, WILLIAM H. MONROE, who was b. in 1841.[1780]

    vi. HANNAH PHIPPEN, b. in June 1847.[1781]

A20 vii. WILLIAM HARRISON PHIPPEN, b. 27 June 1850.[1782]

    viii. LOUISA P. PHIPPEN, b. about 1853; m. at Marblehead, Mass. 20 Jan. 1869, HENRY L. YOUNG, who was b. about 1839, son of Samuel and Sarah (____) Young.[1783]

A8. GERMAN S.³ PHIPPEN (*Robert²⁻¹*) was born at Exeter, New Hampshire, in 1815,[1784] son of Robert and Abigail (Gavett) Phippen. He was a farmer in Malden and Methuen, Massachusetts. He died at Methuen 7 November 1903.[1785] German married, first, **HANNAH D. _____**, who was born at Salem, New Hampshire 23 January 1818. She died at Malden 4 December 1845, of consumption. German married, second, **JULIA F. HAWLEY,** who was born 5 May 1827, daughter of Lyman Hawley of Salisbury, Vermont. She died of consumption at Melrose, Massachusetts 17 December 1852, aged 25 years, 7 months, 12 days.[1786] German Phippen married, third, at Lowell, Massachusetts 30 August 1853, **SARAH MOORE,** who was born in 1830, daughter of George and Sarah (___) Moore.[1787]

    Child of German S. and Hannah D. (_____) Phippen:

    i. ALMENA⁴ PHIPPEN, b. in Feb. 1843; d. Malden 7 Sept. 1843.[1788]

    Children of German S. and Julia (Hawley) Phippen:

    ii. RACKMAN HAWLEY PHIPPEN, b. at Malden 17 April 1847;[1789]

[1780] Mass. VR (1864) 171: 243.

[1781] *Vital Records of Salem, Massachusetts to the end of the year 1849,* 2: 166.

[1782] Mass. VR (1850) 42: 210.

[1783] Mass. VR (1869) 217: 241.

[1784] Mass. VR (1853) 70: 144 (birth year calculated from age at marriage to Sarah Moore).

[1785] Mass. VR (1903) 37: 251.

[1786] Mass. VR (1852) 67: 130.

[1787] Mass. VR (1853) 70: 144.

[1788] *Vital Records of Malden, Massachusetts to the end of the year 1849,* 369.

[1789] Mass. VR (1847) 23: 62; Vital Records of Malden, Massachusetts to the end of the year 1849, 67.

d. there 8 Sept. 1848.[1790]

iii. ROSMAN HAMBLET PHIPPEN, b. at Malden 12 Feb. 1849;[1791] d. there 8 Sept. 1849.

Children of German and Sarah (Moore) Phippen:[1792]

iv. LUZERNE S. PHIPPEN, b. at Melrose 7 July 1855.

v. ARTHUR W. PHIPPEN, b. at Melrose 22 Aug. 1858.

A21   v. GEORGE MOORE PHIPPEN, b. at Methuen 6 Sept. 1862.

A22   vi. BENJAMIN PHIPPEN, b. at Methuen 14 March 1866.

A9. JONATHAN³ PHIPPEN (*Robert²⁻¹*) was born about 1818, son of Robert and Abigail (Gavett) Phippen. He died at Lowell, Massachusetts 28 May 1879, aged 61 years, 4 months, of consumption.[1793] Jonathan married at Salem, Massachusetts 22 September 1844, **JULIA ANN DAVIS,** who was born at Montpelier, Vermont, about 1821 and died at Lowell 6 February 1887, aged 67 years.[1794] Jonathan Phippen's occupation was described as "watchman" in the 1860 census.

Children of Jonathan and Julia Ann (Davis) Phippen may include:

i. SOPHIA or MINNIE⁴ PHIPPEN, b. about 1842, aged 18 years in the 1860 census; aged 38 years in the 1880 census, which places her birth before her mother's marriage to Jonathan Phippen.

A10. ABRAHAM³ PHIPPEN (*Abraham², Robert¹*) was born at Salem, Massachusetts about 1831, son of Abraham and Sarah (Fletcher) Phippen. He married, at Salem 5 April 1855, his first cousin once removed **LYDIA A.⁴ PHIPPEN,** daughter of Abraham W. and Jane (Grover) Phippen (family A7). She married, second, in 1866, **JAMES BULGER.** In 1860, Abraham Phippen Jr. was living with his wife Lydia (Phippen) Phippen; son Thomas Minot Phippen; Lydia Phippen's mother, sister Irene, and her then husband Albert L. Foster; and Lydia's brother George P. and sister Louisa P. Phippen.[1795]

[1790] *Vital Records of Malden, Massachusetts to the end of the year 1849,* 369.

[1791] Ibid., 67.

[1792] Mass. VR (1855) 91: 135 (Luzerne), (1858), 115: 188 (Arthur), (1862) 150: 253 (George), (1866), 186: 242 (Benjamin).

[1793] Mass.VR (1879) 311: 101. The death record indicated that he was married.

[1794] Mass.VR (1887) 383: 118.

[1795] 1860 US Census, Salem, Essex Co., Mass., p. 30.

Child of Abraham and Lydia (Phippen) Phippen, born at Salem:

A23   i.   THOMAS MINOT[4] PHIPPEN, b. 7 June 1856.[1796]

A11. WILLIAM H.[3] PHIPPEN (*Abraham*[2], *Robert*[1]) was born at Salem, Massachusetts about 19 April 1833 (calculated from death record), son of Abraham and Sarah E. (Fletcher) Phippen. He died at Salem 16 November 1877, at the age of 44 years, 6 months, 27 days. He was a farmer.[1797] William H. Phippen married at Salem 22 July 1869, **MARY E. (CARPENTER) CLARK,** who was born 15 November 1837, daughter of James W. and Eliza (____) Carpenter of Troy, Maine, She had previously married Nathaniel Clark (9 February 1864), who was killed in the Civil War. Mary died 19 July 1918.

William was described in his service record as a tanner and a chemist, with blue eyes, brown hair, and a dark complexion; he was 5 feet 7½ inches tall. William died 16 November 1877, aged 44 years, 6 months, 27 days. He enlisted 6 August 1862 in Company A. 1st Massachusetts Heavy Artillery and served to 8 July 1864, when he was mustered out at Petersburg, Virginia. He signed up again 16 November 1864 and was discharged 7 July 1865.[1798]

Child of William H. and Mary (Carpenter) (Clark) Phippen:

   I.   CHARLOTTE[4], b. at Beverly, Mass. 29 Oct. 1877; d. there 4 Oct. 1878, aged 11 months.[1799]

A12. ROBERT C.[3] PHIPPEN (*Abraham*[2], *Robert*[1]) was born 17 January 1839, son of Abraham and Sally (Fletcher) Phippen.[1800] He died at Salem, Massachusetts 17 January 1895, aged 56 years. [1801] The 1860 census shows that he was a tanner.[1802] He served in the Civil War, in the 1st Massachusetts Volunteer Artillery, mustering in 6 August 1862; after being wounded 22 June 1864 at Petersburg, Virginia, he was discharged 8 July 1864.[1803] Robert C. Phippen married at Salem 14 June 1859,

---

[1796] Mass. VR (1856) 96: 257.

[1797] Mass. VR (1877) 292: 274.

[1798] Unattached Co. Mass. Vol. Mil. Vol. 5, p. 268; veteran records of William H. Phippen.

[1799] Mass. VR (1877) 286: 178, (1878) 301: 162.

[1800] *Vital Records of Salem, Massachusetts to the end of the year 1849,* 2: 168.

[1801] Mass. VR (1895) 454: 553.

[1802] 1860 U.S. Census, Salem, Essex Co., Mass., p. 259.

[1803] *Massachusetts Soldiers, Sailors, and Marines in the Civil War,* 9 vols. (Norwood, Mass., 1931-37), 5: 564.

ABIGAIL FINLEY,[1804] who was born at Salem 20 May 1839.[1805] She died there 18 February 1889, aged 49 years, 9 months, 29 days.[1806]

Children of Robert C. and Abigail (Finley) Phippen:[1807]

A24   i.   WALTER A.[4] PHIPPEN, b. 27 Feb. 1862.[1808]
A25   ii. CLARENCE E. PHIPPEN, b. about 1866.[1809]
A26   iii. ALBERT EDWARD PHIPPEN, b. about 1870.

FOURTH GENERATION

A13. ROBERT A.[4] PHIPPEN (*Robert*[4-1]) was born at Salem, Massachusetts 19 April 1832, son of Robert H. and Lydia Ann (Marston) Phippen. He married at Salem **SARAH SKIDMORE,** who was born 1 March 1835, daughter of Henry and Mary (Very) Skidmore.[1810] Sarah died at Salem 4 May 1880, of cancer, aged 45 years, 1 month, 3 days.[1811] In the 1860 census for Salem, Robert A. Phippen was listed as a laborer, age 28, Sarah as 25, and their daughter Ida as 3.

Robert served in the Civil War as a private in the 1st Massachusetts Heavy Artillery; he was 29 when mustered in 5 August 1862; wounded 19 May 1864 at Spotsylvania, Virginia, he was discharged 8 July 1864.[1812]

Children of Robert and Sarah (Skidmore) Phippen, born at Salem:

   i.   IDA FLORENCE[5] PHIPPEN, b. 25 Feb. 1857;[1813] m. at Salem 11 Aug. 1879, CHARLES E. MERRILL, who was b. at Methuen, Mass. about 1855, son of Charles and Lydia P. (Webster) Merrill.[1814]
   ii. MERCY PHIPPEN, b. in Jan. and d. 12 Aug. 1859.[1815]
   iii. ALICE M. PHIPPEN, b. in 1867; m. at Salem 20 July 1896, FRANCIS TORREY UPTON, who was b. at Salem 7 Sept. 1855, son of Eben and Lucy Marie (Carey) Upton.[1816]

[1804] Mass. VR (1859) 126: 217.
[1805] *Vital Records of Salem, Massachusetts to the end of the year 1849,* 2: 165.
[1806] Mass. VR (1889) 400: 352.
[1807] 1880 US Census, Salem, Essex Co., Mass. p. 810D.
[1808] Mass. VR (1862) 150: 276.
[1809] Mass. VR (1891) 415: 469.
[1810] *Vital Records of Salem, Massachusetts to the end of the year 1849,* 2: 169.
[1811] Mass. VR (1880) 319: 285.
[1812] *Massachusetts Soldiers, Sailors, and Marines in the Civil War,* 5: 564.
[1813] Inferred from 1860 Federal Census, Salem, Essex Co., Mass.
[1814] Mass. VR (1879) 307: 283.
[1815] Mass. VR (1859) 129: 176.
[1816] Mass. VR (1855) 90: 239, (1896) 460: 528.

A14. CHARLES HENRY[4] PHIPPEN (*Robert*[3-1]) was born at Salem, Massachusetts about 1845 (calculated from age at marriage), son of Robert H. and Lydia (Marston) Phippen. He married, first, at Salem 29 April 1860, **FRANCES E. DIX,** who was born about 1842, daughter of John and Martha R. (Elder) Dix.[1817] He married, second, at Cambridge, Massachusetts 25 May 1875, **HARRIET E. TRASK,** who was born about 1846, daughter of William and Betsey (____) Trask.[1818]

Charles Henry Phippen was a plumber. He served in the Civil War as a private in the 1st Massachusetts Heavy Artillery; like his brother Robert, he was wounded 19 May 1864 at Spottsylvania, Virginia; he was discharged 19 June 1865.[1819]

Children of Charles Henry and Harriet (Trask) Phippen, born at Salem:[1820]

> i. ARTHUR M.[5] PHIPPEN, b. 14 March 1876; d. at Salem 5 Sept. 1881.
> ii. FRED T. PHIPPEN, b. 4 Dec. 1878; m. at Salem 6 March 1906, BESSIE L. ROWE.[1821]
> iii. JOSEPHINE PHIPPEN, b. 8 Feb. 1880; m. at Lynn, Mass. 20 Feb. 1905 CHESTER L. GIBBINS, who was b. about 1886, son of Lyman O. and Lilian E. (Brown) Gibbins.
> iv. WILLIAM C. PHIPPEN, b. 24 Dec. 1881.
> v. BESSIE E. PHIPPEN, b. 26 Sept. 1883; d. 5 Sept. 1884.

A15. EDWARD A.[4] PHIPPEN (*Edward*[3], *Robert*[2-1]) was born at Salem, Massachusetts about 1836, son of Edward A. and Harriet (Wellington) Phippen. He died at Boston, Massachusetts 7 November 1902.[1822] He married at North Reading, Massachusetts 20 October 1861, **MARY A. THOMPSON,** daughter of Joseph and Susan (Foster) Thompson.[1823]

Edward served in the Civil War, in the 5th Massachusetts Light Artillery. Then a resident of Charlestown, Massachusetts, and a carpenter,

---

[1817] Mass. VR (1860) 135: 243.

[1818] Mass. VR (1875) 272: 58.

[1819] *Massachusetts Soldiers, Sailors, and Marines in the Civil War,* 5: 564.

[1820] Mass. VR (1876) 277: 288 (birth of Arthur), (1881) 328: 294 (death of Arthur), (1878) 295: 297 (Freddie), (1880) 313: 310 (birth of Josephine), (1881) 322: 338 (William), (1883) 340: 340 (birth of Bessie), (1884) 355: 298 (death of Bessie).

[1821] Mass. VR (1906) 562: 641.

[1822] Mass. VR (1902) 22: 19.

[1823] Mass. VR (1861) 145: 136.

he mustered in 3 December 1861, reenlisted 24 December 1863, and mustered out 12 June 1865.[1824]

Child of Edward A. and Mary (Thompson) Phippen:

    i. ARTHUR IRVING[5] PHIPPEN, b. at Charlestown 30 May 1863.[1825]

A16. ROBERT H.[4] **PHIPPEN** (*Niles*[3], *Robert*[2–1]) was born at Salem, Massachusetts 9 September 1850, son of Niles T. and Mary Jane (Grover) Phippen. Robert H. Phippen was a painter in Salem. He married at Salem 19 April 1875, **KATE L. MAHONEY,** who was born about 1850, daughter of Dennis and Catharine (O'Connor) Mahoney.[1826]

Child of Robert and Kate (Mahoney) Phippen, born at Salem:

    i. JANE or JENNIE L.[5] PHIPPEN, b. 10 June 1875; d. at Salem 4 June 1892, aged 16 years, 11 months, 25 days.[1827]

A17. GEORGE LINCOLN[4] **PHIPPEN** (*Niles T.*[3], *Robert*[2–1]) was born at Salem, Massachusetts 16 April 1855, son of Niles T. and Mary Jane (Grover) Phippen. The name of his wife has not been discovered.

Child of George Lincoln and ____ (____) Phippen:

    i. EDWARD JAMES[5] PHIPPEN, b. at St. Paul, Minn. in 1885.[1828]

A18. GEORGE P.[4] **PHIPPEN** (*Abraham W.*[3], *Robert*[2–1]) was born at Salem, Massachusetts 5 January 1841, son of Abraham W. and Jane (Grover) Phippen. He died at Salem 24 June 1884 of pneumonia, aged 43 years, 5 months, 19 days. He was a molder, and an "expressman" (at the time of his marriage). His death record states that he was married and that his mother was born in Maine, his father in Salem.[1829] George Phippen married at Salem 23 October 1864, **MARIA N. MCINTIRE,** who was born in Maine. She died at Salem 4 May 1900.[1830]

[1824] 5th Batt. Mass. Vol. Light Artillery 5: 407.

[1825] Mass. VR (1863) 160: 70.

[1826] Mass. VR (1875) 271: 270.

[1827] Mass. VR (1875) 268: 309, (1892) 427: 495.

[1828] Communication of Walt Breitenstein.

[1829] Mass. VR (1884) 355: 295.

[1830] Mass. VR (1864) 171: 246, (1900) 504: 694.

Children of George and Maria (McIntire) Phippen, born at Salem:[1831]

 i. GEORGE N.[5] PHIPPEN, b. 11 Jan. 1867; m. at Manchester, Mass. 15 Aug. 1900, CHARLOTTE ANDREWS, who was b. in 1862, daughter of George and Olive (Roberts) Andrews.

 ii. ANNA BERTHA PHIPPEN, b. 8 Feb. 1871; m. at Somerville, Mass. 21 Feb. 1894, JOHN HERBERT DAKIN, who was b. about 1873, son of John Dakin.

 iii. JOSEPHINE PHIPPEN, b. 28 Feb. 1873; m. at Salem 20 April 1893, GEORGE A. LUNT, son of William Lunt.

 iv. FREDERIC E. PHIPPEN, b. 7 June 1875; m. at Salem 19 Feb. 1900, HATTIE HUNT, who was b. about 1880, daughter of Fred W. and Hannah (Deland) Hunt.

 v. HATTIE R. PHIPPEN, b. 27 May and d. 22 June 1877, aged 21 days.

 vi. NORMAN PHIPPEN, d. at Lewiston, Me. 13 Sept. 1955.[1832]

A19. OLIVER H.[4] PHIPPEN (*Abraham W.[3], Robert[2–1]*) was born at Salem, Massachusetts in 1845, son of Abraham W. and Jane (Grover) Phippen. Oliver died at Salem 13 January 1883, aged 37 years, of epilepsy.[1833] Oliver H. Phippen married at Salem 24 October 1870, **SARAH J. GILBERT,** who was born at Charlestown, Massachusetts about 1849, daughter of John and Margaret (____) Gilbert.[1834] Following Oliver's death Sarah married, second, at Salem 28 July 1883, **DANIEL W. BRAY, JR.**[1835]

Oliver Phippen enlisted in the military 21 September 1864, as a private in Company E, 61st Massachusetts Infantry Regiment, from Salem. He had blue eyes, was 5 feet 4 inches tall, and was aged 21 at the time.

[1831] Mass. VR (1867) 196: 264 (birth of George), (1900) 500: 493, 339 (George's marriage to Charlotte, and her birth), (1871) 232: 291, (1894) 443: 312 (birth and marriage of Anna Bertha), (1873) 250: 303, (1893) 433: 497 (birth and marriage of Josephine), (1875) 286: 309, (1900) 500: 539 (birth and marriage of Frederic), (1877) 286: 298, (1877) 292: 269 (birth and death of Hattie).

[1832] His age at death is given as 60, which is impossible. He must have been 70 or older. Maine VR.

[1833] Mass. VR (1883) 346: 286.

[1834] Mass. VR (1870) 226: 276.

[1835] Mass. VR (1883) 343: 360.

Children of Oliver and Sarah (Gilbert) Phippen:[1836]

    i.   LILLIE F.[5] PHIPPEN, b. at Salem 3 Jan. and d. there of cholera 1
        Sept. 1874, aged 7 months, 27 days.

    ii. LILLIE FRANCES PHIPPEN, b. at Salem 24 July and d. there 13
        Aug. 1879, aged 19 days.

    iii. BENJAMIN T. PHIPPEN, b. at Salem 10 Jan. 1882.

A20. WILLIAM HARRISON[4] PHIPPEN (*Abraham W.[3]*, *Robert[2-1]*) was
born at Salem, Massachusetts 27 June 1850, son of Abraham and Jane
(Grover) Phippen.[1837] He married at Beverly, Massachusetts 20 August
1874, **MARGARET SEMPLE,** who was born at Dundee, Scotland about
November 1854, daughter of Richard and Elizabeth (____) Semple.[1838]

Children of William Harrison and Maggie (Semple) Phippen:[1839]

    i.   MARY ELIZABETH[5] PHIPPEN, b. at Beverly, Mass. 10 July 1875;
        m. there 13 Oct. 1898, ALBERT ANDREW LEWIS of Calais,
        Maine, who was b. in 1874, son of Thomas L. and Lizzie G.
        (____) Lewis.

    ii. RICHARD SEMPLE PHIPPEN, b. at Beverly 1 Aug. 1882.

A21. GEORGE MOORE[4] PHIPPEN (*German[3]*, *Robert[2-1]*) was born at
Methuen, Massachusetts 6 September 1862,[1840] son of German and
Sarah (Moore) Phippen. He died at Alton Bay, New Hampshire 18
August 1948, of liver cancer. He married 25 November 1911, **HATTIE
DULCINIA ELLINWOOD,** daughter of Daniel Webster and Ann Eliza
(Withington) Ellenwood of Worcester, Massachusetts. Hattie died at
Miami, Florida 6 July 1951.[1841] They had no children.

George Phippen at one time was the owner of the top of Mt. Major
in Alton, New Hampshire, having purchased the land in 1914 for the

---

[1836] Mass.VR (1874) 259: 314, (1874) 265: 265 (birth and death of Lillie F.), (1879) 304:
    285, (1879) 310: 274 (birth and death of Lillie Frances), (1882) 331:319 (birth of
    Benjamin).

[1837] Mass.VR (1850) 42: 210.

[1838] Mass.VR (1874) 262: 179.

[1839] 1900 U.S. Census, North Attleborough, Bristol Co., Mass., E.D. 209, p. 263 (census
    record states that Margaret gave birth to three children, only two of which were
    living at the time of the census; Mass.VR (1875) 268: 186, (1898) 478: 305 (birth
    and marriage of Mary Elizabeth), (1882) 313: 187 (birth of Richard).

[1840] Mass.VR (1862) 150: 253.

[1841] Leonard Ellinwood, *The Ellenwood Family 1635–1963* (Washington, D.C., 1963).

sum of $125. Years later, in the fall of 1925, he built a covered stone cabin on the top of the mountain, equipped with a wood stove, to provide shelter for hikers. The first roof on the cabin did not survive the shelter's first winter, and a stronger roof was built during the following summer. Portions of "Mr. Phippen's Hut" remain at the summit, although the sturdy roof that he built in 1926 lasted only two winters and lies on the side of the mountain nearby, having been blown off by strong winter winds. Today the remains of George Phippen's cabin see limited use as a shelter from the winds of the Belknap Range.[1842]

A22. BENJAMIN[4] PHIPPEN (*German S.[3], Robert[2–1]*) was born 14 March 1866, son of German and Sarah (Moore) Phippen.[1843] He died at Methuen, Massachusetts 1 December 1892.[1844] He married, first, at Methuen 8 July 1892, **EMMA RUSSELL,** who was born 17 February 1866[1845] and died at Methuen 1 December 1892. He married, second, at Lawrence, Massachusetts 27 November 1895, **BESSIE M. CURRIER.**[1846]

Children of Benjamin and Bessie (Currier) Phippen:[1847]

    i.   SARAH A.[5] PHIPPEN, b. at Lawrence, Mass. 3 January 1897.
    ii. GEORGE H. PHIPPEN, b. at Newton, Mass. 16 June 1902.

A23. THOMAS MINOT[4] PHIPPEN (*Abraham[3–2], Robert[1]*) was born at Salem, Massachusetts 7 June 1856, son of Abraham and Lydia E. (Phippen) Phippen.[1848] A stabler, Thomas married at Marblehead, Massachusetts 26 April 1883, **MARY HIGGINS** of Beverly, Massachusetts, who was born at St. Anicet, Canada 18 February 1856, daughter of John K. and Mary (____) Higgins.[1849] Thomas Minot Phippen died at Beverly in 1941, aged 85 years.[1850] Mary died at Beverly 24 December 1920.[1851]

[1842] Paula Tracy, "The Story of Mr. Phippen's Cabin" (2015) (http://www.wmur.com/ article/the-story-of-mr-phippen-s-cabin/5199582, accessed 8 January 2017); Dave Roberts, "Mr. Phippen's Hut" (www.http://belknaprangetrails.org/wp-content/ uploads/2014/04/Phippens.Hut-REV1.pdf, accessed 23 May 2016); *The Laker* [Wolfeboro Falls, N.H.], 15 July 1996, 9.

[1843] Mass. VR (1866) 186: 242.

[1844] Mass. VR (1892) 424: 452.

[1845] Mass. VR (1866) 186: 242.

[1846] Mass. VR (1895) 451: 423.

[1847] Mass. VR (1897) 466: 457 (Sarah), (1902) 520: 476 (George).

[1848] Mass. VR (1856) 96: 257.

[1849] Mass. VR (1883) 343: 203.

[1850] Obituary in *Beverly Evening Times.*

[1851] Questionnaire.

Children of Thomas Minot and Mary (Higgins) Phippen:[1852]

   i. LYDIA E.[5] PHIPPEN, b. probably at Beverly in Feb. 1884; and d. at Salem 5 Jan. 1885.

   ii. MARY LEVINA PHIPPEN, b. at Beverly 8 July 1886; m. in 1914, WILLIAM FELTON; d. in 1971.

   iii. OLIVIA CHRISTINE PHIPPEN, b. at Beverly 22 Dec. 1888; m. in 1916, BERNARD GLIBERT PRIESTLY.

   iv. ISABELLE LOUISE PHIPPEN, b. 21 May 1897; m. at Middleton, Mass. 20 Feb. 1930, PERLEY WOOD.

A24. WALTER A.[4] PHIPPEN (*Robert C.[3], Abraham[2], Robert[1]*) was born at Salem, Massachusetts 27 February 1862, son of Robert and Abigail (Finley) Phippen.[1853] A farmer, he died at Lincolnville, Maine 22 November 1901.[1854] He married at Salem 2 May 1883, **EMMA FRANCES BALLARD,** daughter of George and Louisa Ballard.[1855] They were divorced by 18 June 1900, when she married Fred P. Wiggin at Lincolnville, Maine.

Child of Walter and Emma (Ballard) Phippen:

   i. EVA[5] PHIPPEN, b. at Boston, Mass.; m. 3 April 1912, PERLEY WATTON of Searsmont, Maine.[1856]

A25. CLARENCE E.[4] PHIPPEN (*Robert C.[3], Abraham[2], Robert[1]*) was born at Salem, Massachusetts about 1866, son of Robert and Abigail (Finley) Phippen. He married at Salem 17 March 1891, **BERTHA E. TUFTS,** who was born at Dennyville, Maine in 1869, daughter of William and Mary Tufts.[1857] Clarence married, second, at Danvers, Massachusetts 3 January 1896, **LELIA F. GUPPY,** who was born in Essex County in 1866, daughter of John and Sarah (Crose) Guppy.

Child of Clarence and Bertha (Tufts) Phippen:

   i. LILLIAN GERTRUDE[5] PHIPPEN, b. at Salem 17 April 1895; d. there 24 Oct. 1895.[1858]

[1852] Mass.VR (1885) 364: 181 (death of Lydia), (1866) 367: 211 (birth of Mary).

[1853] Mass.VR (1862) 150: 276.

[1854] Maine VR.

[1855] Mass.VR (1883) 343: 356.

[1856] Maine VR.

[1857] Mass.VR (1891) 415: 469.

[1858] Mass.VR (1895) 448: 521 (birth), (1895) 454: 570 (death).

A26. **ALBERT EDWARD**[4] **PHIPPEN** (*Robert C.*[3], A*braham*[2], *Robert*[1]) was born at Salem, Massachusetts ca. 1870, son of Robert and Abigail (Finley) Phippen. He married **ALICE M. GRAVES,** who was born at Marblehead, Massachusetts ca. 1879.

Children of Albert and Alice (Graves) Phippen, born at Salem:[1859]

    i. ABBIE GERTRUDE[5] PHIPPEN, b. 25 Dec. 1894; d. at Salem 14 Nov. 1895.

    ii. GERTRUDE H. PHIPPEN, b. 3 Feb. 1896.

    iii. ROBERT E. PHIPPEN, b. 10 Nov. 1898; d. 12 Aug. 1899.

[1859] Mass. VR (1894) 439: 538, (1895) 454: 571 (birth and death of Abbie), (1896) 457: 572 (birth of Gertrude), (1898) 475: 604, (1899) 492: 640 (birth and death of Robert).

BIBLIOGRAPHY

Avery, Clara A., *The Averell-Averill-Avery Family, A record of the Descendants of William and Abigail Averell of Ipswich Mass.*, 2 vols. Salem, Massachusetts: Higginson Book, 2000–2010.

Boston Births from AD 1700 to AD 1800. Report of the Record Commissioners of the City of Boston: Boston: Records relating to the early history of Boston, vol. 24 (1894).

Boston Births, Marriages, and Deaths, 1630-1699. Report of the Record Commissioners of the City of Boston: Records relating to the early history of Boston, vol. 9 (1883).

Boston Marriages, 1700-1751. Report of the Record Commissioners of the City of Boston: Boston: Records relating to the early history of Boston, vol. 28 (1898).

Bostwick, Henry A., Genealogy of the *Bostwick Family in America: the Descendants of Arthur Bostwick of Stratford Connecticut.* Hudson, New York, 1901.

Cooke, Harriet Ruth Waters, *The Driver Family: The Driver Family: A Genealogical Memoir of the Descendants of Robert and Phebe Driver, of Lynn, Mass. with an Appendix, Containing Twenty-three Allied Families, 1592–1887.* New York, 1889.

Denny, Christopher C., *Genealogy of the Denny Family in England and America.* Leicester, Massachusetts, 1886.

Derby, Perley, "Inscriptions from the Charter Street Burial-Ground, Salem, Mass.," *Essex Institute Historical Collections* 13 (1877), 67 et seq.

The Diary of William Bentley, D.D., Pastor of the East Church, Salem, Massachusetts, 4 vols. Salem, Massachusetts, 1905–1914.

Ellery, Harrison, and Bowditch, Charles P., *The Pickering Genealogy: being an account of the first three generations of the Pickering family of Salem, Mass.,* 3 vols. Cambridge, Massachusetts, 1897.

The Essex Antiquarian, Salem, Massachusetts: The Essex Antiquarian, 13 vols. 1897–1909.

Essex Institute Historical Collections, Salem, Massachusetts, Essex Institute Press, (1859–1993).

Genealogical Dictionary of Maine and New Hampshire, ed. Sibyl Noyes, Charles Thornton Libby & Walter Goodwin Davis (Portland, Maine, 1928–1939).

Jacobus, Donald Lines, "The Phippen Family and the Wife of Nathan[1] Gold of Fairfield, Connecticut," *The American Genealogist* 17 (July 1940): 1–19.

Jacobus, Donald Lines, *History and Genealogy of Families of Old Fairfield, Connecticut,* 2 vols. in 3 (Fairfield, Conn., 1930-1932; reprinted Baltimore, 2007).

Marston, Nathan Washington, *The Marston Genealogy.* South Lubec, Maine, 1888.

Massachusetts State Archives. Massachusetts Vital State Vital Records (1841–1915). Microfilm & Digital series. Boston: New England Historic Genealogical Society.

New England Historical and Genealogical Register (1847–).

Orcutt, Samuel, *A history of the old town of Stratford and the city of Bridgeport, Connecticut,* 2 vols. New Haven, Connecticut, 1886.

Paul, Edward J., "Notes on the American families of Paul or Paull," 6 vols. (Manuscript, 1897). Boston: New England Historic Genealogical Society, Mss 282.

Perley, Sidney, "Salem in 1700. No. 21, 25, 26, 27, 28. *Essex Antiquarian* 9, 10, 11 (1905–1907).

Perley, Sidney, *The History of Salem, Massachusetts,* 3 vols. Salem, Massachusetts, 1924–1928.

Phoenix, S. Whitney, *The Whitney family of Connecticut, and its affiliations; being an attempt to trace the descendants . . . of Henry Whitney, from 1649 to 1878,* 3 vols. New York, 1878.

Province and Court Records of Maine, 6 vols. (Portland, Maine, 1928–).

Rowell, Roland, *Biographical Sketch of Samuel Rowell and notice of some of his descendants, with genealogy for seven generations, 1754–1898.* Manchester, New Hampshire, 1898.

Vital Records of Beverly, Massachusetts to the end of the year 1849, 2 vols. (Topsfield, Massachusetts, 1906).

Vital Records of Brookline, Massachusetts to the end of the year 1849 (Salem, Massachusetts, 1929).

Vital Records of Cambridge, Massachusetts to the end of the year 1850, 2 vols. (Boston, 1914).

Vital Records of Gloucester, Massachusetts to the end of the year 1849, 3 vols. (Salem, Massachusetts, 1923).

Vital Records of Hull, Massachusetts to the end of the year 1849. (Boston, 1911).

Vital Records of Lee, Massachusetts to the year 1850 (Boston, 1903).

Vital Records of Lynn, Massachusetts to the end of the year 1849 (Salem, Massachusetts, 1905).

Vital Records of Manchester, Massachusetts to the end of the year 1849 (Salem, Massachusetts, 1903).

Vital Records of Marblehead, Massachusetts to the end of the year 1849, 3 vols. (Salem, Massachusetts, 1903–1908).

Vital Records of Middleton, Massachusetts to the end of the year 1849 (Topsfield, Massachusetts, 1904).

Vital Records of Reading, Massachusetts to the end of the year 1849 (Boston, 1912).

Vital Records of Royalston, Massachusetts to the end of the year 1849 (Worcester, Massachusetts, 1906).

Vital Records of Salem, Massachusetts to the end of the year 1849, 6 vols. (Salem, Massachusetts, 1916–1925).

Vital Records of Salisbury, Massachusetts to the end of the year 1849 (Topsfield, Massachusetts, 1915).

Vital Records of Topsfield, Massachusetts to the end of the year 1849, 2 vols. (Topsfield, Massachusetts, 1903).

Wellman, J.W., *Descendants of Thomas Wellman of Lynn, Massachusetts.* Boston, 1918.

White, Lorraine Cook, ed. *The Barbour Collection of Connecticut Town Vital Records.* Baltimore: Genealogical Publishing Co., 2000:

—Vol. 3: *Branford, 1644–1850.*

—Vol. 12: *Fairfield, 1639–1850.*

—Vol. 19: *Hartford, 1635–1855.*

—Vol. 28: *Milford 1640–1850.*

—Vol. 29: *New Milford, 1712–1860.*

—Vol. 41: *Stratford 1639–1840.*